11TH MONTH,

11TH DAY,

11TH HOUR

ALSO BY JOSEPH E. PERSICO

Roosevelt's Secret War

My American Journey
(collaboration with General Colin Powell)

Nuremberg: Infamy on Trial

Casey: From the OSS to the CIA

Edward R. Murrow: An American Original

*The Imperial Rockefeller:
A Biography of Nelson A. Rockefeller*

The Spiderweb

*Piercing the Reich: The Penetration of Nazi Germany by
American Secret Agents During World War II*

*My Enemy, My Brother:
Men and Days of Gettysburg*

11TH MONTH,

11TH DAY,

11TH HOUR

Armistice Day, 1918

World War I and Its Violent Climax

JOSEPH E. PERSICO

Hutchinson
London

Published by Hutchinson in 2004

1 3 5 7 9 10 8 6 4 2

Copyright © Joseph E. Persico 2004

Joseph E. Persico has asserted his right under the Copyright, Designs
and Patents Act, 1988 to be identified as the author of this work

First published in the United States by Random House,
an imprint of The Random House Publishing Group,
a division of Random House, Inc. in 2004

Hutchinson
The Random House Group Limited
20 Vauxhall Bridge Road, London SW1V 2SA

Random House Australia (Pty) Limited
20 Alfred Street, Milsons Point, Sydney
New South Wales 2061, Australia

Random House New Zealand Limited
18 Poland Road, Glenfield
Auckland 10, New Zealand

Random House (Pty) Limited
Endulini, 5a Jubilee Road
Parktown 2193, South Africa

The Random House Group Limited Reg. No. 954009

www.randomhouse.co.uk

A CIP catalogue record for this book is available from the British Library

Papers used by Random House are natural, recyclable products made from wood grown
in sustainable forests. The manufacturing processes conform to the environmental regulations of the country of origin

ISBN 0 09 179503 6

Printed and bound in Great Britain by
Mackays of Chatham plc, Chatham, Kent

To those on all sides who lost
their lives on November 11, 1918

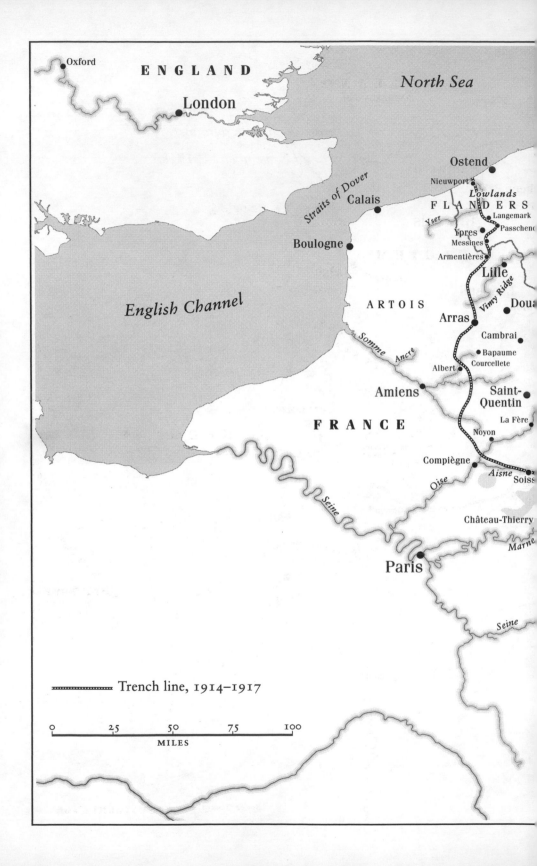

Oxford

E N G L A N D

North Sea

London

Ostend

Nieuwport

Lowlands

F L A N D E R S

Straits of Dover

Calais

Yser

Langemark

Passchen

Boulogne

Ypres

Messines

Armentières

Lille

English Channel

A R T O I S

Vimy Ridge

Doua

Somme

Ancre

Arras

Cambrai

Bapaume

Courcellete

Albert

Amiens

Saint-
Quentin

F R A N C E

La Fère

Noyon

Compiègne

Aisne

Soiss

Oise

Château-Thierry

Marne

Seine

Paris

Seine

▬▬▬▬▬▬ Trench line, 1914–1917

o   25   50   75   100

MILES

Now, God be thanked, Who has matched us with His hour,
And caught our youth, and wakened us from sleeping.

—Rupert Brooke, 1914

————

What passing-bells for these who die as cattle?
Only the monstrous anger of the guns.

—Wilfred Owen, 1917

CONTENTS

Introduction . . . . *xiii*

1. The Desperate Hours 3
2. The Boy Who Blew Up the World 15
3. "A Lovely War" 25
4. "Goya at His Most Macabre" 34
5. Upon a Midnight Clear 43
6. "The God Who Gave the Cannon Gave the Cross" 53
7. The Three Musketeers 61
8. A Scar from Belgium to Switzerland 66
9. Every Inch a Soldier 76
10. "They Shall Not Pass" 80
11. "What Did You Do in the Great War, Dad?" 89
12. "Tomorrow I Shall Take My Men over the Top" 101
13. "Hindenburg! The Name Itself Is Massive" 121
14. "Keeping the World Safe for Democracy" 133
15. "Acts Prejudicial to Military Discipline" 146

16. Doughboys 157

17. "Sweet and Noble to Die for One's Country". 168

18. "Over There" 179

19. "If This Is Our Country, Then This Is Our War" 201

20. Ludendorff's Grand Gamble. 210

21. "A German Bullet Is Cleaner Than a Whore". 225

22. Baptism in Cantigny 231

23. "Do You Want to Live Forever?" 246

24. "I Don't Expect to See Any of You Again" 254

25. "Do You Wish to Take Part in This Battle?". 267

26. A Civilized End to Pointless Slaughter 278

27. A Plague in the Trenches. 292

28. "Victims Who Will Die in Vain". 306

29. "We Knew the End Could Not Be Far Off" 320

30. "Pass the Word. Cease Fire at Eleven!". 327

31. "Little Short of Murder". 337

32. The Fate of Private Gunther 348

33. "This Fateful Morning Came an End to All Wars". 362

34. Greater Losses Than on D-Day. 375

35. "Only the Dead Have Seen the End of War". 385

Epilogue: Marching Home 391

Acknowledgments 401

Appendix: Casualty Statistics 405

Notes 407

Bibliography 427

Index 435

INTRODUCTION

In the fall of 1919, Alvan T. Fuller, a second-term Republican congressman from Massachusetts's Ninth District, received a letter from a constituent, George K. Livermore, one of an accumulating file. Grieving families wanted to know why a son, husband, father, or brother had died on the last day of the Great War when it had been known well in advance, down to the exact moment, that the fighting would end on the eleventh month, eleventh day, eleventh hour. Congressman Fuller, son of a Civil War veteran and raised on tales of soldierly sacrifice, was particularly moved by Livermore's description of a plot of land outside a French village, Pont-à-Mousson, where he had seen "little crosses over the graves of the lads who died a useless death on that November morning."

So numerous were such inquiries that in January 1920, Congress began an investigation into the conduct of leaders of the American Expeditionary Forces, beginning with General John J. Pershing, to find out why so many lives had been sacrificed *after* peace was assured. Casualties that last day were not confined to American forces. Large numbers of French, British, and German soldiers as well died in the final hours, even minutes.

My purpose here is not to offer still another history of the war, though I follow its progression from 1914 to 1918. I am also impatient with presentations of mankind's most violent behavior as if it were a map exercise, with Jones rolling up Smith's flank while the 104th supports a strategic withdrawal by the 105th. And while the role of field marshals and generals is necessarily portrayed, the true protagonists of this story are the men in the trenches for whom what in the map rooms looked like a chess match became transmuted into titanic violations of flesh and blood. The reason I have written an account anchored to the last day of World War I is that the carnage that went on up to the final minute so perfectly captures the essential futility of the entire war. The mayhem of the last day was no different from what had been going on for the previous 1,560 days.

The story is drawn heavily from letters, diaries, and journals of participants, which explains the occasional use of such phrases as "He thought," "He imagined," "She believed." Critics of narrative history understandably question an author's presumption to enter other people's minds. When these phrases are used in this work it is because the people cited wrote that this is what they thought, imagined, or believed.

The Great War, as it was initially known, was indeed global, involving twenty countries on five continents. Yet today, among most Americans, the war is only vaguely recalled, a misty promontory obscured by a war that preceded it and one that followed it, the Civil War and World War II. In surviving images it has something to do with poppies, ghostly figures in gas masks, a rousing tune, "Over There," President Wilson's Fourteen Points, and a fading photograph in an album of an unbelievably young grandfather or great-grandfather wearing a doughboy's tin helmet and a collar that appears to be choking him. Yet, while partially hidden, the Great War still exercises a grip on the imagination. It is futile to argue that one conflict is more horrific than another. The imperative of war is to kill, and thus all wars are exercises in sanctioned murder. For the victim, it is small satisfaction whether he died gassed in the trenches, shot out of the sky in a World War II raid over Berlin, or run through by a Spartan's sword at Thermopylae. Dead is dead. But the First World War's bleak distinction is that it took opposing armies to the outermost limits of man's inhumanity to man, as any honest account of Ypres, the Somme, or Verdun will attest. Of 55 million men mobilized worldwide, nearly 9 million were lost during this war, and far greater numbers were maimed, crippled, and disfigured for life.

The historian Sir John Keegan concluded, "The First World War was a tragic and unnecessary conflict. Unnecessary because the train of events that led to its outbreak might have been broken at any point during the five weeks of crisis that preceded the first clash of arms, had prudence or common goodwill found a voice." But neither prudence nor goodwill did prevail. Obviously, once war began, the aggressor had to be driven from seized territory—but at what a cost—while peace overtures that could have shortened the conflict withered. It has been argued that World War I was a victory of liberal democracy over military autocracy, a temporary victory at best when one considers the subsequent rise of Nazi Germany, Imperial Japan, and the Soviet Union. It has been suggested that the Allied triumph taught "militarism a lesson of restraint." Considering the much magnified destruction of the Second World War, which in part grew out of the First, it seems that the lesson went unlearned. World War I did shift some lines on the map, toppled outworn dynasties, carved out a few unstable and unviable states. It raised, but then dashed, hopes that it was a "war to end all wars." All the scholars on Earth cannot explain the war much better, as it dragged on, than the British Tommies' ditty "We're here because we're here because we're here because we're here." Or as another historian, A. J. P. Taylor, paraphrased it, "They fought because they fought because they fought because they fought." Winston Churchill, serving as First Lord of the Admiralty, wrote as early as April 1915 that his nation's young men were engaged in "the hardest, cruelest, and the least-rewarded of all the wars that men have fought."

To those who study warfare as military science, the Great War did have meaning. It introduced the first battlefield use of radio and telephone communications, as well as most modern weapons: warplanes, tanks, oceangoing submarines, flamethrowers, and poison gas, if these be judged advances in human endeavor. But in the final judgment, it can be argued that the millions from all sides who died at the receiving end of such murderous ingenuity died in vain. It may be that the only value to mankind coming out of World War I was to provide the ultimate test of what human beings can endure under monstrously inhuman conditions and yet maintain their humanity.

Even if the interplay of obstinacy and blindness made war inescapable, can we not question the way in which it was conducted—in battles costing 100,000 or 200,000 or 300,000 casualties in fighting enduring more than fifty months? After more than eighty years, World War I can still arouse outrage over so much squandered life, at generals who could feel every obligation that the profession of arms imposed except sufficient concern for the lives entrusted to them.

For the layman a baffling anomaly remains. One of the great poets of the war, Siegfried Sassoon, wrote of the "doomed and haggard faces" who fought the war. Yet these faces did not necessarily remember their ordeal with horror. Despite the stench of rotting corpses, the filth, the mud, the hunger, the cold, the rats, the ever-present prospect of death, the trenches appear to have exercised a near-mystical grip over men who lived and died in them. Never, many felt, had they experienced such intensity of emotion; never had comradeship—a sense of needing and being needed—struck so deeply and bound prior strangers so strongly in a blood brotherhood. Here was life lived at an adrenaline pitch. A young English officer, Guy Chapman, described the war as "a mistress . . . once you have lain in her arms you can admit no other." The French theologian Pierre Teilhard de Chardin, who served as a stretcher bearer, found in battle a "clarity, energy and freedom that is to be found hardly anywhere else in ordinary life." An anonymous Canadian private put it more simply. The war, he said, had been "the greatest adventure of my life."

In trying to explain such sentiments to the layman, the veteran might well fall back on the cliché "You had to be there." Indeed, those who survived had undergone an etching of the soul that only they understood—and that spouses, parents, children, and other civilians could never fully grasp. It is also striking that beneath the different uniforms, languages, and professed reasons for going to war, the reactions of the soldiers, whether toward their enemy, officers, comrades, or daily life, were not just similar, they were identical.

One hopes that so cruel and pointless a conflict as World War I would, at the very least, have suggested lessons for avoiding a repetition. I thought, as a long-ago college student, that if every world leader was compelled to read Erich Maria Remarque's World War I masterpiece, *All Quiet on the Western Front,* there could be no more wars. We ultimately recognize, however, that those who instigate wars are not blind to their horrors but undeterred by them. The lives lost are only the purchase price that a leader is willing to pay for objectives, noble or ignoble, especially since that leader will likely still be standing at the end. We conclude, finally, that while situations shift, human nature does not. The same impulses—gain, glory, fear, pride, honor, envy, retribution—coupled with short collective memories will continue to propel mankind into a never-ending cycle of conflict occasionally interrupted by peace.

Albany, New York
July 19, 2004

11TH MONTH,

11TH DAY,

11TH HOUR

1

The Desperate Hours

NOVEMBER 11, 1918. The runner, shivering, his breath visible in the morning air, waited for the captain to acknowledge the message. The night had been bitter, the temperature hovering near freezing. The cold had stiffened the mud, caking uniforms and frosting the rim of the trench. Leaden skies threatened snow. A medic moved along the duckboards handing out aspirin to sneezing, hacking men with heavy colds. They gripped tin mugs of coffee, grateful for the warmth, and eyed the runner, wondering what news he bore.

The captain read the message twice. It must be a mistake. True, the night before, the U.S. 26th Division had received Field Order 105 to attack at 9:30 this morning. But at 9:10, just as they had been checking their ammunition and fixing bayonets, word came that the armistice had been signed. Hostilities were to cease at 11 A.M. The attack had been canceled. And here was another message telling the captain that the assault had been reinstated. His watch showed 10:30. A half hour remained in the war.

To Private Connell Albertine, in Company A of the division's 104th Infantry, the earlier word that the assault had been canceled had produced deep, wordless relief. He would live. Rumors that an armistice was imminent had been rife for days. And at 5:45 that morning, the division's radiomen had picked up a message transmitted from the Eiffel Tower in Paris from the Allied commander, Marshal Ferdinand Foch, confirming the signing. That the attack would now go forward, after having been rescinded, struck him as insane, even murderous. Seventeen months had passed since the fresh-faced young New Englander had stood with the crowd reading the bulletin in the window of *The Boston Globe*. A giant keyboard tapped out on an unfolding paper roll, "A state of War between the Imperial German Government which has been thrust upon the United States is hereby declared." President Woodrow Wilson's long agony, his peaceful impulses pitted against the tide of events, had led him to take his nation into Europe's conflict, just five months after he had been reelected president on the slogan "He kept us out of the War." The personal import of the *Globe*'s bulletin was immediately evident to Albertine. He belonged to the Massachusetts National Guard, and its mobilization would be inevitable. "An indescribable feeling swelled within me," he recalled of that day, "driving out all thoughts of my work and daily routine and filling me with an urgent desire to hasten to my gathering buddies and the comfort of my rifle."

Since then, intervening realities had cooled his ardor. In the beginning, war had seemed a romp. The 104th had first entered the trenches in a quiet sector of the western front near Toul in northeast France. In the evenings, the doughboys could hear the sounds of a violin rising from the enemy trenches. When the Germans realized that they were facing Americans, they had behaved as if they had found long-lost family. They came out into no-man's-land offering sausages for American cigarettes, black bread for white. "Hey, Yank!" one called out. "Where're you from?" When the soldier replied, "Boston," the German responded, "I was a bartender at Jake Wirth's." The camaraderie ended abruptly when regimental headquarters at Toul brought court-martial proceedings against twelve soldiers for fraternizing with the enemy. Soon after, the opposing artillery batteries began exchanging fire.

February 17, 1918, stood out starkly in Albertine's memory. He had been crouched in a funkhole clawed from the earth watching geysers of dirt heaved up by exploding shells. A blast over a nearby company tossed up what looked like a rag doll. Albertine watched the stretcher bearers drag a lifeless form from a shell hole. The 104th had taken its first fatality, Private George G. Clarke, Company E.

Soon afterward, through the din of artillery fire, Albertine heard the wail of a klaxon. Gas alert. He pulled his mask over his face just as shells of mustard gas fell to earth with a seemingly innocent thump. They did not explode but issued a pinging sound and then a whistle as the fumes escaped. The gas had caught nearby French troops asleep. Albertine watched the victims being carted from the field, coughing up bits of their lungs, the exposed parts of their bodies blistered, their eyelids swollen shut, blinding them.

Through the months that followed, Albertine had worn the psychological armor that kept soldiers fighting: these things happened to others, not me. That was before the incident in the churchyard cemetery. They had been moving among the graves when shells began exploding close by. As Albertine flung himself to the ground, he felt something cold and hard under his hand, a cast-iron marker blown off a cross. He stared in disbelief. The marker bore the name "Albertine." He flung it aside but, as the months wore on, could never erase its portent from his memory.

The 104th had fought through Château-Thierry and Saint-Mihiel and was now deployed in the Verdun sector. On the morning of the armistice, when it had appeared the assault had been canceled, Albertine could finally believe that he had outlasted the war. He glanced toward Chaplain de Valles, whom he credited with his survival.

John B. de Valles had been born in the Azores to Portuguese parents who had taken him to Massachusetts as a child. He had been ordained in 1906 and became a popular parish priest, first in Fall River and then in New Bedford. When America went to war, Father de Valles immediately joined the Chaplains' Corps. His popularity transferred easily to the 104th. When a soldier found himself short before payday, the priest could be touched for a loan of a few francs—on one condition: he must promise not to use the money for what de Valles called "cohabitation." His orderly kept a ledger in which the loans were recorded. But when payday came around, Father de Valles would tell him to tear out the page. The orderly was Connell Albertine, who looked upon the day the chaplain had chosen him as the luckiest of his young life.

Albertine felt secure in the priest's presence. The previous April, near Saint-Agnant, when Private Burns had been hung up on the wire in no-man's-land, screaming in agony, Chaplain de Valles heaved himself out of the trench and began crawling toward the wounded man. The priest disentangled Burns from the wire, lifted him onto his back, and staggered to the trench as enemy machine-gun bullets tore into the ground around them.

After bloody fighting at Commercy, de Valles had stood mutely watching a procession of carts haul the 104th's dead from the field. Albertine heard Father de Valles curse through clenched teeth, "Kill them! Kill the bastards!" The priest later apologized to his orderly, but the words, he said, had tumbled out and felt right. The incident had bound Albertine more closely to the chaplain, making de Valles as humanly imperfect as his flock.

Now, on this last day, the nightmare of raglike bodies, gas-seared lungs, and unholy shrieks from the wire, he believed, had to end.

COLONEL CASSIUS M. DOWELL commanded another regiment of the 26th Division, the 103rd. That November 11, Dowell was in his dugout bent over a map, marking the point where his regiment could expect to end the war. At 9:45 A.M., his field phone rang. Colonel Duncan K. Major, the division's chief of staff, was on the line informing him that the attack had been reinstated. Dowell was to send his men against German machine guns in a war that would end in a little over an hour. "Why?" Dowell asked. "The French compelled us to do it," Major answered. The 26th was in fact under command of the French II Colonial Corps. Major had experienced his own disbelief when told that the canceled assault was now to go forward. He had checked with the operations chief of the French corps for confirmation. Major, his French imperfect, feared he had misunderstood. An American liaison officer serving with the French came on the line and informed Major that he had heard correctly. The assault was back on. This was the news that Major was now relaying to disbelieving regimental commanders of the 26th.

Cassius Dowell, now in his sixteenth year in the army, was gruff, plainspoken, an officer who had risen from private to his present rank. He was not without compassion for his men, but was a soldier first. He too had learned unofficially from a friend on division staff that the armistice had been signed just after 5 A.M. He had not shared this information with his men "lest it might interfere with their advance during the attack that had been ordered for that day." He had then received word that the assault, except for the artillery bombardment, had been called off. He could not, however, resist one last blow at the Hun. He warned that if any shells were left unfired at 11 A.M., he would court-martial the responsible battery commander.

On learning that the attack had been fully reinstated, "I stood there a few seconds debating as to whether I should send my men forward, having told them that they would not have to go," Dowell later recalled. "I expected my casualties to be very heavy."

Lieutenant Harry G. Rennagel, released from the hospital just the day before, rejoined his unit of the 26th Division to find his men laughing, joking, talking more loudly than they ever dared in the trenches. They were "waiting for the bell to ring," they told him, signaling the end of the war. "When the orders came to go over the top," he remembered, "we thought it was a joke."

Albertine watched Chaplain de Valles move through the trench, deathly pale, comforting the men. An Italian private from Boston's North End asked the chaplain to bless him and kissed the cross hanging from the priest's neck. Other Catholics followed, even non-

Catholics. At 10:35, they began climbing the ladders out of the trenches onto open ground, where nests of German machine guns in defenses called the Trenche de Bosphore eyed them in astonishment.

NOVEMBER 11, 1918, marked the 1,559th day of the war for the British Army. The farthest-advanced forces were pressing the Belgian city of Mons, some one hundred miles northwest of the American 26th Division advancing toward the Trenche de Bosphore. The war, dragging on so interminably, prompted bleak jests in the British ranks. "Ole Bill," the war-weary Tommy created by cartoonist Bruce Bairnsfather, is asked by a pal how long he is in for. "Seven years," Bill answers. "You're lucky," his trench-mate responds. "I'm duration." Even the Americans, in combat for only 167 days, had been infected with the fatalism that the war would go on forever. The doughboys sang a parody to the tune of "Silver Threads Among the Gold" that went:

> Darling, I am coming back
> Silver threads among the black.
> Now that peace in Europe nears,
> I'll be home in seven years.
> I'll drop in on you some night
> With my whiskers long and white.
> Home again with you once more,
> Say in Nineteen fifty-four.

As welcome as the Americans were, to the British and French they remained Johnny-come-latelies. Tommies referred to dud shells as "Wilsons" for their failure to explode, just as President Woodrow Wilson had stalled in bringing America into the conflict.

To the British high command the appropriate place to end the war was obvious. The war had begun for Britain with its retreat from Mons. What better way to mark victory than by retaking the city? And who better to avenge the defeat than the cavalrymen of the 5th Royal Irish Lancers, who had been driven from Mons in August 1914? The 5th Lancers were currently attached to a Canadian infantry division. Though cavalrymen and infantry appeared separated only by a horse, the gulf in their experience of war yawned far wider. Will Bird, of Canada's 42nd Battalion Royal Highlanders, the Black Watch, was serving among the foot soldiers. Bird had been harvesting wheat on the Canadian prairie when war had broken out in 1914. He had tried to enlist but was rejected for bad teeth. The twenty-six-year-old had tried again in 1916 after receiving word that his younger brother, Steven, had been killed in action. By then, demand for replacements had driven the physical standards down, and Bird had been accepted. By December of that year, he found himself in France. For all the romance evoked by these Canadians, who wore kilts into battle, Bird quickly found himself engaged in an inglorious business. On the day his unit arrived at Neuville-Saint-Vaast, a mortar misfired, shredding three men standing next to it, and Bird's first assignment had been to collect their body parts into burlap bags. He had, however, developed emotional calluses against such experiences with a speed that had astonished him, and in time, because he was one of the older men, he had been promoted to sergeant leading his platoon.

On Sunday morning, November 10, Sergeant Studholme entered the farmhouse where Bird and his men were billeted and told them that he was risking his stripes for what he was about to tell them. "On Monday morning the armistice is going to be signed," he confided. "As far as we're concerned, the War is over. But keep it to yourselves." Bird and his pals let out a war whoop and began dancing around the room like Indians. Two brothers, Jim and Tom Mills, hugged each other. They had only recently been reunited when Jim had been transferred into the 42nd Battalion. The others had soon noted the difference between the brothers, Tom garrulous and irrepressible, Jim silent and withdrawn.

They stretched out on the floor, smoking and spinning dreams of what they would do with the war all but over. "I'd buy this place," Tommy Mills said, gesturing around the room, "and make it into a tourist tavern. I'll wear this uniform and tell them that this is where the war ended." Lance Corporal Bob Jones said, "I'm going to set up in the salient; the tourist cabins will be sandbagged and have corrugated iron roofs. Rats will run free, and there will be a gas alarm by the door. Each afternoon I'll read speeches of the brass hats that have been in the *Daily Mail*."

The mood of celebration was broken by the return of a grim-faced Sergeant Studholme, barely an hour later. "Bird," he said, "get your sector in order at once. Battle order."

"What's up?" Bird asked.

"We're going to take Mons. No use to argue about it."

Tom Mills jumped to his feet. "The war's over tomorrow, and everybody knows it. What kind of rot is this?"

"Watch what you say," Studholme warned. "Orders are orders."

THE 5TH LANCERS presented a splendid spectacle trotting along the road from Valenciennes toward Mons. Not since the war had descended into mud and stalemate had Belgian civilians seen anything as dashing as these cavaliers, their weapons glinting in the sun, their sleek, well-fed mounts bearing scant resemblance to the torn, bloated bodies of horses that blighted the roadside. Briefly, it had appeared that the Lancers might be cheated of the glory of re-entering Mons. The Canadian general under whom they served had informed the Lancers' commanding officer that he had no room on his front for cavalry, and he "regretted that no other opportunity arose of making use of the services of this unit." But on the evening of the tenth, the cavalrymen gained a reprieve: they were to ride ahead of the Canadian infantry to scout the enemy's strength before the attack on Mons.

JUST PAST ONE o'clock on the afternoon of the tenth, Sergeant Bird had led his platoon toward its objective, the Mons railway station. They reached an open field before an anonymous, scarred village when German guns opened up. Bird signaled to Lance Corporal Jones and the Mills brothers to follow him into the shelter of an undamaged brick house. Bird judged that the building could take anything but a direct hit. He stood in the doorway while the three men stumbled inside. Jones sat down on a keg, panting heavily. Suddenly a shell burst with a deafening roar, fifteen feet over their heads. Bird was thrown to the floor. He shook himself off and rose unsteadily, shedding plaster and splinters of wood. "That was too close for comfort," he said. No one answered. He turned to see Jones, blood gushing from his temple, topple from the keg. Jim Mills sat on the floor, cradling his brother, Tom, who kept moaning, "I'm hit. I'm hit." Jim set him down and ran to the doorway, screaming for a stretcher bearer. The rent in the man's stomach was too huge. Bird knew that Tom was dying. The war had less than twenty-four hours to run.

Bird left the dead men to the burial detail and led the rest of his platoon through the village. They heard voices rising from a cellar. Bird kicked open the door and found the dank space filled with Belgian civilians, dressed in holiday finery. The fighting had interrupted a wedding, sending the guests scurrying to shelter. The bride sat on the groom's knee. The groom motioned her to get up, took her by the hand, and led her to a doorway, from which he proceeded to urinate. The image, Bird knew, would remain in his memory forever if he lived through the next day.

THE GERMAN MACHINE gunners planted at the Trenche de Bosphore stared over their armor shields. A brown mass was emerging from the American line as if the ground itself were moving. The Germans manned Maxim machine guns, the product of a self-taught American mechanical wizard, Hiram Maxim, who had lived long enough to see his weapon embraced by the German

Army. The Germans had no intention of hauling these 125-pound guns back when the signal came to retreat. To what avail? Their officers had read them the cease-fire order earlier that morning. The war was over and lost. Yet in the meantime, they had orders to fight a delaying action to enable the rest of their unit to retreat back to Germany in an orderly fashion. The American advance struck the gunners as madness. They must know that the war was over. They had only to wait out the next half hour, and they could all go home alive.

Herbert Sulzbach was among those engaged in the German Army's rearguard action. Young Sulzbach was from one of the country's distinguished Jewish families, long since assimilated into German society. Herbert's grandfather, Rudolf Sulzbach, had co-founded the powerful Deutsche Bank. He had been offered a title by Kaiser Wilhelm II. Herbert's father, Emil, had subsequently taken over the family business and contributed so generously to the cultural life of his native Frankfurt-on-Main that city officials had named a street Emil Sulzbach–Strasse. Four days after Germany had gone to war, Herbert, age twenty, joined the elite Frankfurt 63rd Field Artillery Regiment, along with several university classmates. He joked that even the family's huge Adler motorcar had been called up for service. Sulzbach had initially served as an enlisted man but by now was commissioned. A photograph of the tall, handsome, serious-looking officer was prominently displayed in his father's office at the bank.

Sulzbach had been baptized under fire in the Ypres sector two months after his enlistment and decorated for bravery. After being sniped at in house-to-house fighting in Tournai, Belgium, Sulzbach felt nothing but contempt for an enemy who fought "in such a cowardly way. He didn't let us fight properly, man to man, he just fired on us out of a snug hiding place." He had been moved to mingled pride and tears when the regiment buried its first dead.

In those early months, the spirits of Sulzbach and his comrades had been emboldened by a stirring escapade. An official army report released in November 1914 described German student volunteers emerging one morning from a mist, shoulder to shoulder, still wearing their school caps as they charged the French guns. The youths had been cut down like wheat, and, according to the report, they had gone to their deaths singing "Deutschland über Alles." Even those mortally wounded had uttered the national anthem with their last dying breath. Thus had been born the legend of *"Der Kindermord bei Ypern,"* the Massacre of the Innocents at Ypres. German newspapers seized upon the story. The nation thrilled to it. Volunteers were spurred by it to enlist in droves.

It was a myth, however, with only a few shards of truth. Student volunteers did serve in regiments engaged at Ypres but totaled less than 18 percent of the soldiers. At the time of the celebrated charge, more than six thousand reservists were killed, mostly grown men, along with some one thousand students, a terrible toll nonetheless and enough to sow a legend that would magnify these lost lives to mythic proportions.

Now, four years later, the momentum had been reversed. Rather than beardless youths flinging themselves headlong against the foe, grizzled veterans were retreating as respectably as defeat allowed. An orderly withdrawal to Germany was deemed critical in order to stem chaos, Red revolution, and civil war on the home front. Sulzbach was stunned to learn that crewmen aboard the warship *König* had mutinied, shot their captain, hauled down the ship's colors, and hoisted a red flag. Communist workers' councils had seized power in factories and towns. Berlin itself verged on anarchy. Most shattering, on November 9 the kaiser had abdicated, ending the five-hundred-year Hohenzollern dynasty. Germany's bellicose sovereign, wearing civilian clothes, had been ignominiously stopped at the Dutch border and forced to produce his papers as he sought to slip into Holland.

Even in defeat, Sulzbach felt, the army displayed nobility. As the Germans pulled out of the town of Etroeungt, they raised a white flag over the church steeple. It was to warn the advancing Allies not to bombard a town filled with French refugees. "I find this sign of our old-established chivalry most moving," he wrote in his diary. As his men withdrew, Sulzbach called out to the crowd, "Keep a good memory of the Germans." His words were met with murderous stares. Sulzbach had relayed to his men the instructions issued by the general staff to minimize civilian vengeance by people subjected to four years of enemy occupation. "Keep the strictest march discipline. . . . Let no troops lag behind . . . nor may other ranks be sent out alone or billeted alone, and no wounded man may be left even temporarily alone."

As the end drew closer, Sulzbach pondered his personal good fortune amid his nation's humiliation. "I do not believe," he confided to his diary, "that there are many soldiers who were stationed at the front for 50 months and are coming home as I am now, unwounded." Yet, as he contemplated his likely survival, the rearguard machine gunners left behind at the Trenche de Bosphore had no such certainty as they fed their ammunition belts into the guns, adjusted their sights, and, with less than half an hour before the war would end, began pouring fire into the stubbornly advancing Americans of the 26th Division.

2

———

The Boy Who
Blew Up the World

JUNE 1914. The forces that had set Connell Albertine, Will Bird, Herbert Sulzbach, and 10,163,000 other men into mortal confrontation on the western front seemed to confirm the "for-want-of-a-nail" school of history. If a chauffeur had not taken a wrong turn, might World War I never have happened?

On June 28, Archduke Franz Ferdinand, heir to the imperial throne of Austria-Hungary, was making a formal visit to the empire's restive province of Bosnia. The archduke's ostensible purpose was to conduct a military inspection. His subtler intent was to try to pacify the empire's disgruntled Slav subjects and help defuse a radical movement to split Bosnia from Austria-Hungary and make it part of the Slav nation of Serbia. Serbian ultranationalists also hoped to attach two other eastern Slavic outposts of the empire, Herzegovina and Montenegro, into a Greater Serbian Kingdom.

Hard-line conservatives in Vienna saw a simple solution to this festering rebellion: crush Serbia, end its brief independent statehood, and strangle its dreams of Slavic hegemony. The archduke was not of this school. Franz Ferdinand's fierce aspect, his ponderous figure, and his brush-cut hair belied a more conciliatory nature than that of his rigid eighty-four-year-old uncle, the Emperor Franz

Josef. The nephew favored holding the Slavic provinces in the family by granting them a say in the Viennese court and government where currently they had none. And so he had used the pretext of an inspection trip to pay a friendly and flattering call on Bosnian officials in their capital, Sarajevo. He had warned these officials that on entering the city, he wanted none of the usual wall of troops insulating the populace from its future emperor. A few local police would do.

The trip held another attraction for Franz Ferdinand. June 28 marked his fourteenth wedding anniversary to the Bohemian countess Sophie Chotek. Though she was of the nobility, her blood was insufficiently blue for Emperor Franz Josef. The codified snobbery of the Viennese court had thus been harshly applied to the countess. Her marriage was required to be morganatic, compelling her to renounce, for herself and her children, any claim to the Habsburg throne. In public processions, she could not accompany her husband but had to walk behind even the Habsburg dynasty's forty-four archdukes and archduchesses, some mere toddlers. When Franz Ferdinand entertained a visiting sovereign, Sophie had to stay out of sight. A ceremonial place was set at table for a hostess, but the seat remained empty.

However, in the provinces Franz Ferdinand could spare Sophie these humiliations. When he acted as inspector general of the army visiting a provincial capital, his wife would be accorded all the pomp and ceremony due an archduchess. Thus Franz Ferdinand viewed the Sarajevo visit as something of an anniversary present to Sophie.

The archduke's gesture of friendship counted for nothing to four young men strung out along the route of Franz Ferdinand's motorcade. They were members of a revolutionary movement plotting to wrest Bosnia's Slav provinces from Austria-Hungary and deliver them to Serbia. They had acquired six pistols and six bombs from the Black Hand, an ultranationalist secret society operating in Serbia. None had ever handled a weapon before. One of the four was Gavrilo Princip, a slightly built nineteen-year-old with hooded eyes, sunken cheeks, and a pasty complexion, wearing an ill-fitting hand-me-down suit. Princip had been born into a Bosnian peasant family living in virtual serfdom. His father tilled four acres of land and was required to turn over a third of his meager harvest to the landlord. The man could barely feed his family, and six of young Princip's eight siblings had died in infancy.

To the royal couple seated in the rear of an open touring car, the crowd of smiling faces, the waving flags and portraits of themselves hung in shop windows, augured well for a joyful occasion. Suddenly, as the procession approached city hall, the driver spotted an object hurled from the crowd. He stepped on the gas, and a bomb aimed at the archduke's car instead bounced off the back and exploded under the hood of the vehicle behind, injuring two officers. The archduke, though furious and his wife visibly shaken, chose nevertheless to press on. Continuing the visit seemed safe, since the police had immediately seized the bomb thrower. A second would-be assassin felt a pang of sympathy for the stately archduchess and chose to leave his pistol in his pocket. A third, convinced of the futility of the mission, had simply gone home. Only Gavrilo Princip remained, but the motorcade had passed him by before he could fire his weapon.

After the visit to city hall, the archduke was persuaded by Bosnian officials to take a different, safer route out of town. However, the driver of the lead car was not informed of the change and made a wrong turn into Appel Quay. The archduke's driver followed him. When he realized his mistake, he stopped to turn the car around. The vehicle now stood before Schiller's Delicatessen, as did Gavrilo Princip. The time was 10:34 A.M. The young Bosnian had an opportunity he had never anticipated, a stationary target. He leaped forward, raised his revolver, and fired twice at point-blank range. Blood from the archduke's severed jugular vein spurted over his gold-trimmed, sky blue tunic. Sophie, also struck, slumped onto her husband's side, her white dress running crimson. Both wounds proved mortal.

Emperor Franz Josef was not particularly bereaved by the loss of his heir apparent. He had never fancied his glowering, massive nephew. Indeed, in certain Austrian circles, the murders in Sarajevo were seen as presenting an opportunity rather than a tragedy. Nevertheless, the killings aroused shock and outrage around the world, giving the emperor justification for dealing forcefully with "the dangerous little viper," as his army chief, Count von Hötzendorf, characterized Serbia.

Despite its sprawling breadth and a population of more than 50 million, the Austro-Hungarian Empire was a shaky edifice, as fragile as its emperor, now in his sixty-sixth year on the throne. Franz Josef's government dared not take on even the "little viper" with its population of less than 3 million, unless it could count on the support of its powerful neighbor Germany. Indeed, the two Teuton-dominated states shared a mutual dependence. Germany saw itself hemmed in by potential enemies Russia and France, with its cultural cousin, Austria, its only reliable ally.

The emperor and his generals concluded that now was the moment to move decisively against Serbia. Franz Josef wrote a letter in his own hand and entrusted it to his ambassador to Germany, Count L. de Szogyeny-Marich, to deliver personally to the kaiser in Potsdam. What, he wanted to know, would Germany do if Austria attacked Serbia? The answer Szogyeny-Marich relayed back could not have been more pleasing to the emperor's ear. Kaiser Wilhelm pledged that Austria could "rely on Germany's full support." Of course, the kaiser's generals recognized the risk. Attacking Serbia could provoke the Serbs' Slavic big brother, Russia. The kaiser, however, was prepared to take that chance. "Russia," he believed, was "in no way prepared for war." Indeed, both Franz Josef and Wilhelm shared a contempt for Russians. "The Slavs were born to serve and not to rule," the kaiser told the emperor's foreign minister, "and this must be brought home to them."

Before striking at Serbia, Austria needed to make formulaic conciliatory gestures. The formula chosen was an ultimatum delivered on July 23, ten demands that Serbia must accede to within forty-eight hours or face war. Among them: all Serbian officials, military officers, even teachers, who had expressed anti-Austrian views must be dismissed; Serbian radicals named on a list prepared by Austria were to be arrested; Austrian officials must be allowed to enter Serbia to ensure that all demands be met. The conditions represented outrageous infringements on Serbian sovereignty and were intended to do so. Britain's foreign secretary, Sir Edward Grey, described the Austrian ultimatum as "the most formidable document ever addressed from one state to another." The proud Serbs would certainly reject these conditions, and Austria would have its justification for attacking Serbia.

But the Serbians refused to play their part. Instead, they agreed to every demand save one. They objected only to the requirement that Austrian officials take part in a judicial investigation of the archduke's assassination. That, the Serbians protested, was asking too much.

Even the kaiser believed that the Serbian concessions represented an Austrian victory and that war had been avoided. Nevertheless, the single, minor point that Serbia rejected was all Austria needed. Never mind that an official dispatched to Serbia by the Austrian foreign minister had reported back, "There is nothing to prove or even to cause suspicion of the Serbian government's cognizance of the steps leading to the crime." Facts could not displace Austria's objective, a *casus belli*.

On July 28, barely past the ultimatum deadline and one month since the archduke had been shot, Austria declared war on Serbia. The next day, while Austrian guns bombarded Belgrade, Czar Nicholas II of Russia mobilized thirteen army corps as a warning to Austria that Serbia had a formidable protector. The kaiser, bound by his pledge to back Austria, demanded that Russia demobilize or face a countermobilization by Germany. The czar, his cousin, was, in Wilhelm's judgment, a weakling, the sort of man who agreed with whomever he had talked to last. And the kaiser remained convinced that the Russian military was an impotent bear.

Who was this figure standing at the center of a simmering European cauldron? Wilhelm II's life, his very character, were likely molded by a mischance at the moment of his birth. In 1859, in the royal bedchamber in Berlin, the doctors attending his mother's pregnancy had reached a disturbing conclusion: because of the position of the unborn child, they would have to perform a breech delivery. In that age, few infants survived this trauma. Indeed, the child appeared to have been born dead and was handed over to a midwife, while the doctors worked feverishly to save the mother. However, the midwife, a Fräulein Stahl, kept smacking the seemingly lifeless body until, to everyone's surprise, the infant started to squeal. Within a few days, however, a nurse noticed that the baby's left arm never moved. In the course of the birth, the arm had been wrenched from its socket, damaging the muscles. As the boy grew up, the arm withered and became useless. By the time Wilhelm was fully grown, it was six inches shorter than the right arm. Corollary injuries had also occurred at birth. Wilhelm's head remained at a slight tilt, and his hearing was impaired.

As he grew to manhood, the German prince displayed a fierce determination to overcome his handicaps and the indignities they inflicted on him, for example, having to have an aide cut his meat. The positive effect of his iron will was that Wilhelm was driven to excel, particularly in the manly pursuits. He became an accomplished horseman and expert marksman. His left arm might be useless, but he enjoyed shaking the hand of visitors, especially English guests, in the crushing vise of his right hand.

By 1888, when he ascended the throne as king of Prussia and kaiser of Germany, less attractive aspects of this determination to overcome any appearance of weakness became apparent. Wilhelm was bombastic, overbearing, and contemptuous of what he perceived as softness in others. He described Czar Nicholas as "fit only to live in a country house and grow turnips." Wilhelm dismissed his cousin, King George V of England, though only six years younger than himself, as a "nice boy." The most lethal effect of his chronic overcompensating was Wilhelm's desire to play up to the German military, to prove himself as tough as any field marshal or admiral. He supported Admiral Alfred von Tirpitz's plan to challenge British supremacy at sea by launching a naval arms race to see which country could most quickly build the mightiest, fastest battleships, the costly dreadnoughts. In the composite of his character, Wilhem reflected the Germany of the early twentieth century: sensing its power, imagining itself insufficiently respected by other nations, especially Great Britain, and paranoid that it was surrounded by enemies.

On July 30, in response to Germany's threat to mobilize, and under pressure from his own generals, Czar Nicholas moved from partial to full mobilization. The kaiser, egged on by his generals, then issued a stronger ultimatum: Russia must demobilize in twelve hours, or Germany would declare war.

Still, for all their disdain for Russia as a military power—a giant sloth, in their judgment—the Germans faced a quandary. Russia was linked to France in the Dual Alliance. War against Russia meant that France would enter the conflict on the czar's side. Consequently, France must be put out of the way before the sloth could awaken, or else Germany would face the dread prospect of a two-front war. The kaiser's government thus fired off an astonishing demand: What did the French intend to do if Germany and Russia went to war? Even if she chose to remain neutral, France must give over to Germany the fortresses at Verdun and Toul, which had been constructed for the very purpose of protecting France from Germany. The German government demanded an answer within eighteen hours.

Sir Edward Grey had foreseen frightful consequences once the crisis spilled over from a mere Austrian-Serbian squabble. "It cannot but end," the foreign secretary told the House of Commons, "in the greatest catastrophe that has ever befallen the Continent of Europe." On July 29, Grey made a last desperate attempt to stave off disaster. Britain would even accept Austria's right to occupy Belgrade. But after that, mediation by all involved parties was the only course that could avert an international calamity, Grey insisted. When his appeal for such talks was delivered to Wilhelm II, the kaiser scribbled on the message, "That mean crew of shop-keepers has tried to trick us with dinners and speeches." Mediation was out.

On Saturday, August 1, the Russians let Germany's ultimatum expire without response. At 5 P.M. in St. Petersburg, courtly old Count Pourtales, Germany's ambassador to Russia, handed the Russian foreign minister, Sergei Sazonov, Germany's declaration of war. "The curses of nations," Sazonov responded, "will be upon you."

Germany's ultimatum to France expired one hour after the ultimatum to Russia. Instead of knuckling under to Germany's demand to give up two major fortified cities, the French would stand by their treaty obligations to Russia. On August 1, the French Army mobilized. The German general staff now put into play a long-standing strategy. Russia's mobilization would go slowly, the generals reasoned, leaving Germany time to deliver France a knockout blow before they dealt with the Russians. General Helmuth von Moltke, chief of the general staff, had a master strategy, the Schlieffen Plan, for the swift completion of that objective.

The genius of the plan was to bypass France's eastern defenses by simply going around them through Belgium. Moltke predicted that the German Army would be parading through Paris in six weeks. Thus, on August 2 at 7 P.M., Germany fired off another ultimatum: Belgium must allow the German Army to pass through her territory en route to attacking France. The Belgians were given until 7 A.M. the next day to accept, or else Germany would force her way through. The Germans began amassing a persuasive 700,000 troops on the Belgian border. The Belgian Council of State, however, refused to kneel. Instead, the council countered, Belgium would "repel by all means in its power every attack upon its rights." The next day, Germany declared war on France and began to implement the Schlieffen Plan.

Now Britain, more than one thousand miles distant from and with scant interest in a Balkan quarrel, was drawn into the snare. For centuries, an axiom of British maritime policy had been that the English Channel must never be compromised by the presence of a potentially antagonistic power on the Channel's European shore. Consequently, in 1839, Britain had entered into a treaty to defend Belgium's neutrality. Germany's invasion of Belgium constituted precisely such an infringement. Though treaty-bound to Belgium, Britain had no formal obligation to go to France's aid. Britain's leaders nevertheless found both moral and practical motives to support France. A continent dominated by Germany was, to Great Britain, a disturbing prospect.

On the morning of August 4, the kaiser and his generals persuaded themselves that they had no choice if they were to avoid a two-front war and began pouring divisions over the Belgian border. They snatched at a justifying fig leaf: the government claimed to have reliable intelligence that the French had intended to invade Germany through Belgium.

Now came Britain's turn to issue demands. When asked by Winston Churchill, then a member of Parliament, what would happen next, Sir Edward Grey replied, "We shall send them an ultimatum to stop the invasion of Belgium within twenty-four hours," expiring at midnight on August 5. That evening, the British prime minister, Herbert Henry Asquith, along with Grey, David Lloyd George, then chancellor of the Exchequer, and other officials, waited wordlessly in the Cabinet Room at 10 Downing Street, watching the clock creep forward. The silence was finally broken by Big Ben chiming midnight. The ultimatum had expired. Britain was at war with Germany. Austria, reluctantly towed in Germany's wake, declared war on Russia on August 6. The lethal circuitry was complete. Europe's major powers were pitted in conflict. Sir Edward Grey, returning to his chambers at the Foreign Office, stared from his window and uttered a comment long to be remembered: "The lamps are going out all over Europe. We shall not see them lit again in our time."

How could it have happened? Yes, Austria felt it had to thrash a small, troublesome neighbor. But none of the other great powers had a grand motive for an enterprise so charged with peril as war.

Germany wanted to put spine into Austria, its only friend on the continent, despite the risk this support posed of provoking Russia. Russia stood by Serbia. France understandably rejected the outrageous German demands to give up its key fortifications. Britain kept its word to neutral Belgium. There was not a reason in the lot for risking slaughter on the scale that would bleed the world over the next four years. But national insecurities had fostered alliances; alliances had produced rivalries; rivalries led to friction; friction created a powder keg. And Gavrilo Princip had, in assassinating Archduke Franz Ferdinand, lit the fuse.

It was as if a mountaineer, tied by a rope to fellow climbers, had lost his footing and fallen from a precipice, pulling the others down with him. While it can be argued as to which climber fell first, it seems incontestable that the blustering Wilhelm II and an over-eager German general staff made the initial misstep by pushing an Austrian quarrel with Serbia into a confrontation with Russia, then France, then Great Britain. Much of the kaiser's life had been a struggle between his intellect and his ego. In 1914, the ego won.

3

"A Lovely War"

AUGUST 1914. It was as if war had opened on two separate planes. On one, the planners, the generals and admirals, huddling in map-lined rooms, operated on an analytical plane moving chess pieces labeled armies, corps, divisions, and flotillas. On the other, a phenomenon of mass emotion surged forth, fueled by patriotism, a force more mystical, more primeval than the cool calculations going on in war rooms.

Adolf Hitler's enlistment had been the product of this emotional tidal wave, and for this twenty-six-year-old Austrian war marked both an ending and a rebirth. The day that Germany declared war on France, Hitler petitioned the court of King Ludwig III to be allowed to enlist in an elite Bavarian regiment, the King's Own. Initially, it appeared that the pattern of rejection, most painfully his being turned down twice by the Vienna Academy of Art, had followed him to Munich. The King's Own was full. But the next day Hitler received a letter that he opened with, as he recalled, "trembling hands." He had been accepted in a lesser regiment, the 16th Bavarian Reserve Infantry. To the near-derelict Hitler, over at last were the hunger and homelessness, the failure and rejection, that had been his lot. The war spelled salvation. Later he would write, "I am not ashamed to say that, overpowered by stormy enthusiasm, I fell down on my knees and thanked heaven from an overflowing heart for granting me the good fortune of being allowed to live at this time." He was no longer an outcast consigned to a marginal existence but part of something significant, something larger than himself. As he later wrote, the war was not simply "to get a little satisfaction out of Serbia, but Germany fighting for her life . . . to be or not to be."

He completed recruit training with never a complaint, indeed in a daily transport of exhausted ecstasy. A comrade recalled that upon being issued a rifle, Hitler "looked at it with the delight that a woman looks at her jewelry." Though his sloppiness and unmilitary bearing barely suggested a soldier, he never shirked a duty and never failed to offer a comrade a helping hand. He might bore his companions with sanctimonious sermons on the evils of tobacco and drink and never speak of women, but he won over his fellow *Landsern* by a talent for sketching them. They found Hitler an odd duck and a loner but on balance not a bad sort. They called him "Adi," and he liked it.

The attitude of Fritz Nagel reflected a more refined, upper-middle-class version of the same raw sentiments that motivated Adolf Hitler. As war was about to break out, Nagel, son of a wealthy Bremen family in the tobacco business and a strikingly handsome, blue-eyed model Teuton, found himself in ticklish circumstances. On August 3, 1914, German troops were massing on Belgium's border, and Nagel was in the Antwerp railroad station listening to an announcement that all German citizens must immediately report to the waiting room. He was carrying a passport that would reveal him as a German reservist and would surely be arrested. His instant impulse was to get out of Belgium and report to his regiment. As he put it, "Now everything depended upon our armed forces. Germany was completely encircled. How could we prevent hordes of enemies from overrunning Germany? But why, and so suddenly was the whole world determined to destroy us?"

Abandoning his steamer trunk and without a ticket, Nagel

slipped aboard a train bound for Maastricht in neutral Holland. As soon as the train crossed the Dutch-Belgian border, he jumped off and walked the rest of the way to Germany. The next day Nagel reported to his artillery regiment, carried by the tide of optimism evident everywhere, though he confessed, "Nobody really could imagine what a real war would bring us."

The euphoria that swept along an Adolf Hitler and a Fritz Nagel was not, however, universal in the German camp. In July of that summer, Lothar Lanz found himself posted to the garrison at Koblenz. A miner in civilian life, Lanz was now serving in Pioneer Battalion 30 and counting the days until he would complete his two years of obligated service and return home. But the imminence of war dashed all hopes for a discharge. Lanz was struck by the split in the reactions of his comrades. "Part of our men were seized by an indescribable enthusiasm," he remembered. "Others became subject to a great depression." Lanz found himself of the latter sentiment. As he put it, "I could not imagine what interest I could have in mass murder." He argued to his comrades that "war was the greatest misfortune that could happen to humanity." Still, the tide of emotion was so strong that at first it carried Lanz along. "We marched through the streets of the town to the station between crowds numbering in the thousands," he recalled. "Flowers were thrown at us from every window; everybody wanted to shake hands with the departing soldiers. . . . Musicians played songs of leave taking. People cried and sang at the same time. It was a real witches' Sabbath of emotion. Nobody could resist that ebullient feeling."

On the evening of August 2, 1914, the pioneers found themselves bivouacked in a barn on Germany's border with Belgium with no idea why they had been sent there. Lanz was sleeping on a bed of straw when at 1 A.M. he was awakened by the blare of a bugle. The captain strode in, and the men came to attention. "We are at war with Belgium," he announced. They now had a precious opportunity to earn Iron Crosses and bring honor to the Fatherland. As for their conduct toward the Belgian people, civilians were to be treated according to international treaties. "But I want to remind you," the captain advised, "too great considerateness borders on cowardice, and cowardice in the face of the enemy is punished severely."

CAPTAIN VIVIAN DE Sola Pinto, the exotic name apart, felt himself English to the core. When the war began, the gangling, myopic eighteen-year-old aesthete was a student at Oxford. The maneuvering of the great powers had counted as nothing in moving the British populace to embrace war compared to the sense of fair play outraged by the kaiser's invasion of little Belgium. As the novelist Alec Waugh put it, "there was a gallantry to taking the King's shilling," whereas bare months before poverty had been the chief recruiter for the British Army. "Almost any other sort of employment was thought preferable," the historian John Keegan has observed, "for soldiering meant exile, low company, drunkenness or its danger, the surrender of all chance of marriage—the removal, in short, of every gentle or improving influence upon which the Victorian poor had been taught to set such store." In an earlier time, a mother, upon learning that her son had enlisted in the regular army, had cried, "I would rather bury you than see you in a red coat." Overnight that prejudice vanished, not alone among the improvement-minded poor but for all Britons.

The idea of war fired a youthful idealism in de Sola Pinto, "not for imperial aggrandizement or material gain but for justice and liberty. Not only would we save the French and the Belgians, but we would rebuild our own society on a basis of social justice." Rupert Brooke, "a young Apollo, golden-haired," in one description, and judged by W. B. Yeats "the most handsome man in England," a graceful athlete and gifted poet, voiced the spirit of de Sola Pinto's generation. "Now, God be thanked, Who has matched us with His hour," Brooke wrote in an instantly popular sonnet.

Initially, de Sola Pinto's idealism had been thwarted. While at Oxford, he had tried several recruiting offices only to be rejected for poor eyesight. Increasingly, he found university life irrelevant, isolated from what he saw as "a lovely war." De Sola Pinto shuddered at the taunts of young women directed at apparently fit men like himself still in civvies. Just five days after war was declared, *The Times* of London had carried a story about a forty-nine-year-old former infantry captain who had flung himself to his death under the wheels of a van, fearing he would not be accepted for military service. A song had instantly caught on:

> What will you lack, sonny, what will you lack,
> When the girls line up the street,
> Shouting their love to the lads come back,
> From the foe they rushed to beat?
> Will you send a strangled cheer to the sky,
> And grin till your cheeks are red?
> But what will you lack when your mates go by
> With a girl who cuts you dead?

Through the intervention of an officer friend of his father, de Sola Pinto found himself in an army examination room, where a kindly medical officer left him alone long enough to memorize the eye chart. He was accepted and, after completing officer training, was commissioned a subaltern in the Royal Welch Fusiliers.

Class worked for de Sola Pinto but against R. C. Sherriff, a young Englishman equally eager to enlist. In that summer of 1914, Sherriff had just graduated from the local grammar school and had found a job in a London office. He had been an honor student, a team captain in sports, now held a responsible position, and was physically fit. When Lord Kitchener, the secretary of war, issued a call for 100,000 volunteers to supplement the regular army, Sherriff saw himself among the "suitable young men" eligible for a commission.

He took a day off from work, put on his best suit, and reported to the headquarters of his county regiment. He heard the adjutant ask the youth before him, "School?" to which the answer was the prestigious "Winchester." The adjutant jotted down a few details, and the candidate appeared to sail through en route to officer's training. When the same question was put to Sherriff, the adjutant reacted to his answer with a puzzled frown. He pored over a list and said, "I'm sorry, but I am afraid it isn't a public school." Sherriff, aware of the confusing English distinction in which "public" referred to elite private schools, protested that, nevertheless, he had received a good education. "I'm sorry," the adjutant repeated, "but our instructions are that all applicants for a commission must be selected from the recognized public schools, and yours is not among them." Sherriff was shuffled next door to join the enlisted ranks. But as casualties rose appallingly in the first months of the war—with more British officers lost in France than in all the wars in the previous hundred years—the bar had to be lowered, and a candidate of Sherriff's unpedigreed background was accepted into the officer corps.

Years later, as the author of the acclaimed war drama *Journey's End,* Sherriff was capable of putting the early snub into perspective: "Officers had to be made quickly, with the least possible trouble. The Army command had to find some sort of yardstick, and naturally they turned to the public schools. Most of the generals had been public school boys before they went to military academies. They knew from firsthand experience that a public school gave something to its boys that had the ingredients of leadership. They had a good background. They came from good homes. At school they gained self-confidence, the beginnings of responsibility through being prefects over younger boys. Pride in their schools would easily translate into pride for a regiment. Above all, without conceit or snobbery, they were conscious of a personal superiority that placed on their shoulders an obligation toward those less privileged than themselves. . . . It was a rough method of selection, a demarcation line hewn out with a blunt ax; but it was the only way in the face of a desperate emergency, and as things turned out, it worked."

Kitchener had expected that his call might produce the desired

100,000 volunteers in six months. That goal was swamped by a tide of 500,000 volunteers in the first month, and enlistments continued at a rate of 1,000 a month for the first year and a half of the war. In the end more than 3 million Britons would volunteer.

Kitchener had made an inspired promise that produced this flood of recruits: men who joined together could serve together. Thus were born the "Pals," a spontaneous burst of fraternal solidarity never before witnessed in British class history. Pals spanned the social divide. Liverpool's young businessmen enlisted as a battalion; clerks for the Cunard and White Star lines formed their own units; football teams joined together, as did coal miners, artists, and pasty lads from the London slums of Shoreditch, Westham, and Bermondsey. Small towns were depleted of young men who went off together as Pals. Part of the appeal was elemental patriotism. But just as surely, the war offered an escape from humdrum lives, from a desk or coal pit, and the promise of adventure, travel, uniforms, and the admiring glances of girls. Economics, too, was a force. One London clerk earning ten shillings a week was able to receive a continuing five shillings from his employer, seven shillings army pay, plus clothing and food. In the civilian sector, wages rose, unemployment disappeared, profiteers began raking in huge gains, and money flowed freely. H. G. Wells gave it all a moral grandeur. The war was just and inevitable, Wells said, because Germany was a malevolent power, and defeating her would ensure lasting peace. "This, the greatest of all wars is not just another war—it is the last war," Wells proclaimed. And then he refined his words into the phrase that elevated a parochial contretemps beginning in Sarajevo to a global crusade: the Allies were embarked on "the war that will end war."

IN FRANCE, MOBILIZATION exploded as part military operation, part patriotic rally, and mostly pandemonium. Henri Desagneaux had been caught up in the tumult. At thirty-six, Desagneaux was a well-established lawyer, head of the legal department for the Eastern Railway Company. On August 2, the day after President Raymond Poincaré issued the order for general mobilization, Desagneaux, a reserve lieutenant in the Railway Transportation Service, prepared to report for duty. On his way to the railroad station, he watched crowds jamming bank buildings, eager to pull out their savings before the institutions might fail. Desagneaux arrived at the station and waited for the next train to the front. "Women were crying and men too," he recalled as soldiers and families parted. Some of the women had to be torn away from their men. Elbowing his way into a car, Desagneaux noted, "The train is already clearly suffering from every stratum of society! The blinds are torn down, luggage racks and mirrors broken, and the toilets emptied of their fittings; it's typical French destruction." As the train crawled from town to town, crowds alongside the tracks sang "The Marseillaise," handed cigarettes and drinks to the soldiers' outstretched hands, and hoisted homemade signs reading, "String Up the Kaiser," "Death to the Boches."

Desagneaux, a powerful-looking man with a great Gallic nose and an expression that exuded authority, was already plotting how he might escape his rear-echelon assignment for a fighting unit.

PIERRE TEILHARD DE CHARDIN had been called up too, his status as a Jesuit priest notwithstanding. Teilhard had accepted the interruption of his vocation not with enthusiasm but with a philosophic shrug. In any case, everybody knew it would be a short war. Teilhard, age thirty-three, did not enter the army as a chaplain but as an ordinary soldier, the only concession to his clerical collar being an assignment as stretcher bearer with a regiment from North Africa. Eventually, he was one of six brothers called to the colors, the second youngest killed in the first months of the war.

Contrary to Teilhard's expectations, the war did not prove brief. Instead, it spread. Turkey and Bulgaria eventually came in alongside Germany and Austria-Hungary. These four countries formed the Central Powers, arrayed against an eventual sixteen nations comprising the Allies.

General Helmuth von Moltke had succeeded Field Marshal Alfred von Schlieffen as chief of the German general staff. Despite his public optimism that his predecessor's master plan presaged an easy march to Paris, Moltke, a fretful, worrisome personality, saw nothing so simply. He had warned that war among the great powers would descend to a "long, weary struggle" in which the adversaries would never "acknowledge defeat until the whole strength of [their] people is broken."

4

"Goya at His Most Macabre"

NOVEMBER 11, 1918. Four years after he had dropped out of school and memorized the eye test to join the Royal Welch Fusiliers, Vivian de Sola Pinto still retained the gangling, bookish appearance of an Oxford aesthete. He was, however, now a captain commanding a company, a survivor of the debacle at Gallipoli, twice wounded, and on this day back on the western front. The Gallipolli experience had cured de Sola Pinto of any lingering illusions. He remembered a sight there to which "Goya at his most macabre might have done justice": human scarecrows, pants dropped, squatting all day long over stinking ditches, dying of diarrhea and dysentery. This November morning he was marching his company along the road from Tournai to Brussels. Suddenly a staff captain came galloping up alongside shouting, "No firing after eleven o'clock!" De Sola Pinto and his comrades had heard talk of German envoys seeking peace at Rethondes in the Forest of Compiègne. Now it was apparently official. Germany's defeat was confirmed by ragged mobs of deserters happily heading toward Allied POW cages. Still, the morning air was punctuated by artillery and de Sola Pinto eyed stretcher bearers bringing Fusilier casualties to the rear. He ordered the men to fall out and let them stretch their limbs in a shallow trench. He watched another captain rise and trot toward the latrine. A sudden blast showered the men with dirt and rocks. A sergeant, coughing and shaking off clods of earth, stumbled back to the trench. The German shell had scored a direct hit on the latrine, he said. The captain was dead. De Sola Pinto glanced at his watch. It was now 10 A.M. He had only to stay alive another hour.

HENRI DESAGNEAUX had eventually succeeded, though it took two years, in escaping the safety of a railroad service battalion for the peril of the front as an infantry major. He had been cited five times in dispatches and had won the Croix de Guerre with palm leaf, thus far without a scratch. As rumors of a pending armistice swept the trenches, orders were still in place for a major offensive to be launched against the German stronghold and rail center at Metz on November 14. To Desagneaux it had become a race: Which would come first, the end of hostilities or the new offensive? "Revolution is brewing in Germany . . . the Boches are withdrawing everywhere," Desagneaux noted in his diary on November 9. On the eve of the armistice he wrote, "We are excited. We wait and hope."

The French priest Pierre Teilhard de Chardin, with four years of carting broken bodies to aid stations behind him, was also at the front that day, calculating how many stretcher bearers his company would require, based on past casualties, if the Metz campaign went forward.

SERGEANT WILL BIRD and his platoon of Canadian Royal Highlanders faced the end under a double pall, the deaths in the past twenty-four hours of their comrades Bob Jones and Tommy Mills and the awareness that even at this late hour, their own survival remained uncertain. As their battalion, with the 5th Royal Irish Lancers out front, prepared to retake Mons, a bloody four-year round-trip was about to be concluded. For Britain, the war had begun in this city and there it must end.

AUGUST 1914. That the war would descend into the deadly marathon it was to become would have astonished the one figure who had dominated its beginning. By the war's outbreak, the longtime chief of the German general staff, Field Marshal von Schlieffen, had been dead for more than a year, but it was the grand strategy bearing his name that was supposed to deliver a swift German victory. Schlieffen had first originated the concept in 1892. He was single-minded; his all-consuming passion in eighteen-hour workdays was to move the pieces representing armies around the chessboard of Europe, to perfect his plan. On weekends his idea of rest was to read military history aloud to his daughters. Political questions were beyond Schlieffen's responsibility. Those he left to the politicians. What he could tell them was how to overcome their consuming fear that Germany would become trapped between Russia and France. According to Schlieffen's design, the German Army would launch a counterclockwise wheeling maneuver, sweeping across Belgium north of Brussels, then swinging southward into France to catch the French forces between the right wing and a left-wing assault coming through Alsace-Lorraine, a giant pincer movement four hundred miles wide between its two ends.

Schlieffen had died in 1913, succeeded by Moltke. But his strategy lived on, unceasingly war-gamed by the generals. The murder of Archduke Franz Ferdinand and the subsequent mobilization of adversaries provided the rationale to launch the master plan.

According to the Schlieffen timetable, by the forty-first day, September 21, German troops should be marching beneath the Arc de Triomphe. Then Germany could turn her armies east to deal with Russia.

LOTHAR LANZ'S PIONEER Battalion 30 was among the countless anonymous cogs within the Schlieffen Plan machinery. The first clue to the pioneers that they were going into action was the order to cover their gleaming *Pickelhaube,* the traditional spiked helmet, with a dull-colored cloth to prevent the burnished metal from glinting in the sun and revealing their position.

They were deployed in a Belgian field, lying on their stomachs and firing at an unseen enemy, when one of Lanz's comrades rose to his knee for a better look. The man pitched forward, shot through the head. Lanz later recorded his reaction: "When looking at the first dead man, I was seized by a terrible horror. For minutes, I was perfectly stupefied, had completely lost command over myself and was absolutely incapable to think or act." Yet almost immediately, he felt the survivor's euphoria. Someone else had been killed, not him. When the order came to charge, "I ran forward, demented like the others, as if things could not be other than what they were."

The first death Lanz witnessed had been clean and quick. At Donchery, southwest of Sedan, as the Belgians and French fell back, he was initiated into more intimate combat. From a distance, the French troops, in the red trousers and blue coats worn since the 1820s, appeared as rippling waves of color. The Germans rushed forward, as Lanz recalled, yelling in "a good imitation of American Indians." The two forces collided in hand-to-hand fighting in the streets of Donchery. As he described the scene: "You grip your opponent, who is sometimes weaker, sometimes stronger than yourself. By the light of the burning houses you observe that the white of his eye has turned red, his mouth is covered with a thick froth. You stab, scratch, bite and strike about you as would a wild animal. No quarter is given. Exhaustion tries to master you, but that cannot be. You think only of your own life, of death, surprisingly even of home. Old memories rush through your mind. You suddenly remember that you carry a dagger. After a hasty fumbling, you find it. Your enemy bites, strikes, scratches, tries to force you down and plant his dagger in your heart. You use yours first. He is down. You are saved! Still, you must have that dagger back! You pull it out of his chest. A jet of warm blood rushes out of the gaping wound."

THE BARBARISM SPILLED over to civilians. Within months of the war's outbreak, a British commission composed of lawyers and historians investigated charges of atrocities against the Belgian populace. The commission produced the Bryce Report, named for Viscount James Bryce, who led it. Bryce was a respected historian, leader of the Liberal Party, and recently an immensely popular ambassador to the United States. His stature gave credence to accounts of German soldiers bayoneting babies, raping Belgian women publicly in the Liège marketplace, and hacking off the hands of children. "Murder, lust, and pillage prevailed over many parts of Belgium on a scale unparalleled in any war between civilized nations during the last three centuries," the report charged.

Doubtless the document was shaped to exaggerate and inflame. Even Belgian refugees fleeing to England discounted many of the horrors as propaganda. Nevertheless, the Germans' conduct was harsh. As the chief of the general staff, Moltke, observed on the second day of the war, "Our advance in Belgium is certainly brutal; but we are fighting for our lives and all who get in the way must take the consequences." Also on that second day, Private Matbern of the 11th Jaeger Battalion wrote in his diary how his unit had dealt with a village from which hostile fire came: "About 220 inhabitants were shot and the village was burned. . . . It was a beautiful sight." Matbern was likely referring to the village of Andenne, where the churchyard subsequently held hundreds of closely packed graves with identical crosses bearing identical dates of death. More civilian blood was spilled in Tamines, a mining town of 5,000, where 384 people were shot, and in Dinant, where 612 were shot. The bishop of Namur recorded the names and ages of victims from Dinant: Maurice Bettemps, eleven months; Gilda Genon, eighteen months; and Clara Struvay, two years, six months old, among them. More than 5,000 civilians died in the German sweep through Belgium; a few were guerrilla fighters, but most were hostages or people who simply found themselves in the wrong place.

With the Bryce Report translated into thirty languages, Germany's alleged infamy was spread throughout the world, casting the country in the role of villain that would last the entire war.

STILL, AT THIS stage, the slaughter that was to torment Europe for four more years might have been averted but for a strategic blunder by the French. Instead of using the bulk of their armies to block the German path through Belgium, generals Auguste Dubail and Noël de Castelnau saw a golden opportunity to attack eastward toward Lorraine and recover the French province lost to Germany in the 1870 Franco-Prussian War. This maneuver fitted the French military philosophy that the best defense was to attack, attack, attack. Thus, on August 14, to the well-entrenched Germans' surprised delight, waves of Frenchmen clad in greatcoats, their pants stuffed into calf-length boots, their officers in black and gold, surged eastward, shouting *"Vive la France!"* against an army possessing the most machine guns in the world. The French were cut to shreds. Though they would deliver a stinging counterpunch, not only were their casualties staggering in sheer numbers, but those who fell represented the cream of the French Army, her ablest officers and best troops, a blow that can be compared to an individual's loss of a limb.

By August 22, British regular troops had sailed to France and were in position to aid the French and Belgians. The following day, near Mons, British and German units stumbled upon each other. With the arrival of the British, the kaiser was reported to have ordered Moltke to sweep this "contemptible little army" out of his path. Nevertheless, the German assault was stopped cold by well-trained British regulars, who could fire fifteen to thirty rounds per minute up to three hundred yards with their short-magazine Lee-Enfield rifles. So withering was their fire that the Germans believed themselves to be facing machine guns. The British professionals turned the kaiser's alleged gibe around and made it their own, calling themselves the "Old Contemptibles."

Nevertheless, the German juggernaut was too powerful to hold back. By August 26, the British were driven into France, attempting a stand at Le Cateau. The fighting began in Napoleonic style, out in the open, with artillery facing artillery, practically for the last time in this war. German superiority of might continued to tell. A British sergeant, William Edgington, described the retreat, euphemistically designated a "general retirement." "In our hurry to get away," Edgington wrote, "guns, wagons, horses, wounded men were left to the victorious Germans and even our British infantrymen were throwing away their rifles, ammunition, equipment and running like hell for their lives, mind you not one infantryman was doing this, but thousands, and not one battery running away, but the whole of the British Expeditionary Force that took part in the battle of that fatal Wednesday 26 Aug at Le Cateau." Edgington had witnessed, he wrote, "a scandalous sight in the history of Britain, but it will never be published." The French matched the speed of the British retreat. Thus far, Schlieffen's plan was working.

Fritz Nagel's battery was told to prepare for long forced marches to Paris. The men were uncomplaining. Paris should be a paradise. Maybe they would get to stay on as occupation troops. One of Nagel's Bremen comrades had been a portrait painter in Paris before the war and knew the town. "We all looked forward to a good time," Nagel recalled.

By September 5, advance German cavalry units were well across the Marne River, barely twenty miles from Paris. At this point, an audacious French general, Ferdinand Foch, commanding the Ninth Army, supposedly uttered the battle cry remembered in history: "My center is falling back; my right retreats; situation excellent. I attack." What Foch actually said was "The attack directed against the Ninth Army appears to be a means to assure the retreat of the German right wing."

Moltke began to tamper with Schlieffen's plan. Instead of investing 90 percent of the German Army in the French campaign, as required, he began chipping away at it. Russia was mobilizing more swiftly than anticipated; thus he sent 15 percent of the army to defend East Prussia. Moltke did not want the French to retake Alsace-Lorraine; hence another 25 percent of his troops were diverted to that sector. Consequently, only 60 percent of the intended force was thrown against France through Belgium, well below what Schlieffen's pincer envisioned.

Paris, with an enemy so close that the guns could be heard at the Eiffel Tower, now depended for its salvation on one of the more colorful spectacles of the war. Joseph Gallieni, the military governor of the city, an old general with a drooping white mustache and a face suggesting a grandfatherly peasant, rushed reinforcements toward the Marne in taxis. Parisians first stared in astonishment, then cheered wildly, as eleven hundred rickety cabs, festooned with waving soldiers, sped out of the city toward the front. French forces checked the German advance and thus ended the first Battle of the Marne. In succeeding weeks, the opposing armies kept trying to outflank each other to the west of Paris in what came to be called "The Race to the Sea," until they finally ran out of land at the English Channel

No Germans would parade down the Champs-Elysées. Nagel's artist friend would not show his comrades the town. Instead, on September 14, the kaiser sacked General von Moltke for failing to achieve the fruits of the Schlieffen Plan, thus leaving Germany facing its most dreaded outcome, a war on two fronts. Moltke promptly had a nervous breakdown. The stalemated opponents now began digging in. From the North Sea to the Swiss border, some 460 miles distant, they furrowed the earth with trenches. A new form of warfare had begun.

The first two months had delivered a shock to nations believing that the war would be a brief pageant of arms followed by victory. No conflict between major European powers had occurred since 1870, and generals on both sides had no inkling of the effect of modern weapons employed against massed men. The French casualties from August through September—dead, wounded, prisoners, and missing—came to 360,000. Germany suffered 241,000 casualties. The British lost 30,000 men in the first month. The same number of Belgian soldiers, alive on August 5, were dead eight weeks later.

The bloodbath in the east was no less frightful. The Austro-Hungarians, fighting inside tiny Serbia, lost 230,000 men killed, wounded, or missing, roughly 50 percent of the force committed. The Serbians lost 170,000 men, more than 40 percent of their force engaged. In crushing the Russian invasion of East Prussia, the Germans destroyed an entire enemy army and took 50,000 prisoners. The defeated Russian commander, General Alexander Samsonov, committed suicide.

Despite the apparent price, another nation chose to share in the mayhem. Turkey, fearing attack by Russia, took Germany's side and declared war against the czar by bombarding the port of Odessa.

The confusion of generals untested in anything remotely like the war they now directed was captured in an exchange between General Sir John French, commander of the British Expeditionary Force, and his subordinate, General Sir Horace Smith-Dorrien. French, stout, of unimposing stature, and described as "amiable enough though petulant when thwarted," had just given instructions to Smith-Dorrien:

SIR JOHN FRENCH: The British Army will give battle on the line of the Condé Canal.

SIR HORACE SMITH-DORRIEN: Do you mean take the offensive, or stand on the defensive?

SIR JOHN FRENCH: Don't ask questions, do as you're told.

5

Upon a Midnight Clear

OCTOBER 1914. Adolf Hitler would survive to the end, not out of any particular effort to save his own skin, since he repeatedly volunteered for hazardous assignments, but by beating the odds in the roulette of war. His 16th Bavarian Reserve Infantry underwent its blood baptism in Belgium on October 29, 1914, on the Ypres front. Four times the regiment flung itself against British defenders. Four times the Germans were beaten back. On the fifth attempt they succeeded but left the field littered with dead and dying. In four days of fighting, the 16th lost more than 3,000 out of 3,600 men. To Hitler, the bloodletting proved that "our regiment handled itself heroically from the very first day." During the fight his sleeve had been shot off; he had walked out of a tent minutes before it was struck by a shell that killed three of his comrades, the kind of luck that was to save him again and again throughout his life. He was awarded the Iron Cross, Second Class, for heroism under fire and promoted to corporal. Soon after this first engagement, his commanding officer made him a runner, a *Meldegänger,* delivering messages between the rear and the front. Hitler had undergone, he later exclaimed, "the greatest and most unforgettable time of my earthly existence."

IN SOCIALLY STRATIFIED Europe the war juxtaposed unlikely comrades. Hitler's fellow Austrian, the violinist Fritz Kreisler, was already thirty-nine when the war broke out and one of the leading virtuosos of the era, his genius evident since age seven. Kreisler, a reserve officer, unhesitatingly answered the call, carried along by the fever of patriotism that swept Vienna. On the day he reported to his regimental headquarters, he saw a young reservist in uniform seated with his sweetheart at an outdoor café. "When somebody in the crowd spied them, a great shout went up, the public rushing to the table and surrounding them, then breaking into applause and waving hats and handkerchiefs," Kreisler recalled. "They seemed confused, the young girl blushing and hiding her face in her hands, the young man rising to his feet, saluting and bowing. More cheers and applause. There was a sudden silence. He was vainly struggling for expression, but then his face lit up as if by inspiration. Standing erect, hand at his cap, in a pose of military salute, he intoned the Austrian national hymn. In a second every head in that throng was bared. All traffic suddenly stopped, everybody, passengers as well as conductors of the cars, joining in the anthem. The neighboring windows soon filled with people, and soon it was a chorus of thousands of voices."

Kreisler assumed command of a platoon of fifty-five infantrymen, two buglers, and a four-man team of stretcher bearers. He reveled in the swift, easy friendship that developed among previous strangers. The officers he trained, dined, and drank with included a prince, a sculptor, a steel magnate, and a surgeon. In the ranks under him served a painter, a professional singer, a banker, a postal official, and two college professors.

Kreisler was astonished at the physical change he underwent at the front. "My rather impaired eyesight," he noted, "improved in the open, with only wide distances to look at. I found that my muscles served me better than ever before. I leaped and ran and supported fatigue that would have appalled me under other circumstances. In the field, all neurotic symptoms seemed to disappear as if by magic." He wondered what had brought about this altered state and concluded that it was that he had been freed of society's conventions. He shed gentility as if it had been a snake's skin. "It is extraordinary," he later wrote, "how quickly suggestions of luxury, culture, refinement, in fact all the gentler aspects of life which one had considered to be an integral part of one's life are quickly forgotten, and more than that, not even missed. Centuries drop from one, and one becomes a primeval man, nearing the cave-dweller in an incredibly short time. For twenty-one days I went without taking off my clothes, sleeping on wet grass or in mud or in the swamps, wherever need be, and with nothing but my cape to cover me. Nothing disturbs one. One night, while sleeping, we were drenched to the skin by torrential rains. We never stirred, but waited for the sun to dry us out again. All things considered a necessity of civilization simply drop out of existence. A toothbrush was not imaginable. We ate instinctively, when we had food, with our hands. If we had stopped to think of it at all, we should have thought it ludicrous to use knife and fork."

Kreisler's Austrians were facing Russian troops, and he was struck by what he called "the extraordinary lack of hatred" between the enemies. "One fights fiercely and passionately, mass against mass, but as soon as the mass crystallizes itself into human individuals whose features one actually can recognize, hatred almost ceases. Of course, fighting continues, but somehow it loses its fierceness and takes more the form of a sport, each side being eager to get the best of the other. One still shoots at his opponent, but almost regrets when he sees him drop." On the third day in battle, Kreisler was astonished to see "a giant red-bearded Russian whose constant pastime consisted in jumping like a Jack-in-the-box from the trench, crying over to us as he did so. He was frequently shot at, but never hit. Then he grew bolder, showing himself longer and longer, until finally he jumped out of the trench altogether, shouting to us wildly and waving his cap. His good-humored jollity and bravado appealed to our boys and none of them attempted to shoot at him while he presented such a splendid target. Finally one of our men, who did not want to be second in bravery, jumped out

of the trench and presented himself in the full sunlight. Not one attempt was made to shoot at him either, and these two men began
to gesticulate at each other, inviting each other to come nearer. . . .
The big Russian held out his hand which held a package of tobacco and our Austrian, seizing the tobacco, grasped the hand of
the Russian, and then reaching in his pocket produced a long Austrian cigar, which he ceremoniously presented to the Russian. . . .
By this time all precautions and even ideas of fighting had been
forgotten, and we were surprised to find ourselves out of the shelter of our trenches and fully exposed to the Russians, who, in turn,
leaned out of their own trenches and showed their heads in full. This
unofficial truce had lasted about twenty minutes."

His sentimental memories of battle persisted throughout his life
perhaps because Kreisler's war lasted only four weeks after which,
despite the healthful effects of military service, he was invalided
out of the army. In that brief span, his platoon had been reduced
from fifty-five to thirty-four men.

LOTHAR LANZ, a soldier of no social standing, saw the war from
a less romantic perspective. His pioneer unit was assigned to fill in
shell craters along a road to make it passable for the troops. First
they had to clear away the bodies of fallen comrades. As he remembered the work, "Two men would take a dead soldier by his
head and feet and fling him into a ditch. Severed arms and legs
were flung through the air into the ditch in the same manner." If in
the course of this work a man saw a better coat than his own, he
stripped it from the corpse, not always easily since the bodies had
become stiff as wood.

Wounded men who fell between the lines were left to die, often
slowly and agonizingly. To try saving them was to risk adding
oneself to the casualty list. The French had tried to rescue their
wounded by entering the field bearing a Red Cross flag. "We laughed
and shot it to pieces," Lanz noted. The French repaid in kind, and
in the end, in his sector, no side attempted to retrieve its wounded.

In those early months, a Socialist member of the German parliament, back in Berlin and thus a political soul mate of Lanz's, announced that he was volunteering in order to bring humanity to the battlefield. When Lanz read this news to his fellow proletarians, they burst out laughing.

For one brief moment, the war did assume the color and pageantry that Lanz remembered from schoolbooks. His pioneers had taken cover in a field near the French-Belgian border. A comrade nudged Lanz and pointed toward a small woods some five hundred yards ahead. The trees were issuing men on horseback, toy-like figures at first but quickly growing in size as their galloping mounts shrank the distance from the Germans to four hundred, then three hundred, then two hundred yards. Their faces began taking on individual features. The horses' racing hooves appeared not to touch the ground, and Lanz could hear the beasts snorting. One hundred fifty yards, one hundred yards, and then the German artillery began firing point-blank, while the infantry released a storm of lead. The first rank of cavalry dropped, the second and third piling on top of them. Like a tide crashing against a stone wall, the French attack ebbed. What five minutes before had been a spectacle of grace and beauty was now a tangled and blood-drenched heap of more than six hundred men and horses. It was the first and last cavalry charge Lanz would witness in the war.

Lanz's most distasteful duty had not been carried out against enemy soldiers. His unit had been passing through a village when shots rang out from a brick house, wounding four men. An officer sent troops to surround the house and throw hand grenades through the windows. Four French civilians came running out, their arms raised. Three officers formed a court-martial that took ten minutes to pass death sentences on the men.

Lothar Lanz was picked for one of four firing squads. He and five comrades were assigned a tall, lean fellow, a workingman like Lanz, judging from his dress. The condemned man was shoved against a wall and blindfolded. His mouth remained grimly set, and he uttered not a word. Lanz and the others lined up six paces from him. A sergeant shouted out the commands. On "Fire!" the victim was flung back before sinking to the ground, his expression never changing.

All that Lanz experienced—the burial of comrades as if they were animals, the abandonment of the wounded, the decimation of the once beautiful pageant of men on horseback, the shooting of a defenseless man—began raising questions in his mind. "Were these things improper or immoral?" he asked himself. "Again and again I had to return a negative answer. [I and my] comrades had become," he concluded, "no longer human beings, but simply blood-thirsty brutes; for otherwise [we] would be very bad soldiers"—and likely dead ones. Once he had accepted this truth, a seed was planted in Lanz's brain. He had to find a way to no longer face these moral quandaries. There must be a way out of this war.

Still, even if not for Lanz, idealism persisted among men on both sides. Walter Limmer, a student from Leipzig, wrote his mother, "This hour is one such as seldom strikes in the life of a nation and it is so marvelous and moving as to be in itself sufficient compensation for many sufferings and sacrifices." Limmer soon died of wounds. In an opposing trench, British lieutenant Glyn Morgan wrote his father, "My only regret is that the opportunity has been denied me to repay you for the lavish kindness and devotedness you have always shown me. Now, however, it may be that I have done so in the struggle between Life and Death, between England and Germany, Liberty and Slavery. . . . Goodbye dearest of all fathers." Two days later he was killed.

Captain Julian Henry Francis Grenfell, after graduating from Balliol College, Oxford, joined the 1st Royal Dragoons. On October 4, he wrote his mother, "I *adore* war. It is like a big picnic without the objectlessness of a picnic. I have never been so well or so happy." Grenfell later died of wounds at age twenty-seven.

DECEMBER 24, 1914, dawned with a penetrating dampness along the trenches in Flanders. Desultory artillery shelling and machine-gun fire continued throughout the day. But as darkness began to descend in the Wez Macquart sector, where the trenches undulated from four hundred to less than one hundred yards apart, puzzled British troops saw lanterns rising above the German lines. Soon silhouettes of the lantern bearers became visible above the parapet. The Tommies immediately opened fire. As the exposed figures dropped back into the trenches, a voice cried out in English, "Don't shoot! Don't shoot!" More lights began to appear all along the German lines. Another voice called out that he was coming to the center of no-man's-land and invited a Tommy to join him. He was prepared to exchange a bottle of wine, he said, for cigars and Christmas cake. The British were wary. Then one of them leaped out of the trench. His mates watched in wonder as the two figures closed and effected the exchange. Christmas trees bearing candles began to appear all along the German trenches. An English officer from the London Rifle Brigade, just one hundred yards away, described a scene "like the Thames on Henley regatta night." Another German called out, "You don't shoot, we don't shoot." There then rose from the German trenches a guttural rendition of "God Save the King."

Similar scenes were being repeated along the entire front. Lothar Lanz and his comrades, opposite the French, raised small trees, aglow with candles, hung with cookies and cotton taken from medical dressings. They began singing an old carol: "O thou blissful, O, thou joyous, mercy bringing Christmas time. . . ." The shooting gradually died out, producing an eerie silence. Men, long hunkered below ground in freezing knee-deep water, reveled in the opportunity to stand, climb out of the trenches, and stretch their legs without being shot. They began stepping around dead bodies toward the center of no-man's-land. The French met them halfway. They began shaking hands, swapping cigarettes, sausages, candy, wine, Christmas puddings, even their caps.

Officers in the line watched uneasily at the unraveling of discipline, but the flow of men from the trenches swelled beyond their control. In the Wez Macquart sector, a German officer advanced under a white flag to meet his British counterpart. "A truce until midnight tomorrow, when I will fire my automatic and the war will continue," he proposed. The British officer agreed.

As the sun rose the following morning on a cold but sun-filled day, Vivian de Sola Pinto's Royal Welch Fusiliers hoisted a board above their trench reading, "Merry Christmas." Frank Richards, another Fusilier, studied the face of his commanding officer, known as "Buffalo Bill" for threatening to blow out the "ruddy brains" of any man for the most trivial infraction. His comrades regarded Richards with exaggerated deference as "the oldest private in the British Army." It was true that he had held that rank in the regular army back in 1901. But he had left to enter the coal mines. By 1914, he had had a bellyful of the pits when he was, happily, recalled to the Fusiliers at his old rank. On this day he watched horror descend over Buffalo Bill's face as the soldiers emptied the trenches. It was too late to stop them. "The whole of the Company were out now, and so were the Germans," Richards recalled. "One of the men, speaking in English, mentioned that he had worked in Brighton for some years and that he was fed up to the neck with this damned war and would be glad when it was all over. We told him that he wasn't the only one." A German officer came out to meet Buffalo Bill and offered two barrels of beer for his Tommies. Soon, two enlisted men came rolling the barrels across the pockmarked landscape, followed by a soldier balancing a tray with a bottle of champagne and two glasses. Buffalo Bill and his erstwhile foe toasted each other's health.

Word of the truce drove the "brass hats wild," one British soldier remembered. "After they had recovered from feasting in their cushy châteaus, they sent out orders that the soldiers were hereafter to kill each other at every chance, and never to be friendly again." Perhaps the generals had it right. It does not do to give your enemy a human face, a name, with photos of children tucked into his breast pocket, or learn that he plays the piano beautifully—not if you have to kill him. And that, after all, was the whole point. Better a brutish caricature labeled simply "the foe" than a human being in the opposite trench.

Despite the outrage of the senior ranks, the fraternization continued throughout Christmas Day. One British officer happened upon his German barber from before the war and had his hair cut in no-man's-land. A German juggler who had worked the London music halls put on a show in full view of both trenches. The 6th Cheshires produced a soccer ball and organized a match with the Germans. "There was no sort of ill will between us," Private Ernie Williams of the Cheshires recalled. "There was no referee, no score, no tally at all. It was simply a mell." Football games sprouted all along the line with anything kickable serving as the ball—a pickelhaube helmet, an empty ration can, a canteen. Anything handy served as goal markers: cartridge belts, knapsacks, bayonets.

As night fell, songs rose from both trenches, "Stille Nacht" and "O Tannenbaum" from the German side, "Little Grey Home in the West" and "Tipperary" from the British. At midnight, the agreed-upon truce ended and shots rang out.

The following morning, Lothar Lanz, facing the French, listened as his company commander read out an order. "We were forbidden to wear or have in our possession things of French origin; for every soldier who was found in possession of such things would be put before a court-martial as a marauder by the French if they captured him. . . . We were especially forbidden to make use of [French] woolen blankets, because the French were infected with scabies." Unheeding, the men fought over the blankets. Scabies was not fatal, just itchy, and, Lanz reasoned, "What did a man care, if he could only get out of hell."

That morning, Lanz grabbed a young private about to climb out of the trench. "Stay here," Lanz warned. "The French will shoot you to pieces." "I left a box of cigars up there!" the soldier exclaimed, breaking free. His head was barely above the parapet when his cap flew off and he tumbled back, shot through the head.

The death of Lanz's young comrade was added to the total for the first year of the war, a slaughter unparalleled in history: more than 1,000,000 casualties among the French, Belgians, and British; 675,000 for the Germans on the western front and another 275,000 on the Russian front; 1,800,000 Russian casualties;

1,225,000 Austro-Hungarians; and 170,000 Serbians, for a total of 5,145,000 men dead, wounded, missing, or taken prisoner in five months of combat.

RUDOLF BINDING, faithful subject of the kaiser, had left his upper-class life to join his regiment of dragoons as a captain three months before the Christmas truce. Young Binding did not shrink from making hard decisions. During his first time under fire, his men were sniped at from houses. He rejected "the prescribed procedure in this event. To burn the houses—is nonsense, increasing the confusion and the resistance." Instead, "I had two men shot whom I found in two houses from which we were fired on. This had the required effect." He remained a patriot, committed to the war, but an experience like the Christmas truce had planted doubts. "The fraternization that has been going on between our trenches and those of the enemy," he observed, "when friend and foe go to fetch straw from the same rick to protect themselves from cold and rain . . . and never a shot is fired; this is a symptom . . . that there is no longer any sense in this business."

One soldier, however, had not the slightest doubt that what had happened on Christmas Day was wrong. Adolf Hitler did not leave his trench to shake an enemy hand, and he berated his comrades who had done so. "Such a thing," he said, "should not happen in wartime."

The war went on for another forty-seven months after the truce. Many among those who were still alive as the end neared counted the twenty-four hours of December 25, 1914, as the sanest of the war.

6

"The God Who Gave the
Cannon Gave the Cross"

NOVEMBER 11, 1918. Frank Richards marched with the 2nd Battalion, Royal Welch Fusiliers, along a dirt road approaching Mons. Richards had clambered out of the trenches, traded cigarettes and caps, and had his picture taken with his arm around a German during the 1914 Christmas truce. No such truce had occurred in the three Christmases since. And he detected no diminution in the war's ferocity now at the end. Shells continued exploding all morning. One had ripped through the roof of the house where he and his pals had spent the night, just after they had left. Their spirits rose warily when they were told, after days of rumor, that the armistice had been signed that morning. At a crossroads they came upon the smoking wreckage of a cook wagon, with dented kettles and food, still warm, dampening the ground. Alongside the road lay the wagon's two cooks, just killed.

As the shelling increased, Richards's platoon sought refuge in a shattered village. The men collapsed in the garden of a surviving house and broke out their rations. As Richards gnawed at his tinned bully beef, he studied the furrowed, unshaven faces of his comrades. He could count only two who had been with him that first Christmas day of the war. At one point he had calculated the odds of his survival at 20,000 to 1, an exaggeration but not wholly without foundation. The BEF's casualties since the beginning of the war had exceeded the most dire expectations. The 1914 retreat from Mons had almost wiped out the regular army. In the beginning, a man had had to stand five feet eight to enlist. Two months into the war, the need for replacements had driven the standard down to five feet five, then to five feet three. The generals began using the word "attrition" to describe their strategy: meaning which side could bleed the other to death first.

JUST AFTER 10:30 that armistice morning, Chaplain John de Valles and Albertine Connell of the American 26th Division watched the first wave of men the priest had just blessed go over the top. By now de Valles believed he had witnessed almost every contrivance for ending another man's life. All morning he had feared that the Germans in their final retreat might choose to unload their remaining stocks of gas shells. The shriek of artillery winging from their lines suggested the possibility, and the priest shared the terror that gas held for the men. A gas-attack warning, sometimes no more than one guard on duty beating on a cookhouse frying pan, would send the doughboys scrambling to pull on their masks. Every countermeasure to defend against gas seemed only to generate a new measure to penetrate the latest defense. The Germans displayed a particular genius in this deadly game. Knowing that masks donned in time could protect against gas, they began loading shells with sneezing powder, which seeped through the masks' filters. During the Meuse-Argonne offensive, Father de Valles had witnessed the devilish effect of these powders: "Even if we got just a slight smell of them it caused us to sneeze . . . knowing we would not be able to keep our gas masks on." The Germans then followed up with a barrage of lethal phosgene and mustard gas against the unprotected Allied troops. The priest prayed that the men would be spared this agony in the final hours.

APRIL 1915. Gas had first been used sucesssfully on the afternoon of April 22. At the time, Lance Corporal James Keddie, with the Canadian Army, was in a reserve trench on the Ypres front writing to his mother on his twentieth birthday. Keddie felt moderately secure with the support and frontline trenches still in front of his position. Near five o'clock he looked up to see a thick, low-hanging, yellow-green mist drifting toward their lines. As the miasma settled over the trenches, Keddie and thousands of other men abandoned their positions and broke for the rear, clutching their throats, their faces turning blue.

Rudolf Binding was among the German troops racing through the eight-thousand-yard gap opened in the British line by the retreat. "The effects of the successful gas attack were horrible," he said. Binding, who had unflinchingly shot civilians in reprisal for sniping attacks on his men, nevertheless found gas warfare troubling. "I am not pleased with the idea of poisoning men," he wrote in his diary. "All the dead lie on their backs, with clenched fists." He then added, with a gift of prophecy, "Of course, the entire world will rage about it first and then imitate us."

Standing just behind the German lines on the day that warfare entered a new age stood a thoughtful-looking forty-seven-year-old chemist named Fritz Haber. Haber had already won international acclaim for a signal contribution to human betterment. Before Haber, fertilizers to increase food production had depended entirely on a shrinking supply of natural ammonia gathered in Chile from guano, the droppings from seabirds. Haber and a colleague, Carl Bosch, had devised a way to synthesize ammonia in the laboratory for the mass production of fertilizer.

By 1915, with the western front locked in stalemate, both sides had been seeking a breakout strategy. The Germans had turned to Haber, his colleagues, and chemistry. The first canisters charged with nonlethal tear gas had been tested against the Russians on the eastern front on January 3, near Warsaw. The effort failed utterly. The Germans had fired the gas shells, but it was so cold that instead of vaporizing the gas had frozen, and the Russian troops experienced no ill effects.

Undaunted, Haber had pressed ahead. What the Germans unleashed against Lance Corporal Keddie and British and French troops that April afternoon was a gaseous form of chlorine that caused the body to overproduce secretions in the lungs. In effect, the victim drowned in his own fluids. It was Haber, aided by an east-to-west wind, who personally directed the introduction of poison gas on the western front that April day. His wife was so appalled by what she regarded as Haber's prostitution of his genius that she begged him to abandon this work. Haber, an ardent patriot, refused, and Frau Haber killed herself.

The Allies quickly determined that the gas was chlorine, a substance soluble in water. British troops were initially instructed in a crude but reasonably effective defense, water-soaked rags tied around the mouth. The French came up with their own improvement, soaking a handkerchief in urine.

By the end of 1915, the Germans had progressed to using phosgene gas, which also caused suffocation and was eighteen times more powerful than chlorine. The Allies countered with the "box respirator," a mask with huge goggles and a canister dangling from a hose to filter out the toxins. If used in time, the masks could block the gases. They also produced one of the Great War's lingering images, humans reduced to the appearance of grotesque giant insects. The Germans next countered with mustard gas, which burned and blistered any exposed part of the body and swelled the eyelids, causing temporary or permanent blindness. Mustard gas was stubborn, clinging to the ground as long as three days. Heavier than air, it settled into craters and trenches where men had taken refuge. It ruined food supplies. Harold Clegg, a British soldier with the Liverpool Rifles, while recovering in a hospital gas ward, described the effects he had suffered: "Blindness, deafness, loss of voice, inability to swallow, choking, difficulty breathing, and burns." Five years later, he had still not fully recovered from the exposure. The only treatment for chlorine or phosgene poisoning was oxygen, which was effective if promptly administered. No treatment existed for mustard gas.

Binding had been correct. The Allies quickly matched the Germans gas for gas. Indeed, the French devised the most effective long-range delivery system, a shell containing a small explosive that cracked the casing and released the poison. The Germans continued to develop countermeasures, even devising a gas mask for their messenger dogs.

Viewed practically, gas was a limited weapon. If no wind blew, it simply hung in the air. If the wind shifted, it could and did blow back over one's own lines. But the strategists and generals clung to its use since, when it did work, it was a cheap means of killing en masse and denying territory to the enemy. Thus it was used to the war's end.

DR. GEOFFREY KEYNES observed firsthand a key contributor to the death toll. Keynes, at age twenty-seven, had volunteered for the Royal Army Medical Corps immediately upon the war's outbreak, believing that "Great Britain would win the war, it would not last a long time, and that the experience must not be missed." Keynes was of an accomplished family, his father the registrar of Cambridge University, his brother, John Maynard, already en route to his stature as one of history's pivotal economists. A sister, Margaret, had been awarded the rank of CBE, Commander of the British Empire, and her husband, A. V. Hill, was a Nobel Prize-winning physiologist. Along with his medical career, Dr. Keynes had a literary bent and, just before entering the army, had published a book on the seventeenth-century metaphysical poet John Donne.

On August 18, two days after being commissioned, Keynes ran into his friend Rupert Brooke. It was Brooke who had thanked God "Who has matched us with His hour." "He gazed at my uniform with envy and almost with despair," Keynes remembered. "Like many other young men, he was having great difficulty in deciding in what capacity he ought to serve." Brooke soon found his niche in the Royal Navy and wrote a poem that again captured the lyrical romanticism of those of his generation who had yet to taste war. He wrote in "The Soldier":

> If I should die, think only this of me:
> That there's some corner of a foreign field
> That is forever England.

The sonnet was read from the pulpit of Saint Paul's Cathedral, prompting another round of enlistments.

Keynes's first assignment was to a hospital in a converted hotel near Versailles. Trainloads of wounded, delivered in cattle cars, were pouring in from the retreat at Mons. His first patient, his leg fractured by enemy fire, died the next day, much to Keynes's shock and dismay. "We had been instructed," he noted, "not to interfere with apparently clean bullet wounds." The practice had evolved from experience during the Boer War in South Africa. "We soon learned, however, the difference between wounds sustained on the clean South African veldt and those contaminated by European mud." The earth of northern France and Flanders was saturated with "anaerobic bacteria lurking in the soil," Keynes found, and was "responsible for the gangrene which proved to be one of the chief causes of death among men who reached a base hospital alive." On April 23, 1915, his youthful, athletic, passionately patriotic friend Rupert Brooke died under similar septic conditions, from blood poisoning on a ship en route to Gallipoli, hardly the hero's death his poetry had celebrated.

Microbes knew no allegiance. Lothar Lanz recalled the effect of decomposed bodies in no-man's-land contaminating the ground. "If then a man happened to have a tiny wound in his hands his life was greatly endangered." Five of Lanz's comrades had crawled between the lines and subsequently died of septic poisoning.

PIERRE TEILHARD DE Chardin, proud, sensitive, intellectual, understood his station acutely. The priest had not been commissioned a chaplain or assigned to a prestige regiment. Instead, he had been sent to serve as a stretcher bearer with African colonials, the 8th Moroccan Light Infantry and Zouaves. He wrote home, "You feel very insignificant alongside the combat troops, and they make you feel it"—though, as he soon found, machine guns and artillery made no distinction between men who carried a rifle and those who carried a stretcher. His duties, nevertheless, were "looked on as a 'soft number' fit only for weaklings."

Teilhard had entered the front early in 1915 during the Battle of the Yser, the river running from northern France into Belgium. There he had displayed exceptional bravery under fire. He would dash almost up to the enemy wire in search of the wounded. Finding a casualty, he would lift the man onto his back in a fireman's carry and crouch low to the ground, stumbling into shell holes and sprayed by enemy fire, before delivering the man to safety. He wept when he had to leave behind half-crazed, screaming men. Finally his courage and qualities of leadership were modestly recognized: he was made a section leader of stretcher bearers and promoted to corporal.

He remained throughout a priest and a reflective man. He said Mass almost every morning and regretted the occasions when the intrusions of battle prevented him from doing so. He hungered for a rationale that would harmonize his religious beliefs with the horrors he witnessed daily. He came to see the war as "basically a struggle between two moralities." The Germans, he suspected, had "a perverted moral sense." He wrote his favorite correspondent, his cousin Marguerite Teilhard-Chambon, a childhood playmate and an author, "It's Christian justice we are fighting for." Both sides might pray to the same God, but God's cause surely resided in the French trenches, he was convinced.

The lack of religious conviction among the men troubled him. "I am greatly struck," he wrote his cousin, "by this double fact: the very small number of souls in whom the need for religion has awoken, and the extraordinary vulgarity that goes with this atrophy." Even men wanting to believe had their faith shaken, telling

him, "If there were a good God, he would never allow this war."
He admitted to Marguerite, "Many minds, and not all of them
mediocre, are just now greatly exercised by this question." He
began stealing what little free time he had to write a "moral manifesto" to explain the contradiction between God's mercy and war's
cruelty. He wrote his cousin, "If God could make a more perfect
world, why did he not do so? My answer is: you're using 'more
perfect' ambiguously. Every conceivable universe has its own special shade of beauty, which is incommunicable, and by which it is
more perfect than all others. Another universe, with less evil,
would be called by us 'better' because we reason like weaklings
who are terrified of effort. But would it be a fit setting for the
growth of the saintly qualities that are born in the shadow of the
cross?" It was the sort of apologia that might satisfy a fellow Jesuit
and possibly a devout cousin, but not likely one of the wounded
left to die in no-man's-land.

Other believers struggled to reconcile a God who preached peace
with a God who countenanced war. They took solace in these lines:

> Oh! spacious days of glory and of grieving!
> Oh! sounding hours of lustre and of loss;
> Let us be glad we lived, you still believing
> The God who gave the Cannon gave the Cross.

7

The Three Musketeers

NOVEMBER 11, 1918. They knew in London soon after 5:40 A.M. that an armistice had been signed, to go into effect at 11 A.M. Among those waiting was Vera Brittain, age twenty-two, a nurse with the Voluntary Aid Detachment, the VAD, who had spent three years on the western front and in Malta before returning to England. Vera went distractedly about her duties that morning, her thoughts drifting back to a letter she had written to her fiancé, Roland Leighton, when the war had been young. She had been at Oxford at the time and had just heard a performance of Handel's *Occasional Oratorio*. The work portrayed troops mustered for battle, followed by a lament for the fallen and ending in a triumphant finale for the returning victors. She wondered in her letter to Roland, at the time an army lieutenant, "if I shall be one of those who take a happy part in the triumph—or if I shall listen to the merriment with a heart that breaks and ears that try to keep out the mirthful sounds."

JUNE 1914. Awareness of the war had come upon Vera slowly. As she later recalled, "I entirely failed to notice in the daily papers of June 29th an account of the assassination, on the previous morning, of a European potentate whose name was unknown to me, in a Balkan town of which I had never heard." Her mind that summer was afire with the knowledge that in the fall she would be off to Oxford, after a long struggle for her parents' approval. The Brittains were a wealthy paper-manufacturing family from Buxton who, in Vera's view, "represented all that was essentially middle-class in that Edwardian decade." Literature and learning aroused little interest in the elder Brittains. And all that was British middle class had not included higher education for women. Vera's acceptance at Oxford's Somerville College for Women made her "feel as though I were in a dream from which I am afraid to awaken."

Young Vera had led a protected life, so much so that during Oscar Wilde's trial she did not understand the charges of homosexuality and sodomy leveled against an author whose work she loved. Her brother, Edward, two years younger, was a sensitive, dreamy youth with a passion and a gift for music. He played the piano and viola and had composed several songs and concertos. The family comfortably accepted that Edward, unlike Vera, would eventually attend Oxford. In 1914 he was still enrolled at Uppingham in Rutland, a school dedicated to instilling "muscular Christian ideals of athletics, militarism, and morality" in its students. One alumnus remembered his Uppingham days thus: "I was kicked, hounded, caned, flogged, hair-brushed, morning, noon and night."

At Uppingham, Edward formed part of a fast friendship with two others, called by fellow students "the Three Musketeers." The leader was a legendary upperclassman, Roland Leighton, known for his magisterial manner as "the Monseigneur." The trio was rounded out by Victor Richardson, a modest son of a dentist who intended to become a physician himself. For his gentle nature and utter reliability, Leighton had dubbed Victor "Father Confessor."

In April 1914, Edward Brittain brought Leighton home for the Easter break. Roland's reputation had preceded him. The nineteen-year-old was house captain, color sergeant of the Officer Training Corps, editor of the school magazine, a gifted scholar, and also destined for Oxford. Unlike the Brittains, Roland came from an intellectual family, his father the literary editor of the *Daily Mail,* his mother a celebrated novelist. Vera was determined to be unimpressed by Roland. She deliberately arrived late for dinner the day of his arrival and greeted the guest with "a lofty assumption of indifference." It did not last. "I had not been with him for ten minutes," she recalled, "before I realised that in maturity and sophistication he was infinitely the superior of both Edward and myself."

The attraction between Vera and Roland was immediate and mutual. Leighton, not conventionally handsome or physically imposing, projected an appealing combination of forcefulness and sensitivity expressed in soulful eyes and a quiet way of speaking. Vera was small and uncommonly pretty, with a doll-like daintiness. Yet she too communicated strength of character and intelligence to Roland.

On July 14, as the shadow of war loomed, Vera went to Uppingham, ostensibly to see her brother during Speech Day ceremonies at the end of term. She watched in wonder as Roland collected prizes, one after another, for English Essay, Latin Prose, Greek Prose Composition, and Captain in Classics.

Roland went on to Oxford that fall but was soon distracted. After England went to war, he wrote Vera, "I don't think in the circumstances I could easily bring myself to endure a secluded life of scholastic vegetation." He found the prospect of battle "a very fascinating something—something, if often horrible, yet very ennobling and very beautiful." Vera wrote back, with the practicality of her gender, "Women get all the dreariness of war, and none of its exhilaration." A persistent Roland, after first being rejected for poor eyesight by the infantry, artillery, and service corps, finally secured a commission in the 7th Worcestershires.

Shortly thereafter, he and Vera went to dinner, accompanied by Vera's aunt. The conversation, to the aunt's discomfort, turned to burial practices. Vera preferred being burned on a pyre, she said, like Achilles. Roland chose being set adrift on a flaming boat. Vera found herself asking him, "If you could choose your death, would you like to be killed in action?" Her bluntness horrified her aunt.

But Roland replied, "Yes, I should. I don't want to die, but if I must I should like to die that way. Anyhow I should hate to go all through this War without being wounded at all; I should want something to prove that I had been in action."

Toward the end of March 1915, his training completed, Roland was dispatched to the western front. Just before, he and Vera became engaged. At their farewell, he told her that he was not going because he hated the Germans or loved the Belgians, but out of a sense of "heroism in the abstract." Vera's unspoken reaction was "that didn't seem to be a very logical reason for risking one's life." By then, Victor Richardson had also dropped out of Oxford and was serving in the 4th Royal Sussex Regiment. The youngest Musketeer, Edward Brittain, who had also gone on to Oxford, left, and was commissioned in the 11th Sherwood Foresters.

Edward had brought another friend into Vera's circle: Geoffrey Thurlow. Thurlow had been an outstanding student at the Chigwell School, becoming head of school before entering Oxford in the fall of 1914. Initially, the widespread hypnosis of war failed to touch this gentle youth, described as "a non-militarist at heart." However, he eventually succumbed to the pressure of his peers, left Oxford after one term, and also joined the Sherwood Foresters. He met Edward Brittain in officer training, and the friendship was instant. Each bolstered the other's wavering confidence that, despite their nonviolent natures, courage would not fail them when the test came. Soon Vera was corresponding with all four men.

In June 1915, with the closest friends in her life serving, Vera felt she must play her part. She joined the VAD. Her initial tasks, in the military ward of an English civilian hospital, were hardly heroic: emptying bedpans and throwing out pus-filled dressings. She took up these duties, however, with "masochistic delight" since they helped her feel close to Roland, now at the front. She fantasized about him being wounded and brought into her ward while she, in her uniform, tended him.

She was eventually elevated to more challenging duties and described in a letter to Roland "a really terrible amputation dressing

I had been assisting at—it was the first after the operation—with my hands covered with blood and my mind full of a passionate fury at the wickedness of war." Still, she wanted to be closer and began asking for assignment to a field hospital at the front.

Roland's poetic vision of war soon collapsed. Days after entering the line, he wrote Vera, "One of my men has just been killed—the first. . . . I . . . found him lying very still at the bottom of the trench with a tiny stream of blood trickling down his cheek. . . . I have no animosity against the man who shot him—only a great pity, and a sudden feeling of impotence." Within months, the last traces of martial romanticism had vanished. "Let him who thinks War is a glorious, golden thing," he wrote Vera, ". . . look at a little pile of sodden grey rags that cover half a skull and a shin-bone and what might have been Its ribs, or at a skeleton lying on its side, resting half crouching as it fell, perfect but that it is headless. . . . Who can say that Victory is worth the death of even one of these?"

As Christmas 1915 approached, Vera received a scribbled message torn from Roland's field service notebook: "Shall be home on leave from 24th Dec.–31st. Land Christmas Day." On December 24, Vera obtained leave and rushed to Brighton to await him, thinking, "do let us get married and let me have a baby—something that is Roland's very own, something of himself to remember him by if he goes." She checked into the Grand Hotel near the Keymer cottage where Roland's family was housed, all of them waiting throughout Christmas Day for his call.

8

A Scar from Belgium
to Switzerland

1914. History significantly follows technology, and the military technology of 1914 dictated trench warfare. Mass-produced weapons—artillery that could hurl explosives for miles, machine guns that could blanket a thousand-yard-wide field of fire—had driven the adversaries below ground level. The trench became the reality and the metaphor of the war. These ditches, six to eight feet in depth and five feet wide, snaked through the fields, woods, and farmlands of Belgium and France for more than four hundred miles to Switzerland.

Ideally, a trench system comprised three parallel lines: the frontline or fire trench, a support trench several hundred yards behind, and behind that a reserve trench. In front of each trench ran webs of barbed wire, sometimes thirty feet deep. "Saps," short extensions, jutted from the front of the trench for forward observation and emplacement of machine guns. Communication trenches running perpendicular connected the trenches to one another and to the rear.

The front of the trench, facing the enemy, was topped with sandbags, forming a parapet. The sides were shored up with timber planking or corrugated iron. Since water invariably collected in a trench, the bottom was planked with wooden slats called duckboards. Two feet from the bottom, a step allowed the men to see above the trench, fire their rifles, and pitch hand grenades. A trench never ran more than several yards before bending at a right angle, then bending back again, forming a series of indentations. The switches in direction were designed to confine damage from a shell landing in a trench to a short stretch. Further, if enemies entered the trench, their fire would be stopped at the bend. From the air the trench resembled a coarsely stitched border on the hem of the land, rather like a Greek key pattern.

Much of the foregoing description is theoretical, an engineer's rendering of an ideal entrenchment. In reality, the trench might range from all the above features to a hastily clawed rut in the earth. Valentine Fleming, a member of Parliament and army major, wrote his friend Winston Churchill a description of this subworld: "Imagine a broad belt, ten miles or so in width, stretching from the Channel to the German frontier near Basle, which is positively littered with the bodies of men and scarified with their rude graves; in which farms, villages and cottages are shapeless heaps of blackened masonry; in which fields, roads and trees are pitted and torn and twisted by shells and disfigured by dead horses, cattle, sheep and goats, scattered in every attitude of repulsive distortion and dismemberment." Fleming would die in the trenches in 1917, leaving a nine-year-old son, Ian, who would grow up to write of more fanciful wars.

Before the Americans entered the war, the Germans had concocted a piece of propaganda, entitled "The Archives of Reason," to help them understand what they might be getting into: "Dig a trench shoulder-high in your garden: fill it half-full of water and get into it. Remain there for two or three days on an empty stomach. Furthermore, hire a lunatic to shoot at you with revolvers and machine guns at close range. This arrangement is quite equal to a war and will cost your country very much less." The picture might have included the presence of rats—huge, fearless, and clambering over the men as if the trench belonged to them too.

Barbed wire and sandbags became as much a feature of the soldiers' everyday life as a clothesline or pillow at home. Barbed wire was an American invention devised by ranchers in the 1870s to pen in their cattle. In its battlefield incarnation, the wire was originally strung along wooden posts pounded into the ground. The wood was eventually replaced by screw pickets, which could be twisted noiselessly into place.

Sandbags were actually filled not with sand but with dirt or any other available fill. Trench lore had it that one bag would slow a bullet to half speed, and five were required to stop it cold. Guy Chapman served with London's 13th Royal Fusiliers Regiment, which he described as "entirely amateur" with only one regular army officer, who had already been ten years in retirement when the war broke out. Chapman was much amused when the ladies of England took to sewing sandbags as their bit to support the war effort. They "formed a sandbag club for our benefit . . . these sandbags were obviously too good to be put to such humdrum uses as parapets or traverses," Chapman concluded. "Beautifully stitched—hand stitched . . . of colours which the doting Joseph might have dyed for Benjamin, they were too splendid to have mere clay thrust into them." The men found uses the English women would not have foreseen. "A really charming pair kept my boots from soiling my blanket when I slept," Chapman noted. "Another of silken magenta pillowed my head, while a nattier blue affair held my washing tackle."

No-man's-land was the terrain between enemy trenches, a darkly romantic phrase of tangled derivation. The term was believed to have been used originally to define a contested territory or a dumping ground for refuse between provinces and fiefdoms. The *Oxford English Dictionary* contains a reference to the phrase dating to the year 1320 and spelled "nonesmanneslond." It was first used in a military context by Ernest Swinton, a soldier and historian, in his short story "The Point of View."

The greatest scourge to the men in the trenches, wrote Edmund Blunden, a British officer and poet, was "that short and dry word 'raid,' " which he characterized as "nightly suicide." These forays into no-man's-land had initially been introduced by the British and reflected a pugnacious posture—pugnacious at least among rear-echelon officers, who planned but did not take part in them. The army had learned the tactic in India from the tribesmen they had fought in the frontier wars. At its loftiest rationale, the raid was intended to foster "the offensive spirit of the troops, while on the defensive"—in short, to counter any live-and-let-live attitude the men might adopt toward the enemy. Tactically, raids were carried out to detect activity in the enemy trenches, to destroy an installation, to take prisoners for interrogation, or simply as an exercise in "ritualized violence," in Blunden's definition. The first recorded raid on the western front took place on the night of November 9–10, 1914, carried out, appropriately, by the 39th Garwahl Rifles of the Indian Corps.

Second Lieutenant H. E. Cooper of the Royal Warwickshire Regiment, in a letter to his parents, described a typical raid he had led. "Let me try to picture what it is like," he wrote. He had first gone about picking the men for the job: "my favourite corporal (a gentleman, a commercial traveller for the Midland Educational in civilian life) and my six most intelligent and most courageous men." He had next performed a preraid ritual: "Bayonets are examined to see if they slip out of the scabbard noiselessly; my revolver is nicely oiled, all spare and superfluous parts of equipment are left behind." As night descended, the party climbed the ladder and went over the parapet, "tumbling as rapidly as possible so as not to be silhouetted against the last traces of the sunset." Cooper and his men followed a zigzag path through known breaks in the barbed wire. Once in no-man's-land, they began "wriggling through the long grass for a hundred yards or so." Two men crept almost to the German wire, while the others remained a few yards behind. The party waited in brittle silence, during which "tiny noises are magnified a hundred fold—a rat nibbling at the growing corn or a rabbit scuttling along give us all the jumps." Cooper's suspicions were aroused by the silence: "a very ominous sign—no shots are being fired from the trenches in front of us, no flares are being sent up and there is no working party out. This points to only one thing and that is they also have a party out. There is no other conclusion." Soon the Germans could be heard: "My heart thumps so heavily that they must hear it, my face is covered with cold perspiration. . . . I have one solitary thought: I am going to kill a man . . . and the thought makes me miserable and at the same time joyful."

That night they were lucky. The German patrol moved off in another direction, and the British pulled back to the safety of their lines. Cooper was well aware of his good fortune. As he wrote his parents, "The battalion who alternates with us have lost three officers on this business in front of my trenches."

SEPTEMBER 1915. If the German Lothar Lanz had a soul mate in the enemy ranks, it was among *poilus* such as René Naegelen. Naegelen, at twenty-one, was the youngest of seven children of a poor Alsatian baker who had fled to Belfort, France, after the Franco-Prussian War. A precocious mind and love of learning had not spared René from being yanked from school at age thirteen and apprenticed as a pastry chef. What he saw from his father's shop—housewives barely able to afford bread for their children, leaving for work before sunup and returning in the dark, sick children too poor for a doctor's care, awakened in him a passion to fight against injustice. By age nineteen he was already leader of the Socialist Party in Belfort. The war diverted him to what he regarded as simply another crusade. He was yet to learn what his fellow Socialist in the enemy trenches, Lanz, had already discovered of war's pitiless lack of romance.

On September 24, the eve of his first test of fire, the Battle of Second Champagne, Naegelen felt himself intoxicated by the words of his commanding officer. "Soldiers of the Republic," the colonel began. "The hour has come to attack and win. . . . Your onslaught won't be resisted. . . . Fight wholeheartedly for the liberation of your country, for the triumph of justice and liberty!" As he heard the words, Naegelen remembered, "I would not have changed places with anyone, not even for an empire!"

The first obstacle the attacking forces had to overcome was the barbed wire before the German trenches. The French arrayed 2,500 guns to blast away the wire and destroy enemy gun emplacements. The British, launching a companion offensive near Loos, found themselves short of artillery shells and substituted with their first gas attack. It was a disaster. Uncooperative winds blew the poison back, and, in effect, the British gassed themselves. J. W. Palmer of the 26th Brigade, Royal Field Artillery, described the effects of the wayward gas on his comrades: "Their faces and hands gradually assumed a blue and green colour and their buttons and metal fittings on their uniforms were all discoloured."

Subsequent bombardment with conventional shells had scant effect in tearing away the barbed wire. R. C. Sherriff may have been a London clerk before the army deigned to commission him, but he proved an adept student of trench warfare. "You can't destroy barbed wire entanglements with shellfire," he observed. "The more you shell them, the worse they get." After one intensive barrage, he noted that the stakes had been blown out of the ground, but "the wire was still there—all twisted and distorted and more difficult to get through than when it was taut and straight."

Gas was unreliable. Barbed wire stood up to shelling. And one's own artillery produced another unintended consequence. As Sherriff put it, "Land churned up by a massive bombardment of shells was impossible for the rapid advance of infantry." They had to pick a slow and arduous way around the craters, at the mercy of enemy machine guns. So appalling was the slaughter inflicted by machine-gun fire at Loos that the Germans, sickened by the heaps of corpses piling up before them, stopped firing when they saw the beaten British troops finally retreating.

At Loos and in future offensives, British Tommies would fall victim to the generals' impatience with the passivity of trench warfare. To staff officers, a trench was merely a place to assemble until your army climbed out of it to resume the offensive again. Sherriff noted what the generals failed to accept: that "the Germans had built deep dugouts impervious to shellfire. . . . When the barrage lifted for the attackers to advance, the Germans would come out with their machine guns and mow them down."

Though the Allies pointed to gains at Champagne and Loos— Naegelen saw thousands of his comrades fall to take less than two miles of ground, while the British advanced just over two miles— the price was astronomical. By the time these offensives petered out inconclusively, French and British losses totaled 240,000 men, against the Germans' 140,000. To punch one salient two miles deep cost the British Army 16,000 dead, more than four men per yard. A man died to gain a clump of earth no longer than his outstretched body. Some actually saw the toll at Loos as an improvement. An assault at Festubert, five months before, had cost the British nine men dead for every yard gained. Again, the lowly junior officer Sherriff saw it all with depressing clarity. The generals had learned nothing from the horrendous losses at Loos. "They decided that all they needed was another and more copious supply of men and a larger quantity of ammunition."

A POTENTIAL LIFESAVER arrived at the front that September but got off to a suspect start. An engineer, John L. Brodie, had designed the first steel helmet for the British Army, quickly christened, by the Tommies, "the battle bowler." They were first issued only to snipers, and Guy Chapman describes their debut in his London regiment. The first to wear a helmet was "Gerrard, a charming intelligent boy in No. 3. . . . He was killed instantly. A fragment of a shell tore through the steel and pinned his brain." Thereafter, no man would wear the helmet "except under the direct orders and observation of an officer." The men soon found other purposes for the helmet—as a washbasin, as a kettle, and, as Chapman notes, for uses "often of a nature not to be recorded."

In December, as fighting waned for the moment, a poem appeared in the British magazine *Punch*. Its anonymous author turned out to be a Canadian physician, Lieutenant Colonel John McRae, who had served at the Second Battle of Ypres earlier in the year. McRae had noticed that while all else had been laid waste, the fields of Flanders were blooming with red poppies. Indeed, the digging of so many graves helped spread their seeds. The color symbolism struck McRae and inspired perhaps not the best but the best-remembered poem of the war, particularly its hauntingly elegiac opening lines:

> In Flanders fields the poppies blow
> Between the crosses, row on row,
> That mark our place, and in the sky
> The larks, still bravely singing, fly
> Scarce heard amid the guns below.

The second stanza regrets the lives cut so short:

> We are the Dead. Short days ago
> We lived, felt dawn, saw sunset glow,

which suggests that McRae is about to condemn the wastage of war. But even after the staggering losses of 1915, war weariness had not yet set in, and McRae instead calls for renewed effort, blood to avenge blood:

> Take up our quarrel with the foe:
> To you from failing hands we throw
> The torch; be yours to hold it high.
> If ye break faith with us who die
> We shall not sleep, though poppies grow
> In Flanders fields.

THOUGH THE FRONT was relatively quiet that December, collapsed trenches had to be rebuilt, the barbed wire needed repair, raids went on, and white crosses continued to be planted. Back in England, Vera Brittain waited all of Christmas Day for Roland Leighton's call. She went to bed assuming that the telephone lines had been overloaded during the holiday. Her disappointment was shared by the Leighton family, who had stayed up long after dinner, hoping that Roland might still join them. The following morning, as Vera was putting on a blue crepe de chine blouse she thought flattering, a maid informed her that she had a phone call.

Four days before, on the night of December 22, Roland Leighton's 7th Worcestershires had entered the trenches near Hébuterne to relieve another company. The previous occupants had left the wire in such bad shape that Roland's platoon had been ordered to repair it immediately. Roland had gone to scout the damage. The communication trench that he would ordinarily have used to reach the wire unobserved was flooded. Consequently, he had to move above ground, through an opening in a hedge. The Germans were aware of this route to the wire and kept a machine gun trained on the gap. The moon shone full this cloudless night, giving them good visibility. As Roland emerged through the gap, a gunner fired a quick burst. One round caught Roland in the stomach. He lived until the following night, then died at the Louvencourt Casualty Clearing Station.

The phone call Vera expected to be from him on the morning of December 26 was from his sister, Clare, telling her that the family had just been informed that Roland was dead.

A few weeks later Vera visited the Leightons' cottage to find the mother and daughter deeply agitated. They were staring at Roland's open kit, which the army had returned. As Vera described the contents, "the tunic torn back and front by the bullet, a khaki vest dark and stiff with blood and a pair of blood-stained breeches slit open at the top by someone obviously in a violent hurry . . . everything was damp and worn and simply caked with mud." She could not imagine why the army had inflicted these "gruesome rags" on the family.

She wrote a poem about the death of her lover: "Perhaps someday the sun will shine again," it began, and ended:

But though kind time may many joys renew,
There is one greatest joy I shall not know
Again, because my heart for loss of You
Was broken, long ago.

Uppingham School's prizewinner was gone. Three of the men so close to her remained: her brother, Edward, Victor Richardson, and Geoffrey Thurlow.

9

Every Inch a Soldier

NOVEMBER 11, 1918. That morning, the well-ordered mind of Field Marshal Douglas Haig, commander of the British Expeditionary Force, was already planning what must be done once the shooting stopped. He wanted his five army commanders to make sure they had not forgotten a cardinal rule of peacetime leadership. As he recorded in the diary he kept throughout the war, "very often the best fighters are the most difficult to deal with in periods of quiet!" He intended to instruct his chief lieutenants "in a number of ways in which men can be kept occupied. It is as much the duty of all officers to keep their men amused, as it is to train them for war."

But for the Canadians and the 5th Royal Irish Lancers under his command, at that moment engaged in retaking Mons, deadly hours remained before they could turn their lives to footraces and soccer matches.

SEPTEMBER 1915. Douglas Haig had assumed command of the BEF almost three years before the armistice, replacing the first commander, General Sir John French, after French had become, in effect, a casualty of Loos and earlier debacles. Sir John's tally of wins and losses revealed a stunning military mediocrity. In the

1914 First Battle of Ypres, considered an Allied victory, he lost half of the force, at one point taking more than 13,000 casualties in three hours to gain a hundred yards. The inconclusive Second Battle of Ypres, in May 1915, had cost Britain another 58,000 casualties and the French 10,000, against 35,000 for the Germans. After the defeat at Loos, calls for Sir John's head rose to a clamor. Before the year was out, he was gone, his exit greased by General Sir Douglas Haig, commanding the 1st Army Corps.

Before the war, Haig had served under Sir John in a cavalry brigade at Aldershot. French had a taste for high living and the ladies, which had led to his sinking into debt and committing a grievous gaffe in army etiquette: he had borrowed £2,000 from a subordinate—in this case Douglas Haig—which doubtless contributed to the latter's later lack of awe toward his superior.

Haig looked every inch the soldier—erect in posture, stern in demeanor, handsome, with a strong nose above a well-trimmed mustache, a square chin, and a mouth set in a resolute line. His uniforms were beautifully tailored and always immaculate. Haig was ambitious but unobtrusively so, self-righteous but not priggish. Exposed continually to new ideas, he remained essentially rigid and lacking in imagination. He had at various points in his career rated tank warfare as "a minor factor," found bombing munitions factories from the air "unsound," and dismissed the machine gun, before which tens of thousands of his soldiers would die, as "a much overrated weapon." Though Haig was without color or dash, his steady rise nevertheless revealed a quiet talent for army politics. His biographer Duff Cooper said of Haig that he was "as good a general as it is possible for a man without genius to ever become."

Douglas Haig had been born in 1861 into a family that had made a fortune in whiskey. At Sandhurst, the British military academy, he had graduated first in his class, yet was still a plodding captain after fourteen years of service. However, he excelled in sports and became the finest polo player in the British Army. Haig was bitterly disappointed when, in 1893, he failed the examination for Staff College, an absolute requisite for advancement. The setback, however, revealed a talent for social maneuvering. Haig's older sister, Henrietta, was a friend of the Duke of Cambridge, commander in chief of the army. The duke had the authority to nominate candidates to the Staff College without examination, which he did on Haig's behalf. Haig was soon moving in the highest social circles, invited—again through his sister—to shooting parties with the heir to the throne, the Prince of Wales, with whom he became chummy. After service in India and the Boer War, Haig became the king's aide-de-camp. In 1905, he was a guest at Windsor Castle for Ascot Week, where he was paired in a golf foursome with one of Queen Alexandra's maids of honor, the beautiful Dorothy Vivian, daughter of a lord. Miss Vivian soon became Haig's wife in a wedding ceremony held in the private chapel of Buckingham Palace. When a friend commented on the swiftness of it all, Haig responded, "Why not? I have often made up my mind on more important problems than that of my own marriage in much less time."

Though he attended Church of Scotland Sunday services throughout the war, Haig also possessed an unsuspected spiritualist streak. As a young officer he attended seances and became convinced that a medium had put him in touch with Napoleon. He further believed that he was in direct communication with God, who guided his destiny.

In the latter part of 1915, Haig decided to hurry God along. He helpfully explained Sir John French's deficiencies to prominent British officials, including Prime Minister Herbert Asquith. He wrote disparaging reports about French to his old shooting partner, now King George V. The king expressed surprise at Haig's behavior. "If anyone acted like that," he observed, "he would at school be called a sneak." However, Haig believed that far more than fair play was at stake; rather, the future of the empire, which he felt that French's continued command endangered. Haig further judged his conduct justified since French had tried to shift the blame for Loos onto him. Haig managed not only to bring French down but to raise himself up. French was dismissed, and on December 17, 1915, Haig became commander in chief of the army in France.

WHILE STALEMATE MARKED the western front, the British had sustained a clear-cut defeat on another front of this spreading conflict. Earlier that year, on April 25, the British, with French support, had put an amphibious force ashore on the Gallipoli peninsula in enemy Turkey. The thinking was that Britain could gain a cheap navy-led victory, mobilize the Balkans against Austria-Hungary, and buck up her ally, Russia. Lord Kitchener thought it a splendid move that would provide a bonus, protection of the Suez Canal. Winston Churchill, then first lord of the admiralty, also thought it a good idea, since a landing by ships would demonstrate Britain's mastery of the seas. More than eight months later, the British troops evacuated Gallipoli, having suffered a total loss in strategy, manpower, and shattered reputations, particularly Churchill's.

Nineteen-fifteen also marked the year that Italy sought to cash in on opportunities the war opened. In the beginning, in theory, Italy was allied to Germany and Austria-Hungary. But the Allies dangled tempting prizes before her: Tyrol, Trieste, and northern Dalmatia. Furthermore, how could Italy be a great power if it remained uninvolved in the Great War? On May 23, Italy declared war on Austria-Hungary; it would wait a year and then declare war on Germany.

10

"They Shall Not Pass"

NOVEMBER 11, 1918. René Naegelen found himself home on leave at Belfort, happily out of the last-minute fighting still being waged by his division. The mood in town was electric as crowds awaited the ringing of the bells of Saint Christopher's Church, set for 11 A.M. A brass band ambled past the Naegelen family bakery en route to the town square, its tune discordant, its lines ragged, some musicians clearly tipsy. At the citadel on the edge of town, a squad of soldiers hauled an ancient cannon into position in preparation for a triumphal salute.

Naegelen's mother asked him to put on his medal. "You should this day," she said. The Médaille Militaire honored a soldier mentioned six times in dispatches and twice wounded. The mother's effort to share in Belfort's festivity was strained. On the wall, in a gilded frame, hung the photograph of a fixedly smiling soldier, Joseph Naegelen, René's brother. "Joseph had been entrusted with my father's bakery," Naegelen recalled. "He was my senior and had two very young children. My parents had four sons and a son-in-law serving in the infantry. I was conscious of their heart-rending sorrow and of their apprehension concerning my brothers and myself." Of Joseph's death he had learned, "He lay out there beneath his wooden cross. His comrades dug a bed for him, and to prevent the earth from hurting his eyes, put over his face a battered tin plate."

Naegelen's father locked up the bakery, and the family headed toward the square, the young soldier kissed by girls, sobbing old women, even men. Later, he would recall his thoughts at that moment: "I wish you could see what a fool you look. You are walking with such martial strides—chin up, chest thrown out—that your parents can hardly keep up with you. . . . Revel in the fulsome flattery, dear fool! It does not stop war from being a filthy trick."

FEBRUARY 1916. The men of Naegelen's battalion arrived at Verdun in February, his own zeal for battle already having been tempered at Champagne. After France had slipped out of the Schlieffen noose in 1914, the kaiser had replaced Helmuth von Moltke as chief of the German general staff that September with his minister of war, General Erich von Falkenhayn. In his youth Falkenhayn had been a slim, severely handsome soldier with the brush-cut hair favored by Junker officers. By the time Wilhelm II sent him back to the field commanding armies, he had grown heavy-featured, thick-waisted, and leaned on a cane, an appearance in keeping with his attraction to ponderous stratagems rather than brilliant thrusts, most notably at Verdun. In choosing the ancient city, its history dating back to Roman times, Falkenhayn sought no vital bridgehead, rail juncture, or commanding heights. He launched his offensive on February 16, 1916, with the simplest intent: to kill Frenchmen by the hundreds of thousands. France, he reasoned, would never dare surrender an old fortress town possessing Verdun's symbolic potency. The French would hang on and he would grind them down day after day with murderous artillery bombardments, the dead replenished by the living until an entire generation of Frenchmen was annihilated.

The French Army commander, Marshal Joseph Joffre, thought otherwise. He viewed Verdun as a useless bulge in the French front, best given up to achieve shorter lines of communication and supply. The sixty-two-year-old marshal enjoyed a reputation as the leader who had stemmed the German onslaught in 1914. He was held in affection and esteem as "Papa Joffre." What would have surprised his admiring public was that Joffre had stripped Verdun of its guns. France's resources were to be reserved for a great offensive later in the year along the Somme River.

By February 21, 1916, Falkenhayn had amassed 1,240 guns, concentrated on an eight-mile arc of the French front. The kaiser's son and heir, Crown Prince Wilhelm, was given nominal command of the assaults, but Falkenhayn held the reins. That day, as a massive shell exploded in the archbishop's palace in Verdun, the battle was joined. For nine hours, German guns pounded the French positions, the heaviest bombardment the world had yet known. The French prime minister, Aristide Briand, discovered Joffre's willingness to abandon Verdun and was horrified. The marshal might be a soldier who understood strategy, but Briand was a politician who understood the power of symbols. The fall of Verdun would spell the fall of the Briand government. Four days later, the prime minister appeared at Joffre's headquarters at Chantilly and had the sleeping general yanked out of bed. Why was Verdun so poorly defended? Briand demanded to know. Joffre sought to explain that the city had no military significance. The usually even-tempered prime minister exploded. "You may not think losing Verdun a defeat," he railed, "but everyone else will. If you surrender Verdun, you will be cowards, cowards, and I'll sack the lot of you!" An abashed Joffre gave in. "We will fight to the end," he said. General Henri-Phillipe Pétain, the rare French general who believed in defense, was given command of Verdun. Had Falkenhayn been privy to the exchange at Joffre's headquarters, his joy would have been unbounded. The French were playing into his hand, ready to march into his slaughterhouse.

On February 25, Verdun's most powerful symbol, the massive Fort Douaumont, fell. Pétain, determined to stem the advance, uttered the line forever joined with his name: *"Ils ne passerant pas"*— They shall not pass. His pledge would ensure months of just what Falkenhayn had counted on: remorseless attrition.

GENERALS DEALT WITH war at the wholesale level, but troops fought it retail, as René Naegelen again discovered. The fighting ebbed and flowed over the same exhausted ground. The village of Fleury was lost, retaken, and lost again sixteen times in four months. Fort Vaux changed hands thirteen times in one month, with men dying for ground that would not matter a half hour later. Fighting underground was as fierce as that above as both sides honeycombed the surrounding hills with tunnels too low for a grown man to stand in. The foes encountered each other like burrowing animals, clashing with rifles, grenades, even machine guns, their bullets ricocheting off stone walls, tipping end over end, causing horrendous wounds. The miasma of gunpowder fumes and dust in these airless spaces felled men by asphyxiation. The concussive force of grenades rattled men's brains to the point of madness.

Naegelen thought he had gone insane. He had huddled in a shell hole in front of Fort Vaux with two mates when a shell exploded above them, lifting Naegelen from the ground, then slamming him back to earth. He cautiously moved his arms and legs. "Nothing," he concluded with relief. "My two friends, however, lying one upon the other, were bleeding." Both bodies were torn open, and one man "unbuttoned his trousers and died urinating on the gaping wound of his comrade." Amid the madness, Naegelen recalled thinking, "I was twenty and I had never embraced a woman; I had never felt her warm, naked skin against my eager body; I thought I would die on the very threshold of my wretched life."

HENRI DESAGNEAUX HAD managed his transfer from transportation to the infantry in time for Verdun. His 106th Regiment was ordered to recapture a trench seized by the enemy the day before near Bras-Ravin. Desagneaux and his men crouched in a shallow trench, waiting for the barrage that would signal their advance. They watched a seemingly endless procession of stretcher bearers pass by, stumbling under the weight of the bodies they bore to a makeshift cemetery, their work attracting swarms of flies.

As night fell, Desagneaux's unit began its advance. They retook the trench but could not hold it. At daybreak they pulled back and watched an astonishing number of wounded being carried to the rear. Their own artillery barrage had fallen short, dropping shells on their comrades. Desagneaux recorded the scene in his diary: "A machine gunner has been blinded . . . in addition he has lost a leg." A wounded man pleaded with his lieutenant not to let him die; another begged the officer to shoot him and end his agony. "Our time at Verdun has been awful," Desagneaux wrote. "Our faces have nothing human about them. For sixteen days we have neither washed nor slept. . . . Our eyes reveal the horror of it all." His unit had lost more than four hundred men, "and, the positions are the same as before the attack."

JACQUES MEYER SURVIVED Verdun. In the summer of 1914, the nineteen-year-old Alsatian had been accepted at the elite École Normale Supérieure in Paris. But eight days after the war began, Meyer and the rest of his class had left school to enlist en masse. In the early days at Verdun, Meyer, now a junior officer, was puzzled one morning to see a great tongue of fire leap from advancing German troops, turning French soldiers into torches. Verdun did not mark the introduction of the flamethrower, only its perfection. Though initially it was terrifying, the French quickly learned to counterattack. A well-aimed grenade could explode the flamethrower's fuel tanks, causing fire to race up the hose and incinerating the men carrying it. Snipers concentrated fire on these carriers, and when they scored, the flamethrower's nozzle spun about wildly, scorching friend as readily as foe.

Meyer disdained the myth of what the men called the "blessed wound"—not serious enough to maim for life but bad enough to get a man out of the war. There was "no such thing," he concluded. If the wounded soldier was borne on a stretcher, "the danger multiplied with the number of men grouped together, making a target for the machine guns or a 'bundle' for a shell falling on the heap." Often, a man with the blessed noncrippling wound would die from loss of blood, gangrene, or exposure before ever reaching an aid station.

THE PROTRACTED FIGHTING at Verdun dulled human feeling. Troops marching to the rear would taunt their replacements moving to the front with "Hey, look, reinforcements for the cemetery." A nurse moaned to a friend, "This war, it makes brutes of men." She had tried to wash the hands of a soldier about to be operated on. The man had rebuffed her angrily. "No, my hands are covered with the blood of a Boche colonel," he told her. "I killed him myself and I refuse to have the blood washed away!"

An American volunteer ambulance driver recalled his conversation with a housewife living near Verdun. She told him about a German widow who had managed to get a letter through to the mayor of her village, begging that her husband's body be buried where she could find it after the war. "Her thin gray hair hung in wisps over her dirty face, a face lined with a lifetime of toil," the driver recalled of the Frenchwoman, "and at the moment she told me about the letter, I was startled by her demoniacal expression. Her hands, with long curled nails, seemed like claws. Her face was a symbol of fury." She had not the slightest desire that the German widow's request be granted.

THE FIGURE EMERGING most indelibly from the battlescape of Verdun was the *poilu,* the ordinary French soldier. Literally, the word meant "hairy." Its origin preceded this war and had been used by Rabelais and Balzac to depict the unsung men in the ranks, whose hairiness was presumedly a mark of manliness. The defining quality of the *poilu* was uncomplaining fatalism in the jaws of Hell. George Gaudy, an officer with the 57th Infantry Regiment, was moved by his men's acceptance of their fate even as they sang songs depicting their wretchedness. "What struck you," he remembered, "was the physical vigor of these *poilus,* washing up half nude in the snow. Their gaze was calm, the smiles a little mocking." While the word caught the public's fancy, *"poilu"* was rarely heard in the trenches, except by some officers in a cheap bid for camaraderie. The men referred to themselves as *les bons hommes,* the good guys.

In the beginning, Falkenhayn's pragmatic, if ruthless, strategy of attrition had made sense. But though he had wisely judged that Verdun should serve only as the anvil for his annihilating hammer of artillery, Crown Prince Wilhelm insisted on victory. And so the fortress that Joffre had judged not worth saving became a prize Germany found worth taking. German troops were herded into the abattoir as numerously as the French. General Pétain countered with "No retreat. Meet death on the field. Let survivors launch counterattacks!" Thus Verdun became one of the most sustained episodes of bloodletting in the annals of warfare. Scarcely an inch went uncontested. By the end of June 1916, the peak of the German onslaught, French dead totaled 160,000, one death every two minutes; German losses amounted to 218,000 men dead, wounded, and missing. In a single day, 7,000 horses were killed. "Verdun was the most senseless episode in a war not distinguished for sense anywhere," the historian A. J. P. Taylor judged. "Both sides at Verdun fought literally for the sake of fighting. There was no prize to be gained or lost, only men to be killed and glory to be won."

AMONG MORE THAN a quarter of a million Germans lost at Verdun, one name did not appear. Lothar Lanz of Pioneer Battalion 30 had found the wild swings from savage killing followed by a live-and-let-live tolerance morally disturbing. Early in the struggle, he had taken part in shooting Frenchmen trying to rescue their wounded from no-man's-land under a Red Cross flag. Yet at Verdun he experienced numerous tacit cease-fires. At one point his battalion occupied a trench alongside the road from Damvillers to Verdun. The French were dug in three hundred yards opposite. At night, both sides sent patrols ahead to man sentry posts. Wary at first, the "hereditary enemies," as Lanz called them, soon began mingling, "and on the following morning our relieved sentries related to us with pleasure how liberally the Frenchmen had shared everything with them." Both sides drew water from the same well at a farm. The French "used to wait till we trotted off with our cooking pots filled and then they would come up and provide themselves with water." Occasionally, both sides arrived at the well at the same time. "Thus it happened," Lanz observed, "that three of us were at the well without any arms when a score of Frenchmen arrived with cooking pots. The Frenchmen were seven times as numerous as ourselves, the thought never struck us that they might fall upon us." Then, overnight, he would again find himself steeped in savagery. "The spade I found to be a handy weapon," he remembered. "I hit one opponent between head and shoulder. The sharp spade half went through his body; I heard the cracking of the bones that were struck." During another assault, Lanz and his comrades leaped into a trench, flinging grenades at the French defenders. Of eight *poilus,* five were killed outright. Three others began clambering out of the trench. Lanz seized one. "In a trice I was on him. I knocked out some of his teeth. Then he surrendered and raised his hands. . . . He pointed to his wedding ring. He handed me his bottle, inviting me to drink. I told him, 'You've been lucky. A few missing teeth don't matter. For you the slaughtering is finished. Come along.' " As Lanz marched his prisoner to the rear, his strongest emotion was envy.

Lanz and his company were pulled from the line for a rest at Montmédy. The proletarian was disgusted by the number of rear-echelon officers who "loitered about in their faultless uniforms or rode along whip in hand. . . . Many accosted us and asked us rudely why we did not salute them." The harassment, particularly by haughty youths with a touch of gold on the shoulder, made

Lanz and his comrades long for the trenches: "After a few hours we got sick of life twenty miles behind the Verdun front."

Lanz managed to get a furlough. At the end of it, instead of returning to his unit, he went to a friend's home and donned civilian clothes. He removed all identification from his uniform, wrapped it around his rifle, along with his canteen and mess kit, and threw the lot into a river during the night. He followed a zigzag course, taking trains that eventually brought him to Düsseldorf. He was by now several days absent without leave, a deserter subject to the death penalty. He made his way on foot to a woods over the German-Dutch border and slipped across. Lanz eventually arrived in Rotterdam, where "I soon obtained a well-paid position and became a man again who could live and not merely exist." He was one among some twenty thousand German deserters who took refuge in the hospitable Netherlands.

But Rotterdam was still not far enough away. Lanz began scheming to get himself aboard a ship that would take him where he most wanted to be: America.

THE APPALLING WAR in the mud was paralleled briefly by a splendid spectacle on the pristine seas. On May 31, 1916, the British and German fleets squared off near Jutland in the North Sea—twenty-eight British dreadnoughts and nine battle cruisers versus sixteen German dreadnoughts and five battle cruisers. When fog and darkness stilled their guns, the British had lost fourteen ships of all classes and the Germans eleven. The only major naval engagement of the war had ended essentially in a tie of no tactical consequence. But Jutland represented a strategic British victory since the German High Seas Fleet thereafter holed up in port, never again to emerge during the war. Jutland would also have another unintended consequence: with her capital ships essentially out of the fight, Germany turned to submarine warfare, including attacks on neutral vessels, which would eventually contribute to drawing the United States into the war against her.

11

"What Did You Do
in the Great War, Dad?"

NOVEMBER 11, 1918. Father de Valles and his orderly, Connell Albertine, could hear the rattle of the German machine guns as the first wave from the 26th approached the Trenche de Bosphore. Eight months had passed since the 104th Regiment had taken its first casualty, Private George Clarke, felled by an artillery shell. On this last day, the men dropping before the German fire were added to more than 51,000 Americans killed thus far on the western front. That these men were dying, with less than half an hour left in the war, was only marginally more improbable than that they should be in France at all.

MAY 1915. When war broke out in 1914, most Americans saw it as Europe's affair, with their own nation's neutrality standing out as a beacon of sanity in a sea of madness. Robert Frost caught the mood with heavy sarcasm. "You won't catch me complaining of any war," the poet commented, "much less of a great war like this that we wage on both sides like mystics for a reason beyond reason." Yet, as one can rarely watch a fight without eventually favoring one opponent over the other, Germany began early to lose favor in American eyes. From the outset, her violation of neutral

Belgium had the appearance of a schoolyard bully picking on a little kid. The image was reinforced by the widespread credence given to the findings of the 1915 Bryce Report, which were serialized in American newspapers and swallowed whole. The *New York Herald* reported that a German soldier had been seen carrying a bagful of ears. Another newspaper accused Germany of melting down the enemy dead to manufacture soap. A *Philadelphia Public Ledger* editor reflected what most Americans believed: that "the claims of the Bryce Report were factual and final." The calumny stuck to Germany even after the tough-minded lawyer Clarence Darrow visited the war zone and reported that he could find no one who had been the victim of or had witnessed an atrocity committed by a German. When Darrow went home, he offered $1,000 to anyone who could prove that even one child's hands had been lopped off by a German. No takers came forward.

Nevertheless, Germany's reputation as a dishonorable combatant deepened after the country introduced gas warfare in April 1915. But to Americans the greatest sin was committed when Germany discarded a previously unquestioned norm of civilized warfare: that unarmed merchant vessels, whether of belligerent or neutral flag, would not be sunk unless passengers and crew were first allowed to leave the ship. Instead, on February 4, 1915, Germany declared that all waters surrounding Great Britain and Ireland were part of the war zone and that merchant vessels of belligerents *and* neutrals entering it would be attacked without warning. The policy bore its bitterest fruit on May 7. Early that afternoon, passengers aboard the Cunard liner *Lusitania* gazed across clear skies to the Irish coast, just fourteen miles distant. In a matter of hours they would complete the one-week journey from New York to Liverpool. Suddenly the ship shuddered. U-boat 20, commanded by Kapitän-Leutnant Walter Schweiger, had struck the liner with a single torpedo that penetrated the hull just below the waterline. The *Lusitania,* at 790 feet long one of the world's largest oceangoing vessels, sank in eighteen minutes. Ordinarily, the great ship could have outrun the submarine, but the British merchant marine had been drained of manpower by military demands. In peacetime, seventy-seven able-bodied seamen stoked twenty-five of the ship's boilers. On this day, forty-one men fired nineteen boilers, a loss of 24 percent of precious power. Of 1,959 passengers and crew, 1,198 died, 124 of them Americans. Most shocking to world opinion, the *Lusitania* was carrying 129 children, of whom 94 died, including 35 babies. Compounding the horror, German officials committed an act of staggering insensitivity: they struck a commemorative medal with a depiction of the sinking ship on one side and on the other a smiling skeleton under the inscription "Business above all." The words were a mocking accusation that the shipowners had placed profits above people. Germany defended the U-boat's actions, pointing out that notices had been placed in American newspapers on the day of the *Lusitania*'s departure, warning "that travelers sailing in the war zone on ships of Great Britain or her allies do so at their own risk." Further, the vessel was reported to have been carrying 1,250 cases of ammunition bound for Great Britain. Nevertheless, the policy of unrestricted submarine warfare had led to a marginal naval victory for Germany but a public opinion debacle. An editorial in the *Richmond (Virginia) Times-Dispatch* summed up American reaction: "Germany surely must have gone mad." The madness slowly sank in, and by early 1916 Germany had essentially curtailed unrestricted warfare at sea.

Though U.S. citizens had died aboard the *Lusitania*, the incident had not been considered sufficient provocation by the Wilson administration to propel the United States into a European war. Instead the destruction of the ship prompted one of the oddest utterances by an American president. Three days after the sinking, Wilson, in a speech in Philadelphia, declared, "There is such a thing as a man being too proud to fight. There is such a thing as a nation being so right that it does not need to convince others by force that it is right." This locution was perhaps the result of his speaking off the cuff, since the president was using only notes jotted on cards. As interpreted in Germany, his words meant that

America would *not* fight. The presumption was not entirely without foundation. Nearly a year and a half later, Wilson would squeak to a second-term victory with his claim that he had kept America out of war. The notion that the United States would stay out of the conflict was reinforced by a belief that German Americans, then the largest ethnic stock in the United States, would surely not fight against the fatherland of their forebears.

NOT ALL AMERICANS wanted to keep out of the war. Alexander McClintock, a young Kentuckian, became one of 40,000 U.S. citizens who volunteered to fight for Britain, most of them enlisting in the Canadian Army. From boyhood, McClintock had been drawn toward any escape from conventional life. He came from a well-to-do Lexington family who packed him off to the Virginia Military Institute, where he lasted a month before being expelled. He subsequently registered for the University of Idaho but never showed up. His whereabouts in the years immediately before the war are murky until, in November 1915, he appeared at a recruiting office in Montreal, a strapping five-foot, ten-inch, blue-eyed, dark-skinned twenty-two-year-old with a long, unexplained scar across his cheek. The Canadians readily accepted him into the 87th Infantry Battalion, more colorfully known as the Grenadier Guards. McClintock arrived in France in June 1916, just as the Battle of Verdun was peaking and the next big push along the River Somme began gathering force.

As the dead poet Rupert Brooke had captured the spirit of British youth drawn to war, the Americans had produced their own siren singer, handsome, dashing, bohemian Alan Seeger, a Harvard contemporary of T. S. Eliot, Walter Lippmann, and the later Communist champion John Reed, all class of 1910. Seeger rushed to join the French Foreign Legion at the war's outbreak and wrote a poem that made the conflict seem an irresistible destiny:

> I have a rendezvous with Death
> At some disputed barricade,

When Spring comes back with rustling shade
And apple-blossoms fill the air—
I have a rendezvous with Death
When Spring brings back blue days and fair.

The Allies eagerly welcomed volunteers such as the Americans McClintock and Seeger. As the number of casualties overtook that of enlistments, British leaders felt compelled for the first time to introduce conscription. In August 1915, every male citizen between sixteen and sixty-five had to provide details of age and occupation to a National Register. Two months later, a scheme put forth by Lord Derby was adopted requiring eligible males to indicate their willingness to serve if called. When this approach failed to generate enough volunteers, the government, in January 1916, began drafting single men between eighteen and forty-one, later extended to include married men.

At the same time, voluntary enlistments continued heavy, 1.2 million in the very year conscription went into effect. Critics contended, therefore, that coercive service was unnecessary and merely a tactic to heighten the perception of a country wholly committed to victory. The Germans helped contribute to this sense of shared sacrifice when, on January 19, 1915, they began bombing cities in England, first with zeppelin airships and then with long-range twin-engine Gotha bombers.

Whatever the motive, conscription, by thrusting together men from disparate social strata, began to erode British class barriers. The phenomenon was sharpened by a sociological curiosity: volunteers sprang mostly from the wealthiest or the poorest classes, the former on average being five inches taller than the latter. The commingling of classes introduced the privileged and pampered to the common fate they shared with proletarians in the trenches. Stephen Howet, a second lieutenant with the Warwickshires, after censoring letters written by his soldiers, wrote home, "What a lesson it is to read the thoughts of men, often as refined and sensitive as we have been made by the advantages of birth and education, yet living under conditions much harder and more disgusting than my own." Another officer noted in his diary, "I shall never think of the lower classes again in quite the same way after the war."

Good relations between men divided by class depended upon an unspoken, perhaps unconscious, pact, which explained why a thirty-year-old coal miner would follow to the death the orders of a nineteen-year-old officer barely out of Eton. The former had been raised to believe that this boy, by virtue of his station, possessed qualities and knowledge that he did not. Conversely, nothing could more speedily mature a fuzzy-cheeked subaltern than the realization that the lives of other men depended on his conduct.

Lord Moran, many years later to become Prime Minister Churchill's personal physician, told of a subaltern who had gone almost directly from Oxford to the trenches, where he was soon killed by a sniper's bullet. He was buried with his head facing the enemy lines, a mark of honor. The next morning, his commanding officer noticed that during the night the men had bordered the grave with stones and adorned it with wildflowers.

Snobbery, however, did persist, directed at men lacking a pedigree who had managed to crack the officer ranks. "Temporary gentlemen" was the cutting phrase applied by their presumed betters. Men from the dominions displayed a jaunty insouciance toward these social subtleties. A British officer upbraided an Australian trooper for not saluting him, growling, "I'm a colonel!" To which the Australian replied, "Best job in the army. You keep it."

As men from country homes, universities, and vicarages began rubbing shoulders with miners and dustmen, the exposure, as Sir John Keegan put it, "would eventually fuel that transformation of middle-class attitudes to the poor which has been the most important trend in twentieth-century Britain." Britons were beginning to share Oliver Cromwell's long-ago rejection of a world in which "one man shall wear a saddle on his back and another shall sit on it."

BY THE SECOND year of the war, the trenches scarring the western front had settled into a caricature of a normal community. In them the rituals of daily life went on, as through a distorting lens. In this elongated society, with its population shifting between 8 million and 10 million, the inhabitants took their meals at generally regular hours and had a place to sleep, albeit a hole gouged into the side of the trench. Enlisted men watched their affluent neighbors, the officers, retire down rude steps to relatively more comfortable residences in caves lit by candles or oil lamps, where they slept on chicken-wire beds. As one British soldier continued the metaphor, "The firing trench is our place of business—our office in the city, so to speak. The supporting trench is our suburban residence, whither the weary toiler may betake himself periodically for purposes of refreshment and repose." One estimate calculated that the bands of parallel trenches placed end to end would almost match the circumference of the globe, with about 6,250 miles each for the British and French and another 12,000 for Germany. It was claimed that a man could traverse the battle zone from the North Sea to Switzerland without ever lifting his head above ground.

The inhabitants found their way about this netherworld by signs identifying main streets, alleyways, and crossroads. Certain names predominated in British sectors: Piccadilly, Victoria Station, Regent Street, the Strand. Intersections became Hyde Park Corner or Marble Arch. Occasionally the residents watched a play or music hall performance sitting on a sodden field. They took vacations, went to church, prayed to the same God, and asked him to take sides. They frequently attended funerals. They saw their doctor, often about dilatory bowel movements. For this condition, "Number Nine" was the drug of choice, reputed by patients to have the blasting power of dynamite. The reverse complaint was diarrhea. The number of buckets in which the men relieved themselves was invariably too few, so they went wherever they could, with rain floating the mess back into their belowground home. Tommies satirized the famous recruiting poster in which a little boy asks his father, "What did you do in the Great War, Dad?" to which a trench wit rhymed, "I dug latrines for the others, my lad."

It was essentially a law-abiding community. As Alexander McClintock put it, "The only things legitimate to steal in the code

of the trenches are rum and fags [cigarettes]. Every other possession is as safe as if it were under a Yale lock." As often happens in
even the best-ordered community, the soldiers feuded with their
neighbors across the way, who were leading essentially the same
lives as themselves.

The overpowering feature of this community was its stench,
exuding from rotting, half-buried corpses, unwashed bodies, excre-
ment, chloride of lime, and lingering fumes from mustard, phosgene gas, and cordite. Favorite targets of the enemy mortars were
latrines, where direct hits increased the pungency. This miasma
was occasionally penetrated by the pleasant odor of wood fires
and smells rising from cookpots of Maconachie stew, bacon, and
bully beef, canned meat shipped from Argentina. "One of the
great discoveries of this war," McClintock reported, "is that hard
tack makes an excellent fuel, burning like coke and giving off no
smoke." The slate-hard biscuits were burned to heat the bully
beef, make tea, or provide warm water for an occasional shave.
Sandbags were a fixture of trench dining. Food was hauled to the
front in the bags, giving a grittiness to every meal. Coffee and tea
were strained through them. Sandbags were also wrapped around
the soldiers' legs for warmth, swabbed through dirty rifle barrels,
and stuffed under the belt to be filled quickly when men came
under fire. McClintock paid tribute "to the soldiers' most valuable
friend, the sand bag."

He described a daily routine between major engagements as
regular as clerks reporting to their desks in the city. "At a little before daybreak came 'stand-to' when everybody got buttoned up
and ready for business, because, at that hour, most attacks begin."
At that time and at sunset, another likely hour for assaults, the
men became accustomed to what they called "morning and evening hate," fifteen minutes of brisk artillery exchanges. So punc-
tual were these volleys that stretcher bearers lined up just before,
waiting to cart off the casualties. Artillery was feared most. A private with the 1st West Yorkshire Regiment called a bombardment
"the great leveller. Nobody could stand more than three hours of

sustained shelling before they started feeling sleepy and numb. You're hammered after three hours and you're there for the picking when he comes over. It's a bit like being under an anaesthetic." Only marginally less frightening was mortar fire, launched at steep angles and thus capable of dropping straight into a trench. The German *Minenwerfer,* "minniewerfer" to British soldiers, was the most feared mortar, its projectile shooting sparks from its tail and capable of blasting a crater thirty feet wide. Other missiles fired from mortars were named for their noises, "coal boxes" and "whiz bangs," the latter giving off a smell of burning grass as they singed a ridge. Troops who broke through to the German lines were greeted by a hail of "potato mashers," or hand grenades, so called for their resemblance to the kitchen utensil.

The Germans, for their part, particularly dreaded the array of British close-combat weapons, Mills bombs, stick bombs, and egg bombs. But it was nasty business for Tommies to get close enough to use them. Men sent across no-man's-land to toss these missiles into German trenches were called "the Suicide Club." To provide some protective distance, the British came up with an innovation, the Bangalore torpedo, lengths of pipe filled with explosives and screwed end to end until they could reach under the enemy wire. Upon the signal to attack, the torpedo fuses were lit, the resultant blast tearing holes in the wire.

Time spent in the trenches made an enemy's habits familiar, occasionally even entertaining. One story had it that a German machine gunner facing a Canadian unit would rap out the rhythm of the "Maple Leaf Rag" with his weapon. The Canadians supposedly grew tired of the joke and organized a raid during which they silenced the machine gunner and his song. Men could not be kept in the firing trench indefinitely. After three days, at most a week, frontline units had to be relieved and pulled back to the support trench for several days, then to a reserve trench for a week of relative rest and safety. This was the compass of the soldier's life, the cycle in which he moved from fear to renewed hope and back again to fear.

The better the division, the worse the odds of surviving since these units were repeatedly thrown back into battle, some eventually sustaining casualties of 90 percent of their original roster. Actuarially, a man serving in such a unit could not expect to escape being killed or wounded for more than three months. Junior officers, in the vanguard of every assault and easily distinguished by their riding breeches and pistols, had a life expectancy of six weeks.

The raid continued to be the infantryman's terror. Yet volunteers invariably came forward. An officer would dangle inducements: two weeks in a rest camp, the chance to win a medal, the brave example of pals. In preparation, officers concealed their badges of rank, and men blackened their faces to deflect light before they left the embrace of the trench. McClintock recalled how, when an enemy star shell lit up the night as if it were high noon, a raider would freeze in position between the trenches, even balancing on one leg rather than reveal that he was an animate object.

Trench life induced a casual brutality in men who would ordinarily apologize for stepping on someone's toe in a bus. A teenage subaltern in a Highland regiment led a gas bombing raid to flush the enemy from a section of trench. The gas drove the Germans, choking and staggering, hands held over their heads, from their refuge, and they were promptly bayoneted, not out of malice but because the party could spare no one to take them to the rear. "The Western Front was known among its embittered inhabitants as The Sausage Machine," poet and novelist Robert Graves wrote, "because it was fed with live men, churned out corpses and remained firmly screwed in place."

Men were also held in place at the front by an emotional pull that they themselves could barely comprehend. Alec Reader, seventeen years old, serving with the Post Office Rifles, found himself trembling whenever an assault loomed. Then one day it seemed his terror was about to end: the army had issued an order that underage men could return home unless they chose to remain with their units. "The temptation to get out of this ghastly business is far greater than you can conceive," Reader wrote his mother, "but of course there's only one decent thing for me to do, that is to stay here, but OH! It's going to be very hard." Two months later, Alec Reader was killed.

It was not only the contradictions—misery alongside nobility of conduct—that held the men together. "The fineness," one soldier wrote, "came not of war but of the human nature whose strong quality it brings out and reveals. To attribute any nobility to war itself is as much a confusion of thought as to attribute nobility to cancer or leprosy, because of the skill, devotion and self-sacrifice of those who give up their lives to its cure."

Reginald Francis Foster, who at age nineteen abandoned his studies for the Anglican ministry to enlist, described how fear hastened self-discovery. Just commissioned, Foster reported for duty in Flanders on a bitterly cold December day. A captain he identified only as "Bill" led him through communication trenches toward the front line, where their men were scheduled to relieve another unit. Foster felt terrified as machine-gun bullets whizzed overhead, but Bill appeared not to notice. Just before sunset, the older man commented, "Lovely evening," and, to Foster's astonishment, added, "Let's go stretch our legs for a bit." The captain heaved himself over the parapet into no-man's-land, beckoning to Foster to join him. "I wondered whether he had become insane," Foster recalled. He followed the captain through a break in the wire, "My pulses racing and bile in my throat." They zigzagged through successive gaps, emerging onto open ground. About a hundred yards from the German trenches, the captain settled himself onto a blasted stump and lit a cigarette. Foster followed suit. Suddenly, mortar fire erupted around them. "Ah well," Bill said, tossing his cigarette aside, "I suppose we'd better be getting back."

As they returned to the trench, the captain departed with a casual wave to Foster. "When I was alone," Foster recalled, "I knew that during the last half hour, I had undergone the most momentous experience of my life." In the weeks that followed, while leading his first probes into no-man's-land, Foster found himself unafraid. Thanks to the captain, he concluded, "I had become fully integrated, which is to say that I had gained integrity, and that in the future I should invariably live fully—in the present time, leaving the future to take care of itself."

To others, the wisdom of the trenches came more slowly. Guy Chapman, soon after arriving in France, found himself serving on a court-martial that convicted an old soldier of being drunk in the trenches. Chapman hurriedly thumbed through the *Manual of Military Law* to find the penalty for this offense. A major, the president of the court, asked what he had found. "Oh, death, sir, I suppose," Chapman replied. The major then turned to the other member of the court, an officer as unseasoned as Chapman, who concurred, "Death, I suppose." The major shook his head. "But, my boys, my boys, you can't do it." Both his juniors protested. "It says so here," Chapman replied, tapping his manual. Finally, the major talked them out of shooting the old rascal. They instead agreed to break him to corporal. But at that point, when he had yet to set foot in a trench, Chapman believed that the major had failed in his duty.

To British generals, no-man's-land, running narrowly between the trenches, did not officially exist. As one of them put it, "The doctrine of the offensive dictated that any ground short of the enemy's line should be considered to be British, in other words, the German wire was the British front line." This interpretation was not shared by raiding parties crawling about in no-man's-land, where 5,845 British soldiers died during one six-month period in what were recorded in field reports as "minor trench operations."

12

"Tomorrow I Shall Take
My Men over the Top"

NOVEMBER 11, 1918. Herbert Sulzbach, proud German Jew, bitterly resented the imminent defeat. As his once vaunted 63rd Field Artillery Regiment abandoned first La Neuville, then the Ferme de Pavillon, and fell back toward Sedan, gratitude for his own survival thus far warred against his outrage that the cause was lost. "One can hardly find words to express the indignation with which every German must now be filled," he wrote in his diary regarding the terms forced on his country. "They want to humiliate us to death!" How, he wondered, could the Allies "demand conditions of this nature from *us,* a nation which has fought so heroically for over four years, and stood firm against a whole world of enemies! An honorable opponent ought to show regard for us rather than humiliate us by bringing us to our knees." He vented his outrage, after two of his men had been sniped at by civilians, by unleashing every gun in the battery in reprisal against a village, sixty shells from each gun raining down on the inhabitants.

War had brought Sulzbach the finest friend he had ever known. He and Kurt Reinhardt had trained together as twenty-year-old officer cadets. They had pulled out of the train depot in 1914 together, gone into action, and traveled home on leave together. "We understood each other from the very first moment," he wrote of the friendship, "and we were, if you can't find a better word, soul-mates." Feeling homesick on his twenty-first birthday, Sulzbach had just left the gun pit when he heard voices raised in song. Second Lieutenant Reinhardt had organized a serenade. "I was so moved that I almost had tears in my eyes," he remembered of that day.

Sulzbach had experienced a twinge of envy when Kurt escaped the trenches for the life of a pilot. He longed to share the excitement Kurt expressed in a letter describing his first kill. And then, six months before the war was to end, word came from Sulzbach's parents that Reinhardt had been shot down and was dead. "I had never wept before in the war, but I did then," Sulzbach wrote in his diary. "I never had a friend like him." His thoughts drifted to Frau Reinhardt, "who had not only lost her husband in the War, but now her only son."

Now, on this last day, the futility of these sacrifices was nearly intolerable as he turned his guns away from the enemy and hauled them toward the Fatherland. The commander of the Third Army, General Karl von Einem, had sought to put the best face on the retreat. "Undefeated and tested again and again in numerous battles, you are terminating the war in enemy country," his Order 12257 to the troops read. "What you have accomplished in the face of an enemy force many times superior to ours in number belongs to history. . . . With unbroken ranks, each one staunchly in his place, proudly as we left in 1914, so we want to return to our native soil."

Noble words. Still, what had it been all about, Sulzbach asked himself, the *Kindermorde* four years before, when student soldiers had gone to their deaths with "Deutschland über Alles" on their lips, the rivers of blood that had followed, the loss of "our well-beloved Kurt"?

JULY 1916. Since October 1914, Germany had occupied a great swath of northern France, including most of ten departments, among them Nord, Pas-de-Calais, Somme, Ardennes, Meuse, and Vosges. The occupation was more than a national humiliation, as these regions formed France's industrial heart and contained most of the country's coal and iron mines. Recovering this territory was vital to France's continued prosecution of the war. Marshal Joffre had initially resisted defending Verdun early in 1916 because he preferred a decisive offense on the Somme River, one he believed could break the German occupation and end the war. He had settled on this sector since it was here that the British and French lines met. General Haig, handed command of the BEF the previous December, concurred. Haig too believed the war could be won on the Somme. The time chosen for the campaign was the summer of 1916, which should give the British plenty of time to prepare green divisions. Haig's forces, too many of them barely trained Kitchener volunteers led by junior officers just as unseasoned, were as high in morale as they were low in experience. And so, while the French and Germans continued to grind each other to a pulp at Verdun, the British trained for their shining moment.

The battle was to begin on July 1. Haig wrote his wife, "I feel that every step in my plan has been taken with Divine help." Though convinced of God-given victory, Haig did consider precautions should his strategy misfire, a "flicker of sense," as one of his critics put it. He declared that after a massive bombardment, scouting parties must make sure that the guns had leveled the enemy defenses. And, should the attack stall, it must be broken off at once. General Henry Rawlinson, entrusted by Haig with direct command of the assault, resisted. The idea of deep scouting missions, he protested, exceeded his men's capacities. As for breaking off a stalled assault, that outcome seemed far-fetched. The British intended to invest 600,000 men in the offensive, and the French another 150,000.

To HERBERT SULZBACH, inspecting his battery, and to the men in the trenches, the shelling that began on the morning of June 24 stood out from the ordinary din that had become a feature of their daily lives. The British began pounding an eighteen-mile front roughly from Gommecourt in the north to Montauban in the south, the more than two thousand guns expected to tear out the German wire and shatter the frontline trenches. The shelling went on for a week, 1.7 million rounds fired on the first day alone. The Germans sought shelter in their deep dugouts, the men hunched on wooden benches, the officers on rude beds, as the earth above them shuddered. So seismic was the effect that grizzled veterans found their legs shaking uncontrollably, their arms twitching, their minds unable to focus. F. L. Cassel, a German infantry officer in the Thiepval sector, at roughly the middle of the front, recalled thinking, "How long could this last? For a week we had lived with the deafening noise of the battle, and we knew that this went on not only in our sector but northwards almost as far as Arras and southwards as far as Peronne. Dull and apathetic we were lying in our dug-outs, secluded from life but prepared to defend ourselves whatever the cost."

A young British officer, Christian Carver, Royal Field Artillery, barely out of Rugby School, stood on the rim of his gun emplacement in the black of night, "watching the show." A friend turned to speak to him, but "speech was of course impossible, and one could only stand and *feel* the thousands of tons of metal rushing away from one. Impressive enough, but what I shall never forget was a substratum of noise, an unceasing moaning roar, exactly like enormous waves on a beach." In southern England, children in school started at the rattling of windowpanes. When the wind blew westward, the guns could be heard more than one hundred miles distant, across Surrey, Sussex, and Kent. When it seemed that the din could not possibly increase, it did, at 6:30 on the morning of July 1.

Fire was first concentrated between Thiepval and Beaumont Hamel but spread rapidly along the entire Somme front. "The wire has never been so well cut, nor the artillery preparation so thorough," General Haig wrote in his diary that morning. To German troops in their dugouts, attack was obviously imminent.

"It is utterly impossible to describe one's feelings during the hours of waiting for 'zero,' " wrote a private in the Lancashire Fusiliers. "The mind is full of wild thoughts and fancies etc. which are utterly beyond control. Recollections of friends and dear ones, places we have seen and known and different phases of life pass in review before one's eyes." In a barn behind the lines a priest held a communion service, using a raised stretcher as his altar, as men knelt before him, heads bent, thoughts unknowable. Second Lieutenant John Sherwin Engall, 16th London Regiment, prayed among the communicants. His unit had yet to experience combat. The twenty-year-old, just out of St. Paul's School, wrote his parents, "I'm writing this letter the day before the most important moment in my life. . . . I would not back out of it for all the money in the world. Tomorrow morning I shall take my men—men whom I have got to love, and who, I think, have got to love me—over the top to do our bit. . . . I have a strong feeling that I shall come through safely . . . but I am quite prepared to go. . . . I could not wish for a finer death . . . doing my duty to my God, my country and my King." Percy Boswell, a subaltern with the King's Own Yorkshire Infantry, wrote his father, "The Hun is going to get consummate hell in this quarter and we are going over the parapet tomorrow when I hope to spend a few hours in chasing the Bosche all over the place." The twenty-two-year-old, who had grown a sparse mustache to enhance his maturity, closed, "I am absolutely certain that I shall get through all right." Edward Chapman wrote home, "I love the Army—and it is a great game. I haven't seen war yet really, but I know I shall hate it. But Army life is grand, and I wouldn't be a civilian just yet for anything."

In the trenches, mates pooled their cash to be divided among survivors, which they preferred to leaving it to battlefield ghouls. They exchanged addresses so that news of a comrade's death might come from a friend rather than only through the War Office's formulaic telegram.

Private Robert Cude was a twenty-two-year-old with the East Kent Regiment, "the Buffs," admired for his fearlessness as a runner, possessed of a sharp tongue, and an indefatigable diarist recording hundreds of words a day. Cude had sworn to remain a private throughout the war. Being an NCO, he believed, was "too much hard work and no pay for it." Even this bemused skeptic became caught up in the drama of the moment. As he listened to the hiss and whine of shells overhead, Cude told his mates, "Never a German can live over that side I am certain. . . . This must be the beginning of the end."

Zero hour approached. Men pared down to battle dress, stowing packs and stacking blankets to be left in the trenches. They slung their haversacks, regulation-style, just below the shoulder blades, and underneath attached a rolled-up waterproof ground sheet. Each man carried 180 rounds of ammunition, a Mills grenade weighing five pounds in each pocket, a water bottle, and a bag of field rations. The lightest, but by no means least valued, burden was a field dressing tucked into the right flap of the tunic so that a man could treat himself before stretcher bearers arrived. The total pack weighed sixty-six pounds. The rifle added another nine pounds. Some men avoided eating their breakfast rations that morning. It was said that a gut wound through a full stomach could be fatal.

While infantrymen faced the prospect of imminent death, life behind the lines went on as ever. A farm boy, Private Williams of the King's Liverpool Regiment, had been assigned duties in keeping with his past and was milking cows within sight of the men preparing to leave the trenches. Further to the rear, French mill workers ran steam saws day and night, producing stacks of wooden crosses.

Why, apart from coercion by officers, would a man leave the safety of a trench to risk a highly probable death? Alexander McClintock offered his explanation: "I should say that the greatest fear the ordinary man has in going into action is the fear that he will show that he is afraid—not to his officers, or to the Germans, or to the folks back home, but to his mates; to the men with whom he has laughed and scoffed at danger. It's the elbow-to-elbow influence that carries men up to face machine guns and gas. A heroic battalion may be made up of units of potential cowards."

Officers and senior noncoms enjoyed a marginal emotional advantage through these final minutes, their attention directed outward to their men rather than inward to their fears, as they checked packs and gas masks and went over maps, making sure everyone understood the objective. Ten minutes before zero hour, the men were issued a small cupful of strong navy rum. They stood before the ladders, shaking hands, a few making awkward stabs at humor, most utterly silent. Some were plainly drunk.

An infantry lieutenant, A. Grant, described the final moments: "I gave the men a good look. They seemed more or less in a trance. Their eyes were glassy and their faces white as chalk." His batman tried to tell him something, which he could not hear for the roar of the guns. The batman's face was bathed in sweat. The day was already sweltering for men dressed in thick woolen uniforms. Grant studied his company commander standing on the first rung of the ladder, a whistle clenched between the man's teeth, his eyes fixed on his watch.

Suddenly the earth shook, a roar eclipsing even the quarter of a million shells fired in the past hour. Thick columns of earth and rubble sprouted from ten locations over the German lines. British tunnelers, after burrowing for months, had placed huge caches of explosives beneath German positions. So powerful were the blasts that not only the sound but light flashes were visible in Kent, across the English Channel. Their detonation this morning was the signal to attack.

Officers' whistles shrieked along a front now grown to twenty-five miles, and the men began climbing the ladders. They rose above the parapet, rifles held at port, a man every two yards, a second line emerging as soon as the first had advanced twenty yards beyond the trench. They would be moving across flat fields, the only high ground being commanded by the Germans. To men from the southern English counties advancing toward a small forest called High Wood, the landscape was reminiscent of home.

The infantry were to be protected by a creeping artillery barrage moving fifty yards ahead, theoretically shielding them all the way to the enemy lines and keeping the Germans from manning their guns until their positions were overrun. The risk to the defending versus the attacking force, however, remained unequal. One eighth of a man's body was exposed while firing from a trench. For the attacker, exposure was 100 percent.

―――

"THEY'RE COMING," German sentries shouted to their comrades sheltered underground. The detonation of the ten mines had collapsed tons of earth, suffocating defenders by the hundreds. But the seven-day bombardment, unknown to the soldiers crossing no-man's-land, had failed. Unlike a temporary way station, which was how the British generals viewed a trench, the German version was built to last. The enemy had constructed dugouts up to thirty feet deep. Actual staircases, not ruts in the earth, provided access. Floors, walls, and ceilings were lined with stout planks. Men slept in bunk beds and read under electric lights, had water for bathing and drinking, and ate hot meals prepared in underground kitchens. Outside the dugouts, empty shell casings held sprigs of wild flowers. Steel doors guarded the entryways into this subterranean world. Under lesser bombardments, one inhabitant noted, "even the heaviest shells at this depth made no more than a pleasant rumble when we sat there over an interminable game of cards." Most of the gun pits, constructed of concrete reinforced with iron, survived all but a direct hit. The moment the British left their trenches, German troops began hauling machine guns up from the bunkers into firing position with a speed born of endless practice.

Once the British troops had begun their advance, artillery batteries could no longer communicate with them. From then on, the gunners would move the barrage forward according to a timetable to wherever the infantrymen were supposed to be, not to where they in fact were. If the troops were too far advanced, the shells would fall on them. If the artillerymen sought to avoid this danger by firing farther ahead, they would overshoot the enemy defenses, leaving them intact. Further reducing the effect of the bombardment, one out of three shells proved to be a dud. In the end, the millions of shells fired during the earlier bombardment and the barrage this day, instead of obliterating the enemy defenses, delivered a mere pound of explosive over every ten square yards.

AN EARLY MIST had dissolved, and the poet Siegfried Sassoon described the morning as "the kind commonly called heavenly." The officers preparing to lead their troops looked splendid. One major with the Cameroonians wore silver spurs for the occasion. His batman brushed him off as he waited to climb the ladder. In lieu of a revolver, many officers chose to carry walking sticks, Malacca and ashplant canes, or polished black thorn favored by Irish regiments. Once out of the trench, the men moved forward at a deliberate, unrushed pace, the only distinction between this advance and a parade being the uneven ground, the deafening racket, and the flash of guns.

Before Montauban, Captain W. P. Nevill of the 8th East Surreys, after leaving the trench, dropped a soccer ball and gave it a smart kick toward the German lines. The ball was one of four that Nevill had brought back from leave, one for each of the platoons under his command. He had offered a cash prize to the first platoon to kick a ball into a German trench. His kick signaled the East Surrey's advance, its first time under fire.

Immediately, machine guns from the presumably silenced German lines opened fire. The British found themselves facing not inert rubble but Maxims, each spewing up to six hundred rounds per minute. Their fire even reached the parapets, tumbling attackers back into the trenches before they had advanced a foot. Karl Blenk, a German infantryman, gaped in wonder toward the advancing British. "They looked as though they must overrun our trenches," he recalled. "We were very surprised to see them walking, we had never seen that before. . . . The officers were in front. I noticed one of them walking calmly, carrying a walking stick. When we started firing, we just had to load and reload. They went down in their hundreds. You didn't have to aim, we just fired into them. If only they had run, they would have overwhelmed us."

The British maintained their measured pace, heads bent, steps plodding. They began falling like leaves. Men on the ground clutched at the legs of advancing comrades, screaming for help. One cried out, "Leave me, would you? You bastard!" as a mate wrenched his leg free from his grasp. The machine guns continued tearing holes in the formations. The first wave faltered; the second and third waves melted into it. The men began to bunch up out of a primal herd instinct. Weeks of rehearsal vanished in a trice.

Rifleman J. Brown, shot in the back and left on the field, unable to move his legs, recalled, "I laid my head on my arms and laid myself down to die. All I could think of was 'Fancy training more than fifteen months for this!' "

A sergeant of the 3rd Tyneside Irish marched as part of a line running as far as his eye could see. "Then I heard the 'patter, patter' of machine guns in the distance," he recalled. "By the time I'd gone another ten yards there seemed to be only a few men left around me; by the time I had gone twenty yards, I seemed to be on my own. Then I was hit myself."

From the air, the scene below suggested toy soldiers on a counterpane, with tiny figures toppling amid points of light. A flier described his difficulty in believing that what he was seeing actually represented "men going to the glory of victory or death." It was, he said, rather like a "strange, uncanny puppet show."

The Germans had strung ten belts of barbed wire thick as a man's thumb before their trenches. The British, upon reaching this steel bramble, found it intact or blown into an impenetrable jumble, snagging men, who were easily cut down by the hail of machine-gun fire. Still they advanced, propelled, some recalled, by the sensation that their feet were taking them forward rather than that they were moving their feet. The force advanced not as individuals, but more like limbs on a plodding beast. The generals, the architects of this enterprise, had lost all control over the forces they had set in motion. Once the attack began, they were impotent to alter their strategy or deliver an order any more swiftly than could a corporal scurrying between the front and the rear.

A soldier named Manning described the effect of seeing hundreds, even thousands, of one's comrades fall: "A man dies and stiffens like a wooden dummy at which one glances for a second with a furtive curiosity. . . . One forgets quickly. The mind is averted as well as the eyes . . . and one moves on, leaving the mauled and bloody thing, gambling on the implicit assurance each one has in his own immortality." The spectacle offered a perverse consolation: if you could see death all around you, you were still alive.

Men who sought to escape the withering fire faced the "battle police." Troops of the Ulster Division, encountering fierce resistance before the Schwaben Redoubt, began to fall back. They shoved aside a young subaltern trying to block their path. He unholstered his revolver and fired point-blank. A soldier dropped. The Ulstermen turned back toward the redoubt.

As the day ended, the dead and wounded formed heaps before the German defenses. In places, one could walk across no-man's-land on British bodies without ever setting foot on the ground. A Scots sergeant remembered, "We knew it was pointless, even before we went over—crossing open ground like that. But you had to go. . . . If you go forward, you'll likely be shot. If you go back you'll be court-martialed and shot. So what the hell do you do?"

Part of the Haig plan had been to pour the cavalry through gaps presumably punched by the infantry. But no gaps ever opened. Instead, the dashing horsemen were employed to carry the wounded back to aid stations. So overburdened were the stretcher bearers that they could scarcely rescue one in ten of the wounded. The rest were told to crawl back as best they could. A compassionate officer named Seeley observed the last moments of the dying. "It is strange and touching that when men die of dangerous wounds," he recalled, "in almost every case 'mother' is the last word that crosses their lips."

By nightfall, the British Army had suffered its most disastrous day in history. At the deepest point of penetration, the enemy had been driven back less than two miles. The first-day casualties on the Somme totaled 57,470. More than 19,240 men—young, healthy, and alive at 7:30 that morning—were now dead. Men with a likely allotment of another forty to fifty years of life, with the prospect of careers, wives, children, and grandchildren, would never know them. The machine gun had been the great killer, accounting for more than 11,500 of the British dead. The enemy who inflicted this slaughter had lost a comparatively light 8,000 killed.

The French had done somewhat better, having achieved all their first-day objectives. They employed heavier artillery and launched their attack two hours later, thus confusing the German defenders as to when they were coming. However, while initially the Somme was to have been a full partnership, the massive losses at Verdun had forced the French to reduce their involvement. Their numbers were insufficient to overcome the British defeat.

Among the British dead was Captain Nevill. Private Cude had seen the officer hit while his leg was still lifted from kicking the football. Percy Boswell, who had been going to chase the Hun for "a few merry hours," was killed within minutes of the attack. Of 800 men in his unit, 518 had fallen and 21 of 26 officers. Guy Chapman, who had gone into the Somme claiming, "I wouldn't be a civilian just yet for anything," was saying by midbattle, "I hate this business from the bottom of my soul."

Upon receiving reports of his losses, General Haig observed, "This cannot be considered severe in view of the numbers engaged, and the length of the front attacked. By nightfall, the situation is much more favourable than when we started today." The offensive was not to be broken off. A corps commander had his explanation for the failure of the attack: "The men are much too keen on saving their own skins. They need to be taught that they are out here to do their job. Whether they survive or not is a matter of complete indifference." A stunned chaplain present at the moment was prompted to write down the officer's words.

Private S. Cloete described what the scene looked like the following morning: "I remember thinking how untidy the battlefield was. There were hundreds of bodies. There were torn and bloody bandages, burst haversacks, abandoned rifles driven muzzle first into the churned-up soil to mark a body, a wounded man perhaps who had died before he could get help. And paper—there were masses of torn paper, letters, postcards, wrappings from parcels." Private Cloete saw something else, too: "Plenty of souvenirs about, watches, purses, rings and brass hats are kicking around."

Montgomery Belgion, born to English parents in Paris, was a twenty-one-year-old subaltern when he arrived at the Somme with the Honourable Artillery Company. He quickly learned that heroism could be an arbitrary affair. A fellow subaltern he knew only as Kerr boasted to their brigadier that he personally had killed five Germans. Kerr was thereupon awarded the Military Cross. "He neglected to tell the brigadier," Belgion noted, "that the Germans he said he shot were disarmed prisoners being led to the rear." Belgion was to learn later, when assigned to divisional staff, "that decorations came up with the rations, and it only remained to dish them out." An interpreter on the staff, fluent in French, managed a Military Cross for himself even though he had never been under fire.

All the failings that R. C. Sherriff had noted at Loos were repeated on the Somme, vastly magnified. The wire had not been substantially cut, and the pulverized and pitted earth had hobbled the attackers. The bulk of German defenders had survived the bombardment. The lack of imagination in the assault—lining men up in broad daylight and then walking them toward the enemy guns—mirrored the mind of Douglas Haig. The bombardment might have been temporarily halted just before zero hour to fool the Germans into thinking that the attack was imminent, which would likely have lured them from their bunkers up to the defenses. Then the bombardment could have been resumed, raining destruction down on them rather than on empty trenches. Further, the fog of battle produced its inevitable calamities. Near Albert, British troops awaited the detonating of the mines as their signal to advance. Fifteen minutes beforehand, the Germans exploded a mine of their own. Thus, two British regiments, mistakenly believing they had witnessed the attack signal, marched into their own barrage with horrendous casualties.

Immediately upon coming out of battle, the men mustered by unit for the first accounting of losses. An officer called out the names and awaited a response: "Here, sir" or "Dead" or "Wounded," or often simply silence. The 2nd Middlesex had gone into action at a point dubbed "Crucible Corner" with 24 officers and 650 men. The next day, 1 officer and 50 men answered the roll call. Army Form B.104-82a would tell families, "It is my painful duty to inform you that . . ." followed by the longhand insertion of the name of the man killed. Company and platoon commanders were expected to follow up with something more personal. A standard close to these letters read, "You will be relieved to know that your (son's) (husband's) (brother's) death was instantaneous and that he suffered no pain."

Readers of *The Times* became accustomed to seeing column after column of casualty lists. During the fighting that followed the Somme, *The Times* listed the names of the dead for three typical days as follows: August 9, 5,000; August 10, 4,300; August 11, 4,220; and so on, day after day. Every week, local papers carried black-bordered photos of neighbors who had fallen.

VERA BRITTAIN, now assigned to the Camberwell Hospital in London, was called to the phone by the matron. She learned that a Second Lieutenant E. H. Brittain, just arrived in the latest convoy of wounded from the Somme, was asking for his sister. The matron said she would allow Vera to see him if she could be "spared from the ward." Vera rushed off, "half dazed with surging emotions." A few months before, filled with foreboding on a dismal London afternoon, she had gone to see Edward off for France. She had then gone back to Camberwell, feeling "weighted with lead." Soon afterward, she had gone to Fishmonger's Hall Hospital to visit Geoffrey Thurlow, also with the Foresters, her brother's close friend from officer training days, who had been evacuated from Ypres, shell-shocked and suffering from a potentially disfiguring facial wound. Such wounds were feared as much as the loss of a limb or blindness, as suggested in the flowery prose of the time by a newspaper reporter who pitied "those whose dear and familiar features have been transformed into a repellant mask, who never again will be kissed with ecstasy and whose presence cannot fail to bring a shock to those they love best." Now Edward was back, also wounded but alive. She learned that he had led the first wave of his 11th Sherwood Foresters on the morning of the Somme attack. He had been struck in his right arm and right thigh. Upon being carried from the field, he had been taken to a casualty clearing station, where his injuries had been assessed. There a blunt test was applied—triage, from the French Army term for dividing the wounded into three categories: those requiring immediate attention to save them; those who could last long enough to be sent to a field hospital; and those judged beyond hope, who were placed in a tent, known as "the moribund ward," where sedatives and sympathetic nurses eased a man's inevitable end. Edward fell into the second category. He had suffered the kind of wounds many soldiers prayed for, a "blighty," not permanently maiming but sufficient for a ticket out of the war. "Blighty," derived from a Hindustani word meaning a foreign country and adopted by colonial regulars as affectionate slang for England, had come to include the dream wound. The Germans had their own version, the *Heimatschuss,* or "home wound." The *poilu* gratefully suffered the same, called a *filon.* In every case the dynamic was the same: duty discharged, honor fulfilled, the war over.

For his deeds Edward was awarded the Military Cross, his citation reported in *The Times:* "For conspicuous gallantry and leadership during an attack. He was severely wounded but continued to lead his men with great bravery and coolness until a second wound disabled him." The musician, composer, aesthete, and unexpected hero did not regard his injuries as a blighty. He had every intention of returning to his regiment. To Vera, all that mattered was that Edward was alive.

The citations that accompanied medals had a noble, rolling cadence, raising images of fearless heroes depicted in storybooks. A more literal account might describe a twenty-year-old East End Cockney running ahead of his mates, heaving into a trench a Mills bomb whose fragments severed the hand of a thirty-year-old carpenter from Essen with a wife and three children, the Tommy then leaping in and plunging fifteen inches of steel into the throat of a former medical student and shooting an eighteen-year-old officer, his family's only son.

THE FIGHTING IN the Somme sector would drag on by fits and starts for more than four months. Two months were required before the British, with help from the French, overtook the German second-line defenses, which were supposed to have fallen on the first day. "The French and British attacks on the Somme go on continuously," the German artilleryman Herbert Sulzbach wrote in his diary. "They lose 1,000 killed in action and replace them with 2,000 fresh troops. At first it was thought that a battle of this kind would have to be over in a few days but . . . it may even last for months."

On September 12, the British believed that at long last they had found a way to break the stalemate. German soldiers defending a line near the villages of Flers and Courcelette watched in disbelief as what appeared to be iron tortoises rumbled toward them, spitting fire, easily traversing the deepest shell holes, and trampling the wire flat. Ernest Swinton, a multitalented Royal Engineer, historian, and war correspondent, had been appalled by the slaughter he had witnessed from the war's outset. While home on Christmas leave in 1914, he happened upon a tractor towing a gun and had an inspiration. He envisioned a "power-driven, bullet proof, armed engine capable of destroying machine guns, breaking through entanglements and climbing earthworks." The generals, confronted by a new idea, were unmoved. Swinton eventually managed to get his inspiration before Winston Churchill, who, impressed, found the resources to realize Swinton's concept. Less than two years later, the tank, a weapon Leonardo da Vinci had conceived of some four hundred years before, was introduced on the western front. "Tank" had been chosen as the cover name to suggest a container to conceal the true nature of these "land ships" when they were sent from British factories to France. Eleven days after their first appearance, tanks spearheaded a second drive that overtook Thiepval, another objective initially set for the first day. However, the tank proved no more decisive in carrying the day than bombardment or massed infantry assault. The vehicles proved vulnerable to heavy-weapons fire, became mired in the mud, or broke down with dismaying frequency.

The war continued to hatch weapons of ingenious lethality. Still, much of battle remained little changed from ancient times. Major Douglas Pegler, a British officer, described a macabre spectacle he had come across on the same day the tank was introduced. Two dead men, a Prussian and a Coldstream Guardsman, with their bayonets plunged into each other's chests, stood upright, one body supporting the other.

Alexander McClintock, the wry Kentuckian serving with the Canadian 85th Battalion, was assigned to the Somme sector, to what the Tommies called the PBI, Poor Bloody Infantry. Between full-scale assaults, raids went on almost nightly. McClintock took part in a probe by sixty men, for most their first time under fire. The raid was announced by a visit from a splendidly attired staff officer who arrived on horseback. "This is the first time you men have been tested," he said as he dismounted. "You're Canadians. I needn't say anything more to you. You're going to be popping them off at a great rate. . . . Our shells will be going off just six and a half feet from the ground. If you stand up you're likely to be hit in the head, but don't let that worry you because if you do get hit in the head you won't know it." With that he remounted his horse and rode off.

At ten minutes past midnight, the raiding party began crawling across no-man's-land on all fours. Close behind, twelve stretcher bearers waited. Almost immediately, McClintock knew that they had been spotted as German star shells lit the ground with a bluish brilliance. Two men were hit near McClintock, and as they toppled, he found himself taking comfort in the thought that the casualties predicted for the raid had now been fulfilled, and "it seemed the rest of us were safe." But just as they reached the enemy parapet, an explosion rocked the earth. The Germans had detonated a mine placed precisely to drive off such attackers. The surviving Canadians crept back to their lines. The casualties had not yet been reported to battalion headquarters. Consequently, rum rations were provided for the full complement and distributed among the survivors, to which a Canadian Scot in the unit responded, "G-r-r-r-a-nd!" At the roll call it was confirmed that of the sixty men who left the trench, only seventeen had returned. The other forty-three were dead, wounded, or "MBK"—missing, believed killed.

McClintock was struck by the behavior of men under fire. "On our first bombing raid," he recalled, his bayonet instructor, a powerfully built sergeant of commanding presence and voice, "turned and ran back to our own barbed wire." The sergeant was given a second chance but behaved even more cravenly. He was sent to the rear where he resumed teaching others how to deal death with the bayonet. A scrawny lad from Ontario had broken every rule in the King's Regulations and Orders: getting drunk, being absent without leave, disobeying orders. "In France," McClintock remembered, "this chap was worth ten ordinary men. . . . He came out laughing and unscathed from a dozen tight places" and after each immediately resumed his delinquent ways. McClintock could not fathom the thought that had occupied his mind during the raid: Had he lost the address of a girl he had met in London? Would he ever be able to find her?

Among the German casualties during the latter stages of the Somme was Adolf Hitler, wounded in the leg by a shell fragment and sent back to Germany to recuperate. There, the apathy and antiwar attitudes he encountered sickened him. Jews, preaching peace, he believed, were conspiring to undo the heroism at the front. After five months of light duty, which he could have continued, he insisted on being sent back to the line. The British prime minister's son, Raymond, the eldest and considered the most promising of Herbert Asquith's three boys, died on the Somme. To colleagues the loss seemed thereafter to damage the grief-stricken father's capacity to govern. Hector Hugh Munro, best known for his mordantly amusing short stories under the pen name Saki, though forty-six, had refused a commission and entered the ranks of the Royal Fusiliers. Two days before the last day of the Somme, he was crouched in a shell hole, shouting to one of his men to "put that bloody cigarette out," when a sniper killed him.

A year and a half of combat had not dulled the ardor of the American volunteer Alan Seeger. Days after the initial assault on the Somme, the poet wrote a friend of a renewed advance: "I am glad to be going in [the] first wave. If you are in this thing at all it is best to be in to the limit." It was his last letter. He kept his rendezvous with death on July 4, as if he had chosen the date for romantic resonance. Seeger was thirty-two. Seeger's fellow American Alexander McClintock was put out of action permanently on the last day of the Somme, nearly bleeding to death. He was among the 90 percent casualties experienced by his battalion.

The battle effectively ended on November 18 after a final engagement on the Ancre River. On that day, the Allies were still three miles short of Bapaume, an objective set for the first day. Even measured by earlier debacles, the losses over the four and a half months had been appalling: 420,000 British, 205,000 French, 500,000 Germans.

After the war, a monument would be erected at Thiepval containing the names of 73,412 men from Australia, India, New Zealand, Newfoundland, and South Africa, commemorating not the dead but, as the inscription read, only "The Missing of the Somme."

During the Franco-Prussian War, the Germans had used the expression "lions led by donkeys" to describe the generals of the French Army. The term regained currency again as casualties soared during the Great War, leveled most often against British generals. Foremost among those targeted by critics was Douglas Haig. But this carping remained the view of naysayers. Six weeks after the Somme, the government promoted Haig to field marshal.

As THE FIGHTING on the Somme trailed off, it flared in a distant quarter of this global conflict. A slight, inconspicuous British Army captain, Thomas Edward Lawrence, had become an intelligence officer in the British Arab Bureau. On October 16, 1916, Lawrence reported to Jedda, a port on the Red Sea within the Ottoman Empire. His mission was to initiate a friendly liaison with Arab leaders bent on throwing off the Turkish yoke. Lawrence seized this slender reed and transformed himself into a military leader intent on uniting the Arab tribes and achieving their dream of an independent state. Lawrence of Arabia was astonishingly successful. But he was to suffer the enduring pangs of conscience when his victories were manipulated by the British and French, not to liberate the Arabs from the Turks, but to carve up Arab lands into largely artificial states to suit their own strategic and commercial interests.

13

"Hindenburg! The Name
Itself Is Massive"

NOVEMBER 11, 1918. The disbelief experienced by the men of the American 26th Division when ordered to advance at 10:35 A.M. was mirrored in the trenches of the French. A colonel of the 80th Infantry received two nearly simultaneous messages that morning from headquarters: one reported the signing of the armistice; the other ordered an attack at 9 A.M.

The stretcher-bearer priest Pierre Teilhard de Chardin and the infantry captain Henri Desagneaux, the latter haggard, exhausted, and smelly after days without sleep or washing, were among the French sweating out the last hours. For others it was already too late. Second Lieutenant Laurent had just been discharged from the hospital and returned to the 415th Infantry Regiment. Sergeant Holler had been granted leave for the birth of his third child. This was not the moment to abandon his companions, Holler decided, and stayed. In the church of Dom-le-Mesnil, a handful of villagers attended a brief funeral service for Lieutenant Dupin and his telephone operator, Charreton. All four men had been killed on armistice morning.

René Naegelen, who had feared dying without ever knowing a woman's embrace, Teilhard, and Desagneaux were all survivors of the human gristmill at Verdun. Of that experience, Desagneaux described in his diary how it was to serve under "General Mud": men drowning in the suction of the muck who had to be hauled out with ropes; men unable to flee in the midst of a shelling because they were stuck fast. "Let Joffre, the deputies, journalists and senators come and live here a bit with us," Desagneaux wrote. "The war will end quicker." These three had survived the two years since Verdun. They needed only hours more to survive the war.

NOVEMBER 1916. A French legend had been born at Verdun: the Trench of the Bayonets, where a bursting shell had buried men alive, their bayonets still protruding above the earth. The phenomenon was hardly singular. Rifles gripped by dead hands rose from the earth on both sides of the battlefield. As a German survivor saw it, "What a stupendous tragedy! And all to put a feather in the cap of a Crown Prince!" Falkenhayn's strategy of bleeding France white had backfired at Verdun; the French losses totaled 360,000 and the German losses 336,000 men. The Germans were bleeding as profusely as their foe.

A German machine gunner, Wilhelm Hermanns, described Verdun in a bold letter written from a French POW camp addressed to the kaiser in his "palatial setting of the court." Hermanns wrote of how he had been "inspired by your speeches, could not join the Army fast enough." But now, he concluded, he should have listened to Germany's foremost scientist, Albert Einstein, who had opposed the invasion of Belgium, declaring, "Force attracts only men of low morality." Einstein's words "were passed over by your Majesty's courtiers, who sneered, 'Einstein is a moral leper.' " Hermanns offered to guide Wilhelm II on a tour of the battlefield, "where you can see the flesh of your men mingled with the soil." Hermanns offered to introduce the kaiser to some of those who had died because the Hohenzollern dynasty had chosen "to save face, and not retreat from Verdun: Berend, a forty-two-year-old butcher from Berlin, father of five children; Holsten, a twenty-eight-year-old bookkeeper from Danzig; Shroeder, a twenty-year-old former medical student who had already lost two brothers at Langemarck." To his own family he mailed a photo of himself and eight comrades taken in the midst of the campaign. He was the lone survivor.

ODDLY, A FRENCH hero emerged from this inconclusive carnage, General Robert Nivelle, an artillery expert and smooth-tongued charmer who seduced the British with his perfect command of their language and culture, gained from an English mother. Nivelle, the commander on the ground at Verdun, had, by mid-November 1916, regained almost all the territory yielded earlier to the Germans, including the lost forts of Douaumont and Vaux, taking comparatively light casualties. This instant national hero next announced that he had, but was not yet able to divulge, the secret of final victory. The current commander of the French forces, General Joseph Joffre, had become stale, seemingly callous to massive losses. Briand, the prime minister, who had initially pushed Joffre to defend Verdun, kicked him upstairs to become an inert "Marshal of France" and, on December 12, named Nivelle commander of all French armies on the western front.

OTHER CHESS MASTERS changed places before 1916 ended. General Paul von Hindenburg was already sixty-six years old and three years retired from the German Army when, on August 22, 1914, he received a call from the kaiser: the Fatherland needed him. To which the old soldier replied, "I am ready." Forty-four years before, a slim, youthful Captain Hindenburg had ridden on horseback down the Champs-Élyseés, among the victors of the Franco-Prussian War. In the Great War, he had first been given command of the Eighth Army to fight the Russians on the eastern front. Winston Churchill, in a sketch written after the war, caught the field marshal to the life: "Hindenburg! The name itself is massive. It harmonizes with the tall thick-set personage with beetling brows, strong features and heavy jowls. . . . A giant: slow thinking, slow moving, but sure, steady, faithful, warlike yet benignant, larger than the ordinary run of men."

Hindenburg's alter ego was his chief of staff, General Erich Ludendorff, a battering ram, physically overpowering, utterly without fear, immune to the opinions of others, including superiors, thick-skinned, and charmless. The two were character opposites: Hindenburg the aristocratic Prussian, Ludendorff a boorish commoner; one born to the elite, the other clawing his way into it; one steady, the other mercurial; one a plodder, the other a military genius who had revealed his prowess only three days into the war by seizing command of a lost German brigade at Liège and turning it around to storm the city's citadel, for which he had received Germany's highest decoration, the French-sounding Orden pour le Mérite.

After the success at Liège, Hindenburg had pulled Ludendorff from the western front to become his deputy in the east. There they had coauthored signal victories at Tannenberg and Masurian Lakes, repelling the Russian invasion of East Prussia while dealing the enemy staggering losses. "Coauthored" is perhaps generous, since a widely held opinion had it that Ludendorff had provided the brains and daring while Hindenburg had provided the face of respectability to cover up his subordinate's social inadequacies. The eastern front successes, whoever the de facto victor, had won Hindenburg a field marshal's baton.

Hindenburg was too large a man to be resentful or envious of his gifted subordinate and shrewd enough to recognize the complementariness between himself and Ludendorff. He described his relationship with him as "a happy marriage. . . . I realized that one of my principal tasks was, as far as possible, to give free scope to the intellectual powers, the almost superhuman capacity for work and resolution of my chief of staff."

As Moltke had yielded to Falkenhayn over the failure of the Schlieffen Plan, Falkenhayn, for his failure to defeat France at Verdun, was replaced by Hindenburg as Germany's supreme military leader on August 29, 1916. He brought Ludendorff with him to the western front, and the partners quickly sized up the situation they had inherited. Feeling the manpower pinch produced by the extraordinary German losses at Verdun, they adopted a major course change. No longer would German soldiers be fed into the meat grinder at Verdun to gain a few meaningless yards. They would give up territory in order to shorten their line, thus making it more defensible and more easily supplied. Behind it, they began to construct a near-impregnable defense, a thinly held front line to stall an enemy assault, backed by miles of deep, stoutly built trenches, bristling with barbed wire and supplied by railroads running right up to the front. The objective was not to drive farther into France but rather to keep Allied forces out of Germany. This broad belt of iron, wood, earth, and wire would eventually run nearly one hundred miles from Arras to Soissons. Formally, it was called the Siegfried Line, but soon it came to be known as the Hindenburg Line. Here again suspicions circulated that the old man may have received the honor even though Ludendorff had actually provided the vision for the barrier. At the time Hindenburg and Ludendorff moved to the western front, they essentially gained power over both the obstreperous but insecure Kaiser Wilhelm and the flabby parliament. The two essentially became Germany's codictators. They then began to extend their thinking beyond the battlefield and entered the political realm, where their touch was less sure.

Late in 1916, given the abundance of white crosses and the dearth of victories on both sides, President Woodrow Wilson had sought to persuade the stalemated enemies to settle for peace without victory. On December 18, he asked each side to set forth its terms for ending the war. The Allies demanded conditions certain to be unacceptable: withdrawal from all occupied territory and virtual dismemberment of the German and Austrian empires. The Germans wanted the iron ore fields in Lorraine, economic control over Belgium, and the Belgian Congo and Poland as German protectorates. Both sides told Wilson, in effect, no thank you, since each expected to win the war.

Hindenburg, persuaded by Ludendorff, now made a portentous decision. Victory might have eluded Germany on the ground. But German admirals had been claiming that it could be won on the high seas. If given free rein, their U-boats could send Great Britain's food imports to the bottom and starve the enemy into submission in six weeks. After that, France would have to surrender too. Hindenburg was persuaded and on January 31, 1917, announced resumption of unrestricted attacks against any vessel in any waters. The Germans had made a rash gamble. Which would happen first? Would the U-boats drive Britain and France to their knees, or would the destruction of her ships provoke America to enter the war? Four days later, a German U-boat sank the American freighter *Housatonic* in the North Atlantic.

BEFORE THE YEAR was out, Great Britain too had chosen a new leader, the Liberal Party's fiery Welsh social reformer and spellbinding speaker, David Lloyd George. When he became prime minister, Lloyd George was fifty-three years old, a striking if not large figure with a thick shock of undisciplined hair and a heavy mustache, a dapper, tweedy dresser whose style and appearance suggested a model of self-made success. He also possessed the energy to lead a nation while balancing a wife, children, and a mistress. The other woman was Frances Stevenson, a bright classics graduate from London University twenty-five years younger than Lloyd George, who also served as his secretary. He had made clear at the beginning of the affair that he would never commit political suicide by marrying her. Stevenson, nevertheless, remained steadfast out of her love and conviction that she served a man of greatness.

The Welshman's ascent to war leader marked a 180-degree turn from his original position. In 1914, as chancellor of the Exchequer, Lloyd George had argued against Britain's entry into the war, but within six weeks he had mounted the stump speaking as if he had invented the idea, the switch likely prompted by an astute politician's recognition that he was swimming against the popular tide. There followed his appointment in 1915 as minister of munitions, in which office he displayed his contempt for the idea that only generals knew how to run a war. It was Lloyd George that Douglas Haig had told, "The machine gun was a much overrated weapon and that two per battalion were more than sufficient." Kitchener, secretary of state for war, thought four would do nicely. Lloyd George chose his own formula: "Take Kitchener's maximum; square it, multiply that result by two—and when you are in sight of that, double it again for good luck." By July 7, 1916, Lloyd George had Kitchener's job, after the old soldier drowned when the cruiser *Hampshire* struck a mine and sank. Toward the end of 1916, with the war hopelessly bogged down, Lloyd George, forestalling Woodrow Wilson's appeal for peace without victory, called instead for a "knock-out blow." By December 7, he had managed to supplant Herbert Asquith as prime minister. He immediately gathered around him a tightly bound five-man War Cabinet, headed by himself, with a single objective: to win.

Lloyd George was no harrumphing chauvinist. He knew exactly the human cost of war. While still minister of munitions, he had gone to France and stopped by a hospital treating Welsh soldiers to visit the wounded son of a fellow member of Parliament, John Hinds. Young Hinds had been shot through the head, and the bullet had torn away part of his brain. The only life left in the soldier was the agony he underwent before he died. When an ashen-faced Lloyd George returned to England, he told Frances Stevenson, "I ought not to have seen him. I feel that I cannot go on with my work, now that the grim horror of the reality has been brought home to me so terribly. . . . I am too sensitive to pain and suffering and this visit has almost broken me down." Yet he managed to overcome his sensitivity sufficiently to find a rationale for vigorously pursuing victory. How else, he had convinced himself, was the suffering of Hinds and untold thousands of others to be ended?

Completing the triad of new faces was France's latest champion, General Robert Nivelle, with his "secret" plan for victory. It was simplicity itself, if not simplistic: the Allies were to choose a point where the German defenses were weak and attack it with unstoppable force. Evidently, 3,182,400 casualties through 1916, largely through this strategy, were not enough. When each party at conflict is convinced that it will prevail, why trade total victory for a compromised peace? To the generals, the war remained an abstraction, strategies scribbled on stiff white linen napery over lunch in the senior officers' mess, colored pins stuck into a map. The men whose very lives hung on the decisions of these leaders detected little difference when a new signature appeared on the orders from the supreme command. The Tommies simply kept on, singing their circular rationale, "We're here because we're here because we're here because . . ."

To troops lucky enough to be assigned to the rear, the war was a job one went to that offered more or less regular hours in relative safety. To the men at the front, it meant days of boredom, filled with menial chores and relieved by hours of terror. It was a universe where the hunger for survival fostered blind faith, wrapped in denial and tied together with black humor. Flippancy was the soldier's lingua franca, as expressed in the jocular mangling of foreign names and expressions. For Tommies, Belgium's Ypres became "Wipers"; Wijtschate in Flanders, "White Sheet"; Étaples in France, "Eatables"; Loisy, "Lousy"; and Saint-Aignan, "St. Agony." *Vin blanc* metamorphosed somehow into "plonk," a name that outlasted the war, signifying cheap wine. Jesting euphemisms helped take the edge off harsh truths. A cemetery became a "rest camp." To be killed was to "go west" or to "go along the duckboard trail." Stretcher bearers became "body snatchers." Going over the top became "jumping the bags." "Bombproof" meant a safe job behind the lines. Toilet paper, or whatever available was used for that purpose, became "bum fodder," a meaning soon extended to any paperwork issuing from headquarters. The term lives on in the abbreviated "bumf," British slang for red tape.

The British Army, followed later by the Americans, devised a "field postcard" for the tired soldier or one fresh from battle who wanted to notify his family of his situation. The card carried fixed phrases: "I am quite well," "I am wounded," "I have received your letter," "I have received no letter from you." The soldier crossed out the inapplicable phrases and mailed the card. The troops called them "quick firers," or "whizz-bangs" after the feared mortar round because the cards reached their targets so swiftly.

The overworked "fuck" was pressed into service as adjective, verb, and noun, sometimes popping up in the middle of words. Parodies, ditties, and limericks flourished. One of the latter, playing on the men's pronunciation of "Wipers" for Ypres, ran:

> Said a Cockney on furlough from Ypres,
> It's a rotten old village for snypres,
> And the things that they do
> Ain't exactly what you
> Reads abaht over 'ome in the pypres.

The song that best expressed the soldiers' belief that death was for the other fellow was a sardonic version of a presumed old Salvation Army tune:

> The bells of hell go ting-a-ling-a-ling
> For you but not for me;
> And the little devils how they sing-a-ling-a-ling
> For you but not for me.
> O Death, where is thy sting-a-ling-a-ling,
> O Grave, thy victor-ee?
> The bells of hell go ting-a-ling-a-ling,
> For you but not for me.

The soldiers' bitterest scorn was reserved not for the enemy but for generals and home-front politicians. "A politician is a man who gives your life for his country," one popular gibe ran. An anonymous wag perhaps best captured the fatalism of the trenches, writing, "When you are a soldier you are one of two things, either at the front or behind the lines. If you are behind the lines you need not worry. If you are at the front you are one of two things. You are either in a danger zone or in a zone which is not dangerous. If you are in a zone which is not dangerous you need not worry. If you are in a danger zone you are one of two things; either you are wounded or you are not. If you are not wounded you need not worry. If you are wounded you are one of two things, either seriously wounded or slightly wounded. If you are slightly wounded you need not worry. If you are seriously wounded one of two things is certain—either you get well or you die. If you get well you needn't worry. If you die you cannot worry, so there is no need to worry about anything at all."

The necessity of recruiting huge armies produced a few fault lines in the British class system, but the walls remained largely intact. A British officer described the nightly spectacle of trains leaving London's Victoria Station, starting the journey back to France. Six trains were lined up side by side at the departure platforms, in five of which the men and their regimental officers were crowded, "with bulging packs on their backs to sit five a side in badly lit compartments." The sixth train had dining cars and first-class compartments into which obsequious lackeys "guided red-hatted and red-tabbed [staff] officers to their reserved seats where waiters were already taking orders for drinks."

Prejudices were identical on both sides of no-man's-land. Ordinary soldiers hated the war more than each other. At the front, lunatic orders confirmed the conviction that the staff was the real enemy, as when a general insisted on launching a gas attack even when the men could feel the wind blowing in their faces. As for inspirational slogans emanating from the home front, no possible response existed but ridicule. One poster read, "Eat Less, Save Shipping," upon which the soldiers crossed out the last word and substituted "shitting." As the front rocked back and forth over scraps of earth, one Tommy figured the amount of time taken to gain ground at the Somme and concluded that at that pace the Rhine would be reached in 180 years.

Men fastened nicknames on themselves and their enemies, though not always those capturing the civilian imagination. Britons back home and journalists spoke of "Tommies," a term of misty provenance deriving from "Tommy Atkins," supposedly a mythical hero during the Napoleonic Wars. The term was not used by the men themselves except in amused imitation of home-front patriots. As for the enemy, he was "Jerry," "Fritz," "the Hun," or "boche," the latter word borrowed from the French. Even before the war it had had for Frenchmen connotations of a person both bad and stubborn, which to them perfectly caught the German character. To civilian sentimentalists the French fighter remained the *poilu,* as described by one observer: "In adversity, he generally smiles; in the moment of the worst danger, he will often utter a jest which brings forth instant peals of laughter from his comrades; then, when face to face with death, his last words are of his mother and his country." No parallel slang expression for themselves or their enemies seems to have emerged for the ordinary German foot soldier.

After Verdun, a battle veteran and writer, Henri Barbusse, recalled stopping with five comrades in an *estaminet,* one of the rude village cafés that flourished behind the lines. One of the civilian patrons, a woman, dripping sympathy, approached Barbusse's friend Private Volpatte, brandishing a newspaper and pointing to photos from the front. "They ought not to publish these things about the dirt and vermin and the fatigue," she said. Barbusse watched Volpatte blush, "ashamed of the misery from whence he comes, and whither he must return." "No," Volpatte anwered sheepishly, "we're not unhappy." The woman went on, "I know there are compensations. How superb a charge must be, eh? All those masses of men advancing like they do in a holiday procession, and the trumpets playing a rousing air in the fields! And the dear little soldiers that can't be held back and shout '*vive la France*' even laughing as they die." On leaving the café, one of the *poilus* muttered of the civilian patrons, "If I see them again, I'll know what to say to them!" To which another comrade replied, "We won't see them again. In eight days from now, we shall be laid out."

Invalided back home after the Somme, Alexander McClintock, the Kentuckian serving with the Canadians, was asked by *The New York Times* to write about his experiences. "The hardest part of soldiering," McClintock wrote, "is the mental part, and the times when the men are not fighting but just sitting 'round are the hardest to bear. . . . It is the thinking about it all that drives men crazy. I've known men to go all to pieces just sitting around thinking. . . . The only thing to do is to laugh at everything. Keep jolly! Make fun of it all! . . . Give absurd names to everything. The Tommies call the 'R.I.P.' that is put on a soldier's grave 'Rise If Possible' . . . lots of their jokes would seem rather appalling to you people here at home. But they must have their jokes."

Occasionally, behind the rear, in an *estaminet,* after endless raucous choruses of "Tipperary," a lone voice would lift in the poignant "Keep the home fires burning, while your hearts are yearning. . . . There's a silver lining, through the dark cloud shining . . . ," capturing every man's lingering hope.

14

"Keeping the World Safe for Democracy"

NOVEMBER 11, 1918. At 8:56 A.M., Major General Joseph E. Kuhn, commanding the U.S. Army's 79th Division, radioed the brigades under his command, "Hostilities will cease on the whole front at 11 hours today, French time. Until that hour, the operations previously ordered will be pressed with vigor. At 11 hours our line will halt in place, and no man will move one step backward or forward." If anything, Kuhn's subordinate, Brigadier General William Nicholson, relaying the word of the armistice signing to the two regiments under him, the 313th and 314th, heightened the belligerency by adding, "These orders will be strictly complied with and there will be absolutely no let-up in the carrying out of the original plans until 11 o'clock."

Both officers' fight-to-the-end determination reflected the attitude of their superior, the chief of the American Expeditionary Forces, General John J. Pershing. Pershing had wanted no armistice at all. Eleven days before, he had advised the Allied Supreme War Council, "Germany's morale is undoubtedly low, her Allies have deserted her one by one and she can no longer hope to win. Therefore," Pershing urged, "we should take full advantage of the situation and continue the offensive until we compel her unconditional surrender." Pershing had lost that argument under pressure from

President Woodrow Wilson to bring the war to a speedy end. The next best outcome, in the general's view, was to push the enemy back as far as possible and inflict maximum casualties with whatever time was left.

Among the men of the 313th engaged that morning was Henry N. Gunther, in his mid-twenties, a fine-looking soldier with erect posture, a clear-eyed gaze, and a guardsman's mustache that suggested a British subaltern rather than an American private. Gunther, however, had had difficulty with army life. He came from a heavily German neighborhood in east Baltimore where the culture of his forebears remained strong. When the United States had gone to war, Gunther and his neighbors had begun to experience anti-German prejudices. In that poisonous atmosphere, Gunther had felt no impulse to enlist. He was doing nicely at the National Bank of Baltimore and had a girlfriend, Olga Gruebl, whom he intended to marry. Nevertheless, Gunther was drafted five months after America's entry into the war and entered the 313th, "Baltimore's Own." Gunther's closest pal, Ernest Powell, became platoon sergeant in Company A, while Gunther was appointed supply sergeant. "Supply sergeants were traditionally unpopular," Powell recalled. "Army clothing in the war, as they said at the time, came in two sizes—too large and too small." Supply sergeants took the brunt of the soldiers' gripes, and Gunther began keeping to himself, his enthusiasm for army life well controlled. After arriving in France in July 1918, Gunther wrote a friend back home to stay clear of the war at all costs as the conditions were miserable. An army censor passed the letter along to Gunther's CO, who broke him to private. Gunther now found himself serving under Ernie Powell, once his coequal, a chafing humiliation. Thereafter, Powell observed, Gunther became increasingly brooding and withdrawn.

Company A arrived at the front on September 12, occupying a supposedly safe position in reserve. The next day the unit suffered its first casualty, Corporal Edgar Stewart, killed in an insignificant skirmish. Soon afterward, the 313th was sent to the front lines. "On our first day in the trenches," Powell remembered, "a regimental runner came up to my post of command and asked for a runner to operate between regimental and brigade headquarters. Before I could ask for volunteers, Gunther said, 'Sarge, I'll take it.' " Gunther was gone for a week and on his return to Company A bore a wound to his arm that could easily have gotten him out of the line. He chose instead to stay. Powell thought he detected a new attitude in Gunther, propelled evidently by a desire to reha- bilitate himself.

By Armistice Day, the 313th had been engaged in nearly two months of uninterrupted combat. At 9:30 that morning, the regi- ment jumped off, bayonets fixed, rifles at port, heads bent, slog- ging through a marshland in an impenetrable fog in what they hoped was the right direction toward their objective, a speck on the map called Ville-devant-Chaumont. Their advance was to be covered by the 311th Machine Gun Battalion. But in the fog, the gunners had no idea where to direct their fire, and Company A thus moved along in an unsettling silence. Suddenly, German ar- tillery opened up. Most shells sank into the morass, sending up geysers of mud but causing scant damage. A brother company to the north was less fortunate. A runner bringing word of the armistice was killed before he could reach the front line. Sergeant Paul Jenkins died laying down a telephone line. Private Americo Di Pasquale of the 315th, trying to keep two separated units in touch, was fatally struck while midway between them.

At sixteen minutes before eleven, a runner finally reached the 313th's parent 157th Brigade to report that the armistice had been signed. But the message did not say that the troops were to stop fighting yet. More runners were dispatched to spread the word to the farthest-advanced regiments.

Two German machine-gun squads manning a roadblock watched, disbelieving, as shapes began emerging from the fog, forcing them to fire in self-defense. Gunther and Sergeant Powell dropped to the ground as bullets sang above their heads. The firing broke off as the Germans assumed that the Americans would have the good sense to stop with so little time left. Suddenly Powell saw Gunther rise and begin running toward one of the machine guns. He shouted for him to stop. The Germans waved him back, but Gunther kept advancing. The time was 10:59 A.M.

JANUARY 1917. What ultimately placed Ohio farm boys, New York street toughs, Kentucky backwoodsmen, Boston socialites, and a Baltimore bank clerk before the German guns had begun on the high seas and in a code room. At roughly the same time that Germany's military leaders had decided to reinstitute unrestricted submarine warfare and risk provoking America, British cryptographers in London broke a coded German cable that was to prove a bombshell. On January 19, the German foreign minister, Arthur Zimmermann, sent a secret message through his ambassador in Washington, Count Johann Heinrich von Bernstorff, to the German minister in Mexico City. Zimmermann believed that U-boat encirclement was going to strangle Great Britain. Furthermore, France was tired and demoralized. Zimmermann thus offered a deal to Mexico's president, Venustiano Carranza. If America came into the war, he proposed, Germany and Mexico "shall make war together and make peace. We shall give financial support, and it is understood that Mexico is to reconquer the lost territory in New Mexico, Texas and Arizona." Further, he urged President Carranza to persuade Japan to enlist on Germany's side. Zimmermann's telegram represented a marvel of arrogance, provocation, and miscalculation of the American reaction should its contents become known. And they did. On February 4, British code breakers gleefully passed along the decoded cable to the Wilson White House. On February 28, the president revealed Zimmermann's telegram to the press, producing an electric effect on American public opinion. To the already widespread conviction that her army behaved dishonorably and her navy sank helpless ships, proof was now added of Germany's duplicity toward the United States. Robert Lansing, the secretary of state, shocked fellow Cabinet officers with another instance of German depravity, telling them that "the wives of American Consuls on leaving Germany had been stripped naked, given an acid bath to detect writing on their flesh, and subjected to other indignities."

German submarines continued to sink American ships: the *Algonquin,* with huge stars and stripes painted on both sides of its hull; the *Vigilancia,* struck without warning and sunk in seven minutes; the *Illinois,* shelled until it went under. Wilson was no longer "too proud to fight." On the evening of April 2, 1917, the president was driven from the White House to Capitol Hill through a drizzling rain. On his arrival, he was conducted to an anteroom of the House of Representatives. There a reporter observed the president standing before a mirror; "chin shaking, face flushed, he placed his left elbow on the mantel and gazed steadily at himself until he composed his features."

The House, packed with congressmen, senators, Supreme Court justices, Cabinet members, high federal officials, and their spouses, saw the president emerge through swinging doors into the chamber, head held high, gaze resolute. For half an hour they listened to Wilson's cadenced, high-church delivery as he cataloged the reasons why the United States must go to war: Germany's atrocities committed on land, her barbarous taking of innocent lives on the high seas, her plotting against America. Still, the Wilsonian ethic did not permit bringing the United States into war merely to redress grievances. "We have no selfish ends to serve," Wilson went on, reading the speech he had typed himself. "We desire no conquest, no dominion. We seek no indemnities for ourselves, no material compensation for the sacrifice we shall freely make." America must go to war only for a large purpose. Wilson proclaimed that noble aim—"keeping the world safe for democracy"—to thundering applause. Still, the president was unwilling to align America completely with the aggrandizing powers of old Europe. The United States would enter the war not as one of the Allies but as an "associate power," essentially a distinction without a difference.

Back at the White House, Wilson turned to his secretary, Joseph Tumulty. "My message today was a message of death for our young men," he said. "How strange it seems to applaud that." As he spoke, his voice broke and he wept.

Over the next four days, the Senate and House of Representatives debated, then passed, a resolution approving a declaration of war. Belligerence was the dominant but not universal mood. Six senators and fifty congressmen voted against the resolution. Senator George Norris, Republican of Nebraska, claimed that the country had been plunged into somebody else's war. A dismayed Senator Norris saw profiteering underlying Wilson's call to arms and remarked, "I feel that you are putting the dollar sign upon the American flag." On April 6, Wilson signed the declaration. The United States was at war with Germany. Wilson had sought to seize the moral high ground in bringing his country into Europe's conflict because it was the "right thing to do." But harder heads saw another advantage in taking sides in a distant struggle: Britain and France owed massive debts to American companies. If the Allies went under, these firms could go broke.

America was technically at war but in no condition yet to fight. The German military remained unawed. Admiral Eduard von Capelle, secretary of state for the German Navy, assured parliament that the Americans would not even make it to Europe "because our submarines will sink them. Thus America from a military point of view means nothing, and again nothing and for a third time nothing." Capelle's contempt was not groundless. At the time, the U.S. Army numbered some 107,600 men, less than the belligerents were losing in a single campaign. In size it ranked seventeenth in the world. The reserve force, 122,000 members of the National Guard, nearly half of whom had never fired a rifle, was considered a joke. The Spanish-American War aside, American generals had not conducted a serious land battle since the Civil War more than a half century before. Thus, Wilson's first priority was to find a leader who could give America an army capable of fighting alongside and against great European powers. The hunt was on.

THE FRENCH AND British were overjoyed at America's entry into the war. A sleeping giant had been aroused. The question was whether this Goliath would be ready to fight before the British were starved into submission and the French bled to death. In the meantime, the war went on. Three days after America's entry, Field Marshal Haig opened a new front, at Arras, north of the Somme, the battle to be coordinated with an attack by General Nivelle on the River Aisne. This front was new to the British, but Haig's strategy remained old: assemble the guns, bombard for days, mass the men, advance.

For this campaign, various Canadian forces were welded together for the first time as the Canadian Corps and handed a formidable objective, Vimy Ridge, a shelf of land rising some five miles northeast of Arras, believed to be the most strongly held German position on the western front. Two years before, the ridge had been saturated with French blood in failed attempts to dislodge the Germans at a cost of 130,000 Frenchmen killed and wounded. Vimy Ridge, nevertheless, remained a prize worth taking. It commanded the Douai Plain, an occupied area of France whose coal mines and factories were now producing for Germany.

Canada, as a dominion within the British Empire, had come automatically into the war, and Canadians streamed to the colors as if their own broad land had been invaded. During the Germans' first gas attack at Ypres in April 1915, as gasping Britons reeled to the rear, leaving a huge hole in the line, it was the Canadians who held on, braving the deadly fumes. In engagement after engagement, the Canadians had won a reputation as tough fighters willing to take losses. In forty-eight hours at Saint-Julien during Second Ypres, gassed again and protected only by wet handkerchiefs, they held the line while losing one man in three. During the Somme, in July 1916, the Canadians fought alongside men from Newfoundland, then territory still independent from Canada. In that battle, the 1st Newfoundland Regiment formed a human spear point in front of Beaumont-Hamel against near-point-blank machine-gun fire. They had been virtually annihilated within thirty minutes. The losses were so painful that July 1 is still marked as a day of mourning in Newfoundland. All told, Canadians and Newfoundlanders suffered more than 24,000 casualties in the Somme campaign.

Now they were to be awarded a fresh opportunity to lead—or die trying. For months before the attack, Allied troops, led by ex–coal miners, had hollowed approaches to Vimy Ridge with miles of elaborate tunnels, supplied with electricity and water so that troops could assemble unseen before the assault. At 5:30 on the morning of April 9, 1917, the day after Easter, four divisions, nearly 60,000 men, emerged and began moving up the slope against snow, sleet, and a knife-edged wind. The Canadian air ace Billy Bishop described the scene from above: "No-man's-land, so often a filthy litter, was this morning clean and white. Suddenly over the top of our parapet a thin line of infantry crawled up and commenced to stroll casually towards the enemy. To me it seemed they must soon wake up and run; that they could not realize the danger they were in. Here and there a shell would burst as the line advanced and halted for a minute. Three or four men near the burst would topple over like so many tin soldiers. Two or three other men would then come running up to the spot from the rear carrying stretchers, pick up the wounded or dying and slowly walk back with them. I could not get the idea out of my head that it was just a game they were playing at. It all seemed so unreal."

By midafternoon the Canadians had swept the heights commanding the Douai Plain. When the fighting ended three days later, 3,598 Canadians lay dead, including three whose bravery posthumously earned them Britain's highest decoration, the Victoria Cross. The Canadians had achieved that rare event thus far in this inconclusive war, a clear-cut victory. The novel sensation was, however, short-lived. German resistance stiffened, and again the war stalemated. By the time the Arras offensive withered away, the British Expeditionary Force had lost 150,000 men killed, wounded, and missing and the Germans 100,000.

VICTOR RICHARDSON, now with the King's Royal Rifle Corps and once so close to Vera Brittain's late fiancé, Roland Leighton, fought at Arras. One week into the battle, disregarding a wound to the arm, Richardson continued leading his men toward a redoubt called the Harp. He was shot through the head, the bullet passing behind his eyes. One eye had to be removed immediately, and the bullet severed the optical nerve of the other. He was evacuated to a London hospital to determine if any of his sight could be saved. It could not. Vera had just returned from service in Malta when her brother, Edward, cabled her from France of Victor's fate. Soon afterward, she was posted back to London and arranged for Victor's family to stay with the Brittains in Kensington, sharing their son's agony as the young officer sank, rallied, then sank again. Edward Brittain had written to Geoffrey Thurlow, who had also been at Arras and was now recovering from his facial wound, telling him what had happened to Victor, adding, "and he had such beautiful eyes." While Victor was being treated, word came that he was to receive the Military Cross for gallantry. It occurred to Vera that the same valor that had won him the purple-and-white decoration had prevented him from ever seeing it. She found his family innocent of "foreign affairs and politics" and unable to grasp the idea of their son as a hero while still reeling from the shock of his blindness. Victor lingered in an emotional funk for two months, then died.

Edward Brittain's letter to Geoffrey Thurlow was never delivered. Last witnesses reported seeing Thurlow shot by a sniper while trying to make contact with a neighboring unit. His body was never found. Of the original foursome, only Edward remained. His regiment of Sherwood Foresters was soon transferred from France to the Italian front. Vera felt relieved. Her brother should be safer there, she believed. She then returned to the war zone herself, serving in a hospital in Étaples, France. There she was expected to treat wounded German prisoners along with fellow Britons. Having never met a German except a hated mistress at her girl's school, "it was somewhat disconcerting to be pitch-forked, all alone, into the midst of thirty representatives of the nation which, as I had repeatedly been told, had crucified Canadians, cut off the hands of babies, and subjected pure and stainless females to unmentionable atrocities. I didn't think I had really believed all those stories, but I wasn't quite sure. I half expected that one or two of the patients would get out of bed and try to rape me, but I soon discovered that none of them were in a position to rape anybody, or indeed to do anything but cling with stupendous exertion to a life in which the scales were already weighted heavily against them."

THE MAN President Wilson chose to lead the U.S. Army resembled a bronze casting of a military paladin. John J. Pershing was born in 1860, the eldest of nine children of a poor railroad worker on the Missouri frontier. By age eighteen, he could handle a plow, break a horse, pick off a distant squirrel with a rifle, and teach as a country schoolmaster. The schoolhouse was meant to be a stepping-stone to his ultimate ambition, to become a lawyer and then a judge, to which end he took law classes in his spare time at the State Normal School in Kirksville. One day Pershing was picking up some extra cash plowing a cornfield when a younger brother brought him word that would change his life and the country's: a competitive examination was about to be held for entry into the U.S. Military Academy at West Point. Pershing, discouraged that he would never save enough money to finish law school, put aside the plow and at age twenty-two won an appointment to the West Point class of 1886. Academically he was so-so, graduating in the middle of a class of seventy-seven. Militarily, however, he was a standout, achieving the most coveted honor, first captain of the Cadet Corps. Robert Lee Bullard, a year ahead, provides an illuminating picture of the early Pershing: "plainly of the estate of a man while most of those about him were still boys . . . Pershing inspired confidence but not affection. Personal magnetism seemed lacking. He won followers and admirers, but not personal worshippers. . . . His manner carried to the mind of those under him the suggestion, nay, the conviction, of unquestioned right to obedience." The one exception to this portrait of a single-minded au-

June 28, 1914. Police subdue accomplices of Gavrilo Princip, who has just killed Archduke Franz Ferdinand, the Austrian heir apparent, igniting a war in which nearly 15 million soldiers and civilians will die.
akg-images

Britons flock to enlist in Trafalgar Square. Lord Kitchener's 1914 call for 100,000 volunteers was topped fivefold in one month by men expecting a swift, glorious adventure. Some 700,000 Tommies would never return.
Imperial War Museum, London

Adolf Hitler in a crowd welcoming the war. No major conflict had occurred
on the European continent for nearly forty-five years and
the belligerents anticipated quick victory.
Imperial War Museum, London

Vera Brittain, a volunteer
British nurse in a war that was
to take the lives of her brother,
her fiancé, and two close
friends. She later wrote
Testament of Youth, a searing
memoir of the experience.
*William Ready Division,
McMaster University
Library, Canada*

Roland Leighton, Vera Brittain's fiancé, a prizewinning student who left Oxford to join the 7th Worcestershires. He was killed three days before he was to depart on Christmas leave in 1915.
William Ready Division, McMaster University Library, Canada

German and British soldiers gather in no-man's-land during the spontaneous 1914 Christmas truce, which was regarded by the generals as treasonous but considered a rare sane moment by the troops.
Imperial War Museum, London

The 3rd Tyneside Irish advancing on July 1, 1916, the first day of the
Somme offensive. More than 19,000 men, young and healthy at
7 A.M., were dead within hours. Field Marshal Douglas Haig
declared the casualties not excessive.
Imperial War Museum, London

By 1916, thoughts of Christmas truces were long since past. Here British
Tommies eat their holiday rations in a shell hole at Beaumont Hamel
before the hastily dug grave of a comrade.
Imperial War Museum, London

Blinded gas victims. In 1915 the Germans introduced poison gas, developed by Fritz Haber, who had earlier won renown for developing agricultural fertilizers. Gas was unreliable, but cheap and terrifying.

Imperial War Museum, London

Australians who fell at the wire near Peronne illustrate the slaughter advancing men faced against the six-hundred-rounds-per-minute firepower of German machine guns. Note the shell burst on the horizon.

Imperial War Museum, London

Field Marshal Douglas Haig, commander of British forces in France. He disparaged not only tanks and planes but even machine guns. A biographer called him a good general "for a man without genius."
U.S. Army Military History Institute

Field Marshal Ferdinand Foch with General John J. Pershing. Foch wanted Pershing's men as replacements for depleted British and French units. Pershing held out for independent American divisions and won.
U.S. Army Military History Institute

VON LUDENDORFF VON HINDENBURG

The German general staff, led by Field Marshal Paul von Hindenburg,
who projected stolid respectability while his chief of staff, Erich Ludendorff,
was the brains and almost led Germany to victory in 1918.
American Battle Monuments Commission

Corporal Hitler *(right)*
welcomed the war, which
rescued him from a life
of near dereliction. In
four years at the front he
frequently escaped death
and won the Iron Cross,
First Class, a rare award
for an enlisted man.
Ullstein Bilderdienst

French troops during the 1916 battle of Verdun, a shifting charnel house where one village changed hands thirteen times and 7,000 horses died in one day. One historian judged Verdun the war's "most senseless episode."
U.S. Army Military History Institute

Douglas MacArthur, the youngest general in the American Expeditionary Forces. He personally led raids in flamboyant dress, armed with only a riding crop, and once remarked, "It's the orders you disobey that make you famous."
National Archives

thoritarian was Pershing's way with women. In their pursuit he was all charm and wit—and famously successful.

After graduation, he fought in the Indian wars in the West against the Apaches and helped suppress a Sioux uprising. In the 1890s, he served among white officers who led the black 10th Cavalry, the legendary "Buffalo Soldiers." Pershing displayed a knack for being in the right place at the right time and profiting therefrom. Sent to New York's Madison Square Garden in 1896 to attend a National Guard show, he found himself sharing a box with Theodore Roosevelt, then head of the New York City police board. Pershing, as a man of action, particularly one who had experienced adventures similar to Roosevelt's in the Wild West, appealed strongly to the rising politician, and a friendship was born. The following year, Pershing returned to West Point as an instructor in tactics, widely disliked by the cadets as a harsh disciplinarian. They vented their animosity by calling him behind his back "Nigger Jack," referring to his service with black troops. Eventually the moniker was sanitized to "Black Jack" and stuck, since that weapon seemed well matched to Pershing's character.

In 1898, during the Spanish-American War, Pershing returned to the 10th Cavalry and marched with Teddy Roosevelt and the Rough Riders up Kettle Hill and San Juan Hill. Roosevelt later wrote, "I have been in many fights, but Captain Pershing is the coolest man under fire I ever saw in my life."

At age forty-five, Pershing made a loving and advantageous marriage to Helen Frances Warren, a wealthy Wellesley graduate, whose father, Senator Francis E. Warren of Wyoming, chaired the Senate Military Affairs Committee. Equally helpful, Pershing's old comrade of San Juan Hill had become his champion in the White House. In 1906, President Theodore Roosevelt jumped Pershing over 862 more senior officers and made him a brigadier general. Six years later, Pershing was back at West Point, this time as superintendent. By now he had become the father of three daughters and a son, enjoying a home life that the hard-bitten soldier described as blissfully happy.

By 1915, Pershing was back in the field, patrolling the U.S. southwest border to defend against Mexican marauders, when, overnight, his world collapsed. Ordinarily, the general's family traveled with him, but this time they had remained home in San Francisco's Presidio army post. On August 27, 1915, a reporter called Pershing's headquarters with word that smoke from a midnight fire had killed the general's wife and three daughters. Only his six-year-old son, Warren, had survived.

On March 9, 1916, Mexicans believed to be under command of the revolutionary Pancho Villa crossed the U.S. border and killed eighteen American civilians at Columbus, New Mexico. Almost as a blessed distraction from his grief, Pershing was ordered by President Wilson to lead 16,000 American troops on a punitive expedition into Mexico to take Villa dead or alive. Villa eluded his pursuers for eleven months, and on February 5, 1917, American troops were withdrawn. Two months later, the United States was at war, not against ragtag *bandidos* but against a military leviathan. At that point, five major generals were senior to Pershing. He had going for him, however, his formidable reputation, which even the Mexican failure had not dimmed. He also had his powerful friend in court, the father of his late wife, still chairing the Military Affairs Committee. Warren sent Pershing a telegram: "Wire me today whether and how much you speak, read and write French," to which Pershing replied with more confidence than accuracy that he could quickly acquire "a satisfactory working knowledge." He also enjoyed the support of Secretary of War Newton D. Baker, whom he had shrewdly cultivated. Early in May, Wilson named Black Jack Pershing commander of the yet-to-exist American Expeditionary Forces.

Body-hungry British and French military representatives in Washington began swarming over Wilson and Baker. They wanted not an American army but American troops, 500,000 of them, sent to Europe as quickly as practicable to fill out their riddled ranks. Pershing recognized that he was about to face his first adversaries in this war, not the Germans but the Allies, since he had no intention of becoming simply a dispatcher, shipping Americans to serve under foreign generals.

⸻

AMERICA WAS A large country that entered the war under Woodrow Wilson waving the banner of a just cause. A small nation entered the war a few months later for less noble motives. On August 27, Romania declared war on Austria-Hungary, invading the province of Transylvania, drawn by its large ethnic Romanian population. Backing their Austrian ally, Germany and Turkey then declared war on Romania.

15

"Acts Prejudicial to Military Discipline"

APRIL 1917. What had happened to the British at Arras, what was about to happen to the French in their coordinated attack along the thickly wooded ridges of the Chemin des Dames—the Ladies' Highway—quickened the Allies' hunger for American troops. The British assignment had been intended to draw off the Germans some seventy-five miles to the southeast, in the Aisne River sector, allowing the dashing new French commander, General Nivelle, to smash through the German defenses at Laon and "rupture," the general's favorite word, the Hindenburg Line. Nivelle's supreme confidence rang out in his battle cry: "One and a half million Frenchman cannot fail." Thus, one week after the Canadians had secured Vimy Ridge, the lone bright spot in the Arras campaign, Nivelle sent four armies, backed by seven thousand artillery pieces, along a forty-mile front from Soissons to Reims below the Chemin des Dames. This mundane thrust was the secret prescription for victory that Nivelle had boasted about. It was hardly a secret to the Germans, who learned of his attack from French newspapers. Initially, Nivelle scored fragments of victory, taking more than 20,000 prisoners and at one point actually breaching the Hindenburg Line. But the cost had been horrendous—118,000 men cut down by German machine guns and artillery in four days. By the end of April, 29,000 French dead were added to the hundreds of thousands of their countrymen already perished in the war. The writer Richard Holmes described a mounting dissatisfaction: "While French soldiers endured the sufferings of the front line and the dismal conditions in camps behind it, they knew that there was a world of theaters, cafés, and restaurants not far away. It was a world they seldom glimpsed and never sympathized with. The *embusqué*, the shirker, with a soft job, clean fingernails, and another man's wife, was the target of deep hatred, reflected in the trench newspapers, which provide such a valuable understanding of the way the French soldier thought." Indeed, though unable to admit it openly, many frontline officers sympathized with their men for their miserable lot.

The latest carnage was more than long-suffering *poilus* would tolerate. The sheep began to refuse to enter the slaughterhouse. The defiance started on day two of the battle. Ordered to advance, troops of the 108th Regiment refused to leave their trenches. The insubordination spread like a plague. Within weeks, disobedience had infected two thirds of the French Army. In early May, a regiment that had been taken out of the line and promised leave was ordered back into the particularly bloody Craonne sector, where, as one writer put it, "the industrialization of murder had been perfected." The *poilus'* despair was captured in a song sweeping the ranks:

> Goodbye to life, goodbye to love
> Goodbye to all women
> It's all over now, finished for good,
> This awful war.
> At Craonne, on the plateau
> That's where we'll lose our lives
> Because we are all doomed
> We are sacrificed.

For René Naegelen, the butchery of the Nivelle offensive had struck home. It was here that his older brother Joseph had been killed on the second day. The calmest protests involved sending

representatives to confront the officers and explain their dissatisfaction. At their most enraged, soldiers began commandeering
troop trains and taking control of towns. They threatened to bring
down the government and go home. One writer noted, "It was the
war's finest moment." The word "mutiny" was quickly applied to
this collapse of discipline, which suggests violence against superiors. More accurately, what was happening was a strike, a work
stoppage. What Naegelen and his comrades demanded was not the
capitulation of their superiors but more humane treatment from
them. "On the tenth [of May]," he recalled, "my regiment, among
others, agreed to return to the front, provided that it should remain on the defensive."

To the government and the generals, the attack on authority was
intolerable. Obviously, they reasoned, the men had been incited by
civilian antiwar agitators. Obedience to orders must be restored.
The job fell to General Henri Pétain, hero of Verdun, who on
May 15 replaced the disgraced Nivelle. Pétain's mission was to
quell the rebellion and continue prosecution of the war.

In the early stages of the mutinies, the doggedly patriotic former
railroad lawyer Henri Desagneaux had been outraged by insubordination among his men. In one instance, a corporal had persuaded
his comrades to refuse to report for duty, all claiming sickness. "I
had five court-martialled, to get rid of the worst," he noted in his
diary. He described the defendants as "a procession of rogues."
But trying the culprits, he concluded, would be self-defeating since
"that's just what they want . . . to spend a year in prison." Because
of his background, Desagneaux was sent to the rail junction at
Meaux to help put down rioting there. What he witnessed behind
the lines began to alter his sympathies. He saw pampered staff officers chauffeured in fine cars and dining in exclusive restaurants
with women brought in from Paris for "a real orgy." He saw shirkers who had managed to manipulate themselves out of danger. On
his return Desagneaux attended the court-martial of his men and
described General Pétain addressing the court. "Pétain enters, cold,
stern," Desagneaux recorded in his diary. " 'How many deserters in

the division?' he asks immediately. We look at each other. We were expecting something else. And, after asking the amount of losses, declaring that we should not count on reinforcements to bridge the gaps, he finishes with these words, 'You must re-discipline this undisciplined division. Gentlemen, that's all I have to say to you, good-bye.' And he leaves slamming the door of his car. Brute, is that the way to raise morale and to ask people to go and get themselves killed?" What had the mutineers been guilty of, Desagneaux asked, "a moment's discouragement or cowardice?"

The soldier/writer Henri Barbusse swore to this account of punishments meted out to troublemakers. A soldier told him of being chosen for an escort party taking two hundred mutineers to the front who were then ordered to huddle together at a point well in front of the lines. They were told to keep looking straight ahead, while the escort slipped away. Immediately thereafter, French artillery batteries were ordered to fire on a target at the same point. In Barbusse's account, "Two hundred men in the prime and vigor of life" were "transformed into a hash of flesh, bones, and cloth." The account is more revealing of the ordinary soldiers' hatred of "the brutes who commanded us" than of literal truth.

Pétain's severe conduct in the courtroom reflected the fine line the general was treading, working to restore discipline while at the same time removing the roots of indiscipline. The general went to the front, heard the men's grievances, improved their rations, increased their leaves, raised their pay, and, most effective, ceased, for the moment, offensive operations. At the same time, he made clear that disobedience was futile, even fatal. Over the next months, more than 23,000 soldiers were convicted of various court-martial offenses. The question was, how many should be shot? Previously, executions had followed a rough pattern: the more endangered *La Patrie,* the more men who were shot, the intention clearly being to stiffen the incentive of the rest not to shirk. In a not untypical instance, with Paris endangered in September 1914, one regimental commander had seven of his men summarily shot without so much as a hearing, much less a trial. By 1917, when the mutinies began, public sympathy would not tolerate brutal punishment of men who had been pushed to the limits of endurance. Of the thousands convicted in the wake of the mutiny, only thirty men were shot. For the entire war, the number of French soldiers executed for cowardice, including those who wounded themselves to escape the front, is clouded by official reticence. The numbers obtainable range from 133 to 550, most shot in the war's first year.

However widespread the rebellion, press censorship succeeded in keeping it from the enemy. The Germans never knew they were facing a demoralized and disintegrating adversary until it was too late to exploit the situation and order was restored in the French ranks.

HAIG'S ARMY DEALT no less harshly with dereliction of duty. Brutal punishment had been an everyday feature of life in the British regular army. From the outset of the war, career officers were suspicious of the fighting spirit of civilians delivered to them as soldiers. They believed that the influx of amateurs into the ranks intensified the necessity for punishing acts of cowardice swiftly and severely. A brigade commander recommending the execution of a private for desertion defended his actions by saying, "An example is needed as there are many men in the battalion who have never wished to be soldiers, but who were conscripted and who do not understand the seriousness of desertion." The private in question had volunteered at age eighteen and had spent three years in the trenches before his offense. On one occasion, after an officer delivered an inspirational speech to men about to go over the top, and presumably to further strenghen their motivation, a sergeant was instructed to read off a list of men recently executed, including name, rank, offense, and date and hour of their death.

On the eve of a May 1915 assault at Neuve-Chappelle, a Scottish brigade was assembled to hear a sergeant announce that a private in the unit "has been sentenced to death." He then drew a sheet of paper from his breast pocket and announced, "The fol-

lowing men will parade with rifles to form the execution squad."
Upon hearing his name called, Private John McCauley remembered, "a sickening shudder went through me." He wondered about
the condemned soldier: "Was he a married man—a good husband,
a loving father, a respected member of the peace time community?" McCauley spent a sleepless night and was much relieved the
next morning to learn that he was to be a reserve executioner and
not one of the twelve who would pull the trigger.

At sunrise the battalion was mustered and marched to a field
close enough to the front to hear shells whizzing overhead and exploding a few hundred feet away. Otherwise, a heavy silence prevailed. In the middle of the field stood an eight-foot-high blasted
tree stump. Men of the firing squad were ordered to lay their rifles
on the ground and do an about-face. While their backs were turned,
three military policemen alternately inserted live and blank rounds
in the rifles. McCauley spotted four men accompanying a scrawny,
limping, unshaven soldier with head bowed. As the party neared,
he recognized the condemned man. They had trained together at
Shoeburyness. He also knew that several men in the firing squad
came from the man's hometown. Having men shoot one of their
neighbors struck McCauley as harsh and a departure from army
policy. One of the escort party bound the unresisting prisoner to
the tree stump, tied a blue-and-white blindfold over his eyes, and
pinned a white disk over his heart. The firing squad then formed in
two lines, fifteen paces from the prisoner. At an officer's command
the men in the front rank dropped to one knee. At the order
"Fire!" some men hesitated and consequently the shots struck irregularly, knocking the victim about like a rag doll. Nor was there
any doubt, as the recoil kicked, who had fired the loaded weapons.

"The thing that had been a man," McCauley recalled, "sagged
at the stake." Being "compelled to witness the cold-blooded murder of a comrade," McCauley concluded, "even in the wholesale
violence and killing of this war was . . . barbaric."

Execution of a British officer for desertion or cowardice was
rare. Only two occurred throughout the war. One, a young re-

placement with the Royal Naval Division identified only as D, was sent to the front on his first assignment to locate his brigade. Two days later, he was found in a village behind the lines. He claimed to have become lost. He was arrested, court-martialed, and sentenced to death. Subsequently, the court recommended mercy on grounds of D's youth and inexperience. His division commander concurred and recommended commutation of the sentence. General Sir Hubert Gough, commander of the Fifth Army, judged otherwise. If a private had behaved as D had, Gough insisted, he would have been shot. On the eve of his execution, D wrote, "Dearest Mother Mine," asking that the presents his fiancée had given him be returned to her. He closed by begging forgiveness "for bringing dishonour upon you all."

A second lieutenant, thirty-year-old P, enlisted immediately upon the war's outbreak. After three days in action at the Somme, P was knocked unconscious by an enemy shell. He was diagnosed as shell-shocked and found "unfit for duty at the front." But a week later, the clearly disoriented officer was found fit and sent back to the trenches. His battalion was ordered to relieve another in the front line, during the course of which P disappeared. Military policemen found him far behind the lines, dazed and confused. His brigade commander recommended, unsuccessfully, that rather than being court-martialed, P be assigned to administrative duties in England. After P's conviction, all his superiors, up through brigade, division, and corps, favored commuting the death sentence. Sir Herbert Plumer, commanding the Second Army and ordinarily thought to be one of the more humane generals, rejected the pleas, and P was shot with Field Marshal Haig's concurrence.

Perhaps the saddest spectacle involved the execution of three "bantams," all from Durham County, William Stones, Peter Goggins, and John MacDonald. They had originally been rejected by the army because they were too short. When manpower demands drove down the height requirement, they volunteered, becoming part of a "bantam division." They were shot together at dawn on January 18, 1917, for reasons lost in the military archives.

An imaginative leader could turn even an execution into a moment for inspiring the troops. A British officer, Sir Edward Spears, tells of French General de Maud'huy, who came upon a firing squad marching a deserter to his death. "The General then began to talk to the man. Quite simply he explained discipline to him. . . . He told the condemned man that his crime was not venial, not low, and that he must die as an example, so that others should not fail. Surprisingly the wretch agreed, nodding his head. The burden of infamy was lifted from his shoulders. . . . Finally de Maud'huy held out his hand: 'Yours also is a way of dying for France,' he said. The procession started again, but now the victim was a willing one."

The pain and shame of condemned men ended before the firing squad. Not so for their families. In the first two years of the war, next of kin were flatly informed that the soldier had been executed for "acts prejudicial to military discipline." One grave marker in France read simply, "Shot at Dawn." Only after a strenuous campaign by the feminist Sylvia Pankhurst did the military begin informing families that an executed soldier had "died of wounds."

Unreasoning fear could afflict not only ordinary soldiers and smooth-faced officers. In 1916, Lord Kitchener, hero of Khartoum and the Boer War, while serving as secretary of state for war, was conversing with French prime minister Aristide Briand while strolling along the English Channel at Calais. "I don't like the sea," Kitchener remarked. Briand observed, "It is not very rough today, and in any case, you will soon be across." "That is not what I mean," Kitchener shot back. "I am *afraid* of the sea!" Later that year, Kitchener's deepest fear was realized when he went down with the cruiser *Hampshire*. The near-mythical King Frederick the Great, who made Prussia the foremost military power in Europe, in the midst of the Battle of Molwitz, is said to have galloped off the field in panic, even as his army was winning. One of Napoleon's biographers wrote, "He marshalled others to death, but was afraid of death himself."

John McCauley rejected the execution of frightened men as necessary to maintain discipline. "I still say," he later wrote, "that fear of facing a firing squad had little deterrent effect on the man whose nerves were shattered beyond repair and who eventually became panic stricken at the horrors surrounding him."

After the war, Lord Moran, himself a veteran, offered a convincing analogy. He suggested that courage was rather like a bank balance: given enough withdrawals in battle, the balance of courage would eventually be overdrawn, which explained why, among those condemned to death, the names of even once brave soldiers appeared. The number who broke down comprised an infinitesimal proportion of the millions who served in combat, about one half of one percent in the British forces. Most men managed not necessarily to escape their fears but to live with them, often sustained by gallows humor: "Cheer up, cockie. It's your turn next." "Three to a loaf tomorrow, lads." Throughout the war, 3,080 British soldiers were sentenced to death for desertion, cowardice, or mutiny. Of these, 346 sentences were carried out.

German troops faced stresses no less shattering than those of their enemies. Yet, according to the record, only forty-eight German soldiers were executed throughout the war, giving the lie to the contention that executions were essential to good order. Indeed, the German Army went through the war under the most lenient laws of any belligerent. Attempts to stiffen these laws were regularly defeated in the Reichstag. The leading executioners were the Italians, who shot proportionally twice as many of their own men as did the British.

SHELL SHOCK, NEW to medical nomenclature, afflicted soldiers on every side. The condition, minus the name, had been described by the third month of the war in *The British Medical Journal* by Dr. Albert Wilson. Wilson's prescription for dysfunctional soldiers was a stiff drink. Alcohol would supply quickly absorbed calories, and, the doctor observed, a tot of whiskey led to long lives among the Highlanders of Scotland. The actual term first appeared in the medical literature in an article by Dr. Charles S. Meyers, a Cambridge University psychologist, published in the prestigious journal *The Lancet*. While serving in France, Dr. Meyers came to believe that exploding shells caused molecular commotion in the brain; hence the term "shell shock." Early treatments ranged from the bizarre to the barbarous. One division commander believed that at the first symptom of emotional collapse, a soldier should be tied to the barbed wire before the front trench for thirty seconds. Dr. Lewis Yealland believed in "disciplinary therapies." He claimed he could produce a cure in minutes through electroshock. His favorite case was a private who had survived nine campaigns, from Mons to Loos, and then had woken up one day to find himself mute, a condition still present nine months later. Dr. Yealland had locked the patient in a dark room, warning him that he would not be released until he began behaving normally. He then shocked him for more than an hour, after which the soldier uttered a groaning "Ah!" He then stepped up the voltage for another half hour, after which the patient was able to speak in a hoarse whisper.

In the first year of the war, nearly 2,000 men were admitted to hospitals with no visible injury. By 1915, the figure had jumped tenfold, to more than 20,000. Only 3 percent of these men showed any brain lesions. Dr. W. H. R. Rivers, a psychologist and neurologist who directed the British Craiglockhart Hospital for shell-shock victims, described the kind of emotional trauma that could unhinge a soldier. In one case, the force of an exploding shell had flung a man onto the body of a rotting German corpse, pressing the soldier's mouth into the putrescence of the open stomach.

In a curious sociological phenomenon, as the level of responsibility rose, the incidence of shell shock declined. An officer looking after his men, inspecting fortifications, checking on rations—in short, a man whose attentions were directed outward—was less likely to crack than a simple, uneducated soldier left alone on sentry duty or crouched in a shell hole for hours, even days, his thoughts fixed obsessively on his fate. Supporting this observation, some 80 percent of all "mental cases" came from the unskilled labor class.

Even three years into the war, the Americans, upon their entry, treated the shell-shock victim with neither understanding nor sympathy. In the war's last week, the AEF's III Corps issued General Order No. 35, dealing with a private who had cracked. "This soldier absented himself from his organization in time of battle or impending battle, with no apparent cause except fear," the order read. "The foregoing is to be sent as a letter to the father, mother or nearest relative of the soldier; copies will be sent to the postmaster and the mayor of his home town, and to his sweetheart, if she is known. A copy is to be posted on the company street."

Esoteric neurological and psychiatric diagnoses might eventually explain the mounting numbers of otherwise unwounded men reporting to casualty clearing centers rendered mute, blind, deaf, shaking uncontrollably, or inexplicably paralyzed. But a nonmedical officer gave a description as short as it was apt. "The psychological basis of war neuroses (like that of neuroses in civil life)," he noted, "is an elaboration, with endless variations, of one central scheme: escape from an intolerable situation in real life made tolerable by neurosis."

16

Doughboys

NOVEMBER 11, 1918. That morning a thirty-four-year-old army officer whose bespectacled, clerkish appearance belied his firm command of artillerymen leaned over a caisson writing his fiancée. "I just got notice," Captain Harry Truman wrote to Bess Wallace, "that hostilities would cease at eleven o'clock." The regiment's operations officer, Major Paterson, had alerted Truman soon after the armistice was signed but had ordered him to say nothing to his men until the eleventh hour. Rumors of peace, however, were palpable in the air. Truman took deep satisfaction in the fact that in almost seven months at the front, he had not yet lost a man from Battery D, 129th Field Artillery, 35th Division. Barring a last-minute calamity, the battery would survive the war intact. Reminders of others who had not made it were everywhere. A few days earlier, Truman had written Bess from the farmhouse where he was billeted, "There are Frenchmen buried in my front yard and Huns in the backyard and both litter up the landscape as far as you can see. Every time a Boche shell hits in a field over west of here, it digs up a piece of someone. . . . If ever I get home from this war whole I am going to be perfectly happy to follow a mule down a corn row the balance of my days."

Truman had proved an able officer, his battery receiving a com-

mendation from the 35th Division's commanding general for having "the best conditioned guns." And among his men, their unpre-
possessing leader was seen as fearless, an image he adopted rather
than felt. "The men think I am not much afraid of shells," Truman
had once written Bess, "but they don't know I was too scared to
run." By nature he distrusted sentiment. He had found two tiny
flowers blooming in a cleft of rock alongside a trench and enclosed
them in the letter. "A real sob sister could write a volume about the
struggle of these little flowers under the frowning brows of Douaumont the impregnable" was all he allowed himself to write.

Truman wanted the war to end, but not like this. The enemy, he
was convinced, had purchased peace too cheaply. When he had
first heard about the armistice negotiations, he had written Bess,
"I'm for peace, but that gang should be given a bayonet peace and
be made to pay for what they've done to France." In the letter he
was writing on the war's last day, the mild-looking Truman revealed surprising venom. "It is a shame we can't go in and devas-
tate Germany and cut off a few of the Dutch [German] kids' hands
and feet and scalp a few of their old men," he wrote, revealing a
hardness that would manifest itself long years later, when he
would have to make profound decisions to end another war.

Truman put aside his letter to Bess and assembled the battery for
action. The ammunition he had been firing so far with his French
75 mm artillery pieces had a maximum range of 8,800 meters. He
had just received the new "D" shells, estimated to reach 11,500
meters and was eager to test them before the cease-fire. He figured
the grid coordinates for Hermville, northeast of Verdun, at 11,000
meters distance, and began raining shells on the tiny village.

APRIL 1917. Harry Truman's first brush with the military had occurred in 1905. While working as a twenty-one-year-old $40-a-
month clerk at the Kansas City National Bank of Commerce, he
had joined the Missouri National Guard because, he explained,
"After reading all the books obtainable in the Independence and

Kansas City libraries on history and government from Egypt to U.S.A., I came to the conclusion that every citizen should know something about military, finance or banking and agriculture." Twelve years later, when the United States went to war, Truman no longer held a white-collar bank position. His father's death had forced him to take over the family farm, running an Emerson gang plow for ten-hour days whether the heat was broiling or the cold biting. Truman could easily have escaped military service since he was thirty-three—two years beyond draft age—had weak eyes, was the sole supporter of a mother and sister, and as a farmer was engaged in an exempt occupation. None of that mattered as he "made arrangements for a good man we had on the farm to take over its operation." He memorized the eye chart and rejoined the Guard, which he had left as a corporal six years before. He said, and no doubt meant it, that he had been stirred heart and soul "by President Wilson's war messages" to do "a job somebody had to do." Still, the less lofty appeals of soldiering also drew him. He was escaping a numbing, backbreaking life. And there was the romance of it. "I'll never forget how my love cried," he later wrote, "when I told her I was going. That was worth a lifetime on this earth." Bess thought they should get married at once, but Harry said no. He could not tie her to a man who might be crippled or never come back at all. He helped organize Battery D, and when it came time to elect officers, "I was elected a first lieutenant . . . and would have been happy just to remain a sergeant."

WHEN THE UNITED STATES had entered the conflict, the British had been war-weary and the French mutinous. No lethargy of the spirit, however, afflicted the war's newest entrant. Americans in April 1917 exhibited Europeans' euphoria of August 1914. Volunteers flocked to recruiting stations for motives that have propelled young men since the dawn of human conflict: escape from a dull job selling hardware or handling a plow; a change from a one-horse town to the big city, even exotic lands; flight from suffocating par-

ents, nagging wives, or burned-out romances, from wearing over-
alls and cloth caps to donning smart breeches and brass-buttoned
tunics—in short, from stifling predictability to uncertain adventure, all ennobled by patriotism and more often than not a trade of
one form of confinement for another.

When young men did not feel compelled to join, others applied
the pressure. Joe Rizzi, son of Italian immigrants, had watched a
preparedness parade—firemen, masons, the Salvation Army, the
Knights of Columbus—with the marchers lustily singing "Over
There." Yes, the Yanks were coming, but the handsome, open-
faced, good-natured Rizzi preferred to stay home. He hated the
thought of leaving his girlfriend. As for German atrocities, "I did
not believe any of them as I was practically living with a family of
German descent who had always treated me kindly." His sweetheart, however, was unrelenting: "When we did meet she would
show me papers carrying cruelties committed by the Huns. She
called me a coward and said that I was ungrateful by not serving
for our country. She tormented me with the fact that she would
never marry me unless I entered the Army."

Before America went to war, Harry L. Smith, a graduate of the
University of Iowa College of Medicine, had chosen to serve his
internship at Vancouver General Hospital in Canada. "Many
times," he recalled, "a woman would accost me on the street and
ask why I was not in uniform. I would have to explain, over and
over, that I was an American citizen"—a response that convinced
Canadians that not only was this man a slacker but his entire nation was inhabited by cowards. On returning to the United States
after war had been declared and while still a civilian, Smith encountered the same unsubtle pressure.

Mothers were likely to see war less romantically, stripped to its
tragic potential. Arthur Jensen, age eighteen, and his older brother,
Walt, from Lowell, Nebraska, "were both rarin' to go because we
believed we could soon rise to fame and glory." Their mother
squelched their ardor. "I didn't raise you boys to be cannon fod-

der," she said, "and besides you'd better stay in school where you belong till you're dry behind the ears."

Kenneth Baker, a sturdy, fresh-faced twenty-year-old college boy off an Indiana farm, "just couldn't wait" when the country went to war. He and a schoolmate "immediately decided that we wanted to be fliers," he recalled, "but being very naïve, thought that all we had to do was go to some recruiting station and the Army would jump at the chance of getting us to fly one of their aeroplanes. Well, we soon found out that it was not that simple. If we were to get to fly one of their planes we had to know somebody, say like a governor or a senator or at least a judge to endorse us." The boys were disappointed but listened to the recruiting sergeant pitch the Signal Corps. Since fliers were attached to that branch, he explained, they could soon transfer to flight school. "That recruiting sergeant would tell you anything to get your name on the dotted line," Baker observed. He and his friend went back home to think the matter over, their principal concern being how to serve without ending up in the infantry.

Norman Prince, a polo-playing Harvard graduate from a wealthy Boston family, had not waited for his country to enter the war. He met with five friends in May 1916 to form their own air squadron to fight for France. They had a ready-made base, Prince explained, his family's estate in Gascony. The young collegians first called themselves "the Lafayette Escadrille Américaine." But after the German government protested that this name represented a breach of American neutrality, "Américaine" was dropped. The Lafayette Escadrille continued to attract Americans, particularly Ivy Leaguers, who were soon in aerial combat over the western front. By the time the United States entered the war, the poet volunteer Alan Seeger was already dead and Alexander McClintock put out of action. But some 40,000 other Americans were fighting with the British and French.

Concerned that mobilization of National Guard units might fall too heavily on certain states, the army formed a new division, the 42nd, to be drawn from the Guard in twenty-six states and the

District of Columbia. Major Douglas MacArthur, involved in creating the 42nd and possessed of an oratorical flair that would never dim, regarded its geographic span and declared, "The 42nd Division stretches like a rainbow from one end of America to the other." Thus was born the Rainbow Division.

One National Guard unit had already experienced combat of a sort. William J. Donovan, a former gridiron star at Niagara and Columbia Universities and a rising Irish-American lawyer, had gathered socially prominent colleagues from Buffalo, New York, into a National Guard cavalry troop called the "Silk Stocking Boys." The Boys had gone with Black Jack Pershing on the futile hunt for Pancho Villa. The unit had been home less than a month when it was ordered to report to New York City for active duty with the 27th Division. Donovan, however, found a more congenial fit in the Fighting 69th and passed up a promotion to colonel to become a major and battalion commander in this legendary Irish-American outfit. The regiment's ranks began to swell as the 69th employed elemental male psychology to heighten its appeal. Trucks crisscrossed New York with machine guns mounted on the back and signs reading, "Don't join the 69th unless you want to be among the first to go to France." Volunteers streamed to the regimental armory.

The Fighting 69th became subsumed as the green in the Rainbow Division and in the process lost its historic designation. It was now the 165th Regiment, 42nd Division. The Irish flavor of the regiment persisted, but more as symbol than fact, its 3,500-man roster including a Dambrosio, an Ivanowski, a Jaeger, a Believeau, a Rodriguez, a Menicocci, and even a Kaiser. More than sixty men in the regiment were Jews.

The unit's chaplain, Father Francis Duffy, left a sharp-edged sketch of the commander of the 1st Battalion. "Donovan is a man in the middle thirties, very attractive in face and manner," the priest wrote, "the athlete who always keeps himself in perfect condition. . . . He is cool, untiring, strenuous, a man that always uses his head. He is preparing his men for the fatigues of open warfare by all kinds of wearying stunts. They call him 'Wild Bill' with malicious unction, after he has led them over a cross country run for four miles. But they admire him all the same, for he is the freshest man in the crowd when the run is over." As for the origins of Donovan's nickname, Father Duffy claimed to have overheard the men discussing their leader, when one said, "Hell, I'll say this, Wild Bill is a son of a bitch, but he's a game one." Another version had it that while Donovan was with General Pershing chasing Pancho Villa, his men complained about the exhausting pace he set. "Look at me," their commander taunted them, "I'm not even panting. If I can take it, why can't you?" From one of the troopers came a plaintive cry: "We ain't as wild as you are, Bill." In his final judgment of Donovan, Father Duffy concluded, "I like him for his agreeable disposition, his fine character, his alert and eager intelligence." Yet Duffy could not resist adding, "I certainly would not want to be in his battalion."

In the end, Joe Rizzi enlisted in order to win his girlfriend's respect, entering the same 35th Division as Harry Truman, but with the 110th Engineers. "What irony," he noted, "before she was nagging me for being a coward and a slacker. Now she felt that it wasn't right." Dr. Harry Smith went off to the medical officers' training camp at Fort Riley, Kansas, no longer accosted by women wanting to know why he was not in uniform. Arthur Jensen, despite what amounted to a $500 bribe from his father to stay in college and despite his mother's fears, enlisted. "All I thought about was the war," he confessed. Ken Baker took the gamble that the Signal Corps would eventually make him a pilot, signed up, and reported to Fort Logan, Colorado, but would never get off the ground.

AFRICAN AMERICANS JOINED the military before there was a United States, beginning in 1652 with a Massachusetts militia. More than 5,000 blacks served under General George Washington during the Revolution and another 220,000 in the Union ranks during the Civil War, in which 37,500 gave their lives and 14 won the Medal of Honor. Paintings of Teddy Roosevelt and his Rough Riders ascending Cuban heights show not a single black man, though they were there with their leader, Black Jack Pershing, during the Spanish-American War. The black man's willingness to serve a nation in which he could not be served in most restaurants or hotels was not necessarily to defend freedom, of which he had little, or his rights, of which he had few. Rather, he was motivated by a hope that what could not be achieved in a cotton patch or cornfield might be won on the battlefield: acceptance as an American entitled to the full rights of citizenship. So far the strategy had failed. Slavery survived the Revolution. During the War of 1812, Andrew Jackson had promised land to blacks who fought with him at New Orleans in 1815, but the promise had never been honored. The Civil War brought emancipation, but it had been blunted by the rise of the Ku Klux Klan, segregation, and lynchings.

In 1917, blacks were willing to try again. They too flocked to the recruiters. This time they wanted something more—not simply to serve under white officers but to become officers themselves. When the leader of the National Association for the Advancement of Colored People, W. E. B. Du Bois, advanced this idea to Secretary of War Baker, the secretary stalled, saying the army had no place in which to bed black officer candidates. Thomas Montgomery, a black Harvard graduate, countered, "No bedding, Mr. Secretary? We will sleep on the floor—on the ground—anywhere—give us a lift!" Finally Baker relented, and a class of 1,200 black cadets reported to a new camp for training them, Fort Des Moines in Iowa. To sidestep the thorny issue of having blacks ordering white enlisted men, the newly commissioned officers were assigned solely to black units.

Social fraternization posed a more delicate quandary. Major General Charles C. Ballou, commanding the black 92nd Infantry Division, issued Bulletin 35, which stated, "It should be well known to all colored officers and men that no useful purpose is served by such acts as will cause the 'color question' to be raised. It is not a question of legal rights, but a question of policy. . . . To avoid such conflicts the division commander has repeatedly urged that all colored members of the command, especially the officers and noncommissioned officers, should refrain from going where their presence will be resented." Bulletin 35 specifically condemned the conduct of a black sergeant in the Medical Department who had tried to attend a theater, "as he undoubtedly had a legal right to do." That was not the point. The sergeant, upon being given a poor seat, had complained to the theater manager, making him "guilty of the greater wrong in doing ANYTHING, no matter how legally correct, that will provoke race animosity."

Deadlier frictions occurred. On August 23, during America's first summer of war, Lee Sparks, a white police officer in Houston, beat up a black soldier who had tried to stop him from brutalizing a black woman. When a black provost marshal arrived to investigate the incident, Sparks turned on him as well. That night, more than one hundred outraged black soldiers, mostly from the North, stormed out of their base to find Sparks. In the course of their search, they began shooting randomly at any whites they encountered, killing sixteen and wounding eleven others.

Initially, potential American Indian recruits, raised on remote reservations, often still clothed in skins and blankets, ran aground on the army's Stanford-Binet intelligence test, undone by what a later age would call cultural bias in the testing. Still, they were considered more desirable soldiers than blacks. Indians may have been exploited by the white man, but they had not been enslaved. Instead they enjoyed a romanticized image as the quintessential free spirit and natural warrior. Of 33,000 Native Americans of military age, more than 6,000 from fourteen tribes eventually served in the army, 85 percent as volunteers.

For eligible Americans unmotivated to enlist, the nation adopted what Secretary Baker called a "great national lottery." Two and a half months after Wilson procured his declaration of war, Baker stood blindfolded in the Capitol before a giant fishbowl and extracted from 10,500 capsules one containing the number 258. All men assigned that number by their local draft board were to report for examination. Country boys turned out to be the fittest, producing 4.8 percent more able-bodied draftees per 100,000 than city boys. Whites were 1.2 percent more physically qualified than blacks and native-born Americans 3.5 percent more than those foreign-born.

Men inducted were shipped off to hastily constructed training facilities scattered across the country, from Camp Upton on Long Island to Fort Riley, Kansas, where the process began of pounding them from individuals into cogs. They were outfitted at what then seemed an exorbitant $156.30 per man, including $1.25 for an overseas cap and $19.50 for a rifle. The training of leaders proved harder than training followers. Of necessity, tens of thousands of candidates had to be rushed through officers' training camps where, as one career officer put it, "they couldn't make three months in a camp equal four years at West Point." More pointedly, General James Harbord, commanding officer of the 2nd Infantry Division, observed, "You can sew brass buttons on a man, but that won't make him an officer." Recent college boys, now infantry lieutenants and captains, were to lead hundreds of men into the mouth of a hell they had never experienced. Even the highest-ranking army regulars were unprepared for the unprecedented scale of conflict they were about to enter. Senior officers who had never commanded more than a 2,000-man regiment were soon to lead corps of more than 150,000 men. A major who months before had been a hotel manager was now expected to feed 100,000 soldiers in the field. Career sergeants who had served hitches in Cuba, the Philippines, and Panama suddenly found themselves commissioned as officers. A forty-eight-year-old former topkick, elevated overnight to captain, was described by Arthur Joel, one of his subordinates, as "uneducated except in army affairs, he spoke rather brokenly, with the grammatical mistakes of a child." When one of his men got married, the captain was heard to remark, "Anudder guy went an' hung himself." "He would likely never be requested to serve as a model for a bust or portrait," Joel went on. "Yet I'll wager there was not a more popular captain in the regiment. What mattered a gruff voice and a rough appearance when a man had a big heart, a great fund of common sense, an unlimited supply of army knowledge, and was loyal to his men and officers."

The American soldier was almost immediately dubbed a "doughboy," a term of clouded origin. Early in the Civil War, "doughboy" was said to refer to the globelike brass buttons on a Union infantryman's uniform, which resembled a doughnut or dumpling. Another explanation had it that the expression originated during the nineteenth-century Indian Wars, when sweat mixed with the dust of the trail gave soldiers the appearance of having been rolled in dough. Contributing to that explanation, an officer had written of General George Custer's widow, "She was so accustomed to fast riding with our cavalry that she does not know how to treat a doughboy"—that is, an infantryman. Still another explanation had it that "doughboys" was a corruption of *adobes,* the huts men had inhabited during the hunt for Pancho Villa in Mexico. After the United States went to war, the word was said to derive from the fact that an American soldier was paid ten times more than a Tommy or a *poilu* and was thus "rolling in dough." However it began, the term stuck with headline writers and the public, though, like Tommy and *poilu,* not with the men.

On May 28, forty-two days after war was declared, when the rest of the army had barely begun training, General Pershing led a cadre of 177 generals, colonels, majors, captains, and lieutenants, plus a handful of sergeants and infantrymen, aboard the British White Star liner *Baltic,* bound from New York to Europe. They formed the vanguard of a force that, between enlistment and the draft, would eventually make up the American Expeditionary Forces of nearly 2 million men.

17

"Sweet and Noble to Die
for One's Country"

JUNE 1917. At 3:10 on the morning of the seventeenth, British prime minister Lloyd George was jolted from his bed at 10 Downing Street by a shock wave suggesting an earthquake. Lloyd George had just experienced the most powerful man-made explosion the world had yet known.

While American doughboys were still at home practicing the manual of arms and close-order drill, the killing went on in Europe. By the summer of 1917, Field Marshal Haig had fixed on his own win-the-war strategy. It was a large plan, mined with "ifs," but at its heart it depended on the same old mechanism, the frontal attack. He intended to push his armies through Ypres, already the scene of two costly battles, then move along the Belgian coast, taking the ports of Ostend and Zeebrugge. His aim was twofold: to sever the railway lines serving the German armies in Belgium and France and to drive enemy submarines and destroyers harassing British shipping from the two port cities. But first, a natural obstacle had to be overcome. The Messines Ridge south of Ypres ran for miles at a height of 150 to 300 feet. The Germans had occupied it for years. The ridge commanded the Flanders plain and, until it was taken, Haig's offensive was going nowhere.

To take Messines Ridge, he assigned General Sir Herbert

Charles Onslow Plumer, commander of the Second Army. Plumer's outward appearance suggested a caricature of the British armchair officer, an early incarnation of Colonel Blimp. The sixty-year-old was squat, potbellied, jowly, chinless, with a veinous red face, snow-white hair, and a matching mustache. The comic appearance, however, belied the man. Plumer's manner lacked fire, but he was a meticulous planner, not without imagination, and unflappable under the severest pressure. His men trusted him implicitly and felt genuine affection for their commander, calling him "Daddy." Plumer had been planning the Messines assault for a year. He had a full-scale replica of the ridge constructed behind the lines, accurate to every contour, where his army conducted mock assaults. Plumer recognized that artillery alone could not reduce the enemy's defenses. That lesson had been paid for on the Somme with mounds of dead Britons. He needed fresh thinking. Hundreds of former miners served in Plumer's army, and they had talked among themselves about a solution that eventually found its way up to the general. Why not tunnel beneath the German positions on the ridge, place tons of explosives at the terminus, and blow the Jerries to kingdom come before even launching a ground assault? Plumer was persuaded and sappers, excavation teams led by the miners, dug twenty-two tunnels totaling 4.6 miles. As time for the attack neared, the unwitting Germans were sitting atop a volcano, a million pounds of high explosives planted a hundred feet beneath them.

The enemy tunneled too, with each side trying to detect the other's digging. Unseasoned soldiers tried putting an ear to the ground to detect suspicious noises but were easily confused by the welter of sounds. The miners, in their element, would stick a bayonet in the earth, grip it with their teeth, and could distinguish among rats burrowing underground, a stake being pounded, and actual tunneling. Chance encounters of opposing tunnelers proved nightmarish. In a typical instance, the face of a tunnel collapsed in front of British sappers, revealing Germans coming from the opposite direction. The two enemies fought in the dark, cramped space against shadowy shapes, jabbing blindly with bayonets and firing revolvers in a space too narrow for rifles.

On May 21, 2,300 artillery pieces, arrayed along a nine-mile front, began pounding Messines Ridge. The shelling went on unbroken for sixteen days. On the evening of June 6, General Plumer told his staff, "Gentlemen, we may not make history tomorrow, but we shall certainly change the geography." At ten minutes before two the next morning, the guns suddenly went silent, leaving the eerie calm that usually presaged an attack. The German defenders climbed out of their bunkers along the ridge and began to man their guns. But no enemy troops appeared. A British general named Lambert stood in a dugout, watch in hand, and called out, "Three minutes to go, two to go—one to go—20 seconds to go— 9, 8, 7, 6, 5, 4, 3, 2." At "1," the sappers threw electrical switches and Messines Ridge appeared to lift from the earth. Columns of brilliant orange flames shot into the sky, chunks of the ridge the size of houses flew in every direction, and the crest appeared to vanish. The earth shuddered so violently that British infantrymen two miles away were flung to the ground and left gasping as oxygen was sucked from the air. "We saw what might have been doors thrown open in front of a number of colossal blast furnaces," a correspondent for the *Daily Express* reported. "They appeared in pairs, in threes, and in successive singles. With each blast the earth shook and shivered beneath our feet." All but two of the twenty-one mines had detonated. This was the man-made quake that awoke Lloyd George, some 130 miles away in London.

As the roar of the detonations died away, a rolling barrage began to form a steel curtain behind which nine divisions of British infantry responded to the whistles and cries of "Over the top, boys!" The clanking of tanks and the soft plop of gas shells accompanied them. As the barrage crept forward, the attackers stepped over heaps of dismembered enemy bodies and incoherent, glassy-eyed German troops wandering aimlessly among the mine craters. The mines had killed some 10,000 of the enemy before a single Briton had left the trenches.

Ernst Jünger has provided firsthand testimony of what it was like to be on the receiving end of such punishment. Jünger had been among the eager youths who had gone directly from high school to war, camping on the doorstep of a recruiting office for three days to enlist in the 44th Reserve Division. After two months of training, conducted mostly by poorly prepared schoolteachers, Jünger had found himself at the front. After a heavy bombardment, he wrote, "You cower in a heap alone in a hole and feel yourself the victim of a pitiless thirst for destruction. With horror you feel that all your intelligence, your capacities, your bodily and spiritual characteristics, have become utterly meaningless and absurd. While you think it, the lump of metal that will change you to a shapeless nothing may have started on its course. . . . Well, why don't you jump up and rush into the night till you collapse in safety behind a bush like an exhausted animal? . . . There are no superior officers to see you. Yet someone watches you. Unknown perhaps to yourself, there is someone within you who keeps you to your post by the power of two mighty spells: Duty and Honour. You feel, 'If I leave my post, I am a coward in my own eyes, a wretch who will ever after blush at every word of praise.' You clench your teeth and stay."

Jünger recognized an odd kinship with the men who were trying to kill him. "We often talked of the 'Tommy,' " he noted, "and, as any genuine soldier will easily understand, we spoke of him very much more respectfully than was commonly the case with the newspapers of those days. There is no one less likely to disparage the lion than the lion-hunter."

Finally, thanks to Plumer's measured boldness, an attack had succeeded. By noon, British, Australian, Canadian, and New Zealand troops, along with a French army group, stood atop their objective. The Messines Ridge was theirs. By this war's standards, the cost of victory had been relatively cheap. Before the offensive, 85,000 casualties had been predicted but only 17,000 men were killed, wounded, or missing, while the Germans lost 25,000 men, the war's first engagement in which defenders suffered more than attackers. To Haig and the general staff, the two miles gained storming Messines Ridge confirmed their contempt for static trench warfare. Haig now felt validated in preparing for the next phase, the Third Battle of Ypres, more hauntingly to be remembered for the name of a tiny village, Passchendaele.

MESSINES RIDGE may have been counted a victory, but to one young officer it merely perpetuated state-sanctioned murder. Siegfried Sassoon, from a wealthy family, his mother a Christian, his father a Jew, had enlisted at age twenty-eight, two days before Britain declared war, eventually serving with the Royal Welch Fusiliers. Before the war, Sassoon had dropped out of Cambridge with an inheritance sufficient to indulge a life of fox-hunting, cricket, and writing poetry, dreamy verse of which he had published nine volumes at his own expense. His early work may have been rated minor, but in the war he found his voice.

The conflict had struck personally in 1915, when Sassoon's younger brother, Hamo, died at Gallipoli. Five months later, a bosom companion, Second Lieutenant David "Tommy" Thomas, was fatally shot through the throat while on a wiring party. Initially, these losses fired in Sassoon a thirst for revenge. He volunteered for the most perilous raids across no-man's-land, once captured a German trench practically single-handed, and dragged wounded men back to the lines under fire, actions that won him the Military Cross and the nickname, for his disregard for his own safety, "Mad Jack." Frank Richards, who had shaken hands with Germans during the 1914 Christmas truce, believed he had served under every kind of superior and concluded, "It was only once in a blue moon that we had an officer like Mr. Sassoon."

By 1916, disillusioned at seeing lives squandered by the generals and sickened by the complacency of civilians, Sassoon began writing bitterly ironic poetry. One poem read:

"Good-morning; good-morning!" the General said
When we met him last week on our way to the line.

Now the soldiers he smiled at are most of 'em dead,
And we're cursing his staff for incompetent swine.
"He's a cheery old card," grunted Harry to Jack
As they slogged up to Arras with rifle and pack.

But he did for them both by his plan of attack.

Of civilians enjoying the good life, attending the theater while men died in France, he wrote:

I'd like to see a tank come down the stalls
Lurching to ragtime ditties and "home sweet home"
And there'd be no more jokes in music halls,
To mock the riddled corpses of Bapaume.

In June 1916, Vivian de Sola Pinto, fellow Royal Welch Fusilier and budding writer, was thrilled to find himself posted as second in command to his hero. "That splendid erect form with the noble head, mane of dark hair, piercing black eyes and strongly sculptured features," he wrote of Sassoon, "could only belong to a poet."

In the spring of 1917, Sassoon was wounded in the shoulder and evacuated to England to convalesce. When well enough, he spent time at Garsington Manor, the country retreat of Philip Morrell, a Liberal member of Parliament, and his wife, Lady Ottoline Morrell, known for her bohemian flamboyance as "Lady Utterly Immoral." Sassoon's hosts were staunch pacifists, and in their home the soldier met like-minded souls, the philosopher-mathematician Bertrand Russell and a distinguished editor and critic, John Middleton Murry, among them. The persuasive Russell urged Sassoon to take a stand against the war. No one could be more unassailable than a hero who had fought in it.

In July 1917, Sassoon, sufficiently recovered to return to the front, sent to his regimental colonel a letter of decidedly insubordinate stamp. He called it "A Soldier's Declaration" and also released it to the public. "I am not protesting against the conduct of

the war," he wrote, "but against the political errors and insinceri-
ties for which the fighting men are being sacrificed. On behalf
of those who are suffering now I make this protest against the de-
ception which is being practised on them; also I believe that I may
help to destroy the callous complacency with which the majority
of those at home regard the continuance of agonies which they do
not share, and which they have not sufficient imagination to realise."

Sassoon was threatened with a court-martial for trumpeting his
defiance, a fate that he awaited with a martyr's pureness of heart.
Another Fusilier, friend and fellow poet Robert Graves, inter-
vened. Graves persuaded authorities that putting a decorated hero
on trial would raise more suspicions about the army than about
the defendant. Sassoon was instead referred to a medical board,
which sent him to the Craiglockhart Hospital in Edinburgh as a
shell-shock case. In August 1917, Sassoon met another patient,
Wilfred Owen. Owen, the son of a railroad worker, had immediately left a teaching position in France when the war broke out to
enlist in the Artists' Rifles. He was subsequently commissioned a
second lieutenant in the 2nd Manchester Regiment. In May 1917,
his commanding officer claimed he was behaving strangely, and
Owen too was packed off to Craiglockhart as a shell-shock victim.
Sassoon encouraged the younger man, and that fall, Owen wrote
a poem perhaps lacking Sassoon's sardonic bite but possessing
greater emotive power. He called it "Dulce et Decorum Est," taking a line from the Odes of the Roman poet Horace, "It is sweet
and noble to die for one's country," a verse memorized by generations of British public school boys. In Owen's version a group of
soldiers are marching to the rear when suddenly they are attacked
by gas shells. One man fails to get his mask on in time.

> Gas! Gas! Quick, boys!—An ecstasy of fumbling,
> Fitting the clumsy helmets just in time;
> But someone was still yelling out and stumbling,
> And flound'ring like a man in fire or lime . . .

Dim, through the misty panes and thick green light,
As under a green sea, I saw him drowning.

In all my dreams, before my helpless sight,
He plunges at me, guttering, choking, drowning.

If in some smothering dreams you too could pace
Behind the wagon that we flung him in,
And watch the white eyes writing in his face,
His hanging face, like a devil's sick of sin;
If you could hear, at every jolt, the blood
Come gargling from the froth-corrupted lungs
Obscene as cancer, bitter as the cud
Of vile, incurable sores on innocent tongues,—
My friend, you would not tell with such high zest
To children ardent for some desperate glory,
The old lie: *Dulce et decorum est*
Pro patria mori.

An army humor journal, *The Wipers Times,* mocking the prolif-
eration of bards in the trenches, published a notice: "We regret to
announce that an insidious disease is affecting the division, and the
result is a hurricane of poetry. Subalterns have been seen with a
notebook in one hand and bombs in the other absently walking
near the wire in deep communion with the muse. . . . The Editor
would be obliged if a few of the poets would break into prose as a
paper cannot live by 'poems' alone."

Siegfried Sassoon, after four months at Craiglockhart, accepted
that poets were not going to end the war. All that his protesting
had accomplished, he concluded, was to keep him from his duty to
his men. He obtained his release from the hospital and rejoined his
regiment. In the meantime, de Sola Pinto, now a captain, had
taken over Sassoon's former company and his predecessor's bleak
view of the war as well. As Christmas 1917 approached, de Sola
Pinto received a message from division headquarters stamped "Ur-

gent," ordering him to report how many Christmas cards his men would need. He scrawled across the message, "Probably none if present conditions continue."

SIX DAYS AFTER the victory at Messines Ridge, General Pershing and his staff disembarked from the liner *Baltic* and went ashore at the French seaside resort of Boulogne-sur-Mer. One staff officer, Captain Hugh Drum, found himself so moved by the French people he saw in this third year of the war that he wrote home, "The common dress on the street is black. We only see old men or boys, the women are doing the work of the men and indeed are worthy of praise. I have never seen such a staunch class of women. I tell you all this as preliminary to saying that I am glad we are in this war. My heart has gone out to these people. They need and deserve our help."

Pershing's unobtrusive arrival soon gave way to an entrance into Paris befitting the general's flair for the dramatic. On the Fourth of July, at Les Invalides, site of Napoleon's tomb, Black Jack Pershing stood towering over Raymond Poincaré as the diminutive French president presented his nation's flag to an eagerly awaited ally. An army band then led a parade of French infantry along the broad boulevards of the city followed by troops drawn from the American 1st Division's earliest 14,000 doughboys to arrive in France, robust, cocky lads who, like their commander, physically dominated the *poilus*. The parade ended in the Picpus Cemetery at the grave of the Marquis de Lafayette, who had come to America's aid during the Revolution. Pershing's staff had prepared a speech in French for the general, but he was uncomfortable with the language. He had particularly bridled at the final phrase, noting in the margin, "Not in character." He decided instead to make brief extemporaneous remarks and left the reading of his prepared text to a French-speaking staff officer, Colonel C. E. Stanton. The colonel did not find the objectionable sentence at all out of character for himself and rang out at the end of his remarks, "Lafayette, we are here!" The crowd exploded, shouting, laughing, and weeping, surrounding and kissing the Americans. The phrase would forever be associated with Pershing, uttered by him or not.

Just over two weeks later, on July 20, the heads of the British, French, and American armies met over a dinner hosted by Field Marshal Haig. It was Haig's habit before retiring to record the day's happenings in an ordinary field-service notebook that served as his diary. He made carbon copies of whatever he wrote and at intervals shipped them to his wife in England via king's messenger. By war's end, Haig's dutiful entries would total thirty-eight bound volumes. His initial opinion of the Americans recorded in the diary was mixed. Of Pershing, Haig wrote, "I was much struck with his quiet, gentlemanly bearing—so unusual for an American. Most anxious to learn, and fully realises the greatness of the task before him. He has already begun to realise that the French are a broken reed." As for Pershing's staff, Haig found the chief of staff, General James Harbord, and the adjutant general, Colonel Benjamin Alvord, "men of less quality, and . . . quite ignorant of the problems of war." Specifically, he found Harbord to be "a kindly soft looking fellow with the face of a punchinello . . . less mentally alert than the others." Pershing's commander of headquarters troops, Captain George S. Patton, Haig noted, was "a fire eater and longs for the fray." Haig's mildly approving appraisal of Pershing, however, would not last. Pershing, for his part, was already forming his own opinions of British leaders. Just before coming to France, Pershing had met the British prime minister in London and made an instant judgment. He described David Lloyd George as "that son of a bitch."

Pershing had chosen as his headquarters Chaumont, a hilltop town of 20,000 inhabitants 140 miles southeast of Paris. On journeying there, his entourage passed through the village of Soulaucourt, where a granite shaft had been erected to commemorate the town's war dead, thus far 17 men out of a population of 250. With customary Yankee enterprise, sleepy Chaumont was soon sprouting barracks and offices in which typewriters clattered and telephone switchboards hummed in preparation for the arrival in France of 1,300,000 men over the next twelve months.

ONE REASON PERSHING had chosen Chaumont for AEF head-quarters was to limit the temptations of Paris to his staff, to mini-mize what one officer called *la guerre de luxe*. Pershing still grieved and always would over the staggering personal loss he had suf-fered only two years before, when his wife and three daughters perished in flames. Soon after his arrival in France, he confided to a friend, "Even this war can't keep it out of my mind." Yet, the general, at fifty-seven, was, beneath his mask of imperturbability, a passionate, virile man. Before he left for France, he had been ro-mantically involved with Anne "Nita" Patton, the thirty-year-old sister of George Patton, which had not disadvantaged Patton's ca-reer. Soon after Pershing's arrival in France, however, unknown circumstances ended the engagement that Miss Patton presumed she had with the general.

The French government arranged for Pershing to sit for his portrait. The artist chosen was Micheline Resco, a twenty-three-year-old Romanian who had taken French citizenship and had established her professional reputation with official portraits of Marshal Foch and French aristocrats. The chemistry between artist and subject was instantaneous, romantic, and sexual despite the thirty-four-year gap in their ages. Pershing's duties required fre-quent travel between Chaumont and Paris, where a wealthy Ameri-can, Ogden Mills, lent him his mansion at 73 rue de Varenne. In the evening, when freed of his official tasks, the AEF commander had his chauffeur drive him to "Michette's" apartment on the rue Descombes, with the placard displaying the four stars of a general first removed from the limousine's windshield. The older man and the young artist never talked about the war. Pershing instead looked forward to temporary surcease from his crushing burdens and found himself revitalized by the love and loyalty of his youth-ful mistress.

18

"Over There"

JULY 1917. While Pershing and his thus far token force were still settling in, Tommies and *poilus* were preparing for the assault that Field Marshal Haig believed would render the American presence in France irrelevant. With Messines Ridge now in Allied hands, Haig was ready to complete the push through to the Belgian ports, neutralize German ships operating from them, then turn east to throw the enemy out of Belgium, honoring the pledge that had drawn Britain into the war.

In London, a dubious Lloyd George cross-examined Haig. All other frontal offensives, except the secondary victory at Messines Ridge, had failed. Why should this one succeed? Why didn't they wait until the Americans could bear their share of the burden? Why did other respected British generals oppose Haig's strategy? Nothing dissuaded the field marshal. To Haig there simply was not time to wait for the slow mobilizing Americans to be battle-ready. He promised victory before the year was out. Lloyd George's doubts persisted. Still, he had come to power pledging to win the war, and here was the army's chief saying that victory was within their grasp. The prime minister concluded reluctantly that he could not overrule Haig. The Third Battle of Ypres would proceed, later remembered for the obscure Belgian village in its sector,

Passchendaele. General Sir Hubert Gough's Fifth Army, backed by Plumer's Second Army, the victors at Messines Ridge, and the French First Army would lead the attack.

It was as if the three previous years had never happened, as if artillery had never failed, as if the machine gun had never been invented, and as if his troops had never piled up on the wire. Once again, artillery pieces were lined up, only more of them, 4,000 in all, a gun every six yards stretching for fifteen miles. The enemy would be pounded with shells, only more of them, 4.5 million this time. As before, infantrymen, 120,000 of them, would advance over open, featureless terrain. Haig assured Lloyd George and his War Cabinet that he had "no intention of entering into a tremendous offensive involving heavy losses." If casualties were too high and the ground gained too little, he promised, as he had at the Somme, to break off the offensive.

The artillery pummeling began on July 24. Lieutenant A. G. Dixon had been asked by his mother what a bombardment was like. "If you stood on the platform of any railway junction as an express train roared through," he wrote her, "you would have a fairly good idea what it was like." The din was exceeded only by the mine detonations at Messines Ridge and lasted not for minutes but for eight days.

While the guns were still hammering, Paul Maze, a divisional intelligence officer, saw puffs of smoke rising from a shop as he rode alongside troops headed for the front. "A steam saw was cutting rhythmically through wood, working at high pressure with a tearing sound," he remembered. "Seeing the yard in front of the house piled high with wooden crosses and thinking to spare the men, I hurried in to have them removed. The Belgians engaged in the work threw up their hands in despair and pointed through the window to the back of the house and an even bigger pile. Nothing could be done. I watched the men as they passed by. Some smiled, others passed a joke, some wouldn't look. But I knew that they all saw and understood."

In the early morning hours of July 31, the men in the trenches were alerted to stand to. The soil in this part of Belgium was chalky, wet, and had been turned into a clinging clay by recent rains. Belgian farmers had cut canals through the fields in an attempt to drain them. But the ditches had been shattered by previous battles in Flanders. Consequently, the millions of shells, rather than destroying German defenses, had churned the ground between the attackers and the defenders into a boot-sucking bog. British intelligence in London had warned against the terrain chosen for the assault. Haig's own intelligence officers on the scene had questioned it. A later chronicler of the battle wrote, "If a careful search had been made from the English Channel to Switzerland, no more unsuitable spot could have been discovered." Haig had remained unmoved.

His timetable predicted a five-mile advance by the end of the first day. He was holding cavalry divisions in reserve that were expected to swarm over the enemy as soon as the infantry broke through. At 5:27 A.M., the men began to go over the top. The skies opened and delivered a torrential downpour, turning already sodden fields into a sea of mud. As the infantry plodded on, a wary Montgomery Belgion "took the precaution of carrying the blade of my entrenching tool across my private parts."

Instead of making five miles on the first day, the attackers took two days to advance a half mile, littering the morass with 35,000 dead and wounded. Haig was urged to call off a disaster in the making. He agreed only to stop until the playing field dried. The attack was resumed on August 9 and continued through August 27, with another mile gained and another 40,000 casualties suffered.

The problem had been evident from the moment the first Tommy tried to pull himself out of the trench by gripping a rotted sandbag and had fallen back to the bottom. The rain collapsed the sides of trenches, and men had to be heaved over the parapet bodily. Tanks sank, their treads unable to gain traction. As the men finally advanced, they were sucked into mud-filled craters, where many drowned. Edwin Vaughan of the 8th Warwickshire Regiment remembered "faint, long, sobbing moans of agony, and despairing shrieks. It was too horribly obvious that dozens of men with serious wounds must have crawled for safety into new shell holes, and now the water was rising about them."

IN THE PARADOX of the western front, some men died while others, close by, played at games. Haig, a noted sportsman, expected the men to engage in athletics whenever their unit was out of the fight. Robert Cude, the runner with the Buffs and confirmed private promoted against his will to sergeant, described the pastimes that filled a Tommy's free hours. In a diary now running to tens of thousands of words, he wrote, "An amusing part of sports is the one round blindfolded boxing bouts and the tug of war on mules." His brigade won a one-mile relay, and a proud Cude wrote, "I may state that this team has not been beaten yet, and have challenged any unit in the B.E. Force." Some competitions suggested a busman's holiday: bomb throwing, bayoneting, trench digging, rapid wiring, and stretcher bearing. But European football, which Americans called "soccer," remained the favorite wherever a flat patch of earth could be found. Captain Charles May of the 22nd Manchesters exulted in his team's 2–0 victory over the Borders, noting that "Fritz commenced shelling in the wood whilst the game was in progress, the shells were passing our heads and exploding on the slopes above."

Music hall performers came over from England to entertain the troops. "I miss the theatre more than anything else here," Cude recalled. "Mister L. Hay gives us 'Alice, Where Art Thou Now' and 'Come into the Garden, Maude,' both in ragtime and they were enthusiastically received. . . . I thank heaven that there are people that appreciate us for what we are doing and in return help us to live again, if only for a few hours."

Even death could provide a spectator sport. Cude remembered watching a dogfight during which a British aircraft shot down a German two-seater. One enemy flier managed to parachute to safety, but the other's chute failed to open and "he falls like a stone. We watched him all the way down," Cude noted, adding, "He is a magnificent specimen of an officer of the German Army and he must have been 6 feet 3 inches in height . . . his body had driven almost 6 inches into the ground. I think that every bone of his body was broken, for we can roll him up just like a carpet."

Even during a lull, daily life consisted of unrelieved discomfort. A freshly dug trench soon became waterlogged, and men had to remain there, unwashed, unshaven, and caked in mud, for a week until relieved by another unit. They relieved themselves squatting over old bully beef tins, then chucked the waste out of the trench, while keeping the tin. Tea was served from empty gasoline cans still laced with traces of fuel, which led to violent bouts of diarrhea. Boots, never allowed enough time to dry, caused trench foot, which sent more men to the rear than did wounds. To navigate above ground, the men had to walk along narrow duckboards, which the German gunners had sighted with lethal accuracy. Men who slipped off the duckboards risked drowning in the mud.

In late September, a deeply doubting Lloyd George came to France and confronted Haig about the latter's intention of continuing the Passchendaele offensive. The field marshal proved both stubborn and wily. He had his men assemble the most bedraggled POWs in one cage to prove to the prime minister that the Germans were down to the dregs and verging on collapse. Lloyd George returned home, still doubting but unwilling to reverse Haig.

The respite of games for Sergeant Cude and his comrades was short-lived. By August 16, Haig judged the ground dry enough to push on. The next day, Cude wrote, "I move off with an advance party back to the line again." In a subsequent wave on September 20, the Tommies went over the top, gained 900 yards, and took 22,000 casualties. On September 26, they advanced 1,000 yards at a cost of 17,000 men. On October 4, they gained another 700 yards, losing 26,000 men. The British were paying 25 men per yard.

Despite their ferocity toward the foe in the heat of battle, the men could, when fighting halted, show compassion toward an enemy sharing their common ordeal. Edwin Vaughan watched a squad of Germans stagger out of a pillbox, hands raised over their heads. *"Nichts essen, nichts trinken"*—nothing to eat, nothing to drink—"always shells, shells, shells," they cried. Vaughan could not spare a man to take the prisoners to the rear, so he motioned them into shell holes where his own men were sheltered. The Tommies "made a great fuss of them, sharing their scanty rations with them."

Gallantry diminished the farther one went back from the front. A soldier told of seeing German dead near his encampment, "with the whites of their pockets turned out and their tunics and shirts undone" by scavengers. He saw a well-dressed corpse lose first his boots, then his tunic, then his pants, until the body was stripped naked. Occasionally men were shocked by their own behavior. One Tommy bit off the finger of a dead man to get his signet ring and later asked himself, "Did I really do these things? If so, I could not have been in a normal state of mind."

Haig lowered his sights. He had given up his ambition to liberate the Channel ports and drive the Germans out of Belgium. He was now content to gain control of the Menin Road and Polygon Wood and capture Passchendaele. On October 26, the Canadians joined the British for the final attack on the village. To the mud, shells, and machine-gun fire, the enemy added mustard gas, which burned the lungs, blistered the skin, and swelled the eyes shut. The final push opened during another violent rainstorm with the men, rifles held over their heads, struggling to advance against waist-deep muck. The ruins of what had been a quaint village fell, a puny prize after Haig's initial grand designs. Passchendaele ended in breathtaking losses. More than 310,000 British, 85,000 Frenchmen, and 260,000 Germans, a total of 655,000, had fallen in a battle fought over a field five miles wide. Of the 20,000 Canadians engaged, 12,000 were dead, wounded, or missing. "Passchendaele," one observer put it, "had become a Canadian Calvary."

The magnitude of the figures robs them of any sense of personal loss. Better to consider one out of the two thirds of a million men who were lost. Private Jack Mudd, a thirty-one-year-old Cockney from Bow in London's East End, serving with the Royal Fusiliers, wrote his wife, Lizzie, with a sensitivity his betters would not have suspected. God had been with him, Mudd believed, "ever since I have been out here, but we are expecting to go up again in 2 or 3 days, so dearest pray hard for me. . . . How I long for you and the children. . . . I often take your photo out of my pocket and look at your dear face and think of the times we had together, some lovely days, eh love." Mudd spoke of the brotherhood of the trenches. "Out here we're all pals," he wrote, "what one hasn't got, the other has, we try to share each other's troubles, get each other out of danger. You wouldn't believe the humanity between men out here." He lamented the loss of a friend, Shorty, "poor fellow I don't think he even has a grave." It was to be Mudd's last letter. A month after Passchendaele, Mrs. John W. Mudd received Form B.164-82a reporting that her husband was missing and the army "was regretfully constrained to conclude" that he was dead. Private Mudd's body was never found. His would be one of 34,888 names later chiseled onto a Memorial to the Missing at Tyne Cot Cemetery, a half mile below Passchendaele Ridge.

Another casualty had to be counted in the three battles waged over the Ypres landscape, the villages razed, the churches leveled, the art destroyed, nine centuries of civilization demolished in three years.

* * *

AFTER TEN MONTHS at the front, Will Bird, Canadian 3rd Division, watched with a jaded eye the alternating tides of humanity and bestiality flowing over the battlefield. He had come through Passchendaele, as had his close comrades Bob Jones and Tommy Mills, who would later die in the last twenty-four hours of the war. One day Bird had been standing near a cobblestone road when a *Minenwerfer* shell struck, spewing up a geyser of bricks and killing Captain Mason. Bird stayed with the dead man until the stretcher bearers arrived and looked on indifferently as they rifled the captain's pockets, extracting 500 francs. What would be the point, Bird accepted, of burying the money along with the man?

One day, he and his men stopped by the house of a Frenchwoman who spoke passable English. She made coffee for them and asked their names. Upon hearing Mills say, "Tommy," she said that she too had a Tommy, a French one. She disappeared into a room and came back leading a white-haired, shuffling figure by the hand. This was her son, Henri, she said. "He is twenty-three." Henri had been wounded at Verdun, the mother explained, and "a man fell across him and died. In his mind, he is still there." She had had two other sons, she added, but they had both been killed.

In October, in the waning days of Passchendaele, Sergeant Pearce asked Bird if he would like to try his hand at sniping. One of the first battle deaths that Bird had witnessed had been at the hands of a German sniper. A newly arrived officer had started chatting with Bird. "He told me that his name was Larson," Bird recalled, "that he was from Bear River, Nova Scotia, and thrilled with the front line." He asked Bird how close they were to the Germans. Bird was gazing across no-man's-land through a periscope when an enemy sniper shot it out of his hand. "That fellow must be very near," Larson commented. "I'll take a quick look." "Don't!" Bird yelled, grabbing at Larson's coat as the officer rose to peer over the parapet. It was too late. The bullet pierced the man's forehead and sent his helmet rolling and clanging along the trench.

Now Sergeant Pearce was asking Bird if he wanted to be a sniper. Bird, a fine shot, said yes. The next morning was cold and occluded as the two men set themselves up behind a steel shield only one hundred yards from the German lines. Bird began scanning the enemy trenches through a telescopic sight. But as the day went on and no targets appeared, he began grumbling. Pearce told him to relax. It had taken him months, he said, to accumulate his eighteen kills.

The next day dawned sunny and clear. Almost immediately, a

German in full pack, evidently new to the front, rose waist high in his trench. Through the telescopic lens, Bird could count the buttons on the man's tunic. He fired. The German fell backward and slipped from sight. "Great stuff!" Pearce exclaimed, jotting down Bird's kill in a notebook he kept. Within minutes, Bird shot three more men. A fourth German came into his crosshairs. Bird hesitated. "Shoot!" Pearce ordered. "You won't get a chance like this all day." Bird felt a wave of nausea sweep over him. He handed Pearce the rifle. "Go ahead yourself," he said. "I've had enough." He never accepted sniping duty again.

Bird shared the resentment of the other men toward staff officers behind the lines; the farther behind, the greater the resentment. One night, he was sitting on the firestep when he made out an unarmed figure approaching, obviously an officer. Bird rose to his feet, and the man put him at ease. The officer began questioning him in an avuncular fashion. Where was he from, what had he done before the war? Bird began to relax and told of homesteading in Alberta and making a bundle with an odd American duck using Russian wolfhounds to hunt coyotes at fifty cents per head. The older man brought the conversation around to the present and asked if Bird knew who commanded the 3rd Division. "Major General Lipsett," Bird answered. "Does he ever come to the front line?" the officer asked. Bird replied that he did not know. "I'm Lipsett," the man said with a grin. He drew a photograph of himself from his pocket and gave it to the tongue-tied soldier. He shook Bird's hand and left. Bird was still carrying the photograph on the last day of the war.

THE CLEAR-EYED realist R. C. Sherriff was wounded at Passchendaele, and fifty-two fragments were extracted from his body. "One for every week of the year," the surgeon remarked, wrapping the pieces in lint and giving them to Sherriff as a souvenir. After what had happened at Loos, Verdun, and the Somme, Sherriff commented, "I need no souvenir to remind me of the monstrous disgrace of Passchendaele. It was proof, if proof were needed, that the generals had lost all touch with reality." To Sherriff, the only lesson that appeared to be learned was that nothing was ever learned.

For staff officers battle remained not a bloodletting but a test of the ingenuity of their chess moves. A widely repeated story has Lieutenant General Sir Launcelot Kiggell, Haig's intelligence officer, making a visit to the Passchendaele front after the battle. As his staff car lurched through a muddy track lined with bodies, mired guns, and tanks, he supposedly said, "Good God, did we really send men to fight in that?" An officer accompanying him replied, "It's worse further up."

The gulf between what generals and soldiers experienced was cavernous. Joffre enjoyed two-hour lunches; Hindenburg, ten hours of sleep a night; and Haig had roads near his headquarters sanded so that his horse would not slip during the field marshal's morning canters. To Lloyd George, "the solicitude with which most generals in high places . . . avoided personal jeopardy is one of the debatable novelties of modern warfare." He admitted to "honourable exceptions," and in fact fifty-six British generals were killed at the front.

Again, it was Siegfried Sassoon who, in his poem "In the Pink," best measured the distance between the men in the trenches and the officers in their château headquarters:

> Tonight he's in the pink; but soon he'll die.
> And still the war goes on; *he* don't know why.

Winston Churchill, after rejoining his regiment for a brief turn at the front following the Gallipoli fiasco, keenly understood the divide between those who planned the war and those who fought it. The generals, Churchill said, were "fighting machine guns with the breasts of gallant men."

Who was responsible? Lloyd George told of a dinner conversation several weeks after Passchendaele with Philip Gibbs, correspondent for *The Daily Telegraph*. The prime minister believed that what Gibbs had observed at the front was "the most impressive and moving description . . . of what the War in the West really means, that I have ever heard. Even an audience of hardened politicians and journalists was strongly affected." What did he intend to do with this testimony? The next morning over breakfast with another journalist, C. P. Scott, editor of *The Manchester Guardian,* Lloyd George confided, "If people really knew, the war would be stopped tomorrow. But of course they don't know and can't know. The correspondents don't write and censorship would not pass the truth. The thing is horrible beyond human nature to bear and I feel I can't go on with the bloody business: I would rather resign." But he did not resign. Nor did he replace the commander, though by now he accepted that in Haig he had "backed the wrong horse."

Lloyd George simply did not know how to end the war, nor did his adversaries. One side would not give up its gains; the other would not accept its losses. Thus both sides came to the same solution: that the way to stop the killing was to win. And both believed God was on their side. "Such a war is a heavy price to pay for our progress towards the realisation of the Christianity of Christ," a British bishop intoned from his cathedral pulpit, "but duty calls." A German nationalist avowed, "God must stand on Germany's side. We fight for truth, culture and civilization and human progress and true Christianity." Indeed, the belt buckle of a German soldier had stamped on it *Gott mit uns,* "God is with us." "The soldiers," the historian Correlli Barnett noted wryly, "were beating each other's heads with crucifixes."

Haig, himself a religious man, might have his objectives blunted, but never his supreme self-confidence. After his army had taken Passchendaele, a tiny village pounded out of existence, he declared he could now stop because Third Ypres "had served its purpose," a purpose difficult to discern. Haig could perhaps have no other outlook. The professional soldier views the casualties his decisions cost the way a gambler calculates losses: How much is he willing to lose in seeking what he hopes to win? The stakes in this game, however, were counted in lives, not chips.

Living with what seems like hell on earth, ordinary soldiers displayed a surprising duality. "We held two irreconcilable beliefs," Robert Graves recalled, "that the war would never end and that we would win it." Even with the conflict in its third year and the casualties accounted in the millions, the trench worked its bizarre spell. Lieutenant Vivian de Sola Pinto's third wound, suffered at Passchendaele, was the perfect "blighty," a shot through the right arm, badly infected and nasty enough to get him home but not permanently disabling. A proud father squired his hero son to visit friends, clubs, and relatives, where de Sola Pinto was lavishly wined and dined. The young captain listened politely to civilians who always referred to the Germans as "the Hun" and who could not wait for the day when the kaiser was hanged. "As I gulped down their champagne with a fatuous smile," de Sola Pinto recalled, "I felt horribly unreal, a sort of ghost from another world, the real world of the brotherhood of the front line." When well enough, he made no attempt to evade reassignment to the front. Aboard a troopship full of Americans, he was reminded of how long the war had gone on. One doughboy asked him with wonder, "Say lootenant, were you at Mons?"

Guy Chapman felt, when back in London, "as foreign as a Chinese." He shared the hostility of ordinary soldiers toward rear-echelon warriors and complacent civilians. Tales of profiteers getting rich in coal, wheat, wool, and whiskey sickened Chapman. Money had become England's God, he concluded. "It was better in France. There a man was valued rather for what he was than what he achieved." Chapman could describe a life of lice, rat-gnawed clothing, stinking bodies, undisposed human waste, and barely edible rations yet wax poetic about the experience. "In spite of it," he reflected, "there grew a compelling fascination. I do not think I exaggerate: for in that fascination lies war's power. Once you have lain in her arms you can admit no other mistress. You may loathe, you may execrate, but you cannot deny her. No lover can offer you defter caresses, more exquisite tortures, such breaking delights. No wine gives fiercer intoxication, no drug more vivid exaltation." Chapman happily returned to the front.

Only in the trenches was a man free from the harassment of red-tabbed staff officers, the military police, home-front jingoists, gushing matrons, and religious firebrands. Robert Graves recalled that lightly wounded men "soon grew bored with hospital and depot and schemed to get back again, our wounds half healed. The trenches made us feel larger than life: only there was death a joke rather than a threat."

By now, however, the home front was getting at least a desultory taste of mechanized killing. Since 1915, London and eastern England had been bombed by dirigibles, ponderous cigar-shaped airships whose attacks killed 564 people in fifty-seven raids. By 1917, the Germans began using huge twin-engine giant Gotha bombers that killed another 835 people in twenty-seven raids. Sybil Morrison described an experience that had led her to embrace pacifism. She had been standing with fellow Londoners watching an airship that had been hit by antiaircraft fire and was burning. "We'd always been told there was a crew of about sixty—and they were being roasted to death," Morrison recalled, appalled to see her fellow spectators begin dancing, applauding, and singing. When she remonstrated, she was told, "But they're Germans; they're the enemy—not human beings." It came to her in a flash that this was what war was about: "It created this utter inhumanity in perfectly nice, decent, gentle, kindly people."

While their families at home were occasionally threatened by random death, Tommies were dying at an average rate of 450 a day. "Wastage," the staff called it. Still the men bore their burdens stoically. Thousands of soldiers had left the collieries for the army. Thousands more had come from the servant class. A quarter of the army had worked on farms. These were men inured to hardship, hard work, low wages, and being told what to do.

NOVEMBER 1917. From the decks of the *George Washington,* the *President Lincoln,* and the *Leviathan,* a swelling tide of doughboys caught their first glimpse of the ocean and felt the peril of war as they began their journey across an Atlantic Ocean infested with U-boats. Wilbur Peterson, from Marshall, Iowa, described his crossing with 6,000 other men aboard the *President Lincoln,* out of Hoboken, New Jersey. Though ordered to stay below, Peterson sneaked onto the main deck at night for his first and what he feared might be his last sight of the New York skyline. Six more troopships made up the convoy, protected by a cruiser and two ever-darting destroyers patrolling for submarines. When the men were allowed above deck, Peterson could find no room to walk, sit, or stand. The only place to stretch out was back in the fetid, airless compartments, where men were stacked in bunks six high. "Thirteen days of it in all," Peterson remembered. "Days endless with monotony. Days of torpedo scares. Days when the ship seemed to drop from beneath us as the engines stopped to fool wary submarine ears. Days of seasickness when soldiers' faces turned a pasty green. . . . Nights broken by alarms of abandon ship, real or drill we never knew—standing in the blackness ready to jump over the rail into the sea. Jump to what? A couple of dozen lifeboats and two or three score rafts—for six thousand men!"

Ken Baker, his hope of becoming a flier now abandoned, was thrilled to learn that he would be making the passage in presumably comfortable quarters aboard the *Baltic,* the former luxury liner that had earlier carried General Pershing and his staff to Europe. "I think they marched us there to see that we did not desert when we saw our so called stateroom," Baker remembered. Six men and their gear were crammed into a six-by-eight-foot cubicle. Communal toilets, with seats broken or missing, backed up and overflowed. "There was about an inch of water and raw sewage sloshing around on the floor," Baker remembered a voyage that he described as "a horror." The day before they were due to arrive in port he felt a thud and rushed up on deck. Destroyers were crisscrossing the sea while their depth charges sent towering geysers of water into the sky. The *Tuscania,* immediately behind the *Baltic,* had been torpedoed. The following morning, a relieved Baker set foot on land at Liverpool. There the troops learned that 174 men aboard the *Tuscania* had died and a far greater loss avoided only because the ship had taken more than two hours to sink. Other troopships would go down during the Atlantic crossing: the *Moldavia,* losing 56 men, and the *Ticonderoga,* with 215 lives lost. Wilbur Peterson, aboard the *President Lincoln,* had been fortunate in his timing. That ship too was later sunk while returning wounded men to the United States.

EIGHTEEN-YEAR-OLD Arthur Jensen, happily escaped from college, remembered his first sight of men who had actually been in battle. Jensen's unit debarked in a French port alongside a train overflowing with silent, badly wounded Britons enroute to hospitals in England. He saw his first enemies the same day: 600 German POWs guarded by a half-dozen kilted Scotsmen. "The Germans were a dizzy looking bunch," Jensen remembered. "None of them were dressed alike. Covered with mud, they reminded me of tired horses. They were larger than the British and looked as if they might be better soldiers. Compared to us, they looked stronger and heavier, but more clumsy and stupid." One of Jensen's pals said with unconvincing bravado, "Aw hell, they don't look very bad to me!"

Joe Rizzi had lived with a kindly German family and doubted stories of enemy atrocities. On his arrival in France, a curious Rizzi and his pals went to visit a POW cage, where they were supposed to see, "according to the propaganda, hardened and ferocious men who would commit all kinds of atrocious acts." What they found instead were "wretched looking human beings who were being starved. . . . Our sympathy went out to the poor fellows." Before they left, the Americans were pressing packs of cigarettes on the POWs.

To General Robert Lee Bullard, commanding the 1st Division, the Big Red One, America had already come "into the war too late." What he confided to his diary on October 28, 1917, reeked of disloyalty. "We may perhaps save France from a shameful peace," he wrote, "but we cannot beat Germany. She has beaten Serbia, Russia, Belgium and Rumania. She is now beating Italy. . . .

There is just one man responsible for it, and that is President Wilson. He, three years ago, prevented any preparation for war by the United States. Had we last spring been prepared for war we could have had here today in France an army that could occupy fully the German armies. . . . I repeat, we came into the war too late, and Mr. Wilson is responsible for it."

VERA BRITTAIN, NURSING British troops in France, described her first sight of unfamiliar new arrivals marching to the front. "They looked larger than ordinary men; their tall, straight figures were in vivid contrast to the under-sized armies of pale recruits to which we had grown accustomed," she wrote. "At first I thought their spruce, clean uniforms were those of officers, yet obviously they could not be officers, for there were too many of them; they seemed, as it were, Tommies in heaven. . . . I wondered, watching them move with such rhythm, such dignity, such serene consciousness of self-respect. . . . Then I heard an excited exclamation from a group of sisters behind me. 'Look! Look! Here are the Americans!' . . . So these were our deliverers at last."

The Americans were pouring into France at the rate of tens of thousands per month. British and French generals eyed the new arrivals as a bottomless barrel of replacements from which to replenish their own battered ranks. Thus, Pershing's first battle continued to be to keep the hands of his allies off his army. Black Jack did not object to sending his men into the French and British lines under American command, but he did not want them dispersed. He would never deploy them at less than divisional strength, which meant in blocks of 28,000 men. Pershing argued that his policy was vital to the doughboys' esprit de corps and the country's pride in and support of the army, arguments he knew that President Wilson dared not oppose regardless of pressure by the Allies to allow them to draw from the American manpower pool. When the victory parade was finally held, Pershing intended to march alongside and not behind Foch and Haig.

As troops debarked at Brest, Cherbourg, and Le Havre, they

were transported to training camps in Bourbonne-les-Bains, Mont-morillan, Bruyères, and La Courtine. They lacked everything but cockiness. French and British arms makers enjoyed a bonanza as the ill-equipped AEF bought 9,600 Hotchkiss machine guns, 514 tanks, 3 million shells of every shape, weight, and destructive design, and 4,225 cannons, three quarters of them French 75 millimeters, the best field pieces in the war. Some new arrivals were issued an American-made version of the British Enfield rifle. The only wholly American weapon the doughboys brought over was the Springfield 1903, the finest rifle of its day. In the hands of a good infantryman, the Springfield was accurate up to one thousand yards. In the 1908 and 1912 Olympics, marksmen using the Springfield had taken the gold.

The Allies called the newcomers Yanks, Yankees, or Sammies, for Uncle Sam, but "doughboy" was the only label that stuck. As they continued to pour in, a Canadian artilleryman wrote, "Along all the roads of France, in all the trenches, in every gunpit you can hear one song being sung by the *poilus* and Tommies. They sing it while they load their guns, they whistle it as they march up the line, they hum it while they munch their bully-beef and hardtack. You hear it on the regimental bands and grinding out from gramophones in hidden dugouts:

> Over there. Over there.
> Send the word, send the word over there,
> That the Yanks are coming—

Men repeat that heartening promise as tho' it were a prayer, the Yanks are coming."

BRITISH VETERANS BEGAN to train the Americans at camps behind the lines. Doughboy William Triplet recalled the surgically precise direction he received from a no-nonsense Cockney: "He would calmly advise the Yanks to shove a bayonet only a 'hinch' into a man's throat, two 'hinches' into his kidneys, or a couple of 'hinches' into his 'art.' If you git the blade too deep in 'is ribs, you will 'ave difficulty in gittin' it out, and the next Boche will git you." Sergeant Giles, another instructor, advised, "If the blighter's down—stick 'im. If he puts 'is 'ands hup—stick 'im. If 'e turns 'is back—stick 'im."

Triplet had barely turned eighteen when he arrived in France fresh out of Sedalia High School in Missouri, where, with a war to be fought, he had grown restless studying Latin and algebra. Assigned to the 140th Infantry Regiment, 35th Division, Triplet was pulled aside by a British sergeant named Carter. "You Yanks are flymin' 'ot to get into the thick of it now. I can remember 'ow it was with us," Carter told the eager tyro. "But I'll tell you stryte, in six months you'll be bloody well fed up. You'll be stickin' your ruddy 'and h'above the bloody parapet and syin' 'Shoot me, Jerry, if you wish.' " Malingering, however, had to be done with care, Carter warned: "Be sure that Jerry does it for you. And are you right 'anded? Then get your Blighty in your right 'and. If you 'ave a powder burn or bullet in your left 'and or foot you're for it."

The 16th Infantry Regiment of the Big Red One had been the first to arrive in France. On November 2, 1917, after three months' training, the regiment was posted to the Lorraine sector, ten miles northeast of Nancy, where it was to relieve troops of the French 18th Division, to which the Americans had been assigned. The sector had been deliberately chosen to initiate the newcomers gradually into the mysteries of trench warfare. To reach their destination, the doughboys, backs bent under hundred-pound packs, slogged for five hours to cover one mile in a driving rain that had left the trenches floating with duckboards. Once in place, they found themselves eight hundred yards from the German lines. They would have to spend ten days there before being relieved by the French. It was nevertheless a quiet sector. The Germans and French who faced each other there carried on an unspoken truce. They did not snipe at each other. Machine guns were fired perfunctorily only to satisfy an occasional visiting inspector. Artillery shells landed in empty fields. Trenches were deep, well built, and intact since there had been no movement here since 1915. The

French called this sector a "rest camp." One doughboy dubbed this part of the line "home-sweet-home."

The Germans across the way knew from their intelligence that the recent arrivals were unblooded Americans and decided to break the truce to shatter any illusions the doughboys might hold about easy heroics. Soon after midnight, 240 men of the 7th Bavarian Landwehr Regiment loaded their Mauser rifles, hung flashlights and grenades from their belts, stuffed spare explosives into the pockets of their greatcoats, and prepared for a raid ostensibly aimed at seizing prisoners for interrogation. They climbed out of their trenches, trotting hunched over, then midway dropped to the ground and crawled across no-man's-land still undetected.

Among the men in F Company were Corporal James B. Gresham, known for some unaccountable reason as "Boo Boo," and two comrades, privates Tom Enright and Merle Hays. Gresham and Enright were regular army with long service; Hays had enlisted when the war broke out. F Company had been assigned one hundred yards of trench to defend. The site seemed safe enough, but it seethed with lice and rats. Exhausted from their long march to the sector, the men eagerly awaited daylight, when they would be relieved and could retreat to the dugouts burrowed behind the trench for breakfast rations, a mug of coffee, and a quick nap.

Suddenly, the night vanished as Very shells illuminated the American trench. Artillery fire erupted. Even near misses generated "tremendous heat," one doughboy recalled of this baptism of fire. "One feels he is about to burn up." Sickly sweet fumes of picric acid and pungent smoke burned their eyes. Pipe bombs exploded in front of the trench, opening gaps in the barbed wire. The Germans were back on their feet now, advancing within a box barrage that blocked any other units from coming to F Company's rescue. The Germans jumped into the trench, stunning the defenders with grenades. In fifteen minutes it was over. The enemy began withdrawing, dragging their dead and wounded along with every piece of equipment they could lay their hands on and taking eleven American prisoners.

That afternoon a funeral was held within sight of the trenches over three shallow graves in the village of Bathelémont. The French had sent General Paul Bordeaux to eulogize the dead. Compared to France's three-year casualties, the fate of these Americans was inconsequential. That was not the point. As Bordeaux put it, "Here lie the first soldiers of the famous Republic of the United States to fall on the soil of France for justice and liberty. . . . Corporal Gresham, Private Enright, Private Hays, in the name of France, I thank you. God receive your souls. Farewell!" An honor guard of Frenchmen then fired a salute and the ceremony ended with the poignant wail of "Taps." Nine days later, grimy, unshaven, and exhausted, the survivors of F Company turned their hundred yards over to the French.

One of the most promising career professionals on the First Army staff, Lieutenant Colonel George C. Marshall, was sent to investigate what had happened near Bathelémont. After the funeral, the colonel went to thank General Bordeaux for his moving tribute. He had thought to do so in French but then thought better of it. On his arrival in France months before at the port of Saint-Nazaire, Marshall had been greeted by a French officer, and as they drove off, he had decided to test his language facility. It was a fine morning, and the colonel remarked, *"Je suis très beau aujourd'hui."* The Frenchman gave Marshall an odd look. "I mentally translated my remark [I am very beautiful today]," Marshall remembered of that moment, and "I never spoke French again except when forced to."

Given Marshall's report on the skirmish in Lorraine, General Pershing was said to have broken down and wept. Likely, he was more chagrined than grieving. This setback, however minor, weakened his argument that the Americans could handle themselves independently.

RUDOLF BINDING WOULD later entitle his diary *A Fatalist at War*. Fatalism had first infected this German lieutenant during the 1914 Christmas truce, when he had seen the combatants trying to kill each other on December 24, behave with kindness and companionship on the twenty-fifth, then go back to killing each other on the twenty-sixth. Shortly after Passchendaele, a chaplain in Binding's unit had come to him with a tale that had only deepened the young lieutenant's conviction that resignation was the soldier's best armor. The chaplain explained that his only son had just been killed, and he asked for permission to find the spot where the soldier had fallen. "As he spoke to me about his boy his face lit up under his tears," Binding recalled. "To have experienced this grief seemed to him a marvelous achievement. He was proud to have been so rich that so much could be taken from him." The chaplain told Binding that someday "he is going to preach in his parish at home on his great experience. I should like to hear that sermon." Such unalloyed faith collided with the opportunism Binding observed. He remembered an occasion earlier in the year when a training officer whom he identified only as Captain von P—"the family is well beloved of the Supreme War-Lord"—had showed up "to have a good look around here." Binding noted that "the one and only time that he was sent near a shelled area, he turned back remarking that he was not sent there to get killed." On his second day the captain informed Binding that he had seen enough and was leaving. Binding and his friends began betting on how long it would be before Captain von P would receive the Iron Cross, First Class, for his exploits at the front.

WITHIN LESS THAN two weeks of Passchendaele, Field Marshal Haig, unfazed by monumental casualties, ordered General Sir Julian Byng to send his Third Army against the Hindenburg Line, forty-five miles to the south. The assault finally gave champions of the tank the leading role they had argued for, with 476 iron behemoths, the largest number yet placed on a battlefield, spearheading the attack. Their success was spectacular. Germany's vaunted defensive wall was pierced up to eight miles deep and a hole four miles wide was blasted for the infantry to go through. In London, church bells pealed for the first time since the war. The celebration proved premature. Within less than two weeks, the opposing forces were back where they had started. Casualties were a draw, roughly 40,000 for each side. A British court of inquiry investigated the lost victory; the generals were exonerated.

WHILE THE AMERICANS were spilling their first blood and yards were being exchanged at Passchendaele, something happened on the Italian front not seen since 1914, a war of genuine movement. A massive force, fifteen German and Austrian divisions, sent the Italians reeling back seventy miles in a battle known to history as Caporetto. By November 12, 30,000 Italians were dead, another 70,000 wounded, missing, or prisoners, and, most dismaying to Italy's allies, 400,000 Italian soldiers had deserted. The debacle, however, did not put Italy out of the war. Commanding generals were merely changed, and the continued fighting brought Italy not the territorial gains for which she had gone to war but thousands more wooden crosses.

19

"If This Is Our Country, Then This Is Our War"

NOVEMBER 11, 1918. With the end so near, Brigadier General John H. Sherburne expected to look back on a good war. The Harvard-trained Boston lawyer had command of the black 92nd Division's artillery and, at age forty-one, was one of the youngest generals in the AEF, a meteoric rise for an officer with only National Guard experience along the Mexican border. Sherburne was aware that the Allied commander in chief, Marshal Foch, had announced two days before that regardless of armistice talks all offensive orders remained in force. General Pershing had issued a vigorous concurrence to the AEF. But Sherburne was convinced that orders must yield to the realities of the past twelve hours. At 8:30 the evening before, his men had watched a spectacular fireworks display erupt from the German lines all along the front east of the Moselle River—flares, Very lights, rockets, Roman candles—illuminating hillsides and forests all the way to Metz. What could this demonstration mean but that the Germans had accepted terms of the rumored peace talks and were celebrating their anticipated return home? Near midnight, division headquarters had relayed a premature newspaper story that the Germans had accepted the Allied terms. Shortly thereafter, Sherburne's liaison officer with the French forces to his right came to tell him that a message just broadcast from the Eiffel Tower announced that fighting was to cease at 11 A.M. Sherburne now had information from three sources that the war was essentially over. Still he detected an interval of ambiguity. What was to happen until 11 A.M.? Since the day before, the 92nd had been operating under Field Order 5, which called for an advance northward to put the division in a strong position for the push on Metz set for November 14. In view of the latest developments, was the 92nd to stop now and hold its ground, which to Sherburne seemed logical, or keep fighting, which he found inconceivable? Yet, according to the order, at 5 A.M. two regiments of the division, the 365th and 366th, were to attack their next objectives, Champey and Bouxières, villages on the path to Metz. Before them stood Lacotte Hill, a stout German defense studded with machine guns and artillery. To launch that attack, Sherburne knew, would cost inevitable last-hour casualties. Sherburne asked his counterpart, the artillery commander of the French XXXII Corps, what he was going to do in the interval. Nothing, the officer answered, until the armistice was either carried out or called off. The enemy had not shown a spark of offensive spirit for days, he pointed out, but did respond fiercely if attacked.

General Sherburne sought further clarification from his superiors. At 1:30 A.M., he called division headquarters on the field phone but was unable to reach the commanding officer, Major General Charles C. Ballou. The general, a bald, stiff-necked army regular described by one associate as a cold authoritarian with a superficial grasp of the war, had turned in for the night. Sherburne spent an hour talking to a Ballou aide asking why the assault set for 5 A.M. was not being called off. Field Order 5 still stood, he was told. Sherburne next stuck his neck out and went above division to VI Corps artillery headquarters, speaking to a Major Ranghart. Ranghart told Sherburne to hold the phone while he checked. The VI Corps had issued no orders to rescind the attack, Ranghart informed him. Sherburne took the matter even higher. He called Second Army artillery headquarters at Toul, some twenty miles to the rear, and received the same response: the attack order remained in force. Everyone Sherburne had talked to was, however, aware of the impending armistice.

Early that morning, the 365th Regiment received a blessed reprieve: its men were to hold their position on the northern edge of the Bois de Fréhaut but go no farther. Their war was over. But at 5 A.M., the 366th began its advance. At 8 A.M., Sherburne was officially informed that the armistice had indeed been signed at the very hour the black troops had begun to move out of a wood called Voivrotte, which they had taken the day before. He again sought guidance, convinced that the attack by the 366th would certainly be halted. Sherburne received word from the division's operations officer, Colonel Allen Greer, that his guns were to continue to support the infantry's advance. The single star of a brigadier general had been pinned on Sherburne's shoulder just four months before. He was not eager to undo the army's confidence in him. He had done all the questioning he dared. He kept his guns firing.

Sherburne began to suspect that this pointless assault might be another test of the 92nd. The division had had a troubled history. To a degree its creation had been political; it had been raised in response to pressure from black leaders led by W. E. B. Du Bois, the pioneer civil rights champion. "If this is our country, then this is our war," Du Bois had argued. Black Americans might suffer oppression at home, but, he cautioned, "That which the German power represents spells death to the aspirations of the Negroes and all darker races for equality, freedom and democracy. Let us not hesitate. Let us, while this war lasts, forget our special grievances and close our ranks shoulder to shoulder with our own white fellow citizens." His appeal had sent black men flocking to recruiting stations, hoping that their demonstrated patriotism might finally pry open the door to equality.

The 92nd, however, had not been organized until seven months after America went to war, after the first flush of enthusiasm, and was composed largely of draftees. From the moment of its creation the division was segregated, in camps, in training, in off-duty hours.

A black graduate of the segregated Officer Candidate School at Fort Des Moines in Iowa might make captain and command a company but could rise no further. All field-grade officers up to general were white. These officers often balked at assignment to a black division, looking upon it as no advantage to their careers.

In a move to create esprit de corps, the 92nd was designated the Buffaloes, a nod to the black soldiers of the nineteenth-century Indian Wars. The romance of these earlier fighters did not, however, pass on to the 92nd Infantry Division. Its soldiers were shorted in everything from uniforms to guns to up-to-date maps. When the New York 15th National Guard Regiment (later to be absorbed into another black division, the 93rd) marched through the city's streets, only men in the front rank and on the flanks were issued rifles to make it less obvious that most lacked weapons.

Prejudice was exported when the 92nd went to France. To avoid friction between black and white doughboys, General Pershing assigned the division to the French XXXIII Corps. The AEF issued a directive reading, "General Pershing is in some doubt as to the aptitude for command of these Negro officers. He asks that the French command report to him all cases in which these Negro officers appear to be incapable in order that he may immediately take such measures as may be necessary. A suitable method seems to be to place a French officer alongside of each Negro field officer. This method gave good results when applied by the English to the Hindoo officers."

One notch below Pershing in the AEF stood the tall, gaunt, black-booted southerner now commanding the Second Army, Lieutenant General Robert Lee Bullard, whose divisions included the 92nd. Of these black men Bullard wrote, "Our government seemed to expect the same of them as of white men. Poor Negroes! They are hopelessly inferior. . . . If you need combat soldiers, and especially if you need them in a hurry, don't put your time upon Negroes." On another occasion, Bullard claimed, "The Negro is more sensual than the white man." The verdicts of courts-martial appeared to support his view. Six black soldiers in France were convicted of rape and executed, one just three days before the end of the war. General Charles D. Rhodes, when commanding the 157th Field Artillery, observed, "The 92nd Division (colored) has been withdrawn (no good, cowardly) and sent to the rear to work on the roads." Rhodes was right to the extent that whenever brute labor was needed, blacks were pulled out of the line to do it.

The YMCA in France sponsored shows to raise troop morale, and one skit was entitled "A Musical Evening in Coon-Town." *The Stars and Stripes,* the soldiers' newspaper, reported an imaginary conversation between "Rastus" and "Mose" in which Mose tells how, after the war, "I'se gwin to buy me a white suit of clothes, white shoes, white shirt and tie, and I'se gwin to tend de white folks' church, and sit by the white women. What's yo gwin to do, Rastus?" To which his friend replies, "I'se gwin to buy me a black suit of clothes, black shoes, black shirt and tie, and black gloves, and attend yo funeral." The black experience seemed to validate the observation of George Bernard Shaw that America "makes the Negro clean its boots and then proves the moral and physical inferiority of the Negro by the fact that he is a shoeblack."

For all the corrosive prejudice, black soldiers performed acts of heroism and died fighting. The first man from the 93rd to fall was an Ohio farmer, Private Moses Justice, a volunteer picked off while on patrol on September 2, 1918. Another member of the division, Henry Johnson, initially seemed unlikely material for gallant deeds. Johnson, born and raised dirt poor in the South, had drifted to Albany, New York, where the five-foot-four, 130-pounder worked long days as a redcap porter wrestling baggage in Union Station. Johnson was among the black volunteers who marched through New York without a rifle before arriving in France on New Year's Day 1918. His early duties involved unloading ships and digging latrines.

Eventually, his outfit was assigned to, armed by, and trained by the French Fourth Army, which welcomed the black men. By October, Johnson's 369th Regiment was in the trenches in the Argonne Forest. Near midnight on the fourteenth, his second night at the front, Johnson and Needham Roberts, a private from Trenton, New Jersey, were dispatched to man Outpost 29, an early-warning trench poking fifty yards into no-man's-land. Veteran German troops across the way sensed the inexperience of the new arrivals, who were alarmed by the rustling of the wind or the scurrying of a rabbit, which set them firing at tree stumps and shadows. The Germans decided to launch a raid to snatch prisoners.

To Johnson and Roberts the sound of the wire being cut rang out in the dark like a rifle shot. Roberts fired a Very pistol in the direction of the sound, illuminating a dozen advancing Germans, who responded by lobbing grenades into Outpost 29. Both Americans were hit and knocked to the ground, Roberts so badly hurt that he could not move. Johnson staggered to his feet and fired into the figures sliding over the parapet. He emptied the three rounds in his magazine, one bringing down the lead German. He swung his empty rifle with astonishing force for a man his size, cracking the skull of another enemy. He spun around to see two Germans dragging Roberts away. He drew a bolo knife from his web belt and stabbed one of them as the rest began to retreat before his wild thrashing. Johnson began hurling grenades after them. Collapsing and barely conscious from loss of blood, he was carried back to a dressing station, where he was found to have twenty wounds. When the regiment's commander stopped by to check on him, Johnson said, "Don't worry about me, Major. I've been shot at before." General Pershing, citing the incident, issued a statement that read, "Reports in hand show a notable instance of bravery and devotion shown by two soldiers of an American colored regiment operating in a French sector. They should be given credit for preventing, by their bravery, the capture of any of our men." The French showed more tangible appreciation. They awarded Johnson the Croix de Guerre with gold palm.

A black officer, Lieutenant Charles G. Young of the 368th Infantry Regiment, wounded twice by shell fire, refused to leave his post, remaining in an exposed position to defend his battalion's unprotected flank. A rifleman, Robert M. Breckinridge, crawled one hundred yards, though suffering a severe leg wound, to block an enemy attempt to outflank his company, firing until he was killed by German machine gunners. Still, to white officers the weight of evidence continued to prove the black to be no soldier. Black officers, demeaned by whites, had trouble exacting obedience even from their own men. One private resisted an order from his captain, saying, "You are of the same black meat as I am." In the very sector of the Argonne Forest where Lieutenant Young had performed his heroic feat, a white battalion commander, Major J. N. Merrill, described a scene not of bravery but of chaos and cowardice. On September 23, the 368th had been assigned to close a gap between French and American units. Merrill contended that he had to drive the troops forward "at the point of the pistol. . . . Without my presence or that of any other white officer right on the firing line, I am absolutely positive that not a single colored officer would have advanced with his men. The cowardice shown by the men was abject. . . . Under the slightest fire the men either diverged into the forest and laid down, or laid down where they were in the majority of cases without any officers near—who were conspicuous by their absence, the men firing in all directions and even into the trees."

According to General Bullard, blacks "had twice run away in front of the enemy." Consequently, he approved the trials of six black officers charged with cowardice. Five were convicted and sentenced to death, "I felt sure, as any white man would have been sentenced," Bullard commented. He nevertheless foresaw political difficulties. Justice, "if meted out by white men alone," he concluded, "becomes to Negroes injustice and converts them in the eyes of their fellows into martyrs for the race." He subsequently persuaded President Wilson to set aside the convictions of the condemned men.

Black soldiers believed that their honor had been unfairly stained. After the September debacle, officers of the black 367th Infantry Regiment crowded about General Ballou's car during a visit to the front, pressing a petition on the general to judge them not by any other black regiment's behavior but on their own merits. All they wanted, they said, was the chance to prove they were brave Americans or literally die trying.

The enemy, aware of American race prejudice, sought to exploit the situation. One morning black troops occupying a position in the Tête des Faux in the Vosges went scrambling in all directions as hand grenades began raining down on them. But the grenades did not explode. Warily, the men came back. Tied to the grenades were leaflets with a message obviously crafted by someone comfortable with American English. The leaflets were headed "How to Stop the War" and read, "Stop fighting! That's the simplest way. . . . What does it matter to you who owns Metz or Strasbourg . . . so what do you care about them? . . . Your country needs you, your family needs you and you need your life for something better than being gassed, shot at, deafened by cannon shots and rendered physically unfit. . . . The tales they tell you of the cruelties of German prison camps are fairy tales. . . . You better come over while the going is good." The black soldiers put the leaflets to a hygienic purpose.

The French continued to accept black Americans as worthy comrades. Regiments from a black division, the 93rd, served with the French in the Champagne campaign, prompting the French commander of the 157th Division to comment, "During seven months we have lived as brothers in arms, sharing the same works, the same fatigues, the same dangers. The 157th will never forget the irresistible dash, the heroic push of the colored American troops."

Whatever his misgivings about black soldiers, when directed by Pershing on November 9 to commit his entire army, General Bullard did not exempt his segregated division, the 92nd. It was against this backdrop that General Sherburne received the 8 A.M. phone call on the eleventh advising him that the 366th was to continue its advance and that he was to provide artillery support. Sherburne later described his reaction as "one of absolute horror . . . an absolutely needless waste of life."

General Ballou, Sherburne's divisional commander, would later maintain that, after receiving official word that the armistice had been signed, "I at once put every agency at my command in motion to get this order to every element of my command." He also directed that not a shot be fired after 11 A.M. Nevertheless, he did not halt the assault already under way, since "no subsequent orders in any way changed this order."

The 366th's advance from the Bois de Voivrotte that morning was intended to position the regiment for the Metz offensive, which would never take place once 11 A.M. arrived. As the men emerged from the protection of the trees and headed toward Champey and Bouxières, they were met by a storm of machine-gun fire and a foul mist of mustard gas from German defenders on Lacotte Hill. By 9:30, they had been driven back into the woods. Their regimental commander, Major A. E. Sawkins, regrouped them, and at 10 A.M., the war's last hour, they resumed the advance over ground littered with men from the previous failed attempt.

20

Ludendorff's Grand Gamble

NOVEMBER 11, 1918. The morning found Ernst Kielmeyer, a German telephone lineman, huddled with his comrades in an abandoned schoolhouse in Breuthaut, Belgium. The twenty-year-old, looking even younger, wrote in his diary what he hoped would be the last wartime entry, since rumors of a cease-fire were rampant. "We are just killing time," he wrote, "we are thinking and hoping that it is the real thing. Then we won't have to endure another winter out here to suffer, freeze, die and join our comrades who sleep the eternal sleep far from home." His sergeant appeared in the doorway, out of breath and waving a piece of paper. "The armistice has been signed," he called out. "Germany is now a Republic!" To Kielmeyer, the news was an answered prayer. Still, the Allies, especially the Americans, were not letting up, and he feared that his unit might yet be sent to fight a rearguard action.

Kielmeyer had been too young to volunteer in 1914, but even in those early days he had understood perfectly Germany's cause: "To make the world safe for all parties," a sentiment to be echoed later by an American president. A tenant in his home, Eugen Pfander, had immediately been called up by his reserve regiment. On the day of Pfander's departure, Ernst had shaken his hand and said, "I'll soon see you out there." To which the older man replied, "If boys as young as you are needed, then the war is lost."

As time passed and the easy early victories faded, so did Kielmeyer's idealism. Early in 1917, at age eighteen, he was drafted, hurriedly trained, and dispatched to the Ypres sector with the 26th Reserve Field Artillery. He became a telephone lineman, stringing and repairing lines between forward artillery observers and the gun batteries, constantly exposed to enemy snipers. He served under Corporal Gaupp, a man double his weight, whose girth, Kielmeyer feared, would attract fire. Consequently, he volunteered to work alone. As he described his duties, "We start out with one wire in one hand following along the wire. We come to the place where it is ripped apart. We look around to find the other end and splice it together. Then follow it to its destination, which is not always the right one. So back we go, pull the wires apart again. Finally finding another one we put them together. Hope for the best."

During Passchendaele, Kielmeyer and his comrades had undergone the same nightmare as the British. "We fear the mud at night more than we do Tommy," he wrote in his diary. "You just slide a little and disappear forever, and the clerk officially records, 'Missing in action.' " One cold December day after the heaviest fighting had passed, Kielmeyer stood shivering with another soldier in a trench along the Yser Canal watching two Tommies on the opposite bank sauntering along carrying buckets. "They didn't even have their rifles," Kielmeyer recalled. Aiming his Mauser, he turned to his friend and asked, "Shall we practice?" Then he thought better of it, telling his comrade, "You don't shoot at a helpless man." Later, as dark descended, "I went back to thinking about the two Tommies. Were they single or married? Did they have children at home praying the good Lord may bring them back again just as our loved ones do? Some crazy world."

During the lull after Passchendaele, Kielmeyer experienced an instance of the mischief men got into with too much time on their hands. It happened four days before Christmas. He and Ulmer, from near his hometown, were in a bunker looking through a two-inch-wide observation slit. Outside, two of their comrades were amusing themselves by setting dud shells on end and shooting at them from thirty-five yards away, aiming for the detonator fuse. They succeeded. A shell exploded, and a knifelike fragment came through the narrow slit and killed Ulmer outright. How could he explain this to the man's parents when he got home? Kielmeyer asked himself. Better, he decided, to leave it to the usual official notification: "He died for his country. He was a good man."

By now only the most unusual circumstances could jolt Kielmeyer from the casual acceptance of death. He was spending a night in a barn when he was awakened by children screaming. Kielmeyer rushed out to find two little Belgian boys on the ground, writhing in agony. They had been tossing a live grenade back and forth, and it had exploded. Kielmeyer had to take the news to their mother. The father was not at home but at the front, "fighting," Kielmeyer asked, "for what?"

When his regiment was sent to the rear for rest, Kielmeyer's behavior was indistinguishable from that of Tommies or *poilus*. Men who had survived monstrous shelling, been machine-gunned, sniped at, and gassed were put through silly parade-ground drills by officers who never went near the trenches. "We sure hope to get relieved and sent back in the front lines," he wrote in his diary. "There the boys are the boss and not the big shots. . . . It seems they want us to be Bolsheviks. At the rate we are treated, it won't take long."

As the Germans retreated under heavy fire, Kielmeyer began to feel himself to be *Kanonenfutter*, cannon fodder for the Fatherland. He could sense the hatred of the Belgian people as the army fell back. "How hostile they are," he wrote. "They are trying to kill us with their eyes. Would they like to fight? We are fully armed and anxious to leave their land as soon as we can."

To the German general staff, the war was not supposed to end with its army beating a retreat to a homeland slipping into chaos. Less than eight months before Armistice Day, the army had stood at the gates of victory.

MARCH 1918. General Ludendorff had seized upon a convergence of events to fashion a masterful offensive. For three and a half years, Germany, through miscalculation and thwarted objectives, had become locked into the very fate she had most hoped to escape, a two-front war. The Germans had struck France in August 1914 to knock this foe out of the fray before turning east to defeat the greater threat, Russia. But France had not folded, and instead Germany had found herself caught between adversaries. Then, in March 1917, Czar Nicholas II, buffeted by food shortages, soaring inflation, battlefield defeats, and mounting revolution, abdicated, ending the three-hundred-year-old Romanov dynasty. Russia's armies, plagued by indiscipline, desertion, and catastrophic losses, continued to fall apart. By November, Bolshevik revolutionaries had seized power and had begun armistice negotiations with Germany. Russia, effectively, was out of the war. Her removal from the field meant that thirty-three German divisions, some 400,000 men, could be pulled from the east and sent west. The Americans were not yet ready for battle, and Germany, for the moment, could amass a decisive manpower superiority on the western front. Thus a scheme that had been long simmering in Ludendorff's imagination began to take on fine detail. The de facto leader of the German Army was certain he could beat the exhausted French. But the British would still prosecute the land war, and her naval blockade would continue to starve Germany. How long the wobbling Austria-Hungary could be counted on as an ally was uncertain. The immediate solution, Ludendorff told his staff, was obvious: "We must beat the British." The key was to exploit contradictory British and French objectives. The BEF's priority was to hold on to the French ports through which its manpower and resupply flowed. The French saw Paris as the keystone holding up their nation. In effect, the two Allies' priorities pointed in opposite directions, one toward the sea, the other toward the French heartland. Ludendorff intended to break the linkage at the junction where French and British forces hinged, south of Ypres. Once this was accomplished, he could then reach his arm around the British forces in the north of France, take the Channel ports, and shove Haig's army southward in a final crushing embrace. By March 3, the Russian revolutionary government had signed the humiliating peace treaty of Brest-Litovsk, which cost the country Ukraine, Poland, the Baltic provinces, and other chunks of the czar's empire. To Ludendorff, the time had come to strike hard in the west. He intended first to hit General Sir Julian Byng's Third Army and General Sir Hubert Gough's Fifth Army with sixty-three German divisions, knowing that the most the enemy could muster was twenty-six divisions.

An assault on so grand a scale, bruited about for months, had inevitably lost the element of surprise. Haig and Pétain knew an attack was coming, but they knew not where or when. Haig faced a vexing decision. On March 16, his wife had given birth to a son, whom he was eager to see. On March 20, he wrote Lady Haig, "The enemy is rather threatening for the moment. I therefore think that it will be better for me to delay coming over to see you for a week." He had, however, found something to console her with: "The cook is making some soup for you, and I am arranging to send it by King's messenger on Friday."

Lloyd George would not have minded if Haig had come home and stayed there. The prime minister still looked upon the field marshal as a bungler and fought against sending him the additional troops he continually demanded. Yet Lloyd George dared not sack him. Haig had powerful conservative friends and a heroic image with the public, he remained a favorite of King George, and his wife had been a popular maid of honor to Queen Alexandra. Lloyd George was not alone in his lack of enthusiasm for the BEF commander. After a meeting with Haig in March, General Sir Henry Wilson, the chief of the imperial general staff, wrote in his diary, "I have never seen him so stupid and unaccommodating. He is a remarkably stupid, narrow, prejudiced, insular person."

ERNST KIELMEYER KNEW that something serious was brewing when the wire man found himself assigned to an artillery battery early in 1918. On March 12, the artillerymen were given twenty-nine horses to haul the guns forward, and Kielmeyer wrote in his diary that it "can only mean an offensive." The next day a friend, Albert Stegmaier, was picked off by a British sniper, and Kielmeyer wondered how many more friends a grand-scale assault would cost him.

Nine days later, on March 21 at 4:40 A.M., Kielmeyer was jolted awake by a stupendous roar, his ear telling him that the batteries were firing 30.5 mm Austrian Moerser shells. "That is the signal to start the slaughter," he concluded. Soon his own battery commenced its role, sending two hundred gas shells against the enemy lines. The green shells, fired first, were tear gas intended to drive the British into tearing off their masks. The blue shells, fired second, discharged phosgene gas, expected to kill the British once they were unprotected.

Kielmeyer was a cog in an enterprise marshaling three German armies—more than a million men—poised along fifty miles of northern France stretching from Arras southward to Saint-Quentin and La Fère. The cannonade from 6,473 guns and 3,532 mortars, drawing on dumps piled with more than a million rounds, shook the ground with seismic force. The seemingly unsurpassable bombardments of the Somme and Passchendaele had been dwarfed. The shelling strategy was the product of Germany's artillery genius, Lieutenant Colonel Georg Bruchmüller, known as "Durchbruchmüller," Breakthrough Bruchmüller. The artillery officer had mastered the technique of firing accurately in the dark by registering the guns beforehand, that is, determining the variance in each gun for barometric pressure, wind speed, and direction. The artillery could thus fire unceasingly both day and night prior to an attack.

A British private with the West Yorkshires, T. Jacobs, described experiencing Breakthrough Bruchmüller's ingenuity: "you can't put a lot of resistance up. . . . On the other fronts I had been on, there had been so much of our resistance that, whenever Jerry opened up, our artillery opened up and quieted him down but there was no retaliating this time. He had a free do at us." Psychologically, too, the Germans had the best of it. Stress and mental breakdown occurred far more often among defenders under relentless shelling impotently waiting out their fate. Contrarily, neurosis dropped off sharply among men making the attack.

During the bombardment, Lance Corporal William Sharpe was keeping an eye on four replacements just arrived, the eldest aged eighteen, all undergoing fire for the first time. "They cried and one kept calling 'mother' and who could blame him," Sharpe recalled. "Such HELL makes weaklings of the strongest and no human's nerves were ever built to stand such torture, noise, horror and mental pain." A shell went off with such force that Sharpe's trench collapsed. He pulled himself from the debris and looked around vainly for the four youths. He dug furiously into the earth with his bare hands, but they had disappeared.

Watching the grand spectacle from a panoramic vantage point on high ground stood Kaiser Wilhelm II. Officially the offensive had been designated Operation Michael. But, to the emperor's delight, it soon became *die Kaiserschlacht,* "the Kaiser's Battle."

Ernst Jünger, now a company commander serving with the 73rd Hanoverian Fusiliers, stood among the men waiting to attack. Jünger remembered all too well the unnerving sensation during bombardment that the shell that was going to blow him to pieces might already be in the air. Though now on the delivering end of the shelling, he was nevertheless on edge. He tried to light a cigar to appear cool before his men, but the air currents produced by the guns kept blowing out the flame. His orderly handed him a canteen of whiskey, from which he took a long pull that went down like water. At 4:40 A.M., Jünger drew his revolver from his holster and trotted to the head of his company, a bamboo riding crop planted under his arm. As he described the moment, "The overpowering desire to kill winged my feet. Rage squeezed bitter tears from my eyes." Soon a gray mass rose from the German trenches and began flowing forward. Jünger's company stumbled over bomb-pitted ground in a thick fog that abetted Ludendorff's advantage of surprise. Jünger found himself moving among smashed, abandoned dugouts inside the British lines. He encountered his first enemy face-to-face, a wounded Tommy lying on the ground. Jünger pressed his revolver against the man's temple. The trembling soldier pulled a photograph of a woman and children from his breast pocket and thrust it before Jünger. Jünger had come to respect the Tommy as a lionhearted fighter, but here was no lion. The German withdrew his weapon. He could not shoot a man in front of his family.

NOTHING SINCE THE First Marne of 1914 had matched Ludendorff's audacity. The British Third and Fifth Armies linked between Bapaume and Péronne broke according to plan. Over the next two days, German divisions drove the Allies back twelve miles on a front twenty-five miles wide. All the paltry gains at Passchendaele, for which the British had paid so dearly four months before, were lost and another 38,000 casualties added. A shocking 21,000 Tommies surrendered. The Germans had taken even more casualties, but the day's work allowed a beaming Kaiser Wilhelm to return from his perch above the battlefield and announce to his headquarters, "Gentlemen, a great victory." The father of the victory, Ludendorff, proclaimed, "The English Army suffered the greatest defeat in British history. . . . What the English and French had not succeeded in doing we had accomplished, and that in the fourth year of the war."

Men participating at a less lofty vantage point were already at work preparing for the next day. The men in Ernst Kielmeyer's battery had fired off five hundred rounds, sweating so furiously that some worked shirtless in the cool March air. The locks had become so thickened with soot that they had to be scoured to bare metal so that the guns could be fired again in the morning. Bone-weary artillerymen spent the night lugging empty shell cases to the rear and hauling new rounds up to the batteries. Before collapsing in sleep, Kielmeyer described in his diary the appearance of both guns and men: "Just one color, black."

Ludendorff pressed on, and within six days his armies had advanced forty miles and inflicted 240,000 casualties on the British. The victory, however, continued to exact a high price for the Germans as well. Among the dead was Ludendorff's youngest stepson, also named Erich, killed on the second day of the battle when his plane went down. On the night before the offensive, young Ludendorff had written his mother that his dream was also to become a general, but on his own merit. He bitterly resented, he said, whispers that he would succeed because, "naturally, he is Ludendorff's son." The flier was subsequently buried alongside another, older stepson who had already died for the Fatherland.

On April 9, Ludendorff launched a second offensive, and twelve days later Germany lost its most glittering air hero, Rittmeister Baron Manfred von Richthofen, the Red Baron, as he was known for the color of his plane. Richthofen had won for the squadron of Fokkers he commanded the name "Flying Circus" for its speed in getting planes, tents, and equipment swiftly from base to base. The twenty-six-year-old Richthofen was idolized even by men who had to watch his aerial wizardry from the muck of the trenches. Lieutenant Rudolf Binding recalled an earlier visit to Richthofen's quarters, where the flier had shown him his prize possession, the machine gun of an English flier who had shot down thirty-two Germans. "He shows it off as a sportsman might show the head of a stag," Binding recalled. For all his luster, Richthofen was not universally admired in the chivalrous fraternity that bound airmen on all sides. He was seen as a strutting Prussian who, it was rumored, may have inflated his claim of eighty kills.

Downing Richthofen was first credited to Captain Ray Brown, a Sopwith Camel pilot with the newly independent Royal Air Force. Actually, Richthofen, flying close to the ground in pursuit of his eighty-first kill, was shot down by antiaircraft fire from an Australian machine-gun company. RAF fliers who recovered his body treated the air ace with elaborate ceremony. A wreath placed on his coffin read, "To our gallant and worthy foe." Six British pilots served as pallbearers, and the Red Baron was lowered into his grave to a fourteen-gun salute.

Flying still cast its spell. The death of the Red Baron, if anything, inspired Lieutenant Herbert Sulzbach. The day after Richthofen's burial he wrote in his diary, "My old enthusiasm for flying is starting up again. . . . Curiously, though I feel moved every time an air hero dies, I just couldn't imagine what it would be like if it happened to me." But it had happened to Sulzbach's closest companion. It was shortly after Richthofen's death that he learned Kurt Reinhardt's plane had gone down. Still, death was death, ever present, and to Sulzbach there was scant preference between being blown apart on the ground and being shot out of the sky.

MASS SURRENDER OF British troops was safer than men giving up singly or in small groups. The interval between being a fighter and becoming a prisoner could be the most dangerous a soldier faced. Despite the fact that Hague Convention Regulation 23(c) forbade executing prisoners, shooting them, especially when they were few in number, had a brutal battlefield logic. Sending men to take a handful of prisoners to the rear in the heat of battle meant reducing one's own strength. Lugging wounded prisoners to aid stations drew off even more manpower. Shooting POWs, however, had its downside: the enemy forces would likely return the favor or, expecting to be killed, become less inclined to give up.

Surrendering also raised risks from one's own side. During the heat of Ludendorff's first advance, some British units had retreated pell-mell before the field gray avalanche, littering the ground with jettisoned weapons. Lieutenant Colonel Graham Seton Hutchinson spotted forty men preparing to give up and shot thirty-eight of them. "Such an action," Hutchinson observed, "will in a short time spread like dry rot through an army and it is one of those dire military necessities which calls for immediate and prompt action." As one wry observer put it, "Had he shot two men and inspired thirty-eight, there would have been greater logic in his action. To shoot thirty-eight and inspire two does not make any sense."

Corporal Adolf Hitler distinguished himself by capturing prisoners during the Ludendorff offensive. Armed only with a pistol, Hitler is supposed to have shouted with such authority to the French opposite him that four of them came forward, hands up, fearing that they faced an entire company. Hitler led them back to his regimental commander, Colonel von Tubeuf, who commended the runner for again "volunteering for the most difficult, arduous and dangerous tasks." For this and earlier feats Hitler was decorated with the Iron Cross, First Class. Iron Crosses, Second Class, were handed out almost as freely as field rations in some units. But First Class, the highest medal eligible to enlisted men, was not awarded casually. The decoration was recommended by and presented to Hitler by his battalion adjutant, Hugo Guttmann.

Guttmann, a Jew, must have been outstanding to have risen so high. Rudolf Binding recalled the commanding general of his brigade once looking for an aide-de-camp. Binding had sent him Lance Sergeant Koch. Within weeks, the general put Koch up for an Iron Cross and told Binding that so intelligent, able, personable, and physically impressive a man—and a good horseman to boot—must not "run around any longer without the silver epaulettes of an officer." Binding prepared the necessary paperwork and set it before his superior. All went well until the general reached the question "Religion," to which Koch had answered, "Hebrew." The general became apoplectic. Koch's application must be withdrawn immediately, he said. The matter dragged on for days, during which time the once model aide was now found by the general to have "unbearable Jewish qualities—only Jewish qualities in fact." Binding himself believed that Jews, because of inbreeding, were unfit officer material. Yet he recognized in Koch an exception and dared argue with the general that since Koch was a Jew, why would he have any other than Jewish qualities? The general, thrown by this logic, reluctantly signed the application.

LUDENDORFF'S SUCCESS ON the western front was mirrored in the Balkans. By May 7, the Central Powers had knocked an Allied nation out of the war. Romania surrendered. Her dreams of profiting from the war lay reduced to ashes. Instead of gaining territory, some 80 percent of the country fell under enemy occupation. Proportionate to population, the Romanians suffered the highest casualties of any belligerent: 219,000 dead, tens of thousands perishing in POW camps, and another 120,000 wounded.

For all the ground gained, one of Ludendorff's two objectives had not succeeded: his troops had not smashed through to the coast to drive the British from the Channel ports. Still, the Allies had paid a stiff price to thwart him. Gough's Fifth Army of fifteen divisions, which had guarded the hinge between British and French troops, was no more, with whole elements destroyed, the remnants handed to another force, and Gough sacked. The ports had been denied, but the way south was now open to sweep to the Marne and take Paris. The French capital may not have fallen to the Schlieffen strategy in 1914, but Germany was getting a second chance. With the head severed, the body must fall, Ludendorff reasoned, and the war would be won.

The people of Paris had recently received a foretaste of conflict firsthand. In a wood outside the city of Laon, the Krupp Works had unveiled its latest weapon, the "Paris gun," a monstrous affair with a barrel rising to the height of a ten-story building. Two days into Ludendorff's offensive, the first six Paris guns began lofting shells twenty-five miles into the atmosphere that in less than three minutes fell on the French capital, seventy-five miles distant. Over the next several weeks, the guns sowed panic in the capital. But the nightmare was short-lived. After only forty-five firings the colossal barrels were worn useless. Some 256 Parisians were killed, and the guns were more damaging to the city's sense of security than to its survival.

Despite Ludendorff's early momentum, Allied reinforcements managed to halt his armies before the Marne. The interval gave the Allies a breathing spell in which to correct a failing that had plagued them from the war's outset. Since December 1916, Ferdinand Foch had been vegetating in semiretirement, the penalty for the staggering casualties his earlier leadership had cost France. Foch now had an unlikely champion, the usually domineering Douglas Haig. The German sweep and the threat to Paris had made abundantly clear to Haig that the defensive mind-set of the current

French commander, Henri Pétain, was unsuitable. And so at a hurried meeting at Beauvais on April 3, the British, French, and Americans signed an agreement giving Foch "all powers necessary" to coordinate their forces. By April 14, the vague role of coordinator was dropped and Foch formally became Allied commander in chief on the western front. Haig had championed his rival for practical reasons. Spine had to be restored to the French Army if the German tide were to be reversed. And Foch, whatever his other failings, had a backbone of steel.

The feisty seventy-six-year-old French premier, Georges Clemenceau, was delighted to have an equally pugnacious Frenchman running the war. Though a Socialist, Clemenceau had drawn support from right and left when, in November 1917, the nation sought a warrior to direct a war. "The Tiger," as he was aptly named, had paid a visit to the American lines early in 1918 and immediately captivated Major General Bullard, then commanding the 1st Infantry Division. Struck by the American's full name, Robert Lee Bullard, Clemenceau recounted how he had been a country school teacher in Virginia and had watched General Grant's army march into Richmond in 1865. He had also once been married to an American. His hero, Clemenceau said, was Andrew Jackson, to which Bullard replied that he saw a strong resemblance in the characters of the Tiger and Old Hickory. Visibly pleased, Clemenceau replied, "Perhaps, but I never fought a duel on horseback."

Just before Foch became the Allied commander, Clemenceau visited the front with Winston Churchill, now Britain's minister of munitions. They toured Amiens, the key rail junction joining the British and French forces, before which the Ludendorff offensive had been halted. The French leader, cloaked in a black cape, and the Englishman, sporting a trilby hat, fed on each other's indomitability. When they later returned to the Ministry of War in Paris, Clemenceau told Churchill, "I will fight in front of Paris; I will fight in Paris; I will fight behind Paris." The pledge suggests the roots of Churchill's pledge twenty-two years later when Britain stood in similarly desperate straits: "We shall fight on the beaches, we shall fight on the landing grounds, we shall fight in the fields and in the streets, we shall fight in the hills; we shall never surrender."

Haig realized that he also had to stiffen the spine of his own battered forces as they fell back before the second Ludendorff offensive. In April he issued an order "To All Ranks of the British Army in France and Flanders." Despite the appearance of defeat, he stressed that the Germans had failed in their objectives to divide British and French forces and take the Channel ports. Yet the peril of the moment could not be denied. "There is no course open to us but to fight it out," Haig declared with Nelsonian grit. "Every position must be held to the last man; there must be no retirement with our backs to the wall and believing in the justice of our cause each of us must fight on to the end." His words electrified his countrymen. Even Vera Brittain, whom the war had caused such grief, was moved by Haig's call to exclaim, "After I had read it I knew that I should go on, whether I could or not. There was a braver spirit in the hospital that afternoon." However, in the British trenches, the image of Haig fighting from his château headquarters with his "back to the wall" provoked good-natured derision.

THE REASON WHY Ludendorff's seemingly unstoppable offensive had stalled was not immediately apparent to the Allies but was becoming obvious to frontline German officers. Amiens was just miles away, its cathedral clearly visible to the attackers. German airmen reported no enemy troops there and only the most sporadic artillery fire from in front of the city. Amiens had been expected to fall like a ripe fruit. Yet it had not fallen. The offensive, quite literally, had run out of gas. And there was another reason. Lieutenant Rudolf Binding was dispatched by his commanding officer to find out what had halted the momentum. Binding took a staff car to nearby Albert, which the Germans had captured. "I began to see curious sights," he recalled. "Strange figures, which looked very little like soldiers, certainly showed no sign of advancing." He watched in disbelief as men draped in looted curtains, sporting top hats, carrying chickens under their arms, and driving cows through the streets reeled drunkenly past him. He turned into one alley to find it running red with wine and demanded to know of an officer emerging from a wine cellar what was going on. To which the officer answered, "I cannot get my men out of this cellar without bloodshed." When Binding insisted that he order his men back to the fight, the officer walked off, suggesting that Binding try himself. Discipline was similarly cracking all along the front. Beneath the surface disarray lay a darker truth. The *Feldgrauen* had been led to believe that U-boats had destroyed Allied supply lines and that the enemy was about to fold under the Kaiser Battle. But as they overran the enemy positions, they knew they had been lied to. Stocks of food, drink, and munitions were mountainous. The exhausted, half-starved Germans thus threw discipline to the winds and indulged in an orgy of drunkenness and gluttony. The strongest army on the western front had begun to unravel.

By April 29, Ludendorff's advance had ground to a halt. For all its initial successes, the price had been exorbitant: 50,000 Germans killed and 350,000 wounded in just a month. Yet the general remained convinced that his armies had merely paused and that total victory still lay within his grasp. Discipline, of course, must be restored and overextended supply lines consolidated. But beyond the Marne, just fifty-five miles distant, the prize of Paris still beckoned. He began planning the next drive for May 27, less than a month away. Ludendorff would not accept that he was repeating the delusions of Joffre, Haig, and Nivelle, whose offensives had brought not victory but fleeting gains and ultimate stalemate at horrendous cost. Both sides had become gamblers, afraid to leave the table, believing the next turn of the cards could produce victory.

21

"A German Bullet Is
Cleaner Than a Whore"

APRIL 1918. While the opposing armies were inflicting a half-million casualties on each other at Albert, Saint-Quentin, Soissons, Armentières, and a half dozen other battlefields of the Ludendorff offensives, AEF doughboys continued to flood into France to begin their apprenticeship in the mechanics of killing. By the spring, troop transports disgorged 12,000 to 15,000 healthy young Americans at French ports nearly every other day. The money in their pockets would have been paltry back home. But compared to *poilus* earning a quarter of a franc per day in a country where an egg cost one franc, the doughboys were rich. Soldiers debarking at Saint-Nazaire spent two weeks in port being processed, during which time they spent so freely that one madam was depositing $15,000 in her bank account every month.

Since most of their men were not likely to see France again, senior officers wanted them to have the opportunity to experience the cultural attractions of Paris. The plan first tried was to truck in an unlimited number of soldiers to enjoy a tour of the city's highlights. Along with the edification, this approach was expected to cut down on the alarming number of doughboys going AWOL to experience Paris on their own. General Foch objected vehemently to General Pershing, insisting that "large numbers of American soldiers not be allowed to visit Paris because of the already over-crowded conditions . . . and because from the very fact of their extreme popularity, their easygoing ways, and their unfailing gen-erosity, they would find themselves exposed in this city, more than ever, to exploitations which the French authorities, ambitious for the good reputation of Paris, wish to avoid." In short, keep the doughboys out and the prostitution and venereal disease down. In the end, a compromise was reached: three-day passes but issued to a sharply limited number of men.

The War Department launched an educational campaign of as-tonishing bluntness to protect the men from their folly. One poster proclaimed, "A German bullet is cleaner than a whore." Another asked, "You wouldn't use another man's toothbrush. Why use his whore?" The French and British authorities chose to accept rather than resist human nature, the former by sanctioning approved brothels, the latter by keeping their eyes half closed. Every British base could be counted on to have its semiofficial bordello servicing Tommies from 6 P.M. to 8 P.M., with military police keeping the queues orderly. The going rate was two francs, though the madams soon learned that they could extract up to thirty francs from the better-paid troops from Canada, Australia, New Zealand, and the United States.

The Americans continued to try to eliminate rather than regu-late vice. Private Joe Rizzi had been shamed by his girl into enlist-ing in the 35th Division, and he missed her sorely. Still, the good-looking, virile Rizzi hungered for companionship. He bri-dled at the fact that in the French town where his 110th Engineers were posted, the YMCA maintained a restaurant where officers monopolized "American nurses, pretty, trim and full of life." Yet military police were posted outside houses of prostitution to block enlisted men even from paying for their pleasures. "So, instead of helping us as they thought they were doing," Rizzi complained, "they drove the men to the places where there were no health in-spections and the consequences of a ruined life!"

Arrivals from the New World discovered that French attitudes toward sex were earthier than back home. Will Bird, who had learned the facts of life working with rough characters on the Canadian prairie, found that the French could still surprise him. Early in his service, he was sitting in the kitchen of the house where he was billeted, chatting with the owner, when she began filling a tin washtub with water. While questioning Bird about life in Canada, she "began stripping off her clothes. Soon she was naked and standing in the tub." His astonishment grew when the daughter, a sooty coal miner, arrived home, undressed, and joined her mother in the tub. "Before I had finished," Bird recalled, "father arrived, stood in the tub, and was scrubbed by Madame."

Bird's education was further advanced the next day when an attractive girl passed by the house, drawing whistles and shouts from his comrades. Bird's landlady told them, "You waste your time. That is the priest's girl." The disbelieving Canadians pointed out that priests were celibate. "Stupid," she replied, "she is his girl, she sleeps with him." Furthermore, she added, it was a great honor for the girl and her family, especially since she had lasted eight months while ordinarily the priest changed mistresses every two or three months.

Eighteen-year-old Arthur Jensen, now a wagon driver, a "mule skinner," remembered how his mother back in Lowell, Nebraska, had tried to block his enlistment, warning her son that he was "still wet behind the ears." But Jensen's first sight in France, a trainload of wounded British soldiers, quickly taught him the fragility of life where he was headed. He too had a girl back home, his Eva, but found it increasingly difficult to suppress his carnal impulses. Off duty for the first time in a small French town, he and a pal were wandering the streets when a small boy came up and offered his sister for "*jig-a-jig, très bon.*" Jensen declined, but his companion went off with the boy. On his return, an hour later, the friend described the experience to Jensen. He had been taken to a shabby one-room house where the father, mother, and an eighteen-year-old daughter were sitting. The mother had drawn a dirty curtain across the room to give the soldier and the girl privacy. On the doughboy's way out, the mother collected the money.

For all his small-town roots, Jensen came to display considerable maturity about the mores of the host country. He wrote in a "War Log" he had started, "most of the Americans mistake the frank attitude of the French people on matters of sex for vulgarity. . . . Some of the boys say there isn't a decent woman in France while the rest of us argue that there are as many good women in France in proportion to the population as in America. Here if you ask a decent French woman to go to bed with you, she'll politely say no, and instead of being insulted, will tell you where to go to get what you want—always keeping herself above reproach. Ordinarily we get acquainted with the lowest class here just as we did around Ft. Leavenworth or Kansas City." He recalled back at Leavenworth a pal showing him an ugly eruption on his genitals, explaining that he had caught "a dose of sif. I got it off a wench in Kansas City. . . . And I'm engaged to the sweetest little girl in the world back home. . . . So it's my contention," Jensen concluded, "that we can't judge the women of France by the scum we meet around here." As for French frankness, Jensen believed, "Their young people will grow up more able to intelligently meet the sex problem which perplexes Americans so much."

He did become involved while posted in the town of Saint-Dié with "Andrée, age sixteen—one of the cleanest, sweetest, most wholesome girls I have seen anywhere," whose father owned the local textile mill. After a summer of long walks, picnics, and learning French from the girl, Jensen was ordered to the front. "I had been kidding Andrée about taking her to America after the war; so last night she said she had asked her folks and they said she could go," he wrote in the War Log. "I didn't realize she had been taking me seriously. It hurt me to think I had deceived someone who had such confidence in me. I wasn't ready to get married. What would I tell Eva? What would my folks say?" He found a solution. "I told her if the 'Boche' didn't finish me, I'd be back." He would write Andrée a few times, then stop to "let her think I was killed; which is what I feel I deserve."

Not only callow Americans suffered pangs of conscience. Herbert Sulzbach, of the good German Jewish banking family, could sound like a guilt-ridden schoolboy. After a spree in Brussels, Sulz-bach wrote in his diary that though it had been marvelous to escape the front briefly, "you still feel disgusted with it when it's all over, and long for the German style of being clean, I mean thinking in a clean way."

The American army continued to try to regulate the doughboys' conduct, and the men continued to behave like soldiers ever since the armies of Alexander. One order coming down from an AEF division headquarters displayed exquisite military logic: "Officers are not permitted to be seen in public with women of bad reputation; and a woman of bad reputation will be considered to be any woman who may be seen in public with an officer."

Coming from a land where the forces of prohibition were already on the march and destined within a year to succeed, the doughboy was denied even a bracing shot of whiskey at the front. The Big Red One's commander, Robert Lee Bullard, a tough old frontier Indian fighter, ridiculed the ban. The French and British issued wine or liquor to their troops, "who could not have continued the war without it," Bullard observed. "It consoled, cheered and braced them for their hardships and labors. . . . It gave them physical courage to face death in the fearful 'jump-off.' " Americans served alongside French soldiers who maintained, *"Pas de pinard, pas de soldat"*—no wine, no soldier. Though forced to abstain at the front, the men compensated when off duty. An officer with the judge advocate general's branch wrote home, "It's hard to convict officers of drunkenness. There is sympathy for them, especially if they are young and come to headquarters after a hell of a time in the trenches. . . . At the same time, it is destructive of discipline to have them drunk in the street and all the enlisted men laughing at them."

The doughboys went on drinking, fracturing the French language—"Jenny's pa" for *"Je ne sais pas,"* teaching girls obscene American phrases while claiming they meant "How do you do" or "Nice to meet you," and concocting endless ribald verses to their favorite song, "Mademoiselle from Armentières." Perceptive officers understood that high-minded behavior and good soldiering did not necessarily go hand in hand. British captain James Agate set down observations that could apply to all armies in all ages: "The man who enlists for his sweet country's sake is a bit of a nuisance. The fellow who does it for a lark, or because everybody else is enlisting, or for a jumble of reasons, or for no reason at all, is the man we want most." What made good soldiers, Agate concluded, was "1) Good feet, 2) Good digestions, 3) Good teeth, 4) A sense of humor, and 5) Strong appetites of all sorts." "The more ribald the song," Agate added, "the shorter the march." One mindless popular ditty that the Tommies sang while marching reflected Agate's point:

> Wash me in the water that you
> Washed your dirty daughter in
> And I shall be whiter than the
> Whitewash on the wall.

22

Baptism in Cantigny

NOVEMBER 11, 1918. General Hay faced the situation an officer dreads most, interpreting unclear orders upon which the lives of his men rested. William H. Hay, age fifty-eight, West Point class of 1886, had come halfway around the world to enter this fight after commanding a cavalry unit in the Philippines. He had received his first star just eleven months before and been given command of the 28th Infantry, the "Keystone" Division of Pennsylvanians, only eighteen days previously. Since the previous morning, the 28th had been in action in the AEF's southernmost sector, some fifteen miles southeast of Verdun. The division had taken the town of Haumont and was advancing against stubborn resistance along the shallow banks of Lake Lachaussée. During the night, Hay moved up reinforcements to continue the assault the following morning. Just before 8:30 A.M., he was informed that the armistice had been signed and was to take effect at 11 A.M. At this point, his forward regiments were nearing the German line, with some men already inside the enemy wire. Knowing that the fighting would end in two and a half hours, Hay found himself in a decisional no-man's-land. The attack order in force since the day before had not been rescinded. Should he fight on? Should he stop? What he decided would affect the fate of more than 28,000 men under him in a division that had already suffered 2,874 killed and more than 11,000 wounded since it had gone into action six months before. Hay concluded that he could order his division to cease fire only at 11 A.M., and he began putting the word out by telephone and runners.

The attack under way had been spearheaded by Hay's 55th Brigade under Brigadier General Frederic D. Evans. General Evans, a fifty-two-year-old Illinoisan and, like his superior, a West Pointer and Philippine veteran, had been pushing the brigade toward the town of Lachaussée, on the northeastern edge of the lake. Evans too had learned that the armistice had been signed and at that point checked with Hay to ask what he should do in the time left. As he recalled that moment, "The division commander definitely ordered me not to stop the fight, until I heard from him or until one minute of eleven." And so, for Evans's men, the war went on.

In the time remaining, Lieutenant Francis Reed Austin led a platoon against a German position defended by ten machine guns. Austin's force was driven back and the lieutenant wounded seriously. He nevertheless continued to direct the evacuation of other wounded men before letting the medics treat him.

At 9:15 A.M., Evans received another call from Hay, one that filled him with relief. Hay had no authority to stop the fighting but had decided to stick his neck out. He made the decision, he said, because "I felt, since the Armistice had already been signed . . . that no good could be accomplished by continuing the attack but that if it were continued I would sacrifice the lives of hundreds, perhaps thousands, of my men and accomplish nothing except the gain of a few hundred meters of territory." He ordered Evans "to hold all ground already taken but to make no further advance." Hay, so briefly in command of the division and knowing he potentially faced a charge of insubordination, informed his superior, General Bullard, now commanding the Second Army, of what he had done, ready to face the consequences. To his surprise, his decision was not countermanded. Evidently, in Bullard's Second Army, commanders had the unspoken choice to end the war immediately for the men under them or keep fighting.

Besides breaking off the advance, General Evans recalled, "I stopped our machine gun and artillery fire in hope that the enemy would do likewise. This he did," he noted happily. But Hay, though he had halted the attack, ordered Evans to resume firing his artillery. Evans protested that this would only invite retaliation. He was overruled, and his guns began again. The Germans, with fifty minutes now left in the war, returned fire. Evans's men continued taking fatal casualties, including Lieutenant Austin, whose wounds proved mortal.

MAY 1918. The AEF's involvement in the war had not begun in earnest until May, when the earliest-arriving Yanks had already been in France for eleven months. The first American artillery shell had been fired at 6:05 on the morning of October 23, 1917. The French 75 mm gun that the Americans used lofted a shell five thousand yards toward a German battery concealed behind a village called Réchicourt. One artilleryman recalled, "We never knew just what damage, if any, the first shot wrought." The Americans had occasionally suffered battle deaths, the first being the losses of Enright, Gresham, and Hays in the Vosges sector in November 1917, but nothing remotely resembling the bloodbaths of Verdun or Passchendaele. An American unit conducted a tyro raid on March 9, 1918, at the Salient du Feys, led by a thirty-eight-year-old West Pointer conspicuous for his appearance. He wore no steel helmet, only a visored cap with the wire removed, letting it drape over his brow at a rakish angle. He wore a sweater with a black "A" for "Army" knitted into the front, awarded to him at the academy. Wound around his neck was a four-foot-long muffler knitted by his mother. His riding breeches, even in the trenches, remained immaculate, and his boots possessed a mirror-like sheen. He was Douglas MacArthur, first in the West Point graduating class of 1903, who had originated the 42nd Division's popular designation, the "Rainbow," in which he now served as chief of staff with the rank of colonel. The raid's objective was to capture prisoners for interrogation. The tactic was old hat to French and British troops, who accepted that invariably a raid cost a few men killed, occasionally many. Without bothering to inform the division's commanding officer, Major General Charles T. Menoher, MacArthur decided to lead the raid himself, a mission below his pay grade by at least three ranks. As the men waited for the signal to go over the top, another officer turned and asked MacArthur why he was not in regulation dress. "It's the orders you disobey," he replied, "that make you famous." As soon as MacArthur's party exited the trenches, the Germans sensed something was afoot and opened up with their artillery. MacArthur strode before his men, armed only with a riding crop, a cigarette holder clamped jauntily between his teeth, without the slightest suggestion in bearing or movement that he was under fire.

The raid was a marginal success, with several casualties taken and one German officer captured. MacArthur's bravado was not universally applauded. His peers saw him as an exhibitionist obsessed with drawing attention to himself. MacArthur countered that he did not want his men to think he would ever send them on a mission he would not undertake himself. Further, he wanted the Germans to understand that American officers were not headquarters-bound but had the guts to lead.

The MacArthur of 1918 was almost unrecognizable from the remote godlike figure who would emerge in the Pacific in the next war. In 1918, because of rapid promotion, he was closer in age to the men than were most high-ranking officers. He deliberately shared the doughboys' discomforts and dangers. He encouraged them to call him "Buddy." The men idolized him. A fellow officer wrote of MacArthur that it was "hard for me to conceive of this sensitive, high-strung personage slogging in the mud, enduring filth, living in stinking clothing and crawling over jagged soil under criss-crosses of barbed wire." But to a military romantic like MacArthur, the mud and filth of the trench lent the war a heroic nimbus.

THE FABLED FIGHTING 69th had been formally redesignated the 165th Infantry Regiment within the Rainbow Division in order to fit into the army's table of organization, though the old name stuck. The unit was led by Colonel Frank McCoy, but its most vivid member remained the 1st Battalion's commander, William J. Donovan. The 165th had been training in France since November 1917. There Donovan earned a reputation as a hard-charging leader, sensitive to his men's needs but intolerant of slackness. Lieutenant Colonel Hugh Ogden, like Donovan a lawyer in civilian life, described meeting "a bully fellow at the mess the last two days, Major Donovan. . . . He's a corker, enthusiastic and efficient, takes his men out on cross country runs, etc. and is a live wire generally."

The regiment's chaplain, Father Francis Duffy, stopped by Donovan's headquarters one day to find the major outside forming up his men for a run. The priest kept himself out of sight until Donovan disappeared, leading the battalion over rusted barbed wire, half-collapsed trenches, and fields littered with the detritus of battle. On their return, a seemingly unwinded Donovan, spotting the chaplain, called out, "Father, why didn't you get here earlier? You missed a fine time." To which Duffy replied, "My guardian angel was taking good care of me, William, and saw to it I got here late."

Donovan's chronic exuberance wore the priest down, but the man's gift of leadership was undeniable. In March 1918, the 165th was at the front, in the Lunéville sector, undergoing its first bombardment. A *Minenwerfer* shell landed on top of a bunker, shattering the supporting beams and sending rock and clay cascading into the cavity. Beneath the rubble twenty-five men of Company E lay trapped. Donovan rushed to the scene and found soldiers digging with entrenching tools, bayonets, and bare hands trying desperately to reach the men crying out beneath the rubble. He quickly grasped that the shelling likely presaged an attack and that the rescuers had left a sector exposed. Donovan broke them into two groups, one to continue digging; the rest, led by the soldier he considered the coolest in the battalion, seventeen-year-old "Little

Eddy" Kelly, he ordered to return to the line and plug the gap. It proved too late for the men in the collapsed bunker and a shell killed Kelly, for a toll of twenty-five dead in the battalion's introduction to fire.

On Saint Patrick's Day, Father Duffy, standing on a hillside dotted with birches, said Mass for the fallen. He reminded the men of what the Irish would be doing back in New York on this day and then echoed Henry V at Agincourt. They were better off in the battlefields of France, he said. "Every man in the town would be saying he wished he were here and every man worth his salt would mean it." They had answered the call "to fight for human liberty and the rights of small nations," earning a permanent claim on their country's gratitude. With mass over, the chaplain recited a poem entitled "Rouge Bouquet," written by a sergeant named Joyce Kilmer. Duffy had placed one bugler alongside him and another off in the distance. As he read, the buglers alternately sounded the phrases of "Taps," creating an echo effect:

> In a wood they call the Rouge Bouquet,
> There is a new made grave today,
> Built by never a spade or pick,
> Yet covered with earth ten meters thick,
> There lie many fighting men
> Dead in their youth prime.
> Never to laugh or love again,
> Nor taste the summer time.

Duffy watched men brush tears aside. Then, in a quick shift of tempo, he signaled the regimental band to strike up a medley of rollicking tunes, "Gary Owen," "Let Erin Remember," and "O'Donnell Aboo." "It is the only spirit for warriors with battles yet to fight," Duffy later explained. "We can pay tribute to our dead but we must not lament for them overmuch."

Joyce Kilmer, born Alfred Joyce Kilmer, was the rare poet in the AEF ranks, unlike the BEF, where poets abounded. In August

1913, the magazine *Poetry* had published Kilmer's "Trees." Hardly a great poem, "Trees" nevertheless struck a popular chord and made Kilmer's fame. He had volunteered for the Fighting 69th at age thirty-one, after teaching, editing a dictionary, and writing for *The New York Times Magazine*. The poet was as much at ease with doughboys as generals and clearly preferred the company of the former. Kilmer's proudest moment, Duffy believed, was when he had made sergeant. The chaplain respected Bill Donovan, "but my chiefest joy in life," he said, "is to have Joyce Kilmer around."

Three nights after the Saint Patrick's Day memorial, the men of the 165th in the Lunéville sector were startled by a sentry clanging a steel pipe against an iron ring. A gas attack was imminent. They scrambled to pull on their masks as the thud of shells hitting the ground was followed by the deceptively pleasant aroma of new-mown hay. By now, the use of gas had become so common that it had lost, if not its horror, at least the novelty of its horror. More men were put out of action by gas than by rifles, pistols, and grenades combined. In one German attack launched against a neighboring division, gas shells rained down in the thousands for sixteen hours, causing more than eight hundred casualties. One of them, Sergeant Howard Cooper, recalled trying to repair telephone lines while half suffocating under a mask. Cooper started work with 125 repairmen. In the end, 21 were still standing. When they could finally remove the masks, "Our bodies were burnt by the gas," Cooper recalled, and their flesh gave off a pungent stench.

Gas attacks froze those caught without warning in grotesque tableaus. A German flier, Hans Schröder, wanted to see what war on the ground looked like after Ludendorff's first offensive. He described what he had found in the overrun British lines: "They lay as they fell when the fatal gas surprised them. The butt ends of their rifles pressed against their cheeks; their right hands still grasped hand grenades. There were whole lines of sharp shooters in this position. Then we came to a machine gun nest, with the gunner still taking aim while the second and third men worked the belt, and the officer lay there with his glasses on his eyes."

Prime Minister Lloyd George had asked the American artist John Singer Sargent to do a series of paintings celebrating Anglo-American unity in the war, to "be handed down to posterity as a series of immortal works." Sargent, at age sixty-two, went to France and was in the Arras sector looking for subjects when he came upon a sight that chilled him, a medical orderly leading a file of mustard-gas victims toward a dressing station. He immediately began taking notes and making sketches. The result was likely the most haunting image to come out of the war, the blinded men, their eyes masked with lint, each with his hand gripping the shoulder of the man ahead, moving with faltering steps toward the aid station. Sargent entitled the work simply *Gassed*.

The scene was repeated at Lunéville following the gas attack on the 165th. "One after another they began to feel its effects on their eyes, to cry, and gradually go blind," Father Duffy noted, "so that by dawn a considerable number had been led all the way back and were sitting by the Lunéville Road, completely blind."

WHEN NOT BEING shelled or gassed, infantrymen existed in a twilight suspended between fear and tedium. They found pet expressions for the various configurations of steel that took their lives. The Germans' barrel-sized *Minenwerfer* became the "GI" can, standing for "galvanized iron," which on impact, according to Father Duffy, "made a hole like the excavation of a small cottage." The men broke up the boredom by battling the one ever-present enemy. "Most of the day we waged war on the rats," Ernst Hinrichs, an American Signal Corps sergeant, recalled. A huge rat had darted into a hole at the back of Hinrichs's bunker. While the men tried to lure the rat with scraps of "corn willy," canned corn beef, a soldier named Pompie waited with bayonet poised. Bets were taken as to which would be faster, the rat or the bayonet. Suddenly, the bayonet flashed, a squeal sounded, and Pompie collected his winnings. "He performed a dance of triumph with the rat dangling on the bayonet," Hinrichs remembered, "and then we held a mock funeral service." Hinrichs found the war against rats oddly satisfying. "Here, at least, one saw the enemy once in awhile and got into personal encounter."

The doughboys absorbed the wisdom of the battlefield from toughened *poilus* and Tommies. Machine gunners facing capture were warned to tear off their insignia since the weapon was so feared that the Germans might kill a prisoner simply because he had manned one. Eighteen-year-old Bill Triplet of the 140th Infantry listened closely, having been much impressed by the Cockney who had earlier instructed him in the intricacies of the bayonet. In the beginning, Triplet fell victim to the greenhorn's impulse to overreact. One night, he sought to light up no-man's-land, firing off twenty-one white parachute flares. Realizing he had only three left, he sent a man to the rear for more, only to be told that the French had already given his unit its month's supply. The next delivery would occur in two weeks. A panicked Triplet feared his position would be overrun in the dark. But the French, who rationed themselves to one flare per night, would send no more. Triplet's twenty-one-flare barrage had illuminated only a single rat, on which his squad had expended fifteen hand grenades. "The Jerries," Triplet commented, "were laughing their heads off," and he had been cured of his profligacy.

Triplet volunteered for high-risk employment as a runner and quickly rose to a teenage sergeant. He learned that in the trenches talent could be turned on its head. In choosing runners, he wryly observed, "Illiteracy, while not essential, helps a lot. If you give a hasty verbal message to a Rhodes scholar, he will waste valuable time fumbling for his notebook and pencil, and will ask you to repeat certain points he has forgotten already. He will read his notes back and make indicated corrections. He will then proceed with intelligent caution and get himself killed on the way." The illiterate, on the other hand, was accustomed to getting by on observation and memory. "He will take off and deliver the message as accurately as a carbon copy to include tone of voice, gestures, blasphemies and state of mind of the sender."

The Yanks' rawness prompted occasional derision from battle-scarred veterans. R. G. Dixon, a British officer, was sitting on a box of ammunition in the Ypres sector, puffing his pipe, when "a long column of men hove in sight, infantry, all wearing very broad brimmed hats, and marching in a very sloppy manner." Dixon wondered, "Who the hell could they be? Not Australians, not Canadians." The new arrivals halted and one of them with a cigar clenched between his teeth, an officer, Dixon presumed, though he could not be sure, came up and said, "Say, buddy, how far is it to this l'il old shootin' gallery of yours?" It was now clear, Dixon concluded, that they must be Americans. "My hackles rose," he recalled. "I disliked this guy—all Americans are guys, are they not?—instantaneously. . . . We had heard that the Yanks had at long last, after waiting on sympathetic sidelines, got some troops to France." Dixon glanced at his watch and advised the officer, "It is now three minutes to eleven, and at eleven precisely, Jerry puts down a carefully bracketed shoot of high velocity shells upon that stretch of road you have halted upon." He added, "Your chaps ought to be wearing their tin hats, you know." The shelling began as punctually as a German train schedule. "I regret to have to write this, but those highly startled and distressingly raw troops from across the Atlantic," Dixon recalled, "scattered all over the countryside" in a manner "unnecessarily undignified."

The French were more charitable and more grateful. "We had the Americans as neighbors and I had a close up view of them," wrote the priest–stretcher bearer, Pierre Teilhard de Chardin. To Teilhard, the doughboys were "first-rate," possessed of "wonderful courage." He had only one complaint: "They're too apt to get themselves killed. . . . When they are wounded, they make their way back holding themselves upright, almost stiff, passive and uncomplaining. I don't think I've ever seen such pride and dignity in suffering."

ON MAY 27, 1918, the indefatigable Ludendorff launched his third offensive. His objective again was to split the Allies by striking first at the French along the Aisne River, then resuming the fight against the British to the north. In picking the battleground, Ludendorff chose wisely. The French did not expect an attack at this point, and the British forces consisted of battle-weary divisions pulled from Flanders for a rest. Haig's ranks were now heavily manned by men who would have been rejected for military service four years before. The age for conscription had been raised to fifty, and the trenches were filled with graybeards and downy-cheeked boys. Thrice-wounded men were patched up and sent back to the front. Against this soft spot the Germans unleashed 4,600 cannon and 400,000 men. The shells and gas tore a gaping hole in the Allied front, and the German infantry poured through.

THUS FAR, FIELD Marshal Haig had barely concealed his contempt for the AEF and Black Jack Pershing. After a Supreme War Council earlier that May, Haig had found Pershing's insistence on a "great self-contained American Army" ludicrous and the man himself "obstinate and stupid." American soldiers belonged under seasoned British control, Haig maintained, and "it is ridiculous to think such an army could function unaided in less than two years." Pershing held fast, and the AEF was about to make its solo debut at Cantigny, once a picturesque village nestled amid chalk cliffs, now a skeletal ruin. Cantigny possessed no strategic value and was occupied by third-rate German troops, the 82nd Reserve and the battered 25th Reserve. Thus this speck on the map would provide a perfect proving ground for Pershing since victory would boost troop morale and defeat represent no serious setback.

The Big Red One, then commanded by Major General Bullard before his ascent to Second Army chief, was to make the attack. Bullard addressed his staff with the drawling accents of his native South Carolina, but his mind was quick and his character decisive. "I remembered the tradition of loss of heart, aggressiveness, and morale of the Confederates shut up in the trenches," he had said upon taking over the division. "I remembered, too, from my boyhood, a one-armed brother-in-law licking a big two-armed opponent by starting the fight before the other fellow." Striking first was precisely what Bullard intended to do at Cantigny.

On May 28, the Americans opened with a fierce one-hour barrage followed by five minutes of smoke and gas shells. At 6:45 A.M., the men, each burdened with a rifle, 220 rounds of ammunition, three grenades, three empty sandbags, a shelter half, two canteens of water, two chocolate bars, and a lemon and chewing gum to quench thirst, began going over the top. They wrested Cantigny from the Germans, who had taken it in the Ludendorff offensives. The enemy counterattacked, but the Americans held on to the town. The next day they tallied their losses. The casualties bore out Ernst Jünger's observation about who fought best: "The notion that a soldier becomes hardier and bolder as war proceeds is mistaken. As troops remained in the line, they became wilier, not braver. They left the heroism to unbloodied fresh troops still retaining illusions of immortality. For this reason, I consider that troops composed of boys of twenty, under experienced leadership, are the most formidable." In twenty-four hours the 1st Division counted 1,600 casualties at Cantigny, including a third of the 28th Infantry Regiment. The attack had left an acceptable 199 dead, though to men new to combat, the rows of bodies laid out behind a small church seemed endless. One officer wrote home, "When the wind is right, you can smell Cantigny two miles away." Bullard kept the victory in perspective. It was "a small fight. Hundreds greater had preceded and would follow it in the mighty war." But the effort had served its purpose. "To both friend and foe Cantigny said, 'Americans will both fight and stick.' "

The baptism passed, and the men engaged at Cantigny settled into the hit-and-run raiding tactics that their allies employed to break up the monotony of stalemate between battles. Jim Duane, commanding a company in the 26th Infantry Division, was struck by the historic parallel of his first raid, launched from Cantigny on May 31, Memorial Day. "Back in America, our old buddies of the Grand Army of the Republic and the veterans of the Spanish-American War were decorating the graves of their comrades," he remembered. The raid was the type the French called a *coup de mad,* which the doughboys found apt. "Prizes of several francs were offered to the one man or unit who took the largest number of prisoners," Duane remembered, "also a trip back to America with Chaplain Rollins was offered." The force was relatively large, well over 100 men. They were trucked toward a town called Seicheprey and during the ride spent the time fashioning a weapon of their own invention, barbed wire coiled around a billy club. By 1:30 A.M., they were in the forward trenches. Their hope that they would be undetected grew slim as the enemy lit the sky with flares. A half mile behind them, in a dugout serving as a command post, the regiment's colonel bent over a table set on wooden horses over which a map had been spread. He puffed at his pipe as he waited for the field telephone to ring, reporting that the raid was under way.

Telephone linemen had laid out five redundant lines, more than ten miles of cable snaked around craters and through barbed wire and back to the command post. At least one should survive German shelling. Wire cutters crouched in no-man's-land, spurting ahead between bursts of German machine-gun fire. They first cut gaps in their own wire to let the raiding party through. Another team followed, lugging thirty-foot-long torpedo tubes inside no-man's-land, to be fired the moment the attack started to breach the wire. "The party now being ready, adjusted equipment, fixed bayonets, and with a slightly nervous feeling, awaited the signal," Duane recorded in his journal. H-hour was set for 2:30 A.M. As the minutes ticked by, the men, face muscles taut, waited in eerie silence. Then "the heavens opened. Never in our lives had we heard such a noise before." It was merely a raid, but the two hundred artillery pieces poured out more fire than at Gettysburg. Their pattern formed a "box barrage" that enclosed the targeted stretch of enemy trench to prevent German reinforcements from getting through. "On the signal of the first shell of our barrage the boys leaped out of our trenches," Duane recalled, "and over the top with a yell and were on their way." Trailing close behind were stretcher bearers. Ahead, at an unnerving fifty yards, a rolling barrage preceded the infantry. The doughboys were soon inside the enemy wire, locked in hand-to-hand fighting. All thoughts of winning prizes vanished in murderous thrusts of rifle butts and bayonets. The force and suddenness of the raid had stunned the defenders, and a half-dozen Germans surrendered. Before the attack, their American commander had told the men, regarding prisoners, that they "might kill all but one, and he would give sufficient information. . . . Several prisoners being taken back to our lines by the boys showed signs of fight and the result was that they remained in no-man's-land dying there of bullet wounds." In less than an hour, it was over and the men were back in their lines with their single prisoner. Because so much ordnance had been expended, the men dubbed the foray "the Million-Dollar Raid." The colonel, back in his dugout command post, judged the mission's cost acceptable: two American dead, five wounded, and one man missing who was never found.

What the Americans exhibited at this stage was the untested optimism that Britons and Frenchmen had displayed before the brutal lessons of Verdun, the Somme, and Passchendaele. A young American officer, Adrian Edwards, not long removed from his law practice in Carrollton, Illinois, wrote home, "My Dear Mother, I am about to go into battle and have instructed the company clerk to send you this letter in case that I become a casualty." Edwards was thirty when America entered the war and need not have volunteered. He did so, he said, because "someone must make the sacrifice, some mother must lose her son." Should she receive this letter, he wrote, "rejoice that you have given a son in sacrifice to make the greatest military caste of all time lay down the sword— to save civilization, to prevent future wars, to punish the huns, who have disregarded every law of God and mankind, whose only God is the God of War and military force—to make the world safe for democracy." He reminded his mother of the mothers of Sparta, who, when their sons went into battle, said, "Either come home proudly bearing your shield before you or upon it." Mrs. Edwards's son fell on May 4, 1918, while leading a charge. The company clerk followed the young officer's last wish and posted the letter left in his care. The final line read, "Goodbye, Mother, I will see you in the next world."

To the southeast, the real battle, Ludendorff's current offensive, raged on. The French Sixth Army disintegrated before its fury. By June 4, Soissons and Château-Thierry had fallen. As Ludendorff had planned, the German Army was again on the Marne, threatening Paris.

Exhausted and supposedly beaten, the flame of duty still burned inextinguishably in some Frenchmen. Georges Gaudy, studying for the priesthood before the war, had initially been rejected by the army as too scrawny. He thereupon gorged himself on sweets until he was fat enough to be accepted. By the time he was among the troops falling back at Soissons, Gaudy had been in almost continuous combat for more than two and a half years. Yet, upon receiving a soldier's grimmest order, to fight a rear-guard action while the main body escaped, Gaudy experienced near-religious ecstasy. "We would have to hold out to the last man without the slightest hope of relief, like the fighting men of Carthage," Gaudy later wrote in his war memoirs. "Wire entanglements barred the entrance to the shelters so that no one would give way to the very strong temptation to take refuge in them. . . . We were the country's living shield. The sacrificial fate filled my soul with a holy joy. It was," Gaudy recalled, "one of the happiest periods of my life."

23

"Do You Want to Live Forever?"

NOVEMBER 11, 1918. To Rudolph Binding, the imminent end was as much a personal as a national humiliation. Five months before, he had been among Ludendorff's field gray swarm poised to take Paris, defeat France, and force the Allies to the peace table. When the German troops had begun to lose momentum, looting, drinking, and cavorting foolishly in places like Albert, he had tried to stop this unraveling of discipline. But now, at the end, this miraculously unscarred survivor of four years of warfare, a boy grown to manhood in a junior officer's uniform, found himself laid low by that least heroic of a soldier's afflictions, dysentery. Binding had been pulled out of the line in the latter part of August delusional and spouting gibberish, with a raging fever and a pulse rate of 120. Two and a half months later he was still convalescing at a military hospital in Baden-Baden as the sacrifice of millions of Germans, living and dead, was about to come to naught. On the morning of the armistice, he wrote in his diary, "The news from the front about the retreat of my division and the Army was hard to bear." This upper-middle-class German found the reports of workers, soldiers' councils, and socialists at home seizing power preposterous. "I find all their acts, even demands, so absurdly superficial, so half-boiled, that I cannot conceive of any sort of stability in this form," he wrote. He was particularly incensed that the rallying anthem, "Wacht am Rhein"—"To the Rhine, the Rhine, the German Rhine"—had been parodied by the defeatists into "We're going behind the Rhine-line, the Rhine-line, the Rhine-line." The only achievement of the new socialist order that Binding observed in the hospital was that "today we had no sweet for dinner!" How had victory, once so near, slipped so completely from their grasp?

JUNE 1918. It was a hilly little forest no more than a mile square, thick with second-growth trees and scrub brush sprouting among its stone outcroppings. Surrounding it, an amber skirt of wheat dappled with poppies swayed in the wind. It was called Belleau Wood. In June, it would mark America's full-scale entry into the war.

Though achieved against inferior troops, the AEF's triumph at Cantigny had sounded an alarm to the Germans. In three offensives thus far, Ludendorff had failed to knock out the French and British, and now the Americans were becoming a force with which to reckon. One Ludendorff division commander issued a proclamation to his men warning, "Should the Americans on our front even temporarily gain the upper hand, it would have a most unfavorable effect for us as regards the morale of the Allies and the duration of the war." The issue now "was whether Anglo-American propaganda that the American Army is equal to or even superior to the German, will be successful." Black Jack Pershing was eager to answer and to put into action on a major scale his doctrine of open warfare: get the men out of the trenches, overrun the enemy lines, and march on to Berlin and total victory. Pershing wanted no more "quiet sectors" for the AEF. The German and American armies were on a collision course. They would collide in Belleau Wood.

Pershing assembled the 2nd Division, a mixed force composed of one army and one marine brigade—26,665 men all told—to take the wood. To command the marine brigade, he assigned an army regular, his former chief of staff, Brigadier General Jim Harbord. He was getting "the best brigade in the army," Pershing told Harbord, "and if it fails, I'll know who is to blame."

On June 5, French villagers awoke to an extraordinary sight, more than a thousand trucks snaking along the road toward Belleau Wood filled with raucous, cheering, waving doughboys as if en route to a party. Gaunt, hollow-eyed French veterans watched from the roadside, among them Captain Henri Desagneaux. To the onetime railroad lawyer, survivor of the abattoir of Verdun, the Americans were "great strapping fellows, sappers, admirably turned out with brand new equipment." Clifton Cates, a second lieutenant and one day to be the commandant of the Marine Corps, described the scene in a letter to his family. The roads were packed with refugees, "plodding their way back and old men, women, and children: some walking and others on carts trying to carry their valuables back—it was the most pitiful sight I have ever seen, and there is not a man in our bunch that didn't grit his teeth and say 'vive la France.' . . . The mother that can furnish a boy should say—'America, here's my boy, God grant that he may come back, if not, he died for a noble cause, and I am willing to give him to you.' "

The force reached Belleau Wood on the evening of June 5. The next morning dawned chilly and shrouded in mist, the quiet broken only by topkicks barking orders at drowsy doughboys. The men rose to their feet, slung packs over their backs, and laughed uneasily at black-humored wisecracks. The 5th Marine Regiment, lined up in parade-ground formation not seen on the battlefield since 1914, led the advance into a wheat field before the wood. The French had told the Americans that the Germans held only the wood's northeast corner. The Yanks had been misinformed; the enemy did not occupy a corner of Belleau Wood but was entrenched throughout with four divisions in the marines' immediate path. Enemy machine gunners blinked in amazement at the easy targets and began cutting down marines in rows as neat as their marching formation. Blood began to mingle with the red of poppies in the wheat field. Pinned down by the murderous fire, a fifty-year-old gunnery sergeant, holder of two Navy Crosses, was about to add to Marine Corps legend. Nineteen years in the corps, Daniel Joseph Daly, a five-foot, four-inch knot of hickory, glanced at an order to advance handed to him by a runner and rose up amid a hail of gunfire. Swinging his rifle overhead, Daly yelled to his company, "Come on, you sons of bitches!" They hesitated. He roared again, "Do you want to live forever?" The men rose, and a frightful number immediately had the question answered. Sergeant Dan "Pop" Hunter, another veteran leatherneck, heard someone shout, "Hey, Pop, there's a man hit over here!" "Goddamnit! He ain't the last man who's gonna be hit today." Before the day was out, the thirty-year veteran would himself be dead. By the end of the day, two battalions of the 5th Marine Regiment, nearly 3,000 men, were out of action and the third battalion was barely able to muster a token force.

Among replacements rushed up the next night was a twenty-year-old who looked fifteen. Elton Mackin had grown up in a working-class family in Lewiston, New York, from which one could look across the Niagara River into Canada. Soon after America entered the war, Mackin read an article in *The Saturday Evening Post* about the Marine Corps and decided he must become a leatherneck, the term originating with the leather stock once worn around the neck to keep the head erect. Marines like Mackin found themselves in France because the corps's leaders persuaded Secretary of War Baker that they deserved a piece of the action. Though absorbed under army command, the marines strove to maintain their individuality, even sewing the corps's globe-and-anchor buttons and insignia onto their army-issue uniforms.

Mackin and the others sent to replace casualties in the 1st Battalion, 5th Marine Regiment, entered Belleau Wood on June 8, weaving around bodies not yet recovered from the previous fighting. The novices moved with their eyes fixed straight ahead, Mackin noted, shooting sidelong glances, checking the expressions of their comrades, most of whom wore a mask of impassivity. Shells screamed overhead, exploded in the treetops, and sent spear-tipped branches plunging into the men below. Mackin wished it was darker so that he might hide the terror that he felt his face must betray. As they came under fire, Mackin fought an urge "to flee, to get away. Suddenly," he later remembered of that moment, "we didn't want to die." The enemy counterattacked. A gray silhouette rose up before Mackin, and the training pounded into the young marine produced a reflex reaction. He fired and, in his first hour in battle, killed a man. Germans continued to emerge from the pall of smoke blanketing the field. Sergeant McCabe could be heard bellowing over the din, "Fix bayonets! Fix bayonets! And watch that goddamn wheat field!" Ever since training, the prospect of using the bayonet had horrified Mackin. As he slotted the long blade into his rifle, his knees trembled.

The days that followed became an exercise in coarsening the senses. Mackin's company had reached a fork in a path just beyond the captured hamlet of Lucy-le-Bocage. A German corpse lay in the juncture, arm raised, hand palm forward, as if fending off death. A doughboy had stuck a piece of scribbled cardboard between the corpse's fingers reading "Battalion P.C.," with an arrow pointing west. Men laughed as they slogged past. Though the death of a comrade became commonplace, Mackin found the death of a horse somehow more jarring. Men died quietly if they died quickly enough. Only after the initial merciful numbness wore off did their cries begin. But, Mackin wrote in his memoir, "Have you ever watched a gut-shot horse, screaming, drag his shell-killed mate, his dead driver, and his wagon down a bit of road before he dies? Horses die more noisily than men."

Mackin had formed a friendship with another marine from Cleveland named Hiram Baldwin. Mackin, with only a high school education, believed that Baldwin's years at Ohio State may have posed a hindrance. "It's a revolting business for an educated man," Mackin observed. "They were pitiful sometimes, these men who took clean sportsmanship and decency to France. It's such a poor way of preparation."

During the Belleau Wood fighting, Mackin was summoned by

Sergeant McCabe, who told him that Frederick "Itchy" Fox, the battalion runner, had been killed the night before. They needed a replacement. Since the sergeant and Mackin were both called "Mac," the young marine's name had popped into McCabe's mind. Mackin knew the dismal survival rate for runners. The men called them the Suicide Squad. He also knew by now the trench ethics governing this situation. No one had to take a runner's job. If a man lacked the stomach for it, no questions would be asked. "Want the job, son?" the sergeant asked. To Mackin, McCabe's gaze also posed an unspoken query: Are you brave or a coward? Mackin did not want the job. He nevertheless found himself saying, "Sure, Sergeant, I'll take it." It was, he concluded, "easier that way. You couldn't face the question in his eyes and tell the truth." He was struck, however, by the chance nature of fate. He might die because his nickname was Mac.

Belleau Wood dragged on for three brutal weeks. Thirty-eight years before, General William Tecumseh Sherman, reflecting on his experience in the Civil War, had told an audience, "There is many a boy here today who looks on war as all glory, but, boys, it is all hell." The doughboys at Belleau Wood discovered that nothing had changed in the interval. They prevailed, but at a steep price. The 2nd Division lost 9,272 men dead, wounded, or missing. Fifty percent of the Marine Corps officers engaged fell in and around a square mile of woods.

A private named Aitkin, one of twenty-five survivors of his company, drew burial detail. The grave diggers first prepared a shallow trench, six feet wide and long enough for forty bodies. "We had to go out with stretchers and pick them up very carefully," Aitken recalled, "and roll them into the trench in a very careful manner after having been searched for personal effects etc. One tag was left on the body, the other attached to a rude cross at the head." While the chaplain read a simple service, German shells began dropping, killing two men in the burial party. "We buried the pieces and said some hurried prayers," Aitken noted, concluding, "C'est la guerre."

General Bullard credited his commanders at Belleau Wood with having rescued the Allies from defeat, and with saving Paris. Premier Clemenceau was on the scene two days after the battle, determined to elevate Belleau Wood to a triumph that would continue to inspire his new ally and at the same time lift the spirits of his war-worn compatriots. He again reminded his hosts that he had entered Richmond five days after General Grant and had now witnessed the valor of the ordinary American soldier repeated fifty-three years later. Adding what Pershing most wanted to hear, the Tiger described Belleau Wood as a victory planned, executed, and won independently by the AEF.

The most convincing proof of the Americans' successful rite of passage came from across the lines. The Germans had previously regarded the Americans as little more than an armed mob. After Belleau Wood, the corps commander who had faced the attackers arrived at a reappraisal: "The 2nd American Division can be rated a very good Division. . . . The various attacks of the marines were carried out smartly and ruthlessly. The morale effect of our fire did not materially check the advance of the infantry. The nerves of the Americans are still unshaken." A German corporal, Earl Recklinghausen, put it more bluntly: "If those in front of us are fair specimens of the average American troops, and there are as many as they say there are, then goodbye for us." Indeed, there were 700,000 doughboys in France at the time of Belleau Wood.

A victory had been won, rather more than minor and something less than epic. But it had been conceived and carried out as if Pershing and his generals had never heard of the French at Lorraine or the British at Passchendaele. Men carrying rifles over open ground had marched against men firing machine guns. The war had become a classroom in which the teachers were dumb and the students deaf. Pershing, however, appeared to have absorbed one bleak lesson: casualties proved that his army could take it.

THE AMERICANS AT Belleau Wood had been supporting actors in the French-led counteroffensive to stop Ludendorff's fourth campaign on the Marne, launched on June 9. The Germans, after gaining five miles, were again stopped. Ludendorff ended this effort on June 13, only to begin plans for a fifth offensive. The old seesaw went on—a mile gained, a mile lost, and bodies in between. Ludendorff waited just over a month, until July 15, for the next push. History would remember it as the Second Battle of the Marne.

24

"I Don't Expect to See
Any of You Again"

NOVEMBER 11, 1918. Elton Mackin had survived 156 days at the front. Whether he would survive the last day would depend heavily on the actions of General Charles P. Summerall, commander of the 5th Army Corps, of which Mackin's marine regiment was a part. No doubt clouded the general's mind as to how all this talk of an armistice should be treated. The day before, he had gathered his staff officers behind the lines and told them, "Rumors of enemy capitulation come from our successes." Consequently, this was not the time to relax but rather to tighten the screws. Summerall, a fifty-one-year-old southerner, had spent three years teaching school before entering West Point. By the time he arrived on the western front, he wore ribbons from the Spanish-American War, the Philippine insurgency, and China's Boxer Rebellion. He was a severe, unsmiling, some said brutal man who liked to turn out in a prewar dress uniform with copious medals, gilded sashes, and fringed epaulettes suggesting a viceroy of India rather than a plain American officer. Because he had taught English, Summerall prided himself that he possessed a literary turn of phrase. "We are swinging the door by its hinges. It has got to move," he told his subordinates regarding the necessity of crossing the Meuse River. "Only by increasing the pressure can we bring

about his [the enemy's] defeat. . . . Get into action and get across."
His parting shot was "I don't expect to see any of you again, but
that doesn't matter. You have the honor of a definitive success—
give yourself to that." Was he referring to ending his present command over them or foretelling their fate? In either case, Summerall
was spurring them on to the defeat of an enemy, whatever the cost,
that was already defeated.

On the night of November 10–11, Private Mackin's regiment
stumbled out of the Bois de Hospice, a wood on the west side of
the Meuse. The night was shrouded in fog and drizzle as the
marines slid down a steep hillside and crossed a railroad track, trying to find their way to the river in the thick gloom. Army engineers had gone before them, throwing flimsy bridges across the
water by lashing pontoons together, then running planks over the
top. The first signs that the marines were headed in the right direction were the bodies they stumbled upon, engineers killed attempting to construct the crossings.

Near 4 A.M., the marines reached the first pontoon bridge, a
rickety affair thirty inches wide with a guide rope strung along
posts at knee height. They could see roughly halfway before the
bridge disappeared into the mist. Beyond, nothing was visible but
the flash of enemy guns in the darkness. The marines began piling
up at the bridgehead, awaiting orders. A marine major blew a
whistle blast and stepped onto the bridge. As the men crowded behind him, the pontoons began to sink, the water sloshing about the
marines' ankles. The engineers shouted to them to space themselves before the span collapsed.

Enemy shells began spewing up geysers, soaking the attackers
with icy water. Machine guns opened fire, the rounds striking the
wood sounding like a drum roll, those striking flesh making a
sock, sock, sock sound. The span swung wildly in the strong current. Mackin saw the man ahead of him stumble between two
pontoon sections, topple into the black water, and vanish. Enemy
Maxims embedded in the hills on the opposite bank continued
knocking men off the pontoons like ducks in a shooting gallery.

Still they kept coming. By 4:30 A.M., the marines and infantrymen of the 89th Division had taken Pouilly on the east bank. The task now was to mount the heights above the town and clean out the machine-gun nests. As day broke, Mackin watched a runner come sprinting across the bridge. The message from General Summerall's headquarters said only, "Armistice signed and takes effect at 11:00 o'clock this morning." To career-minded majors and colonels, the safer interpretation was to keep pressing the attack.

JULY 1918. On the fifteenth, the unrelenting Ludendorff embarked on his fifth offensive, to propel a battering ram against the Allies across the Marne between Château-Thierry and Épernay. Paris lay a tantalizing forty-two miles away. The exhilaration of imminent victory lasted only three days before the French counterattacked, forcing Ludendorff to abandon the fight. Instead of smashing the enemy ramparts, the battering ram itself had broken. Ludendorff's five offensives since March had cost Germany nearly half a million irreplaceable men, while the Americans continued to arrive in a torrent.

WHILE THE JULY fighting raged on, the war was temporarily suspended for Connell Albertine, and he briefly forgot the moment when he had found his name on a grave marker in a French cemetery. Albertine's l04th Regiment had been sent to a rest area, where the young Bostonian reveled in the respite. "We spent our nights in cafes, eating beefsteak and pommes de terre, drinking wine and beer, playing cards, having a good time with the French," he recalled. As clerk to Chaplain de Valles, he watched with amusement as the priest continued to dole out small loans to the men, admonishing them that they must not spend the money on "bad women." As Albertine filled his spare hours poring over mailed copies of *The Boston Globe,* the war seemed to be taking place on another planet and he felt indescribably happy. Just days before, he had watched a burial detail of black soldiers loading men from his regiment into rude coffins and then onto trucks, blood oozing between the boards. He had assisted Father de Valles at a burial ceremony held so close to the front that the priest told the mourners to leave before they joined the dead. Now Albertine found himself playing the fiddle with a French cornetist and trombone player as doughboys and Frenchwomen, young and old, brightly dressed or in mourning black, danced in the streets. "The weather was so nice here and the smell of new-mown hay so invigorating," he wrote home, that war seemed a bad dream.

The idyll ended when the 26th Division was pulled into the French counterattack against Ludendorff's fifth offensive. On July 17, the 104th found itself going against the Prussian Guard, "the finest soldiers in the German Army," Albertine judged. They stormed the enemy defenses and fell to hand-to-hand fighting. In the midst of the frenzy, Albertine was surprised to hear the vaunted Prussians shouting *Kamerad, Kamerad!* while throwing down their rifles, and raising their hands. The victors now faced the all-too-frequent dilemma: "who was going to escort these prisoners to the rear. Before we knew it, the prisoners were either shot or bayoneted, by whom no one seemed to know." Soon afterward, heavy German machine-gun fire drove Albertine's company back, forcing the Americans to abandon their dead and wounded. Upon retaking the ground, "The wounded we had left on the field had all been bayoneted by the Boche," Albertine recalled. "We all vowed revenge and did not take a prisoner but let all the Boches we came in contact with have it."

WAR IN THE sky remained a more chivalrous affair. On the day before Ludendorff launched his latest offensive, a pilot named Quentin Roosevelt, fresh out of flight training, took off with a squadron of French-made Spads. His flying career would be brief. The youngest son of former President Theodore Roosevelt was shot down by a Fokker and died on Bastille Day, July 14. Colonel

Frank McCoy, commanding the Fighting 69th, had served as military aide in the Roosevelt White House and had known Quentin as a child. McCoy told his staff that he wanted the body found.

Quentin Roosevelt had crashed just north of Château-Thierry behind German lines, in an area that was subsequently retaken by the Americans. Chaplain Duffy and McCoy set out to find a small orchard near the village of Chamery where they had been told Quentin was buried. Upon reaching the grave, they found that the Germans had put together the long end of an airplane propeller and a broken-off shorter end to form a cross over the grave. The two officers further learned that the Germans had laid the young flier to rest with full military honors. Father Duffy conducted a brief service at the site and afterward wrote, "We erected our own little monument without molesting the one that had been left by the Germans. It is fitting that enemy and friend alike should pay tribute to heroism."

Quentin was one of four Roosevelt brothers in uniform. Their father had chafed impatiently during America's neutrality, labeling President Wilson "a coward" for keeping the United States out of the fight. The death of Quentin, said to be his father's favorite, did not transform Roosevelt into a pacifist overnight, but did replace his military romanticism with a grim fatalism. He subsequently wrote of his surviving sons, "Archie is badly crippled; whether permanently or not it is not yet possible to say. . . . Ted was seriously wounded. . . . If the war lasts long enough he will either be killed or crippled. . . . Kermit is trying to get with the machine guns in the infantry; if he succeeds he will do admirably, but will at no very distant time share the fate of his brothers."

THROUGHOUT JULY, THE Fighting 69th joined in the French counterattack against Ludendorff. The cockiness of these big-city boys occasionally grated on doughboys from small towns and farms. They dismissed the Irishmen, actual or adoptive, as a bunch of "micks." Father Duffy came to be known as "the Vicar of

Times Square." Southern boys were chagrined, however, to find these street urchins their match in stealing chickens.

Wild Bill Donovan, the 1st Battalion's commanding officer, had won a reputation that teetered between fearlessness and "gaudy recklessness," as Alexander Woollcott, the rotund unlikely war correspondent and future literary eminence, described him. After the regiment's first exposure to battle, another legend began forming around Donovan: that his derring-do acted as a magnet for death. The Ourcq River runs roughly east–west some eleven miles north of Château-Thierry. The Germans had dug in on the river's north side to await the Allied counteroffensive. On July 27, the Fighting 69th was ordered to cross the Ourcq and take a hill designated as "152," its slopes studded with Maxim machine guns. To achieve surprise, the Americans began advancing with bayonets only. Trailing Wild Bill across the Ourcq was the poet-sergeant, Joyce Kilmer. Kilmer, now attached to the battalion's intelligence section, could have remained behind the lines. He had instead chosen to volunteer as Donovan's sergeant major. Inside his pack Kilmer carried a poem he had written for his wife, Aline, a poet herself. The last lines read:

> I have no vision of gods, not of Eros with love-arrows laden,
>> Jupiter thundering death or of Juno his white-breasted queen,
>> Yet I have seen,
> All of the joy of the world in the innocent heart of a maiden.

Barely across the Ourcq, Donovan's battalion began taking fire from three sides. One bullet grazed Wild Bill's thigh; another tore off the heel of his boot. A shell fragment would surely have killed him had it not struck the respirator of his gas mask. Donovan's adjutant, Lieutenant Oliver Ames, ran forward and flung himself down alongside the major, joined by a mess cook, John Kayes. A sniper's bullet whizzed past Donovan and struck Ames in the head, killing him instantly. Kayes was fatally riddled by machine-gun fire. Donovan reached out toward the men and was shot through the hand. Two days later, still deployed along the Ourcq, Donovan, with Kilmer at his side, crept to the northern edge of a wood for a better view of the enemy's position. Suddenly he realized that Kilmer was not with him. He retraced his steps and found the sergeant sprawled on the ground, a bullet through his brain.

The Fighting 69th served under the 42nd Division, whose chief of staff, Colonel MacArthur, planted himself in the thick of the struggle along the Ourcq. He later described the experience in what was becoming the patented MacArthur prose style. As the men mounted the heights above the river, "A flare suddenly lit up the scene for a fraction of a minute and we hit the dirt hard," he wrote. "There just ahead of us stood three Germans—a lieutenant pointing with outstretched arm, a sergeant crouched over a machine gun, a corporal feeding a bandolier of cartridges into the weapon. I held my breath waiting for the burst. But there was nothing. They were all dead—the lieutenant with the shrapnel through his heart, the sergeant with his belly blown into his back, the corporal with his spine where his head should have been." Calculating that at least 2,000 bodies lay sprawled about him and hearing the cries of the wounded, MacArthur observed, "I could but think how wrong I had been on a bright day at West Texas Military Academy when I had so glibly criticized Dante's description of Hell as too extreme." During the Ourcq engagement, MacArthur won his fourth Silver Star and a tribute from his comrades. "The staff nearly broke my heart," he recalled, "when they presented me with a gold cigarette box with the inscription, 'The bravest of the brave.' " He was soon thereafter promoted to brigadier general, the youngest in the army.

In the end, the 42nd Division wrested the heights above the Ourcq from the Germans and continued across open ground against waiting machine guns at an appalling cost. From Wild Bill Donovan's battalion of some 1,000 men, more than 600 were dead, wounded, or missing. One regiment of the 1st Division, the 26th, suffered more than 80 percent casualties. For the entire AEF, the campaigns at Cantigny, Belleau Wood, Château-Thierry, and the Ourcq started to approach the bloodletting of past western front battles, with 67,000 men fallen.

The larger the number, the less personal the sense of loss. The closest that Ken Baker, telephone lineman and thwarted pilot, had thus far witnessed death was seeing the troopship behind his own, the *Tuscania,* torpedoed on the Atlantic crossing. Being trucked to the front during the July 1918 Allied counteroffensive, he saw his first dead American, a doughboy sprawled in a ditch. He was sickened. And then he saw another, and another, and another. "I started counting," he recalled and reached 252 before he tired of the exercise.

The sense of having experienced hell began to produce in the Americans the same emotions—or rather the same emotional numbness—that had psychologically shielded Tommies and *poilus.* Courage, even among the bravest, it appeared, was finite. Sergeant Bill Triplet, 140th Infantry, had become sufficiently seasoned to no longer set the sky ablaze with flares at the sound of a rat. Now, sharply attentive to his men, the youthful noncom became something of a mother hen. One morning, after a shell exploded near him, Triplet heard a soldier shrieking, "My God! Oh my God!" To spare the man shame, Triplet later identified him pseudonymously as "Wharton." Previously, the fellow D Company soldier had rarely spoken but had proved fearless and uncomplaining during the hardest fighting. This day Triplet found Wharton crouched in a ball shrieking hysterically but apparently unhurt. "Where're you hit?" one man asked. "Oh my God," the soldier kept screaming. "Next one of them things that bursts near me is gonna get me. I know it, my God, I know!" His wailing, Triplet observed, was more words than he had ever heard the man utter, and he wondered at what point Wharton's stoicism had been exhausted. In the same engagement, he came across another man, dead, but without a scratch on him and with no sign of concussion injuries. "It sure looked like he had wished or willed or scared himself to death," Triplet concluded.

Another D Company infantryman had gone down with a piece

of shrapnel the size of a pie plate driven through his back. Triplet knew the soldier was doomed, and he puzzled over the ethics of the situation. "If I had a horse or dog in that shape," he observed, "I'd pat it on the head and put a quick bullet through the back of the neck. But the law and custom says you can't help a human friend like that, you have to prolong his pain to his last miserable moment." Triplet had arrived at another bit of trench philosophy: "I've noticed that a man that's hit his thumb with a hammer generally complains about it much more than a man who's lost a leg or taken a bullet in the belly."

Still, the romance of war died hard among those who had not yet known it. Arthur Jensen, mule skinner, kept his War Log protected by a rubber bag and occasionally sneaked pages of it past the censors by hiding them in the doughboy newspaper, *The Stars and Stripes,* which he mailed home. Thus far the closest Jensen had come to the enemy was seeing German POWs on his arrival in France. In one entry in his log he described a red semicircle of shells glowing over the distant horizon. "It made my blood tingle," Jensen confessed. "Anyone knows it's foolish to risk your life when it isn't necessary; but there is something fascinating about war. It must appeal to a primitive instinct. . . . I believe most men fight because it relieves the humdrum of their existence."

There were indeed moments etched in memory that the boys back on the farm or clerking in a dry goods store would never experience. Captain Will Judy was relaxing near 33rd Division headquarters, a commandeered château, when a friend shouted, "Hurry, here comes the king!" A limousine, black and gleaming, pulled up alongside the château. Out stepped England's King George V, assisted by fussing aides and followed by General Pershing and General Tasker Bliss, the American representative on the Allied Supreme War Council. As the dignitaries began moving toward a parade ground lined with British and American troops, Judy stared in amazement. He was looking at a sovereign, by the grace of God, King of Great Britain and Ireland and the dominions beyond the sea, Emperor of India, nevertheless a disappointing figure, Judy found, no taller than five feet four, with dark rings under baggy eyes, whose every movement betrayed ennui. Movie cameras rolled as the king pinned British decorations on twenty American soldiers. A band struck up "God Save the King," then "The Star-Spangled Banner" and "Illinois" for the state that had given its sons to the 33rd. The ceremony over, Judy watched King George's aides "as they placed him like a child in the automobile." An irreverent Yank called out, "So that's the big stiff?" Judy, however, judged the day unforgettable: "I saw a king for the first time. I saw together the only two full generals of the United States Army. It had been a great day for the 33rd Division."

Back in a London hospital, a wounded captain, Henry Maslin, awoke to hear a sugary drawl call out, "Anybody here from Virginia?" Maslin, a member of the "Metropolitan 77th" Division, answered, "I'm from New York." With a blinding smile, the woman responded, "You poor miserable Yankee." She was, Maslin thought, the most beautiful woman he had ever seen. "We have a way of getting square with you fellows," she said, moving among the cots. "We marry you. I married one." She also confessed that she had four half-Yankee children. "That's why you, a mother of four children, look so young and full of sunshine," Maslin replied. He learned only afterward that the visitor was Virginia-born Lady Astor, the first woman to sit in the House of Commons.

BY AUGUST 6, 1918, the Second Battle of the Marne had ended in Allied counterattacks and disaster for Germany. All the bitterly purchased German gains of five offensives had essentially been lost. Two days later, Foch launched another Allied counterstrike, spearheaded by 456 British tanks. Gordon Hassell, a captain involved in the drive, described the small hell inside a tank: "noisy, hot, airless and bumpy! . . . As we had no springs and had thirty tons' weight, any slight bump and crash was magnified. . . . Instinctively one caught at a handhold, and got a burn on the hot engine. . . . In action if the tank was hit slivers of hot steel began to fly—bullets hitting the armoured plates caused melting and the splash, as in steel factories, was dangerous to the eyes. For protection we used to wear a small face mask."

The Anglo-French push proved a signal success, hurling the Germans back ten miles. Most devastating to Ludendorff, 15,000 German soldiers surrendered in a single day. Earlier, in the second summer of the war, a badly mauled regiment, the Royal Scots, had finally overcome their tormenters near Ypres and reportedly slaughtered 300 prisoners. But prisoners coming over in the thousands enjoyed safety in numbers and lived to be escorted to the rear. The official German history noted, "As the sun set on the 8th of August on the battlefield, the greatest defeat which the German Army had suffered since the beginning of the war was an accomplished fact." Informed of the scale of the loss, particularly the mass defections, Ludendorff put it more bluntly: it had been "the black day of the German Army." Simultaneously the cracks on the home front began to widen.

Princess Blücher, an Englishwoman married to a titled German and living in Berlin, wrote in her diary, "It is sadly tragic to look on and see the slow fate of Germany overtaking her. I who have watched the people struggling, and seen their unheard-of sacrifices and stolid resignation, cannot but pity them in my heart. In spite of their odious officialdom, which makes the Prussian so disliked everywhere, the whole world must admire them for the way they have held out." The German populace was living on bread made from potato peels and sawdust powdered with chalk instead of flour, plus the rare bit of meat, including the flesh of dogs and cats. German newspapers carried advertisements for a new drug that offered relief to people "made ill by hunger between meals." Fuel was so short that people slept in their overcoats.

Within a week of the latest Allied push, Germany lost another 46,000 men killed or wounded and 33,000 more who surrendered. The Allied losses were no smaller, but with one difference: the unstoppable flow of Americans went on, producing a net gain in manpower. Germany, in contrast, had to dip into the class of

1920 two years early to bring another 200,000 men to the front. George Goethals, earlier the chief engineer on the Panama Canal project and an authority on logistics, noted that where the "Huns" were still finding men and munitions "continues to be a mystery."

On August 15, Ludendorff made a stunning admission to his staff: the war could not be won. Germany could only hope to negotiate its end far short of victory. He described the Americans in something of an oblique compliment. "Their attacks were undoubtedly brave and often reckless," he wrote in his memoirs. "They came right on in open field and attacked in units too closely formed. Their lack of field experience accounts for some extraordinarily heavy losses." But their entrance into the war, he accepted, was proving fatal to Germany. "The tremendous superabundance of pent-up, untapped nervous energy which America's troops brought into the fray more than balanced the weakness of their Allies who were utterly exhausted."

That the United States was making war against them seemed incomprehensible to Germans, almost a betrayal of kinship, given their common roots with so many Americans. Karl Friedrich Rudolf Nagel, known as "Fritz," an artillery officer, came from a well-to-do Bremen family that had made its money in tobacco, much of the business involving American growers. Nearly all his father's foreign friends were American. An older brother had emigrated to the United States in 1908 and was now serving in the American army. "Many German people who had lifelong dealings with Americans felt vaguely that they simply would not fight us, even if their government told them so," Nagel recalled. His father, a frequent visitor to Virginia and Kentucky, had assured his son, "Americans would make poor soldiers because they were unable to subject themselves to rigid discipline. . . . Furthermore, so my father thought, America had no Army to speak of and there was nothing in its history to suggest a military mind." Young Nagel, however, had read history and knew that in the American Civil War each side had fought with disciplined ferocity, both sides shedding blood copiously. "That we now had to face all these

American soldiers," Nagel concluded, "was proof to me that our diplomats must have been the worst in the world. It was unbelievable."

THE LATEST ALLIED victories convinced Foch that the time had come to break the enemy's back. Even as his armies were shattering Ludendorff's last offensive, even before Germany's "blackest day," Foch summoned Haig, Pétain, and Pershing on July 24 to his headquarters to lay out the endgame. It was to be three-pronged, spanning the entire western front, the British attacking from Ypres in the north, the Americans from the south near Verdun, and the French keeping up pressure in the middle until the ends were bent backward and snapped, leaving the enemy vanquished. Confidence in Foch ran strong among the Allies. On August 10, the French government accorded him the same rank as his German counterpart, Hindenburg. He was now Marshal Foch.

ONE SOLDIER IN the German ranks remained undaunted. Despite nearly four years of frontline service, Adolf Hitler, sloppy in appearance, slouching in posture, refusing to click his heels at an officer's approach, remained a corporal. According to his superior Captain Fritz Wiedemann, Hitler lacked "the capacity for leadership." Fearless in combat, however, he continued to be decorated. In May 1918, he had received two more commendations, the regimental diploma for outstanding bravery and another for being wounded. The defeatism breaking out into the open enraged him. Hitler, a comrade remembered, "became furious and shouted in a terrible voice that pacifists and shirkers were losing the war." When a fellow noncom suggested that it was stupid to keep on fighting, Hitler beat him up.

25

"Do You Wish to Take Part in This Battle?"

NOVEMBER 11, 1918. With minutes remaining before the cease-fire, Sergeant Ernie Powell watched, uncomprehending, as Henry Gunther rose from a shallow indentation in the earth and began charging the German machine-gun emplacement. Their 313th Infantry Regiment, Baltimore's Own, had suffered its first casualty scarcely two months before on the second morning after arriving at the front, when a sniper had shot Corporal Edgar Stuart dead. Stuart's fate was quickly followed by other Baltimoreans, including many of the city's socialite volunteers, Major Israel Putnam, namesake of his Revolutionary War hero ancestor, among them. The place where they died was called Saint-Mihiel.

SEPTEMBER 1918. The French called it "L'Hernie," the Hernia, a triangular bulge jutting into the Allied front some twenty miles southeast of Verdun, its lower-left angle anchored by the city of Saint-Mihiel. The Hernia was located in a wide swath of France that the Germans had held since 1914. It stood sentinel before Metz with its rich iron mines and coal fields. It was here that General Pershing had wanted to commit his expeditionary force from the moment he had arrived in France, sensing that victory at this place could spell victory in the war. Further, he wanted that victory won independently by his army and believed that he had Marshal Foch's concurrence. Pershing's ambition had been temporarily thwarted by the first Ludendorff offensive of March 21. At that time, the AEF commander recognized what Foch needed most and offered "infantry, artillery, aviation, all that we have are yours, use them as you wish." But after the counteroffensives that eventually stopped Ludendorff, Foch shifted ground. On August 28, he descended on Pershing, virtually telling him he would have to abandon the Saint-Mihiel offensive and again put troops under French command as part of his three-pronged strategy for breaking Germany. Pershing resisted, and a violent argument flared. Both men jumped to their feet, exchanging curses. Foch, with a sneer, asked, "Do you wish to take part in this battle?" Pershing shot back, "While our Army will fight wherever you decide, it will fight only as an independent American army!" Days passed, tempers cooled, and on September 2 the two men reached a compromise: Pershing could have his cherished Saint-Mihiel offensive, but immediately thereafter he was to turn his forces north to the Argonne Forest to form the southern jaw of Foch's vise.

STRATEGIC WRANGLES IN the map rooms of châteaus behind the front were far from the thoughts of Pershing's doughboys. Their ever-present enemy was a six-legged creature the size of a grain of rice. The lice fed twelve times a day, clinging tenaciously with tiny claws to the men's clothing while sucking blood from their flesh. The itch drove men to distraction. Arthur Jensen recorded in what he now called the "War Log of an Underdog" that he had scratched himself until he was covered with bleeding sores that then became infected by the bacilli of boils, impetigo, and ulcers thriving in the soil of France. The doughboys called them "cooties" and fought back, taking off their clothes, searching the seams, and crushing the lice between two thumbs until they popped. It was a losing battle. Each louse laid at least five eggs a day, so small that they were barely visible before growing to feeding size. The only real relief was from the delousing van. The van, invariably arriving on the coldest day, required soldiers to strip naked and throw their clothing into a tank on the back in which steam boiled the lice to death. Still, relief was short-lived. One soldier sent from the front to a hospital behind the lines broke down and cried upon discovering that the pests had followed him there. Another soldier, as a permanent memento of his misery, pulled a cootie from his undershirt, dropped it on the letter he was writing home, and dripped candle wax over the louse.

Rivaling the battle against lice in gripping the soldiers' attentions was food. Cook wagons routinely had to travel up to ten miles over rutted roads, between trenches, and around craters to deliver rations to the front. German artillerymen charted the hours and routes the wagons followed and laid down murderously accurate fire. If a shell struck a cook wagon, the units to be fed from it were "SOL," "shit out of luck," in the parlance of the trenches. The rations, if they did arrive, were stowed in burlap bags, each marked with a platoon number. They were usually cold, with bits of lint or cloth clinging to the food. Soldiers joked of first having to give their meals "a shave and a haircut." Cooks suffered perpetual abuse. They were taunted by doughboys filing through the chow line with "What's this, a sample?," "I'll eat it if it kills me, which it probably will," or "Chuck a few Boche helmets in. That stew's damned tasteless." After rations were distributed, the same wagons hauled the dead to the rear. How well one ate was the luck of the draw. While the frontline troops picked shreds of burlap from their mess kits, Draper Dewees, in a cushy clerk's job at V Corps headquarters, remembered, "those army meals have been good. . . . There is nothing better in the world than three or four big flapjacks with lots of syrup and a couple of slices of bacon, eaten from a mess kit under a tree. . . . This is practically an outdoor life and it will do me a lot of good after being tied down to a desk for ten years."

Tobacco was rated not a luxury but a necessity. Even behind the lines, Dewees found smokes hard to come by. "Tailor made cigarettes and pipe tobacco are very scarce. Cigars are almost extinct," he wrote home. Doughboys learned to roll their own from a weekly ration of Bull Durham tobacco. A Fifth Avenue specialty shop in New York did a handsome mail-order business selling an item called "the Makings . . . in khaki or navy blue," a waterproof tobacco pouch with cigarette papers and a matchbox fitted into the lid, price $1.50. Toilet paper was also treasured. One doughboy gratefully recalled, "Each letter from home contained a few sheets. On arrival in France, there was a lack of bungwad and letter paper was too smooth."

Wilbur Peterson composed an impressionist portrait of an existence far removed from life back in Marshall, Iowa: "with a single cupful of water, brush our teeth, shave, wash out our towel and handkerchief . . . half a dozen times a night, crawl out of our blankets for gas alerts, often all of them false . . . two wheeled French cars that took back a load of dead men and returned with a load of unwrapped bread . . . your throat dry as cotton from wearing your gas mask for a couple of hours. . . . Rats eating up your rawhide shoe strings . . . drinking hot, heavily chlorinated water out of canvas bags . . . falling asleep so quickly you wake up the next morning with a burned-out cigarette stub in your mouth."

They sang whenever they safely could. A rouser such as "Over There" was left largely to the folks back home. But at nightfall, in a reserve trench, doughboys, to the accompaniment of a harmonica, would join in singing "Keep the Home Fires Burning," "Little Grey Home in the West," or, in a cheerier vein, "Goodbye Broadway, Hello France," along with a borrowed British favorite, "Pack Up Your Troubles in Your Old Kit Bag" and increasingly ribald versions of "Mademoiselle from Armentières." In an effort at comradeship with the French alongside whom they served, they would stumble through the *poilu* favorite "Madelon."

ON SEPTEMBER 1, 1918, Kaiser Wilhelm, his withered arm tucked out of sight behind his back, a gilded pickelhaube helmet planted across his brow, an Iron Cross dangling from his tunic, addressed thousands of workers at the Krupp armament plant in Essen. The German monarch told the crowd that he was speaking as "the country's father." The sacrifice and suffering of his people, Wilhelm said, was not unknown to him. "I have spoken with many a widow, many a farmer . . . whose hearts were heavy with cares." Who, he asked, bore the blame for the trials of the German people? "How did such a thing happen? Why did we have to undergo such a thing after forty years of peace? . . . The German people were industrious, thinking, assiduous, imaginative in all domains. They worked with body and soul." But this their enemies could not abide, as "we gained on them through our profitable work, and the develoment of our industry, science and art. . . . Envy induced our enemies to fight, and war came upon us." But Germany, Wilhelm assured them, had the ultimate ally: "Each one of us has received his appointed task from on high. You at your hammer, you at your lathe, and I on my throne . . . and is it to be thought that the good God will abandon us there at the last moment? . . . We often at home and at the front and in the open air have sung, 'Ein feste Burg ist unser Gott' ['A Mighty Fortress Is Our God']. . . . a nation from which such a hymn is originated must be invincible." The kaiser asked the workers to promise "to fight and hold out to the last, so help us God." The crowd answered with a thundering *"Ja! Ja! Ja!"* The curious part of Wilhelm's speech at this stage of the war was that no longer was victory mentioned, though the appeal to stand fast was well timed. Within days, his army would feel for the first time, at Saint-Mihiel, the full force of the American Expeditionary Forces.

THE GERMAN HIGH command had decided to start pulling out of the Saint-Mihiel salient on September 11 in order to shorten the front and lessen the drain on its shrinking manpower reserves. At that moment the Americans, unaware of Ludendorff's intended withdrawal, were gearing up to attack, planning to open with a 3,000-gun artillery barrage, more than half a million troops supported by 110,000 Frenchmen, and 1,481 planes, the largest air armada yet assembled. The aircraft were commanded by a brash, not particularly tactful exponent of aerial warfare, Colonel William "Billy" Mitchell, who riled regulars with his claim that the day was dawning when airpower would win wars.

As the battle of flesh against flesh loomed, both sides continued a war for their enemy's soul. German planes carpeted the American front with leaflets urging them to "get out and dash to safety. If you don't you stand a slim chance of ever seeing Broadway or the old home again. The Wall Street millionaires may like this war because they are becoming billionaires. But you will have to pay for it . . . with your blood and taxes and the tears of your loved ones at home. . . . Quit it!" One German plane risked a low pass over a stretch of trench, dropping leaflets that attempted a note of kinship: "To the American Soldiers of German Descent. Do you think it is honorable to fight the country that has given birth to your fathers and forefathers?" it began, and went on, "We are fighting for everything dear to us, for our homes, for our very existence. What are you fighting for, why did you come over here, four thousand miles from your own home? Did Germany do you any harm, did it ever threaten you? . . . It is an everlasting shame that twenty millions of German-Americans could not prevent that man Wilson, who never was a genuine American but rather an English subject in disguise, to raise his hand against their mother country!" The futility of this appeal could be seen in the Schmidts, Mullers, and Schultzes who studded the American casualty lists.

The Americans counterattacked, dropping ten thousand leaflets a day declaring, "Your fight is hopeless, America will cook your goose. Your submarines are no use. We construct more ships than you sink. Your trade is destroyed. . . . Germany's industries must famish." In a September 6 manifesto, a rekindled General Ludendorff retorted, "Germany and her allies are not to be vanquished by arms alone." Germany's army had forced Russia out of the war, "and in the west we are strong enough to do so despite the Americans." He ended with a petulant racial innuendo: "Why does the enemy incite colored people against German soldiers? Because he wants to annihilate us."

Whatever public face Ludendorff chose to present, intelligence officers of the 42nd Division were sure they had discovered deep fissures in German morale. They found a sack of unmailed letters stowed in a command post previously occupied by the once elite, now battered German 10th Division. In one letter, an infantryman complained, "We few fellows cannot hold up to this superior might and must all go helplessly into captivity and of course most of the prisoners are murdered." A grenadier wrote, "Every evening strong patrols are sent out to bring in prisoners, but they are always driven off by the Americans." A corporal concluded, "The Americans are said to have assembled tremendous numbers of tanks and troops on the other side. In that case we are lost." Another wrote, "You have no idea how bad I feel. We get such bad food, worse than a dog, and the men have no more courage." And, on the eve of the Saint-Mihiel offensive, another told his family, "The men are so embittered that they have no interest in anything and they only want the war to end, no matter how."

The order to withdraw had not yet reached all German units in the salient. Consequently, in launching their offensive on the morning of September 12, the Americans were about to battle for ground that a day or two later they could have walked through unopposed. The remaining Germans would, nevertheless, be fighting from stout defenses constructed during their four years of relatively unchallenged occupation. Barbed wire was sown so thickly that it was possible to place boards on it and walk on top. Colonel George Marshall, calculating the artillery required to breach the wire, concluded it would take "five hundred shots . . . to cut a gap five meters wide and ten meters long."

The American guns began their bombardment at 1 A.M. Rain had been falling steadily for four days, the damp and cold soaking through the army wool of shivering doughboys. At 5 A.M., they clambered from the trenches and began slogging through the sodden terrain, embarked on thus far the largest wholly American of-

fensive of the war. The men forming this mass had made an unconscious surrender of individuality. Thousands moved as one or-
ganism. Coercion had played the least part as they advanced into
the killing field. Rather, the desire to keep the respect of one's comrades and sheer momentum carried them along as if by an irresistible tide. Had they been in the British ranks, their courage
would have been bolstered by a tot of rum that morning. The
Yanks moved ahead, cold sober, sustained only by herd instinct.

This day, they were lucky. The Germans fought back but only as
men planning to withdraw anyway rather than as diehards making
a last-ditch stand. By the evening of the thirteenth, nearly all the
AEF's objectives had been taken, and within four days the Saint-
Mihiel salient had been pinched off, with a creditable bag of 15,000
prisoners. By the measure of this war, America's losses were light,
fewer than 9,000 men killed, wounded, or missing. Victory, however, was paid for not only in blood. Brigadier General Charles
Rhodes, then commanding a field artillery regiment, wrote in his
diary about a recent raid, "Last night was satisfactory to the authorities who planned it. But it seemed to me rather barren of results: one prisoner captured alive. . . . 56 American casualties, one
killed in action; estimated cost, $200,000."

General Pershing now had what he wanted: proof that the AEF
was the equal of its allies and the enemy. British generals, however,
were less than awed by the American success at Saint-Mihiel. Since
the Germans had intended to abandon the salient anyway, the
Yanks, as one Briton put it, had not so much defeated the Germans
as relieved them. In explaining the victory to his intelligence officer, Colonel Dennis Nolan, Pershing displayed an unexpected bent
for sociology. "Wave after wave of Europeans," Pershing maintained, "dissatisfied with conditions in Europe, came to seek liberty." This migration had acted as test of character. "Those who
came had the will power and the spirit to seek opportunity in a
new world rather than put up with unbearable conditions in the
old." Through this filtering process, coupled with democracy and
the incentives of individual enterprise, "we had developed a type

of manhood superior in initiative to that existing abroad which, given approximately equal training and discipline, developed a superior soldier."

What doughboys saw in the two hundred square miles they had conquered was an eye-opener. They were all too familiar with the glorified ditches that passed for trenches along the British and the French fronts. But the Germans had built redoubts both sturdy and comfortable, homes away from home. Behind the lines, German soldiers cultivated gardens of fresh vegetables and kept dairy cows. Some had started second families, fathering children with Frenchwomen.

As a mule skinner moving between the rear and the trenches, Arthur Jensen was struck by the swings in human behavior he witnessed. When the infantrymen prepared to go over the top, they abandoned all their possessions except for rifle, helmet, and gas mask. "I had lots of fun snoopin' into what they'd left behind," Jensen confessed. He was surprised in his roaming to come upon "trench buzzards," men "too yellow to follow along. They were eking out an existence on stuff they found lying around, mostly corned beef and hard tack." Equally disgusting to Jensen were displays of safe bravado. On the first morning of Saint-Mihiel, Jensen watched German prisoners pouring to the rear. "One kid in our outfit was so determined to kill a German," Jensen recalled, "that he told me he was going to hide somewhere and shoot a prisoner as they marched by." Jensen told the soldier that "the one he'd kill would probably have a sweetheart over in Germany who would be crying her eyes out while he was bragging about killing his German. After a little thought he decided not to."

During Saint-Mihiel, Jensen saw his first fatality, a German corpse crouched in a dugout, his face blue-black and bloodstained, one hand clutching his heart, the other reaching out. "So this was war," Jensen wrote in his log. "I was ready for hostilities to cease right there." Yet just days later, the mule skinner found himself succumbing again to the imagined romance of living on the cusp of mortality. He longed to enter the trenches before it was all over. In the meantime, he became something of an authority on postbattle conditions, especially the stench. Most nauseating, he found, were long-exposed bodies of fellow soldiers. "I don't mind the smell of dead horses," Jensen noted, "but it drives our horses wild. Cattle are the same way. I've heard them stand bawling over ground stained by blood of their own kind. It seems as if every animal is terrorized by the smell of its own dead."

He was sickened to see a doughboy yank the boots off a German body and begin strutting around the cook wagon. "We thought that was terrible," he recalled, "until one of the cooks took a chisel and a pair of pliers and knocked out his gold teeth for souvenirs." Souvenir hunting had become a mania: rings, bayonets, cartridge casings, insignia ripped from enemy uniforms, and fabric torn from fallen airplanes. A fellow mule skinner was sentenced to cleaning stables for hiding piles of German helmets in a wagon, imposing a useless burden on the horses. Draper Dewees wrote home from V Corps headquarters after Saint-Mihiel, "I have found out what the war is about: France is fighting for 'La Patrie'; England is fighting for commerce; Italy is fighting to get a slice of Austria, and America is fighting for souvenirs." In the end, the constant movement and the limits to what a man could carry returned most souvenirs back to the earth where they had been found. It was just as well; French veterans warned the doughboys against going into battle bearing souvenirs. If they were captured carrying them, the Germans could be harsh. But that risk worked in both directions. A German prisoner found with a pack of Camel cigarettes and a dollar bill, Dewees recalled, had been beaten to death.

Two Saint-Mihiel veterans were already displaying a flamboyance that would become the hallmarks of their subsequent careers. Douglas MacArthur, though now a brigadier general, had been the first man over the parapet, leading the 84th Brigade of the 42nd Division. Also engaged in the assault was an early champion of the tank, the equally theatrical Major George S. Patton. MacArthur dismissed Patton's tanks as useless, as vulnerable in the mud as an overloaded doughboy. At one point during the battle, the two men found themselves standing together, stiff-backed, eyeing each other warily in the midst of a bombardment. "We stood and talked," Patton later recalled, "but neither was much interested in what the other said as we could not get our minds off the shells." In MacArthur's version he saw Patton flinch, whereupon the general observed dryly, "Don't worry, major, you never hear the one that gets you."

26

A Civilized End to
Pointless Slaughter

NOVEMBER 11, 1918. With each crash of artillery, Corporal Clarence Johnson gathered himself more tightly into a fetal coil. For the men of the 321st Infantry Regiment, this was their first day under fire and would be the last. The men had been trucked to the front the day before through terrain where the battle for Verdun had been fought in 1916. Johnson, a graduate of the University of North Carolina, recorded his impressions: "the utter desolation, the completeness and thoroughness of the destruction. Nothing was left standing, not a tree or even a bush." Most macabre, "The barren, shell-torn hills were literally strewn with bones of French and German dead blanched white after two years exposure to the elements." On this last day, Johnson felt conflicting emotions. After all the training, the ocean voyage, the letters home hinting at danger to be bravely met, to return as untested as when they had left would have been unfulfilling, even embarrassing. The prospect of not returning at all, with so little time left, was, however, more disturbing.

In the hours before dawn, Colonel George McIver, commanding the brigade of which the 321st formed part, upon hearing rumors that an armistice was imminent, had sent a message to 81st Division headquarters asking for clarification. What was he to do now? Word came back from Major General Charles Bailey, the 81st's commander, that at 6 A.M. he was to "move forward the attack." The general wanted Ville-en-Woevre, a small town two and a half miles in front of the division, taken. McIver sent runners to relay this order to the two regiments under him. The commander of one, Colonel Frank Halstead of the 321st, added his own belligerent note before relaying the order to his officers: "Aggressiveness must characterize the attack at all stages." At 8:20 A.M., word reached the 321st that the armistice had been signed and that hostilities were to end at 11 A.M. But nothing had been said about stopping before then.

At 9:20 A.M., a runner reached Colonel Thomas Pearce, commanding the other regiment in McIver's brigade, the 323rd, with word of the signing. Pearce told his men to take shelter wherever they could from the fierce artillery fire still falling. Within ten minutes, his order was countermanded. "You will," the message from brigade read, "advance at once." By the time Pearce got word out to his scattered units to regroup, it was 10:40 A.M. The men muttered, expressing disbelief, but rose and began moving forward through a dense fog that Pearce hoped would at least rob the enemy guns of visible targets. To mark their advance through the mist, he ordered the men to drop anything disposable along the way: "towels, socks, underwear, handkerchiefs, and mirrors."

Corporal Johnson's 321st Regiment reached the enemy trenches at five minutes before eleven. Leaping in, they bayoneted seven fleeing machine gunners. At eleven o'clock, "Runners finally managed to reach the 321st with word to stop firing. But in the heat of battle," as Colonel McIver put it, "the movement was arrested with some difficulty." Johnson glanced back and saw their recently covered path strewn with slain doughboys.

SEPTEMBER 1918. These regiments of the 81st Division, pressing the Germans to the very last instant, were simply completing their role within Foch's six-week-old strategy of applying pressure at both ends of the Hindenburg Line, thus breaking Germany's spine and leaving no exit but defeat. The part assigned the Americans, flushed with victory after Saint-Mihiel, had been to wheel northwest of Verdun and drive the enemy out of the hills and woods between the Argonne Forest and the Meuse River. The French were to push the Germans back over the Aisne River in the center, while the British would press the attack from Ypres in the north toward Saint-Quentin.

The northern offensive had begun on September 27 near Cambrai, announced by the customary artillery barrage backed by a huge British force of forty-one divisions. A Canadian infantryman, Sterling Chesson, recalled, "At 5:22 A.M. all hell broke loose." Crouched in a funkhole, Chesson described what he heard above his head: "It sounded like a combination of a hundred express trains rushing over steel bridges, a boiler factory filled with lunatics, and an orchestra of a thousand bass drums gone mad. Interspersed with that was the sound of machine guns hammering away like hell itself and it could only be compared with a million typewriters all hammering away at full speed. . . . If my nerves ever got to the breaking, they came damn close to it during those thirty-five minutes of hell." Then Chesson went over the top.

The attackers ran up against a formidable obstacle, the Saint-Quentin Canal, a lengthy inland waterway, two miles of which had been tunneled under hilly country from Bellicourt to Bony. Ventilated and electrically lit, located just behind the Hindenburg Line, the tunnel had proved a godsend for its German occupiers, a bombproof shelter in which men could be housed, fed, and supplied unobserved. At intervals the Germans had constructed stairways through which troops could rush up from the tunnel out into the open and meet the enemy.

The American 27th and 30th Divisions had been assigned to aid French, British, Australian, and Canadian troops in the north. They fought with what was fast becoming their trademark: heedless, costly advances over open ground. A British barrage intended to provide cover for the American assault on the Saint-Quentin tunnel overshot its mark by 1,100 yards, leaving the doughboys naked to the German guns. Troops of the 30th Division neverthe-less reached the terrain on top of the tunnel, only to have the Germans rise from their underground passageways and wreak havoc on the rear of the unsuspecting Americans. On September 29, the 27th Division's 107th Infantry Regiment took 985 casualties—337 killed—the largest one-day loss for an American regiment thus far in the war. Six doughboys won Medals of Honor in this fight, two of them awarded posthumously.

Eight days after the northern battle had begun, the Hindenburg Line in that sector was breached and abandoned, despite belts of barbed wire running ten miles deep, antitank ditches, machine-gun nests embedded in concrete, devilishly deployed artillery, and the Saint-Quentin tunnel. Sir Arthur Conan Doyle, creator of Sherlock Holmes, serving as a correspondent for *The Times* of London, described German prisoners streaming to the rear in language more palatable on the home front than the battle front: "The prevailing impression was an ox-like stolidity and dullness. It was a herd of beasts, not a procession of men. It was indeed farcical to think that these uniformed bumpkins represented the great military nation, while the gallant figures who lined the road belonged to the race that they despised as being unwarlike."

THE FOCH STRATEGY for breaking the southern end of the Hindenburg Line in the Meuse-Argonne was launched on September 26, the burden of the mission falling to Pershing's AEF. The German Army's lifeline in France was a skein of railroads running behind and roughly parallel to the front. These lines converged near the city of Sedan, some thirty-four miles in front of the Americans. If Pershing's divisions could take Sedan, they would sever the German jugular and leave the enemy to bleed to death. The Germans, well aware that they faced a defend-or-die situation, had hardened the Meuse-Argonne sector of the Hindenburg Line with seven ribs of trenches, bunkers, and antitank ditches. To smash through this cordon, the United States had marshaled the largest force in the history of American arms, one that would eventually reach one million doughboys mobilized along the Meuse-Argonne front.

The respite between the American victory at Saint-Mihiel and this latest offensive was a brief ten days. In the interim, men were marched or trucked to forward positions, huge ammunitions dumps were stacked up by black service troops, rations were heaped in unappetizing piles, and the doughboys groused. While death waited in the offing, their immediate distress had more banal roots: bodies unwashed and plagued by lice, food contaminated, the air fouled by the dead, a smell that clung to army wool. One private was inspired to rank the soldiers' nemeses. At the top he placed "our officers . . . arrogant and unreasonable. They have so much power that they can have us shot for nothing. . . . I call them our arch enemies." Next was the weather, "because in these leaky clothes, the cold rain and mud are slowly sapping the life out of us." Mules followed, "so dangerous that the civilians sold them to the Army to get rid of 'em." Steel helmets were of scant use, sitting "on our heads like pie-pans instead of coming down over our ears where they could do some good." Added to the hate list were lice, canned potato-and-meat hash, "because it gives us heartburn," and "homesickness." At the bottom was the enemy—"if it wasn't for them we could go home."

In their obsession with food, the doughboys came to respect German ingenuity. They learned to ransack the packs of dead Germans for a bread-based cube, sweet-tasting and loaded with nourishment. A canned yellow powder became another item of prized booty. When mixed with water, it produced a surprisingly tasty custard. Bill Triplet, with the 140th Infantry, devised his own energy-packed ration. Filching the ingredients from a field kitchen, Triplet emptied his toilet articles from a tin container, crumbled French field bread into it, then poured bacon grease over the top, creating two pounds of congealed calories, fat, and roughage.

Operating close to the lines, the Salvation Army won the doughboys' affection. The V Corps headquarters clerk Draper Dewees stood in a line a block long to buy chocolate bars, packs of gum, and lemon drops from a Salvation Army Nell for four francs, "which is reasonable when you consider how far that candy had come. . . . Without detracting from the credit due the YMCA and the Red Cross . . . there is one organization that is going to receive my contributions when I get home, the Salvation Army."

The mood before battle wore two faces, one by those who would fight and the other by those who would watch. An army chaplain wrote to his congregation in Watertown, New York, "Let me assure you, our boys count it a great privilege to die for their country. It is no sacrifice to them, no matter how you may regard it." The farther from the war, the more patriotism blazed. Carleton Simon, 26th Division, from a prominent New York family, after coming through Saint-Mihiel and awaiting the Meuse-Argonne, received a letter from his mother that read, "We are very proud of our brave soldier and we knew full well that when your time came to fight, you would. Sweetheart, I want you to go forward with a stout heart and the same trust and courage you have always shown in the past. *Don't fear* you are in the hands of God."

But the seasoned veteran Captain Will Judy, though he had thrilled to see the king of England, was acutely aware of the gulf between lofty sentiments and what he lived daily. The week before the offensive, he wrote in his diary, "I have not heard more than a half dozen times during my year in the Army a discussion among the men, or even the officers of the principles for which we fight. . . . Nor do we sit in dugouts studying tactical maps, discussing the plan of coming battle, and arguing the merits or demerits of this or that campaign. . . . The soldier does not know whether ten thousand men are in the attack and whether the goal is Berlin or Jerusalem. . . . Almost nine tenths of the soldier's conversation concerns stories about women, the location of wine shops, the next trip to the bath-house, . . . what is the popular songbook in the United States, and what's the idea of fighting for France when they charge us high prices, and above all other subjects—'when do we eat?' "

Counterbalancing the physical discomforts and the overhanging

threat of death or mutilation, the men came to prize the camaraderie of the trenches. "We give away anything we have if we
think the other fellow needs it more than we do," Arthur Jensen
noted in his War Log. "Money has no value here. Each man's fortune consists of what he carries. . . . I like the unselfish attitude up
here so much that, in many ways, I wish I could live on the front
forever." What had brought out the best in men—selflessness,
love, caring, loyalty—had come about through the basest human
employment, killing their fellow man.

At 5:30 A.M. on the day of the Meuse-Argonne attack, the U.S.
Army, flanked on the right and left by French troops, began to
move northward from a point seven miles northeast of Verdun.
Artillery had been firing for the previous two and a half hours,
3,980 guns crammed two hundred to the mile along a twenty-five-
mile front. To one granted the perspective of distance, the scale of
it all, the masses of men, the blinding light bursting from flares and
cannon mouths, the ear-numbing cacophony presented a magnificent spectacle. Yet the universe of the man on the ground was
tightly circumscribed, limited to the men to his left and those to his
right. As the soldiers prepared to abandon the protection of their
lines, a man's future could be measured not necessarily in years,
months, or even days but in minutes, even seconds.

Troops of the 37th and 79th Divisions were arrayed before
Montfaucon, a hill dominating the center of the front. Its earth
was steeped in ancient blood. More than a thousand years before,
men had died on its slopes in battles between warring tribes. Rain
appeared to be the inevitable concomitant of a new offensive on
the western front, including this day. Numerous creeks crisscrossing the region flooded and turned fields into quagmires. Troops
dumped tens of thousands of sandbags into washed-out roadbeds
to allow supply wagons to reach the front. The infantrymen had to
lay down duckboards to advance.

For Joe Rizzi, one molecule in the olive drab mass comprising
the 35th Division, the day would mark his initiation into battle. As
he waited for zero hour, a corporal handed Rizzi an ax and wire
cutters. His squad was to move to the front of the first wave, the

corporal told him, and cut the enemy wire for the troops to pass through. Officers repeatedly checked their watches and at precisely 5:30 A.M. unholstered their pistols, blew their whistles, climbed the ladders, and stepped over the sandbagged parapet into open terrain. Sergeants followed on their heels, waving their rifles overhead and cursing at the men in their platoons to follow them. To Rizzi, the spectacle had a ferocious beauty. The magic of the moment was shattered, however, when, as he tried to pull himself out of the trench, the muddied earth gave way and "ass over head I landed back in the trench." A corporal, pointing over the parapet, shouted, "Hey Wop, we're going this way!"

Once out of the trench, Rizzi took his leading place in ranks as regular as the cratered ground permitted. He wondered why they were marching as if on parade rather than running to shorten their exposure to enemy fire. Rizzi soon understood the necessity of advancing at a steady pace. The first wave initially encountered light resistance and reached its objective ahead of schedule. Whistles again blew, signaling the men to halt. To keep advancing would mean walking into their own rolling barrage, dropping just feet ahead of them. Rizzi had heard tales of the effects of fear on bowels. "I felt the seat of my pants and it was dry," he noted with relief. At the other end of the front, Connell Albertine, with the 26th Division, fared less well: "It just came out, trickled down and lodged at my knees . . . because of the wrap leggings. Soon we could all smell this stool odor from each other." Sergeant Triplet, advancing with the 35th, noted the prevailing posture. "It's odd how a man under fire will tilt his head forward and lean into his helmet like it was an umbrella in a hard rainstorm. It would take four helmet thicknesses to bounce a bullet." Triplet understood the futility of the gesture even as he did the same: "It felt safer, peering from under the brim—stupid."

Rizzi's squad moved ahead as ordered and began chopping down the wooden posts supporting the enemy wire. But before they made much headway, the second wave bore down on them. Rizzi flung the ax and wire cutter aside and clambered over the snagging barbs to catch up with the first wave. As he did so, the corporal who had taunted him tripped over the wire and went sprawling. "Thisaway, Corporal," Rizzi mocked him through the din, "notta data way!"

Among the guns supporting the 35th's advance was Captain Harry Truman's Battery D. Truman had been given the battery in July, an agglomeration, as he described it, of "wild Irish and German Catholics" who had already gone through four commanders. Taking charge of this rabble in uniform, he later confessed, had been at that point the most frightening experience of his life. Surprisingly, the rowdies took to their mild-looking, bespectacled captain, who quickly displayed the essentials of leadership, firmness and fairness. The men began calling him "Captain Harry," and Truman liked it. Battery D had not fired in anger until September 1918, five months after arriving in France. The first five hundred rounds unloaded on the German lines in the Vosges prompted return fire that killed two horses and dropped one shell fifteen feet from Truman. Afterward, he wrote his fiancée, Bess Wallace, "Please don't worry about me because no German shell is made that can hit me."

Truman made an ignominious entry into the Meuse-Argonne sector on the third day of the battle. He was galloping on horseback toward his battery's assigned position when a tree limb knocked off his glasses. Without them he could scarcely see the guns, much less the enemy. After pawing fruitlessly on the ground, a distraught Truman was relieved when one of his men found the glasses clinging to the horse's hindquarters. The rest of the day went more fittingly for Captain Harry; his guns destroyed one German battery and put two more out of action. Two days later, while Truman was firing near Cheppy, a breathless runner approached. Air reconnaissance had spotted a German force moving upon an unsuspecting American battalion huddled at the base of a hill. The runner, Paul Schaffer, gave a sharp picture of Truman, the warrior: "He was a banty officer in spectacles, and when he read my message he started runnin' and cussin' all at the same time, shouting for the guns to turn northwest. . . . I never heard a man cuss so well or intelligently, and I'd shoed a million mules. He was shouting back ranges and bearings. . . . It was a great sight, like the center ring in Barnum and Bailey . . . slapping shells into breeches, and jerking lanyards before the man hardly had time to bolt the door. . . . Then Captain Truman cussed 'em to fire even faster. . . . There were groups of Germans on the edge of the woods, stooping low, coming on slowly with machine guns on their hips, held by shoulder straps. Whole legs were soon flying through the air. He really broke up that counterattack."

The airmen who had spotted the German maneuver failed to awe Harry Truman. "They fly around a couple of hours a day, sleep in a featherbed every night, eat hotcakes and maple syrup for breakfast, pie and roast beef for supper every day, spend their vacations in Paris or wherever else suits their fancy, and draw 20 percent extra pay for doing it," he wrote Bess. "Their death rate is about like the quartermaster and ordnance departments and on top of it they are dubbed the heroes of the war. Don't believe it, the infantry—our infantry—are the heroes of the war."

Among the admired infantrymen of Truman's 35th Division was Sergeant Bill Triplet, now a dispatcher of runners. On the second day of the Meuse-Argonne, Triplet's D Company found itself hemmed in by machine-gun fire of unseen origin. He scrawled a message explaining the situation to the company commander and gave it to a runner. "A single bullet took him in the side of the head and cartwheeled him ten yards back down the slope. God damn," he recalled, "I'd had two constructive ideas that morning and each one had cost a man." Triplet decided to wait for the CO to come up and discover the situation for himself. The next day, D Company advanced. Triplet's company clerk had worked out beforehand the mathematics of surviving machine-gun fire. "A Jerry bullet travels 2,700 feet per second and their guns fire . . . 10 rounds per second," the clerk had calculated. "That means there's one bullet every 270 feet, that's 90 yards apart. Any fairly active man," he concluded, "should be able to step between two bullets that are near a city block apart." The numerous men shot down that day apparently lacked that agility.

After the action, amid the corpses, Triplet picked up a German helmet with a hole drilled through it, the lining caked with blood. A stout Red Cross official, immaculately dressed and wearing polished boots, stepped gingerly through the mud and asked to see the helmet. Examining it, he noted gleefully, "That's the coat of arms of the Fifth Prussian Guards." He seemed especially pleased at the hole, which indicated that "that's one Kraut they can write off the roster." The official asked how much Triplet wanted for the helmet. Suddenly, the ghoulishness of the situation, the "head-hunting, scalp-taking . . . instinct that is so close under the epidermis of the most civilized men" revolted Triplet. He handed the man the helmet and told him he could have it. The official pressed a half dollar into his hand. Triplet flung it into the mud. The man glared at him but picked up the money and left with his prize.

The fighting slowed momentarily the way exhausted boxers clinch until they regain strength. Triplet's squad sought refuge in a tunnel, its wide mouth blocked by sandbags and a supposedly gasproof door. Gas, thus far, had caused up to a third of American casualties. The choices were to leave the door open and enjoy fresh air yet risk being gassed, to sleep uncomfortably in gas masks, or to leave the door closed and breathe a stench compounded of four years of occupancy by unwashed *poilus,* abandoned latrines, and the still-clinging foulness of earlier phosgene and mustard gas barrages. They chose to leave the door open and wear the masks that, Triplet complained, led to "whooping cough and bronchitis."

The Germans had by now developed gas warfare to a wicked art. In the Argonne, they would begin blanketing a sector with gas at night. The Americans would put on their masks until the vapors settled into the ground and, when the danger appeared to be over, take them off. But when the sun rose the following morning, the earth would warm and the gas would rise again, poisoning the unprotected doughboys. Triplet remembered the dilemma described by a Cockney who had trained the Americans in gas warfare: "Be careful with your gahs mahsk," the Tommy had warned, "h'and if you do get a touch of gahs, never show it. We courtmartial our gahs cases for self-hinflicted wounds."

After a week of fighting in the Meuse-Argonne, the Americans had penetrated seven miles into German territory, every inch of which the enemy yielded grudgingly. Behind the American lines, chaos reigned. Monumental traffic jams choked the roads, stalling ambulances and leaving the wounded to wait on bare ground. Stragglers, honestly lost or shirking, wandered about in undisciplined packs. General Pershing managed to weave through the disorder in a massive Locomobile limousine with double wheels in the back and license plates adorned with four stars. Despite gains at the front, what he saw in the rear outraged this iron disciplinarian. Pershing ordered that any man found fleeing battle was to be shot. The irascible Premier Clemenceau, while himself trying to inspect the front, became bogged down in the bedlam, assigned the blame to Pershing, and threatened to fire him. The confusion, recriminations, second-guessing, finger-pointing, and faultfinding were hardly unusual. It was war at its most typical.

ON OCTOBER 6, momentarily out of the line, Harry Truman wrote Bess, "The papers are in the street now saying that the Central Powers have asked for peace, and I was in the drive that did it!" The report was rooted in truth. Nine days before, on September 28, General Ludendorff, at the headquarters of the German high command in Spa, feeling the full weight of the American involvement, raged against every perceived internal enemy: the kaiser, the Reichstag, the home front. Germany's chancellor, Count Georg von Hertling, had said of Ludendorff that the general was magnificent only "at a time of success. If things go badly, he loses his nerve." Ludendorff's aide judiciously closed the door to shut out the general's defeatist tirade. That evening an emotionally drained Ludendorff went to the quarters of his nominal superior, Field Marshal von Hindenburg, and said that the Americans had struck at the army's vitals, morale was crumbling, and the manpower bottom had been scraped. There was no choice; they must seek an armistice. The weary old man offered no objection. As

Hindenburg admitted in his memoirs, "It was plain the situation could not last. Our armies were too weak and too tired. Moreover, the pressure which the American masses were putting on the most sensitive point in the region of the Meuse was too strong." The next day, the two men met with the kaiser. A staff officer, Colonel von Thaer, penned in his diary an eyewitness account of the moment: "Ludendorff stood up in our presence, his face was pale and filled with deep worry, but his head was still held high. . . . He said roughly the following: 'The Supreme Army Command and the German Army were at an end. . . . Bulgaria had already been lost. Austria and Turkey, both at the end of their powers, would also soon fall. . . . Some troops had proven so unreliable that they had had to be quickly pulled from the front. If they were replaced with other troops willing to fight, they would be received with the label strike breakers.' " The weight of the Americans would throw victory to the Allies. "Therefore, the Supreme Army Command demanded of His Majesty, the Kaiser, and of the Chancellor that a proposal for the bringing about of peace be made to President Wilson of America without delay on the basis of his Fourteen Points."

The Fourteen Points referred to the American president's highminded attempt, first floated the previous January, to bring a civilized end to senseless slaughter. The points essentially propounded an international order in which relations between nations must be transparent, colonial peoples should determine how and by whom they would be ruled, the seas would be open, free trade was to prevail, and a world government, a league of nations, would be formed. The Fourteen Points also set the price Germany must pay for peace. It must give up every inch of territory taken in this war as well as Alsace-Lorraine, seized from France nearly a half century before.

One deep fissure had already foretold the breakdown of the Central Powers. On September 30, as feared, a German junior partner, Bulgaria, its forces *hors de combat*, had pleaded for an armistice. Wilson had given the beleaguered Germans a handhold with which they might pull themselves out of the morass of failed hopes with a shred of honor, if not victory. On October 3, the kaiser turned to his respected fifty-one-year-old cousin, Prince Max von Baden, bald, handsome, with a twirling mustache, to succeed Georg von Hertling as imperial chancellor. Prince Max was a proven liberal. He had opposed the resumption of the unrestricted submarine warfare that had drawn America into the war, thus sealing Germany's fate. Surely, the kaiser reasoned, Max would be palatable to Wilson. On October 4, the German government requested an armistice, not from its foes in the field but rather from the American president, based on his Fourteen Points. Max's move was adroit. By accepting these terms, he had in a single stroke appeared to lift Germany from bullying aggressor to Wilson's moral high ground. Wilson had hoped for a peace with neither victors nor vanquished, and here was the German chancellor embracing this sensible solution to the slaughter while Wilson's own allies resisted the president's formula.

Prince Max, however, recognized one obstacle. He could not play peacemaker as long as Ludendorff, the de facto military dictator of Germany, remained in power. The kaiser must choose between his royal cousin and the plebeian general. Wilhelm ordered Ludendorff to Berlin and on October 26 accepted his resignation without a syllable of thanks. Ludendorff returned home a broken man who had already given two stepsons to this lost cause. He fled Germany for Denmark, disguised with an ill-fitting false beard and dark glasses. General Wilhelm Groener replaced him as chief of staff. Groener, a transportation expert, was well suited to Germany's immediate task, to get the army back home in an orderly retreat rather than a rout. Within a day, word was on the street in France that Germany was seeking peace, and it was to these reports that Harry Truman referred in his letter to Bess.

27

A Plague in the Trenches

OCTOBER 1918. To Connell Albertine, chaplain's clerk; Vivian de Sola Pinto, in the British sector near Mons; Pierre Teilhard de Chardin, carrying broken Frenchmen to aid stations; and Herbert Sulzbach, German Jew caught up in his country's retreat, the war the day after the kaiser's government asked President Wilson for peace looked no different from the war the day before. Shell fire still dismembered bodies, snipers picked off the unwary, gas blistered the lungs. And mule skinner Arthur Jensen came close enough to the front to experience briefly the involvement he craved. "You can tell a gas shell when it comes over," he wrote in his War Log, "because you can hear the liquid that's going to be gas slopping around inside—blob, blob, blob."

On October 7, Major General Hunter Liggett, commanding the I Corps, put a bold scheme before General Pershing. In the Meuse-Argonne fighting, German artillery was pouring murderous fire into the flanks of American divisions to the right. Liggett's idea was to have another of his divisions, the 82nd, swing north alongside the enemy line, and catch the unsuspecting Germans on their flank rather than head-on. Among the troops carrying out this stratagem was acting Corporal Alvin York, 328th Infantry Regiment, a Tennessee backwoodsman, farmer, and blacksmith with a third-grade education. Before the war, York had abandoned a life of hell-raising, moonshine swilling, gambling, and brawling to become what would one day be called a born-again Christian. At the time he was drafted, the reformed York was choirmaster at his church, with strong scruples against killing. He was also a sure-shot marksman who could plug a half-inch target from one hundred feet. The corporal, now a squad leader with Company G, jumped off with his men at 6:10 A.M. on the morning of October 8 from Hill 223 on the eastern edge of the Argonne Forest. Their objective was to put out of action thirty machine-gun emplacements on an opposing ridge. Doing so required crossing a valley, within which the Americans took fire from both sides. Stopped cold, York recalled, "Our boys just went down like the long grass before the mowing machine at home." The remaining seventeen men decided to try to swing around to the German rear. But the enemy machine guns merely tracked them, killing six more and wounding three others. York, now in command as the senior noncom, observed that every time a German gunner began to resume fire, he first had to raise his head above the parapet. The Tennessean's extraordinary coordination of hand and eye began to tell. York's Enfield rifle never missed. As he put it, "Every time a head done come up, I knocked it down."

A German major, spotting the source of their torment, led five men out of a trench, bayonets fixed, headed toward York in single file. York employed an old turkey-shooting trick, hitting the last man first, then the second to last, and so on, so that the Germans kept plowing ahead, oblivious to the fate of the men behind. York took the major captive and yelled over the din of the guns for him to signal to the Germans still entrenched to surrender, or "I would take off his head next." The major, duped by York's performance into thinking he must be facing a far larger force, did as commanded. Corporal York began to play the Pied Piper to obedient German troops emerging from half a dozen defenses, hands held high. Before the day was done, he found himself marching 132 prisoners to the rear, while 28 others lay dead, which, York noted, "is just the number of shots I fired," adding, "At that distance I couldn't miss." When his commanding officer realized what York had achieved, he promoted the acting corporal to sergeant on the spot. The Tennessean was awarded the Distinguished Service Cross, subsequently upgraded when General Pershing draped the Medal of Honor around York's neck, and America had a hero of immortal legend.

The other indelible legend born in the Meuse-Argonne was that of the Lost Battalion—more accurately, the Surrounded Battalion. On October 2, units from the 308th and 307th Infantry Regiments, plus gunners from the 306th Machine Gun Battalion, a total of 554 men, were cut off by the enemy while descending into a steep ravine. There they remained for five days, trapped in a pocket 350 yards long and 75 yards wide, while food ran out and their only water to drink was from mud puddles. As German machine gunners, mortarmen, and riflemen continued to thin their ranks, the battalion's only hope for seeking help was via four carrier pigeons. Even when word of the battalion's plight did get through, the food and medical supplies dropped by plane fell outside the men's reach. On the fifth day, the German commander sent an escorted American POW into the ravine to deliver an ultimatum that his countrymen surrender or face annihilation. Major Charles W. Whittlesey, surrounded by starving men, untended wounded, and the dead, sent back his answer: "Go to Hell." At seven that evening troops of the 77th Division finally broke through and the Lost Battalion was rescued. Of the 554 men who had entered the ravine, 194 hollow-eyed, unshaven figures staggered out. For their indomitability, Whittlesey and two of his subordinates received the Medal of Honor.

American Indians in AEF ranks produced their own Alvin York, Private Joseph Oklahombi, a Choctaw from southeastern Oklahoma serving with the 141st Infantry Regiment in the Saint-Étienne sector. Oklahombi, whose name in Choctaw meant "mankiller," ran two hundred yards through barbed wire and, according to his citation, "rushed on machine-gun nests, capturing 171 prisoners," then turned the captured guns upon the enemy. Joe Young Hawk, a Sioux, taken prisoner during a raid, slew three of his captors with his bare hands, and marched two others back to the American lines. During the first American engagement at Cantigny, a Mojave Indian named Bluebird picked off six German soldiers, according to a war correspondent, "with the same emotions with which he lit cigarettes." The Indians' heroism fed the white men's romantic notions of the red man as a born warrior. Unlike blacks, who bore the stigma of slave ancestry and were treated accordingly, the Indian was seen as a free spirit, swift of foot, keen of scent, stout of heart. Indians were presumed to be natural scouts, snipers, and runners, all high-risk occupations that they were too proud to turn down. An Indian in the 167th Infantry was sent on patrol into no-man's-land for twenty-one successive nights, until he was killed. Reporters seized on such exploits to mythologize Indians in language approaching comic-strip stereotypes. According to one story, "Red Indians from Wyoming or Colorado were stoics of high explosive shells and poison gas as if the calumet went round at the council fire or the drums beat to a dance." Indians scenting trouble "ran through the woods like deer." Jess Fixon, a Cherokee, reportedly claimed that he had enlisted to "bayonet the Kaiser all by himself," explaining that Wilhelm II, "killum papoose, killum squaw, so Jess Fixon will find this Kaiser and stickum bayonet clear through. Ugh!" Another Sioux, Joseph Cloud, reportedly complained that he had yet "to lift any German's hair." In living up to the warrior image, the Indians paid a stiff price. While the AEF was losing 1 percent of its men to battle deaths, the Indians who had volunteered lost 5 percent. Pawnees in uniform saw 14 percent of their number killed. Indians reaped medals commensurate with their exploits, especially from the French, who regarded them with wonder as storybook figures out of the Wild West.

Doughboys from the Choctaw tribe provided an unexpected advantage to the forces in the Saint-Étienne sector. No German could be expected to speak their several languages. Thus fourteen Choctaws were trained to relay orders in their native dialects over field telephones. These ancient tongues, however, required curious adaptations to meet the demands of modern warfare. The machine gun was thus rendered by the Choctaws as "little gun shoot fast." Ca-

sualties became "scalps," and a unit, the 3rd Battalion, for example, was identified as "three grains of corn." Indian code talkers
would gain far greater fame in the next world conflict, but the
practice began in the trenches of France in 1918.

WHILE DOUGHBOYS OF whatever color won an early reputation
for courage bordering on recklessness, General Bullard found the
number of shirkers shocking. "French villages," he complained,
"were full of them . . . deadbeats, deserters and evaders of battle
and danger." Marine Corps private Elton Mackin, who had witnessed near-unalloyed heroism in Belleau Wood, subsequently discovered cracks in the corps's armor. During an after-action roll call
in the Meuse-Argonne, he remembered hearing the sergeant shout
out, "Gil Bradow." "Dead," the answer came back. Not from
enemy fire, Mackin knew, since "he had been caught rifling the
pockets of the dead of his battalion. . . . There are some laws that
must not be transgressed." Stripping the enemy dead was, however, a different matter. Mackin, though tempted, had shrunk from
taking a ring from a dead German's finger. A comrade did not hesitate, explaining, "Robbing German dead don't count in heaven."

Mackin found in war that the sordid and the sublime alternated
with jarring swiftness. While his company was halting in a village,
an old woman approached him, holding a tiny crucifix suspended
from a piece of string. A fellow marine sneered, "Why didn't ye'
pay 'er las' night? Now she wants her franc!" The woman hung
the cross around Mackin's neck and ran a wrinkled hand along his
cheek. "My son," she said, smiling, "you won't die."

FROM THE MOMENT the Meuse-Argonne campaign was launched
on September 26 through the end of October, the fighting continued bloody and unremitting, with the Germans contesting every
crag and farm as if they were defending the *Vaterland*. The price
was horrific. In slightly over a month, the AEF took 98,000 casu-

alties, with 26,000 dead. High costs were predictable given the pugnacity of generals such as Charles P. Summerall. The main objective of the armies in the Meuse-Argonne was to cut the German-controlled rail line that ran from Mézières through Sedan to Metz. Between their present position and the objective stood a formidable stretch of the Hindenburg Line, the Kriemhild-Stellung. Upon taking command of V Corps, Summerall, atop a sleek black mount, addressed his senior officers. "Way up to the North is a railhead. Go cut it for me," he told them. "And when you cut it, you will go hungry if you try to feed the prisoners you will take." Nothing was to divert them: "Never mind the goddamn souvenirs . . . now on those ridges, all your officers may be down, but you keep going. I want to sit back in my headquarters and hear that you carried all your objectives on time." He closed, warning again against misplaced compassion: "Remember this, on those ridges, take no prisoners, nor should you stop to bandage your best friend." He gave his horse a sharp dig in the flanks with his heels and trotted off. As he disappeared, a sergeant muttered, "Bastard. And he's gonna sit and watch our progress on a map, eh?"

The Rainbow, the 42nd Division, was among those under Summerall's command. Its 84th Brigade was led by newly minted Brigadier General Douglas MacArthur. From a map spread over a wall in his farmhouse headquarters, MacArthur studied the point at which he was expected to break the Kriemhild-Stellung, at high ground called the Côte-de-Châtillon. While MacArthur waited for two days for the attack order, the Germans saturated his position with mustard gas and tear gas. The general, disdaining a gas mask, was so overcome that his adjutant begged him to go to the rear for treatment. MacArthur refused. On the night of October 12, General Summerall arrived at MacArthur's headquarters to announce what he expected. "Give me Châtillon or a list of 5,000 casualties," he said. MacArthur answered, "If this brigade does not capture Châtillon, you can publish a casualty list of the entire brigade with the brigade commander's name at the top." Summerall next stopped by the headquarters of the 83rd Brigade, also committed to the assault on Châtillon. He expected results, he said, "no matter how many men were killed."

On October 14, MacArthur personally led his brigade into battle. He described the engagement with his customary flourish: "Officers fell and sergeants leaped to the command. Companies dwindled to platoons and corporals took over. At the end, Major Ross had only 300 men and six officers left out of 1,450 men and twenty-five officers. That is the way the Côte-de-Châtillon fell." For this feat Summerall nominated MacArthur for the Medal of Honor. But as the recommendation moved up the chain of command, MacArthur's shooting star leveled off and the general had to be content with his second Distinguished Service Cross. The citation read in part, "On a field where courage was the rule, his courage was the dominant factor."

During the fight, the men under MacArthur imagined they had witnessed every permutation of human suffering until they observed the fate of Private Jim Gallagher, 168th Infantry. In an enemy night attack illuminated by star shells, a flare lodged in Gallagher's gut. There was nothing his comrades could do to remove the hissing projectile but watch the man die in agony.

The Fighting 69th was among the regiments ordered to attack the Kriemhild-Stellung. Major Bill Donovan's assignment was to lead his battalion across two miles of exposed ground, then strike rugged rises defended by three belts of trenches. The practice before such engagements was for officers to remove any marks of rank or at least pin them on an inside shirt pocket so that they would not become prime targets of sharpshooters. Similarly, runners did not salute officers upon delivering messages, which also would identify them for the enemy. Donovan, however, intended to go into battle wearing full officer's regalia so that, he claimed, his men would always know who and where he was. The month before, on the eve of Saint-Mihiel, Donovan had strolled among his battalion, exclaiming, "There's nothing to it. It will be a regular walk-over. It will not be as bad as some of the cross-country runs I gave you in your training period." On the eve of Kriemheld-Stellung, he remained as outwardly cocky as ever, though by now the men had seen enough holes in their ranks to know that while their commander was fearless, they were not immortal. On the morning of October 14, waving a pistol overhead, Donovan put himself at the head of the advance. Immediately his men were cut down by withering machine-gun fire. Wild Bill strode among them, shouting encouragement in the manner of the cool Columbia University quarterback he had once been: "Come on, we'll have them on the run before long," and to a hesitant private, "Come on, old sport. Nobody in this regiment was ever afraid." He stood on the lip of a crater in which his men had taken refuge, reading a map with seeming nonchalance while machine-gun bullets kicked up dirt around his feet. Stuffing the map into his pocket, he shouted, "Come on, fellows. It's better ahead than it is here!" The battalion reached the first German wire, chest high and twenty feet thick. The 69th's engineers, crawling on their bellies, tried to cut the wire while infantrymen provided cover. The bodies of men began to drape the wire like rags strung on a clothesline. Donovan went down, struck behind the right knee by a bullet that tore out nerves and blood vessels. From the smoke drifting over the field, gray-clad enemy infantrymen began emerging. The American line started to sag. Donovan, on the ground and bleeding profusely, shouted, "Come on! They can't get me and they can't get you." At his cry, the battalion rose up and beat back the German advance. Donovan remained prostrate for five more hours, directing the troops, refusing to be evacuated. He finally allowed himself to be carried off on a blanket, a man lugging each corner. At the aid station, Donovan was met by Father Duffy and said with a grin, "Father, you're a disappointed man. You expected to have the pleasure of burying me over here." "I certainly did," Duffy answered, "and you are a lucky dog to get off with nothing more than you've got." For his action before the Kriemhild-Stellung, Donovan was promoted to lieutenant colonel and subsequently awarded the Medal of Honor.

Untested romantics still dreamed of sharing in the glory. Arthur Jensen, brushed so far only by a whiff of gas and reveling in the camaraderie of the front, listened like an awed little boy to stories told by men who had actually faced the enemy. He wrote in his war log, "One fellow said they layed in shell holes for two days while the Germans made the ground *boil* around them. He said there were only seven men left in his battalion. He told it so terrible that it hurt me to think I was missing the very thing I had suffered all these months to see!"

THE AMERICANS AND French in the Meuse-Argonne had breached the Hindenburg Line, as had the British to the north, driving the Germans back seventeen miles at the deepest penetration. The American casualties continued to be staggering, in no small part because among the AEF's junior officers enthusiasm generally outran their experience. One lieutenant formed his company in parade-ground ranks and led the men across a bridge that had been registered with hairbreadth precision by German artillery. Waiting until the bridge was full of Americans, the enemy unleashed one perfectly aimed round that landed in the middle, killing more than a hundred doughboys. A more seasoned officer would have sent the men spurting over in small groups at irregular intervals. But a West Point education was not to be gained in a four-month officers' training course.

Early on October 4, the 5th Marine Regiment, engaged southeast of Verdun, was practically annihilated by precise, unceasing enemy artillery fire. Private Mackin, serving as battalion runner, carried messages through walls of fire with robotic indifference. As he later put it, he was sure he had to die, so why do anything to prevent it? For his feats, he earned the Silver Star and the Navy Cross. Among the marine dead was his closest chum, the college boy Hiram Baldwin, shot between the eyes.

For Mackin, the war had become a constant test of his mettle, even when the fighting abated. Just two weeks after the slaughter where he had so distinguished himself, Mackin and two other marines were posted on guard duty over recently taken prisoners, including a German captain, who moved among his fellow POWs smiling, offering words of encouragement. The officer sauntered out of the pack and approached Mackin. "I'm glad you fellows captured me," he said casually. "I'm from Chicago." Mackin stiffened and told him to get back. The captain continued, saying that he had been in Germany when the war had broken out and had had to be dragged into the army. He offered Mackin a cigarette. The young marine realized that he was being tested in full view of his comrades. "How did he know me for a softie?" the decorated marine recalled, reproaching himself. "Me, trying all these weeks to win a place with men. . . . He knew somehow that I didn't know my trade." Smiling slyly, the German moved still closer, holding the cigarette pack out to Mackin. Again the marine told him to step back. The German advanced two more paces. Suddenly Mackin found himself ramming his rifle butt hard against the man's jaw. The prisoner went sprawling onto his back. Two other POWs came forward and dragged his unconscious form away. No other prisoner attempted to be familiar with Mackin that day. Looking back on the incident, he remembered feeling admiration for the man's coolness, still absent in himself, and hoping his victim "didn't die."

LIEUTENANT COLONEL GEORGE Patton could not drive from his mind the face of a dead German he had seen on the battlefield. Haunted by the thought that his foe was also made in God's image, Patton wrote a poem that began:

> Yet that damned Boche looked just like Him
> Leastwise he looked like me
> So why God should be partial
> I don't rightly see.

AS THE GERMANS fell back, ghosts of battles past were exposed on fields from Flanders to the Meuse River. In mid-October,

P. H. Pilditch, a major in the British Royal Field Artillery, bicycled with a friend over old battlegrounds, looking for the grave of a friend killed in October 1914. "It was a morbid but intensely interesting occupation," Pilditch recalled. "The progress of our successive attacks could be clearly seen from the types of equipment on the skeletons, soft caps denoting the 1914 and early 1915, then respirators, then steel helmets marking attacks in 1916. Also, Australian slouch hats, used in the costly and abortive attack in 1916. There were many of these poor remains all along the German wire."

While taking life, the war provoked advances in saving it. Most of the time, the battlefield surgeon's lot remained an unremitting contest against filth, contamination, disease, and wounds in infinite variety, a battle fought with a crude armamentarium. "It was unpleasant amputating those men's legs, and we had to sharpen a knife from a man's kit for it, but what could one do otherwise?" one field surgeon recalled. Hardest to bear, he found, was "the dying faces that come to me of the men of the command . . . men whose letters I had censored so I knew all about them and their homes and worries and dependents."

Major Geoffrey Keynes, in his fourth year as a field physician, found the battlefield a crude laboratory for medical experimentation. At an American casualty clearing station he met a visiting team of physicians from Harvard and learned the latest advances in blood transfusions. He became so intrigued by the possibilities that he began experimenting, matching donor and recipient by blood type and using sodium citrate to prevent coagulation of the blood. Lightly wounded men were offered two weeks' leave to participate. Volunteers lined up in droves. "Rejection was almost regarded as a slur on their integrity, the scientific requirements being incomprehensible to the average soldier," Keynes recalled. Since anesthesiologists were rare at the front, Keynes found that by giving a transfusion first, he could strengthen a man sufficiently to carry out major amputations by himself using only a spinal analgesic.

Keynes wondered about the potential of transfusions for pa-

William J. Donovan of the "Fighting 69th" *(left)* with Chaplain Francis Duffy. Donovan won the Medal of Honor and in World War II became America's first spy chief as head of the Office of Strategic Services.
National Archives

No. 50 873

AMERICAN
EXPEDITIONARY FORCES
Corps Expéditionnaires Américains
IDENTITY CARD
Carte d'Identité

Name HARRY S TRUMAN
Nom

Rank CAPTAIN 129 FA
Grade

Duty
Fonction

Signature
of Holder

Signature Harry S Truman
du Titulaire

Major, AGD USA
Adjutant General

Artillery Captain Harry Truman, whose battery fired until minutes before the war's end. Truman opposed the armistice as premature, displaying the sternness later evident in his decision to use the atom bomb in World War II.
Truman Library

Men of the 167th Infantry Regiment. The number of doughboys in France ultimately approached 2 million and, with French and British troops exhausted after four years of fighting, tipped the scales in favor of Allied victory.

U.S. Army Military History Institute

With clanging alert sounded, American soldiers rush to don gas masks.
As gas tactics advanced, more men were put out of action by
phosgene and mustard than by rifle fire and grenades combined.
National Archives

Americans go "over the top." General Pershing scorned
trench stalemate, favoring open warfare. There were 26,000
men killed in the Meuse-Argonne offensive, which was
then America's largest loss of life in a single battle.
AP/Wide World Photos

Alvin G. York was a corporal in the 82nd Division when he killed 28 Germans and captured 132, exploits for which he received the Medal of Honor and emerged as a World War I legend.
U.S. Army Military History Institute

Chaplain Duffy *(center)* conducts a service over the grave of flier Quentin Roosevelt, youngest son of former president Theodore Roosevelt. One of four brothers in uniform, the pilot was shot down on Bastille Day 1918.
U.S. Army Military History Institute

Chaplain Lyman Rollins administers communion to men of the 101st Infantry in a cave near Chemin des Dames. Within the hour, they would be out of the trenches and advancing into enemy fire.
U.S. Army Historical Institute

British dead near the war's end. Their families at least knew the soldiers' ultimate fate. After the war, a monument was erected at Thiepval containing the names of 73,412 British Empire men, "the Missing of the Somme."
Imperial War Museum, London

Private Henry Gunther *(arrow)*, killed at 10:59 A.M. on November 11, was officially the last AEF battle death. Had the fighting stopped during armistice negotiations, some 6,600 lives would likely have been saved.

Baltimore Sun

British soldiers of the Staffordshire Territorials carpet a bank of the San Quentin Canal toward the war's end. Several can be seen holding German helmets.
Imperial War Museum, London

After the armistice, General Charles P. Summerall crosses one of the pontoon bridges over the Meuse River over which he sent men during the last morning of the war. The cost: 1,130 casualties, including 127 dead.
National Archives

GERMANY HAS SURRENDERED;
WORLD WAR ENDED AT 6 A. M.

Troops in Berlin Desert to Workers; General Strike On

Three Killed as Reds Take Over Public Buildings and Barracks After All Factories Are Closed by Walkout—Rebels Parade Town

..., Proclaiming New Regime, Promises Peace, Urges Restraint

Ex-Emperor, Heir and Staff All Fugitives

WASHINGTON, Nov. 10.—William Hohenzollern has arrived in Holland and is proceeding to the town of DeSteeg, near Utrecht, according to a dispatch received by the American General Staff to-day from, The Hague.

LONDON, Nov. 11 (12:31 a. m.).—The former German Emperor's party, which is believed to include Field Marshal von Hindenburg, arrived at Eysden, on the Dutch frontier, at 7:30 o'clock Sunday morning, according to "Daily Mail" advices.

Virtually the whole German General Staff accompanied the former Emperor, and ten automobiles carried the party. The automobiles were bristling with rifles. All the fugitives were armed.

The ex-Kaiser was in uniform. He alighted at the Eysden station and paced the platform, smoking a cigarette.

Chatting with the members of the staff, the former Emperor, the correspondent says, did not look in the least ...

The engine returned to Vise, Belgium, and brought back a second train in which were a large number of staff officers and others, and also stores of food. The German Consul from Maastricht arrived soon after 8 o'clock. Dutch railway officials soon made their appearance and many of the inhabitants came to the station attracted by curiosity.

Many photographs were taken by the people of the imperial party. On the whole, the people were very quiet, but Belgians among them cried out: "En voyage à Paris?" (Are you on your way to Paris?)

The "Daily Mail" remarks that if the party arrived in Holland armed all of them must intern.

A dispatch to the Exchange Telegraph Company from Copenhagen quotes the "Politiken" as saying the former ruler was accompanied by the former Empress.

De Steeg is on the Guelders Yssel, an arm of the Rhine about forty miles east of Utrecht and twelve miles from the German border. The Chateau Middachten, to which the ...

Armistice Signed By Hun Envoys At Midnight

Official Announcement From Washington Declares End of Great Struggle—Hostilities Cease on West Front as Germans Yield to Allied Terms

Germans Must Withdraw Soldiers Immediately From Alsace-Lorraine

Similar headlines appeared all over America, followed by feverish celebration. However, the war had not ended at 6 A.M., and in the hours before 11 A.M. men were still fighting and dying.

New York State Library

The 105th Field Artillery after firing its last round on Armistice Day. Long ropes were tied to the lanyards of many guns so that hundreds of doughboys could pull them and claim to have fired the last shot of the war.

U.S. Army Historical Institute

tients in the moribund ward. These were men judged beyond hope and on whom medical officers were not to waste time. "I made it my business," Keynes noted, "to steal into the moribund ward, choose a patient who was still breathing and had a perceptible pulse, transfuse him, and carry out the necessary operation. Most of them were suffering primarily from shock and loss of blood, and in this way I had the satisfaction of pulling many men back from the jaws of death."

Once they entered the fight full scale, the Americans too began producing shell-shock cases, the wounded without wounds. An American major, Raymond F. Hodgdon, 71st New York, though a soldier and not a medical man, appeared to grasp the root cause of the condition. Of men who went through hell yet escaped shell shock, "God in his mercy," Hodgdon noted, "has so constituted the human mind that it cannot retain those frightful scenes and experiences for any length of time." But not every soldier could forget, and Hodgson concluded, "I am convinced the average case of so-called shellshock is nothing more than inability to throw off these mental pictures."

FOR ALL THE destructive ingenuity of men, nature proved to be the far superior killer. Plague struck in 1918, called, for no justified reason, Spanish influenza. The pandemic may have originated in the American military post at Fort Riley, Kansas, where a dust storm whipping about tons of incinerated manure had sent hundreds of coughing, stumbling doughboys diagnosed with influenza into the post hospital, where many died. Soon after, American troopships disembarked at Brest and Saint-Nazaire, and French *poilus* began to fall ill, then British soldiers. Then, as the malady rolled across France, German troops were stricken. The fatality rate was appalling. In the AEF, roughly one out of every three soldiers with influenza died, far worse odds than a man faced in battle. The doughboy death toll from influenza eventually accounted for nearly one third of all the Americans who would die in the war. More than 3,600 Britons succumbed and 10,000 French. Ludendorff blamed the failure of his final offensives, in part, on the numbers of men lost to the flu. In Hamburg, deaths averaged 400 a day. Prince Max, in the midst of waging peace, was felled by the illness for two crucial weeks. Civilian deaths dwarfed those in the military. In the last week of October, while 2,700 doughboys in France died from all causes, 21,000 Americans died of influenza at home. Deaths in Britain would eventually total 225,000. No comparable mortality had been experienced since the bubonic plague nearly five hundred years before, and modern medical science stood impotent before the pestilence.

Oddly, the disease struck hardest at the fittest, particularly young men in their prime. Troopships laden with men packed closely together became floating pestholes. An American convoy arriving at Brest on October 8 in the midst of the Meuse-Argonne campaign had 4,000 men disabled by the flu, with 200 already buried at sea. Two hundred of the sick carried off the *Leviathan* died within days. Major Keynes wrote, "I can never forget the sight of our mortuary tents with the pathetic rows of bodies of men killed by one of the most lethal epidemics ever known." Subsequently, a theory evolved that the agents of human flu and swine flu, not usually fatal by themselves, had synergized to produce a new strain of terrifying lethality.

The epidemic posed a dilemma for President Wilson. Since military camps had become hothouses for spreading the infection, orders for 142,000 men scheduled to report for induction late in September were canceled. Should he, Wilson wondered, also cancel the embarkation of troopships? On October 8, he met with the army's gruff chief of staff, General Peyton March, to ask his guidance. Both men accepted that to cram soldiers into the ships was to pass a death sentence on thousands of them. But Pershing was pleading desperately for replacements, especially since he had 150,000 men down with the flu. Just two days before Wilson and March met, Prince Max had made his appeal to the president to bring about peace. Wilson and March recognized that the surest guarantee of defeating the Germans was to continue the deliveries of Americans to France, now swelling to an average of 50,000 weekly. How might the Germans react if they learned that the pressure was off because the American manpower pipeline had shut down? March told Wilson, "Every such soldier who has died [from influenza] has just as surely played his part as his comrade who has died in France. The shipment of troops should not be stopped for any cause." The troopships continued to sail.

Toward the end of October, as inexplicably as it had arrived, the scourge began to fade, but not before it had taken more than 21,640,000 lives worldwide. Influenza had achieved in some four months a mortality greater than it had taken men four years of war to compile. With nature relenting, it was time for the armies to continue the killing.

GERMANY WOULD GO on for the time left with two less partners. Turkey's Ottoman Empire had begun to collapse like a house riddled with dry rot. Jerusalem had fallen to the British Army the previous December, under Christian control for the first time since the Crusades. The Turks suffered another near-fatal blow when rebellious Arabs, organized by the charismatic British officer T. E. Lawrence, cut the critical Damascus-Medina railway and seized the port of Aqaba. Added to the successes of Lawrence of Arabia, General Edward Allenby, called behind his back "the Bull" for his irascibility, defeated the enemy at Megiddo and then took Damascus, breaking the back of the Ottoman Empire. On October 30, Turkey asked for an armistice and left the war.

Four days later, Austria-Hungary was defeated by Italy at the Battle of Vittorio Veneto. On November 4, the tottering imperial regime also sought an armistice. As the grip of the Habsburgs over their subject peoples loosened, the Balkans began to erupt into eth- nic and religious strife among Croats, Bosnians, Serbians, Mon- tenegrins, Moslems, and Christians in the very corner of the world where the war had begun.

28

"Victims Who Will Die in Vain"

NOVEMBER 1918. At 8:30 on the evening of the seventh, French soldiers of the 171st Infantry Regiment, playing cards near the front lines at Haudroy, were startled by an odd four-note bugle call. Fearing they were about to be overrun, they abandoned the game and moved cautiously toward the increasingly loud blaring. Out of the mantle of fog three automobiles, their headlamps blazing, emerged, their sides gilded with the imperial German eagle. A French sergeant recorded the moment: "Standing on the running boards of the [first] car, there were two Boches, each sounding in turn cease-fire with a silver bugle, at least five feet long, much like a Jericho trumpet. While one was blowing, the other one was waving a large white cloth by way of a pennant."

The astonished Frenchmen had encountered a German mission that Marshal Foch had agreed to see. The delegation, chosen by Prince Max, was led by a rotund forty-three-year-old former schoolteacher turned politician and peace advocate named Matthias Erzberger, head of the German Catholic Center Party. The rest of the mission was composed of midlevel representatives of the foreign ministry, army, and navy, thus sparing Germany's top leaders the ignominy of seeking surrender. At Tergnier, south of Saint-Quentin, the delegates left their automobiles and were transferred to a railway coach that the French had deliberately chosen because it had once belonged to Napoleon III, whom the Germans defeated in the Franco-Prussian War. In the early-morning hours of November 8, the train backed onto a siding near Rethondes in the Forest of Compiègne, forty miles from Paris. As daylight filtered into the car, another coach could be seen on a parallel siding. At 9 A.M., Foch's aide, General Maxime Weygand, came to lead the Germans to the other car on duckboards placed over the rain-soaked ground. The delegates, still in the clothes they had slept in, were hungry, rumpled, unkempt, and on edge. They entered dining car 2419D, converted for the occasion into a makeshift conference room. Before them stood a small, erect man who fixed them with a withering gaze, Marshal Ferdinand Foch. After cool introductions, Foch opened the proceedings with a question that left the Germans agape. "Ask these gentlemen what they want," he said to his interpreter. When the Germans had recovered, Erzberger answered that they understood they had been sent to discuss armistice terms. Foch stunned them again: "Tell these gentlemen that I have no proposals to make." The French-speaking Count Alfred von Oberndorff, second man in the German delegation, sought to mollify Foch. They were there, he said, as a result "of a note from the president of the United States." Then he proceeded to read a message that Wilson had sent to the German government two days before, stating that Foch had the authority to set armistice conditions. Foch cut him off and insisted that the Germans admit it was only they who sought the armistice. After the delegates assented to this humiliation, General Weygand read aloud the Allied conditions, each of which struck the Germans like a hammer blow: all occupied lands in Belgium, Luxembourg, and France, plus Alsace-Lorraine, held since 1870 by Germany, must be evacuated within fourteen days; the Allies were to occupy Germany west of the Rhine and bridgeheads on the river's east bank thirty kilometers deep; German forces must be withdrawn from Austria-Hungary, Romania, and Turkey; Germany was to surrender to neutral or Allied ports 10 battleships, 6 battle cruisers, 8 cruisers, and 160 submarines. She was to be stripped of heavy armament, including 5,000 artillery pieces, 25,000 machine guns, and 2,000 airplanes. The next demand threw the German delegation into despair. Though their people already faced famine, the Allies intended to paralyze the country's transportation by continuing the naval blockade and confiscating 5,000 locomotives, 150,000 railway cars, and 5,000 trucks. Weygand droned on through thirty-four conditions, the last of which blamed Germany for the war and demanded she pay reparations for all damage caused.

On average, 2,088 troops on both sides were dying on the western front every day the fighting went on. The German Army delegate, Major General Detlev von Winterfeldt, asked that while the mission communicated the Allied terms to its government, fighting be suspended to save "numerous victims who will die in vain at the last minute and who might be preserved to their families."

The railroad car stood in the midst of French villages that the war had effaced from the earth. The Germans were confronting an Allied leader who had learned of the death in battle of his only son and his daughter's husband in a single day. Foch remained cold to all entreaties, reflecting not only his own fixedness but orders from his equally unforgiving superior, Prime Minister Clemenceau. Foch informed Erzberger that he had seventy-two hours to obtain the consent of his government to the Allies' terms. "For God's sake, Monsieur le Maréchal," Erzberger pleaded, "do not wait for those seventy-two hours. Stop the hostilities this very day." The appeal fell on deaf ears. Before the meeting, Foch had explained to his staff his armistice posture: "to pursue the *Feldgrauen* with a sword at their backs."

No U.S. representative was present in the car in the Compiègne Forest. And to one American, the very idea of an armistice was repugnant. From the moment in October that the Germans had signaled Wilson that they were prepared to talk peace on the basis of his Fourteen Points, General Pershing had argued instead for unconditional surrender. Well before the Erzberger delegation had come to Compiègne, Pershing had sent a telegram to his senior commanders disputing the president's peace moves. The language verged on the insubordinate and leaked to the public. Germany was obviously on the ropes, the general insisted. "Their request is an acknowledgment of weakness and clearly means that the Allies are winning the war. . . . Germany's desire is only to regain time to restore order among her forces, but she must be given no opportunity to recuperate and we must strike harder than ever." Negotiations? Pershing had one response: "There can be no conclusion to this war until Germany is brought to her knees." His French and British allies might be exhausted and longing for peace. But Pershing saw his army akin to a fighter ready to deliver the knockout punch who is told to quit with his opponent reeling but still standing.

Eight days before Foch met with the Erzberger delegation, Pershing had advised the Supreme War Council, made up of representatives of Allied heads of state, that no matter what the casualties suffered by continued prosecution of the war, the relentless infusion of American troops would make up the difference. Conciliation now would only lead to future war. A negotiated peace rather than a peace dictated by the Allies "would jeopardize the moral position they now hold and possibly lose the chance actually to secure world peace on terms that would assure its permanence." Black Jack had powerful allies back home. *The New York Times* published a statement issued by former president Theodore Roosevelt that read, "I hope the President will instantly send back word that we demand unconditional surrender and that we refuse to compound felony by discussing terms with the felons." The conservative Senate Republican leader, Henry Cabot Lodge, introduced a resolution to block any dealing with the Germans except to arrange total capitulation. But now the Allies were talking peace, and the only consolation Pershing found coming out of Compiègne was Foch's insistence that the fighting continue unabated until the last minute before an armistice went into effect.

When Marshal Foch had first agreed to meet with the Erzberger delegation, he had arranged a brief local cease-fire to allow the Germans to pass safely through the French lines. The marshal had conveyed this information to the Germans at 2:30 A.M. on November 7 through a radio message transmitted from the Eiffel Tower. This single transmission set off a chain reaction felt round the world. The French intelligence service, the Deuxième Bureau, had somehow gained the impression not that talks were about to take place, but that a full-fledged armistice was to go into effect at 2 P.M. that day. The news swiftly reached the American Embassy in Paris, where the naval attaché telegraphed it to Admiral Henry Wilson, commander of American naval forces in Brest, the principal port of debarkation for U.S. troops. As chance would have it, Roy Howard, head of the United Press wire service, was at that moment paying a call on Admiral Wilson before sailing back to America. The admiral showed the telegram to Howard, who instantly recognized that he held in his hand the scoop of a lifetime. The UP chief asked, "Admiral, may I use that?" Wilson hesitated, but finally said, "Why, I suppose so." Howard bounded from the office "touching only about every tenth step," a witness recalled, and cabled his home office in the Pulitzer Building in New York. The UP immediately sent out a bulletin on the wire: "Paris, Nov. 7.—The Allies and Germany signed an armistice at 11 o'clock this morning. Hostilities ceased at 2 o'clock this afternoon." Back in Brest, the U.S. Navy band broke into "There'll Be a Hot Time in the Old Town Tonight," setting off a celebration that would spread to the four corners of the earth. From Harry's New York Bar in Paris to French villages, glasses were raised to peace. In New York, thousands poured from their offices as ticker tape cascaded down from Wall Street windows. Crowds marching in the streets in Washington brought trolley cars to a standstill. Troops at a Royal Air Force school in Kent, England, broke into a canteen and carried off pails of beer for a victory party.

Official refutation of the armistice story was slow to overtake the frenzy. The French War Ministry issued a denial, noting that the German mission had not yet met with Marshal Foch. The American secretary of state, Robert Lansing, released a statement that the armistice had not yet been signed. Deflated, the revelers went home and resumed the life of nations still at war.

CAPTAIN HARRY TRUMAN had written Bess about a German pilot downed behind his battery who had suffered only a sprained ankle in the crash. The flier had, however, been sufficiently immobilized that he was stripped nearly naked by souvenir hunters, one of whom, an officer, "I am ashamed to say," Truman wrote, "pulled the boots off the injured man." What struck Truman most, however, was that the downed pilot insisted, confidently, that the war would be over in ten days. The date of his capture was November 1.

Proof that Foch intended to keep prodding his sword into the backs of the field gray was evident in the war planning going on simultaneously with the peace talks. Allied strategists were mapping fresh offensives extending into 1919. The next major push was to be launched on November 14 against Metz on the Mosel River. Metz was as much fortress as city, the German counterpart of Verdun, thirty-five miles away, a vital rail nexus thick with defending troops. Its symbolic value was also potent. The ancient town, with its winding streets and six-hundred-year-old cathedral, had been taken from France during the Franco-Prussian War. The planned attack on Metz was no surprise to the Germans. The secret had been extracted from recently taken Allied prisoners. This knowledge, however, served the purposes of peace rather than war. The German general staff grasped that the tide of Americans, now just shy of 2 million men in France, could push into Lorraine and overrun Metz, then the Saar, thus scattering Germany's armies. The Germans pressed for peace at this time, before their military was completely shattered, to avoid leaving their homeland unprotected against rioters and revolutionists.

While the German delegation swallowed gall in the dining car in the Compiègne Forest, preparations for the Metz offensive went forward, with Pershing amassing his divisions alongside French General Charles Mangin's French Tenth Army in the Meuse-Argonne. Towering fourteen-inch guns, originally built for American battleships, were transported to the front to give the preliminary barrage fresh destructive power. Pershing was quoted as saying, probably apocryphally, "Boys, we'll be in hell or Hoboken by Christmas."

SERGEANT WILLIAM TRIPLET was in the hospital at Vittel with a shoulder wound when the chief medical officer came into his ward and announced, "Men, the infantry units are getting shorthanded and replacements are not coming in fast enough." Any man who considered himself sufficiently recovered to return to the front should stand at the head of his bed. As Triplet put it, "I'd learned in the Argonne that I wasn't bulletproof after all." Yet he felt an unreasoning compulsion to rejoin his outfit. "I was getting homesick for the company," he remembered, "supposing that there were any of them left." Triplet, at that moment, was also waiting out orders to report to Officer Training School on November 15, but nevertheless he moved to the head of the bed. He noted, out of the corner of his eye, that only seven men held back. He soon learned through the doughboy grapevine that he had returned in time for the push on Metz. He observed uneasily the numbers of hurriedly trained replacements in his regiment. He calculated that in five days fighting in the Argonne his platoon had suffered 86 percent casualties. As the date for the Metz offensive neared, Triplet thought, "I'd go to the cemetery or the hospital instead of OTS."

To some men, calculating their odds of surviving was harrowingly personal. To others it meant bookkeeping. As the preparations for Metz mounted, Draper Dewees, clerking at V Corps headquarters, wrote home, "My job is keeping me pretty busy." His task was to compile, from the various divisions in the corps, the numbers of men killed, wounded, missing, or taken prisoner. He recognized the fallibility of his records. A man might see a pal blown to pieces by a shell who could be reported definitely as "killed in action." But the witness might himself soon fall, and thus his vanished comrade would be incorrectly listed as "missing in action." Some cases could be trickier, as when Dewees was reporting on prisoners taken and found among those listed a girl in German uniform. Since the form provided only for "officers" and "men," "I included her with the men." Mobile hospitals began projecting their needs for Metz based on past experience. One medical unit calculated that it had treated 250 patients in the previous week's engagements, of whom half had died within hours. These data were used to forecast the beds, medical supplies, and coffins required for the upcoming offensive.

THE DOUGHBOYS, THOUGH by now well blooded, were still Johnny-come-latelies compared to their Allies, and morale in the AEF continued strong. The Tommies, their original high spirits long since ground down by years of burying their mates, had become resentful of those who had managed to stay home and prosper, a sentiment captured in a trench parody to the tune of "I Wore a Tulip":

> I wore a tunic,
> A dirty khaki tunic
> And you wore civilian clothes.
> You were with the wenches
> While we were in the trenches,
> Facing the German foe.
> You were a'slacking
> While we were attacking
> Down on the Menin Road. . . .

The doughboys knew the tune but had yet to succumb to its sentiment.

WHILE PRESSING THE fight at full throttle, armistice pending or not, Pershing had his eye on the prize of Sedan, located at the northern tip of the Meuse-Argonne sector. Sedan would be the largest French city liberated by the AEF. The appeal of Sedan was sharpened for Pershing by the fact that the Germans had held it since 1870, and he knew that Foch was eager to retake the city himself. Major General Hunter Liggett, directly under Pershing as commander of the First Army, was, at sixty, overage, overweight, and arthritic but a bulwark of common sense. Liggett questioned his superior's priorities and believed the French ought to be given the honor, particularly the IX Corps, which had originally been driven from Sedan. Liggett did not prevail, and two divisions under him, the 42nd and the 77th, were assigned to take Sedan. Pershing added that the offensive was to be "assisted on the right by the 5th Corps" and, astonishingly, that the boundaries that ordinarily kept units from stumbling over one another need not be observed.

In another burst of map room heroics, the V Corps commander, Major General Charles Summerall, spotted a gateway to glory. Rather than merely "assisting," he would take advantage of the flexibility Pershing's order provided and violate a commandment of battlefield tactics. He intended to send elements of his 1st Division, under the equally fiery Brigadier General Frank Parker, through ground currently held by the 42nd and 77th Divisions in order to beat these rivals to Sedan. The chaos that ensued was illustrated when General MacArthur was temporarily arrested by men of Parker's division as a suspected German spy. The outraged Liggett subsequently told Summerall and Parker that what they had committed was no less than a "military atrocity." The only reason he would not court-martial them, he said, was that, luckily, the potentially disastrous consequences of their glory hunting had not occurred. As for taking Sedan, Foch had the last word. Just as the Americans seized the hills before the city, Foch sent his Fourth Army to relieve them. Frenchmen eventually liberated Sedan.

Pershing never chastised any of the parties responsible for what could have been a calamity. Instead, Liggett found Pershing amused at the rivalry his order had provoked. There was more than a little suspicion that Pershing, while visiting Summerall and Parker on the night he issued his orders, had egged them on.

———

WHILE THEIR COUNTRYMEN continued to fall before the unrelenting Allied pressure from Mons in the north to the Bois de Fréhaut 148 miles to the southeast, Erzberger and his mission waited in their railroad car in a state of nervous impotence. At 11:30 A.M., at the end of the first day's meeting, Foch gave Erzberger permission to radio a message to the German high command at Spa reporting the Allied commander's seventy-two-hour deadline. Erzberger added an apology that he had failed to achieve a halt to the fighting in the interim. He closed noting that because he did not want the harshness of the terms to leak to the German people via radio, he was sending Foch's full text to Spa via courier. Selected to deliver the document was a twenty-two-year-old aristocrat captain, Count Wolf-Heinrich von Helldorf, who set out from Compiègne with a French escort at 1 P.M. Upon reaching the German lines, Helldorf's party sounded the cease-fire bugle call. The response was murderous shooting from their own guns. They waved white flags, to no avail. By nightfall, as Foch's deadline melted away, Helldorf still had not been able to pass through the German lines.

In the meantime, Erzberger radioed a coded message to Spa to be relayed to Berlin, informing the government that any hope of the Allies softening their terms appeared doomed. Twenty-six precious hours were lost before this message got through to the revolt-ridden capital. As they awaited further instructions, the Erzberger delegates killed time drafting counterproposals to soften the Allied demands, which they knew were futile.

In their isolation, what they could not know was that the success of their mission now turned on the fate of the kaiser. That the Allies would accept an armistice leaving Wilhelm in power was inconceivable. At this point Wilhelm was at Spa, the imperial head full of foolish fantasies of how, as soon as an armistice was signed, he would lead his loyal armies back to Germany and restore order. What Prince Max back in Berlin recognized was that, far from a solution, Wilhelm's return *was* the problem. In Metz, the Allies' next target, 10,000 German soldiers had reportedly mutinied, formed a Soldiers' Council, and taken over the city. Similar overthrows of the old order were erupting all over Germany.

To upper-class officers at the front, the rebellion of the lesser breeds was baffling. Fritz Nagel, of the well-to-do tobacco family, masked his concern with scorn. "Some of the simple minded soldiers in the army thought a new, wonderful way of life had arrived," Nagel wrote. "But before they could exploit this new life fully, they had to get rid of their officers, and after they had chased them away or killed them, all the pleasures of life would be theirs." He himself was taking no chances. "I had not carried a revolver," he noted, "since I was promoted to officer rank because sidearms handicapped movements." But now, eying the men around him with suspicion, he began carrying his pistol again.

Peace seekers inside Germany accepted that the only act that would prevent the masses from swinging over to the radicals was removal of the country's discredited monarch. Prince Max dispatched an emissary, Herr Drews, the Prussian minister of the interior, to Spa on a thankless task, to explain this situation to a descendent of Frederick the Great. Wilhelm's response was instantaneous: he had "no intention of quitting the throne because of a few hundred Jews and a thousand workmen. Tell that to your masters in Berlin." On the evening of Friday, November 8, Max telephoned his cousin personally, employing the familiar *du* form of address. "Your abdication has become necessary to save Germany from civil war and to fulfill your mission as a peace making emperor to the end," Max said. He then braced himself to deliver the hardest blow: "The great majority of the people believe you to be responsible for the present situation. The belief is false, but there it is." Max went on for another twenty minutes in his most persuasive vein, arguing that if the kaiser sacrificed his throne and thus averted civil war, "Your name will be blessed by future generations." But the kaiser would have none of it. Max, he said, might be incapable of halting the contagion of Bolshevism, but he, Wilhelm, at the head of his still-loyal soldiers, would crush the rabble. The chancellor, recognizing that Wilhelm had lost all touch with reality, begged to resign. The kaiser answered huffily, "You sent out the armistice offer. You will also have to accept the conditions."

It fell to loyal old Hindenburg to deliver the bitter truth to his sovereign. Accompanied by Ludendorff's successor, General Groener, Hindenburg began a slow shuffle from Spa's Grand Hotel Britannique to the staff car that would take him to the emperor, waiting in the nearby Château de la Fraineuse. At 10 A.M., they were received into the kaiser's presence. Heavy curtains kept out the light. A wood fire failed to defeat the chill in the room. Wilhelm stood shivering, his back to the fire, his withered left arm behind him. As Hindenburg started to speak, his voice cracked and tears began rolling down his cheeks. Unable to go on, he nodded toward Groener. His deputy spoke with unabashed frankness. The battle front was collapsing and the home front in revolt. No choice existed but to yield to any armistice terms the enemy demanded. "I shall remain at Spa," Wilhelm countered, "and then lead my troops back to Germany." Groener responded with breathtaking bluntness: "Sire, you no longer have an army for it no longer stands behind you." A downcast Hindenburg added that he too was "unable to take upon himself responsibility for the trustworthiness of the troops." The words finally penetrated Wilhelm's regal armor. If it could be proved that he no longer commanded the army's loyalty, he said, he would abdicate. Senior officers were then summoned to the supreme commander's headquarters in the Hotel Britannique and asked if their troops would follow the kaiser to put down rebellion at home. One responded, "Yes," but twenty-three said, "No."

One last indignity awaited Wilhelm. As he was studying a draft statement of his abdication, he was informed that the Wolf Telegraph Agency in Berlin had just reported his renunciation of the throne. The news agency's scoop was Prince Max's doing. Worried that Wilhelm's intransigence would outlast any hope of quelling revolution, Max had taken it upon himself to proclaim, "The Kaiser and King has resolved to renounce the throne." Wilhelm, nearly apoplectic at this final betrayal, shouted, "Treason, gentlemen! Barefaced, outrageous treason!" The answering silence banked his outburst. The only question left was how to avoid the ignominy of a Prussian monarch being taken prisoner by the enemy or being seized by rioting mobs of his own people. Hindenburg asserted his quiet, heavy authority: the kaiser must take refuge in neutral Holland, only sixty miles away.

It vas 3:30 P.M., Saturday, November 9. The German Empire had been in a race with revolution, and revolution had won. Germany, a monarchy for its entire existence and essentially a military dictatorship since the war had begun, was now a republic. Prince Max, his duty done, turned over the chancellorship to Friedrich Ebert, leader of the Social Democrats.

That same Saturday, Foch issued another war cry to his allies to give the Germans no respite: "The enemy, disorganized by our repeated attacks, is withdrawing along the whole front. It is important to maintain and hasten our action. I appeal to the energy and initiative of the commanders and their armies to secure decisive results."

WHILE THE WORLD outside turned upside down, Matthias Erzberger and the other delegates, confined to a railroad car in a French wood, continued whiling away the hours writing and rewriting a document grandly entitled "Observations on the Conditions of an Armistice with Germany." It cataloged the hardships the German people would suffer in accepting the Allied terms, a document that, in their hearts, they knew would go nowhere. On Sunday evening, the tenth, at 7:30 P.M., with scarcely sixteen hours of Foch's deadline left, Erzberger was informed that French monitors had intercepted a message from the new government in Berlin, stating that "the plenipotentiaries are authorized to sign the armistice." The instruction was confirmed by a message from Hindenburg suggesting that Erzberger should still try to wring a few concessions from Foch, but failing that, it "would nevertheless be advisable to conclude the agreement." The war, in effect, was over, except that the killing must go forward until a fixed time, even after a handful of men in a railroad car affixed their signatures to a piece of paper.

EARLY THAT SUNDAY, near the village of Eysden, an insistent honking of horns woke a Dutch sergeant dozing in the customhouse. He dragged himself out to find four massive automobiles idling their motors before the chain barrier blocking the way into Holland. He demanded passports from the brilliantly uniformed arrivals, examining them with maddening slowness. He knew that Dutch border regulations permitted one person in the party to put through a telephone call to a higher authority. One of the kaiser's aides managed with difficulty to track down a Dutch official, who granted permission to the Germans to enter Holland. The sergeant then let the automobiles pass. Once across the border, a member of the party dressed in civilian clothes and slouched in the second car was recognized by the crowd the motorcade had attracted. He was greeted with catcalls: *"Ah, Kamerad Kaputt!"* *"Vive la France!"* Thus did Kaiser Wilhelm II, the last of the Hohenzollerns, leave the throne and the war and begin a life of exile.

29

"We Knew the End Could Not Be Far Off"

NOVEMBER 1918. On the seventh, the day that the train carrying the German delegation had rolled toward the Forest of Compiègne, six men of the 24th Battalion, Royal Fusiliers, trudged to the edge of the French village of Romeries in a drizzling rain that never seemed to stop that fall. They flanked Private Ernest Jackson, who moved between their two files, his steps faltering, his face impassive, the insignia stripped from his uniform. The thirty-two-year-old Londoner had first deserted in September and been given a two-year suspended sentence. But when he had run away again, the court-martial board judged Jackson an incorrigible shirker and condemned him to death by firing squad. His plea that he descended from a family plagued by mental illness was unavailing.

Private Louis Harris, a Jew from Leeds, volunteered in 1915 but had been rejected on medical grounds, only to be conscripted when physical standards dropped. The studio photograph he sent home to his family showed a small, sharp-eyed, well-turned-out soldier. Harris was serving in the 10th Battalion, West Yorkshire Regiment, when he too was condemned to death for desertion. Harris was twenty-three.

Both men had lost against highly favorable odds. Few men in the British forces who were sentenced to death, most for desertion, cowardice, quitting their post, being asleep on duty, and throwing away their arms, saw the sentence carried out. Jackson and Harris were both shot on November 7 with four days left in the war, the last Britons to be executed. As the end neared, executions in the French Army also slowed to a trickle. The codified killings had fallen off sharply as the war ground on, arousing sympathy for men who broke under protracted stress.

Five months before the armistice, the German Reichstag unanimously passed reductions in the already relatively light penalties for dereliction of duty. As the minister of war put it, "We do not fear this greater leniency will cause any erosion of discipline." Doughboys were executed too, but the AEF restricted the ultimate penalty to criminal offenses—rape and murder—which cost ten men their lives in France.

IF THE OFFICIAL British military history is to be believed, most Tommies faced the prospect of peace with heightened truculence. "Rumours that an armistice had been concluded were current on the 10th," the history reported, "and this had been a factor in the desire of the troops to press on and kill as many Germans as possible before the whistle blew." The Tommies' letters home and their diaries reflect a rather different hope. For Robert Cude, who had witnessed the inane bravado of officers kicking footballs on the Somme, who had seen the appalling effects of the first flamethrowers, and who had survived repeated risks as a runner, his apprehension rose that he might die in the remaining hours. The recent fate of a pal, Teddy, was burned into his memory. The man's wound had been unusually horrendous. A gas shell had exploded in his face. A replacement had just arrived and, standing next to Teddy, had become so unhinged at the sight that he had had to be packed off to the rear. As his comrades buried Teddy, Cude noted in his diary, "No parson was present. Do not see many up here." While they shoveled dirt into the shallow grave, Cude thought, "How long will it be before it is my turn?" Four days before the talks began in the Compiègne Forest, Cude's 7th Battalion of the East Kent Buffs was ordered to take part in a British-French offensive in an area called the Forest of Mormal in France. "Not one of us, but have not the certainty in our own minds, that this is to be the last attack," Cude wrote in his journal, "and now that we are so near to the finish, we begin to wonder, if our luck, that has brought us right through up to now, will hold out, and thereby enable us to live."

The closer the end, the greater the anxiety among men on both sides. Georg Bücher, a German "front hog" since 1914, had lost almost all of his early comrades, and the order to return to the line for a rearguard stand filled him with foreboding. "It was all the harder for us since we knew the end could not be far off," Bücher recalled. "We ducked at the sound of every explosion—which we had never bothered to do before. The old hands fought for the deepest, safest dug-outs and did not scruple to leave to the young recruits the hundred and one things which were risky. . . . The thought of an attack was more terrifying to them than to the young soldiers who were still so inexperienced, so touchingly helpless, yet in spite of everything, so willing."

The final clashes were being fought with the same compound of bravery and lunacy, achievement and futility that had marked the previous four years. On the day before the end, near Tournai in Belgium, British troops flattened a building just within the German lines that had been suspiciously belching smoke for days. The fumes could signal a German field kitchen, a tempting target. And so British Stokes mortars reduced the building to debris. When it was overrun, the place turned out to have been a religious printing plant. Smoldering among the ruins were charred copies of Bibles and hymnals. Near the ruined site, the Tommies came upon the bodies of six men of the 17th London who had fallen in their regiment's last raid of the war.

The German front from Antwerp to the Argonne Forest became a patchwork of last-ditch stands and chaos. Captain von Helldorf spent precious hours trying to get through the iron wall of fire from German troops to deliver Erzberger's report of armistice terms to Spa. Disciplined withdrawals alternated with surrenders by the thousands and mass desertion. Army truck drivers began selling their vehicles and soldiers their weapons to civilians for food, wine, and clothes. Inside Germany, guards simply walked away from prisoner-of-war camps. One prisoner recalled a purple-faced camp commandant at Friedrichsfeld cursing and brandishing his sword in a hopeless attempt to keep his guards at their posts. A soldier from a New York State regiment described German POWs as "an oddly assorted crew of old men and young boys, plainly showing wear and tear. Many were sorely afraid, apparently thinking they were going to be shot." One of the youngest prisoners began to cry, pleading that he had always been a good boy in school and never skipped a day. "Everybody was kind to the little duffer," the New Yorker recalled. "He was frail looking like a little girl."

NOT UNTIL FIFTEEN hours before Foch's deadline did Erzberger's mission receive Berlin's official authority to sign the armistice. The delegation continued tinkering with the draft Allied terms, particularly hoping to end the blockade and save innocent civilians from starvation. At 2:10 A.M. on Monday, November 11, they were again taken over the duckboards through the dark to Foch's car. For the next three hours the adversaries wrangled, with the Germans invariably losing every argument. On only two points did they win any concessions. How could they turn over 2,000 aircraft when they possessed fewer than 1,700? the Germans asked. Foch granted the merit of this position. As for the blockade, Erzberger pleaded that its continuance would harm mostly women and children. He managed to win one limp concession: the Allies "would contemplate the provisioning of Germany during the Armistice as shall be found necessary." By 5:10 A.M., with nothing left to discuss, Foch and the British representative, First Sea Lord Sir Rosslyn Wemyss, signed the final draft of the armistice, followed by the Germans. It would take effect at 11 A.M., when all firing was to cease. Erzberger attempted to lessen the sting of defeat with a final comment. "The German people, which held off a world of enemies for fifty months," he said in a trembling voice, "will preserve their liberty and unity despite every kind of violence. A nation of seventy million people suffers, but it does not die." *"Très bien"* was Foch's expressionless reply. The official time of signing was set back to 5:00 A.M. so that the armistice would take effect in six hours, precisely at the expiration of Foch's deadline: the eleventh month, eleventh day, eleventh hour. At that moment the bloodiest war thus far in the history of human conflict, now in its 1,560th day, would end. Foch adjourned the meeting at 5:30 A.M., and the dining car emptied with not a handshake exchanged.

Foch had word of the armistice sent out immediately to commanders on all fronts via telephone and radio, including a transmission from the Eiffel Tower. The message read, "Hostilities will cease on the entire front beginning at 11:00 A.M. November 11. The Allied troops will not pass the line reached at that date and at that hour without a new order." Upon learning that the armistice had been signed, General Groener issued an instruction to Groups of Armies in the West. "The discipline of the troops must be maintained by every possible means," he ordered. "Fraternization of our men with enemy troops must be prevented." He closed, needlessly it would seem, with "No furloughs will be granted."

General Pershing learned that the armistice had been signed at 5:45 A.M. after Signal Corps radiomen picked up the Eiffel Tower message and relayed it to his Chaumont headquarters. By six o'clock, the general received a confirming call from his liaison officer at Foch's headquarters, Colonel Bentley Mott. To Pershing, the news was unwelcome. By now he had 1,200,000 men in the Meuse-Argonne who had hurled the enemy back thirty-two miles on a front ninety miles wide. It was this success, he had no doubt, that had driven the Germans to the conference table. In just seventy-two hours, the offensive against Metz was to have been launched. Tracing his finger along the map covering one wall of his staff room, he sighed, "What an enormous difference a few more days would have made."

Even before the signing, when it appeared inevitable that the Germans would bow to his terms, the implacable Foch had issued a press-them-to-the-last-minute order to his own forces, the British, and the Americans: "Our advance should be kept going and speeded up." The order had gone out at 2:30 P.M. on Saturday, November 9. It had not been rescinded even after the armistice signing. The Allies still had nearly six hours of fighting left.

Pershing had known in advance the conditions that Foch would demand of the Germans. Thus, he knew that the enemy would be compelled within fourteen days to withdraw from territory they now occupied and pull back inside Germany. Consequently, any ground gained between the signing of the armistice and 11 A.M., at whatever cost in lives, would be handed over at no cost within two weeks. Still, Foch had said to keep up the pressure until the last, and Pershing was all too willing to oblige. Before the signing, he too had ordered all attacks planned and in progress to go forward, even those set for November 11. According to Pershing's chief of staff, the objective was "to take every advantage of the situation." After the signing, Pershing merely passed along Foch's order to stop the fighting at 11 A.M. What was to happen in the hours between the signing and the end was not addressed. Pershing, who had no love for the armistice, was not about to tell his subordinates to stop.

A twenty-three-year-old American pilot, Norman Archibald, apparently shared the general's implacability. Upon learning of the pending armistice, he wrote, "Victory is at hand. A well-earned, blood-soaked victory. Men, sobbing in agony, left the world too soon. . . . They died for victory. . . . That goal has not, quite, been reached. Only a few feet more and a sacred pledge to the dead is fulfilled. We are the winners! Must we stop before we have won all?" The war may have looked more romantic from the air.

After receiving word only to stop at eleven, American commanders found themselves left in a decisional vacuum as to what to do until then. They had two choices: to stop fighting, save lives, and risk censure for not pressing on to the very last; or to keep fighting, spend lives, avoid potential disobedience, and perhaps gain victories, even promotion. To many of the professional caste, the choice was obvious. The approach of a momentous hour in history aroused their competitive instincts. What laurels were yet to be won in the time remaining? Whose final burst to the finish line would be most brilliant? Colonel George S. Patton, in a hospital recovering from machine-gun wounds, had no intention of being on his back with victory so tantalizingly close. He bribed an orderly to let him out and commandeered a car to take him to the front. Colonel George C. Marshall, chief of staff for Liggett's First Army, saw the attitudes of his fellow careerists as "a typical American 'grandstand' finish." How a general viewed his duty would determine over the final five hours whether a doughboy would live out the normal ages of man or die at the first stage of manhood.

30

"Pass the Word.
Cease Fire at Eleven!"

NOVEMBER 11, 1918. The AEF weather service predicted a low temperature near freezing and a high of no more than 40 degrees Fahrenheit for the day. The battle front was expected to be shrouded in fog from 3 A.M. to 10 A.M., with visibility dropping in places to zero. Nearly 10 million men from seven nations inhabited this cold, damp, elongated land stretching some four hundred miles. Some lived safe from the distant rumbling thunder and others amidst lethal blasts, the sounds recorded by microphones installed along the front in "sound ranging stations." A needle traced the reverberations on graph paper, the results resembling the recording of an endless earthquake. The tracings looked no different after the armistice had been signed than before. Within these narrow confines, more than 3 million men had thus far perished.

BRIGADIER GENERAL JOHN SHERBURNE had bucked the army chain of command as only a National Guard officer who was still a civilian at heart would dare. No superior, however, would call off the advance under way by the 92nd Division's 366th Regiment. It was not until 10:30 A.M. that a runner made it through to the 366th reporting that the armistice had been signed, but still with no order to stop before the eleventh hour. Major Warner Ross, a white battalion commander, was in a shell hole when he received the word. He looked around at his men as he broke the news that they were still to advance and read the disbelief in their faces. German machine guns resumed fire as the black doughboys moved out of the protective Bois de Voivrotte for the third time.

TO FELDWEBEL GEORG BÜCHER, the Americans were behaving with a ferocity that suggested they did not know the end was imminent. Bücher and his comrades crouched on their haunches in a trench, overcoat collars turned up against the cold drizzle, letting battle-innocent replacements take the risks. A soldier just returned from leave asked, "Why did we serve and freeze and starve? To return home in shame?" Just after 7 A.M., they noticed a commotion at the far end of the trench and spotted their company commander weaving his way through the huddled bodies. "Cease fire at eleven!" he shouted. "Pass the word. Cease fire at eleven!"

To Bücher, in the fight since 1914, the words seemed a dream too long denied to be believed. The hours passed with agonizing slowness. One recent replacement, a boy Bücher knew only as Walter, clung to him as if to a life raft. An American pilot flying a Spad VII swooped low and dropped a bomb over their position. Walter was hit and badly wounded. He clutched at Bücher's sleeve. "I won't die now that there's an armistice, will I?" he pleaded. Bücher attempted to reassure the youth. As he spoke, gas shells began laying a poisonous cloud over the lines. Bücher pulled a mask over Walter's head, then over his own. Through the goggles he could make out shapes emerging from the odorous haze as the black Americans continued their attempt to breach the line. Bücher stole a glance at his watch. It was two minutes to eleven.

THE ARMISTICE MESSAGE that had gone out that morning to all British units reflected Marshal Foch's command to all Allied forces that pressure be applied to the very last. "Hostilities will cease at 11 hours today, November 11," Field Marshal Haig's signal read. "Troops will stand fast on the line reached at that hour. . . . There will be no intercourse of any description with the enemy until receipt of instructions from GHQ." Haig's order was to "stand fast" not where you are, but where you might be at the last hour.

German resistance continued to present a hodgepodge of fanaticism amid disorder. A British patrol entering a deserted village east of Valenciennes in the northern sector came across a wounded German lieutenant propped up against the wall of a house. He told them, in flawless English, that his men had abandoned the town two hours before and he hoped a British field surgeon might treat him. Given this information, the leader of the patrol began marching some two hundred men into the village square. As they arrived, machine guns appeared to sprout from every window and a church tower. More than a hundred dead Tommies piled up in the square. Such zealotry among the Germans was a vanishing impulse. More commonly, the *Feldgrauen* were surrendering in droves, 10,310 to the British alone in the past week.

To French farmers, their fields used as killing grounds for years, the uniform on a body made little difference. Lieutenant Montgomery Belgion, now commanding an infantry platoon in the British Third Army, in the final hours found a private "half-sitting, half-crouching. . . . He seemed to be waiting and looked as lifelike as any figure in the waxworks. But, of course, he was dead." Some time later, Belgion had to retrace his steps. The dead man was stripped, his belongings now the "possession of a French peasant."

With peace in sight, the ordinary Briton's mood was evident in the diary entry of Robert Cude: "11th November, we are staggered to read the news that, commencing at 11 A.M. today, an armistice will be in force at Jerry's asking." Cude credited the report only when an erratic cacophony erupted, telling him that the artillery "do not mean to be saddled with spare shells and so right up to the last minute they are pumping shells as fast as they can." Cude was fascinated yet wary. "I would not miss the sport at any price," he wrote, yet "I am as nervous as a kitten. If only I can last out the remainder of the time, and this is everyone's prayer. I am awfully sorry for those of our chaps who are killed this morning and there must be a decent few of them too."

Harry Bessborough, in his forties, was reckoned to be the oldest man in the British 111th Company, Machine Gun Corps. As a fervent member of a fundamentalist religious sect, Bessborough had survived, as he put it, "under angelic protection." His section was setting up a Vickers gun in a sunken road when a runner came, shouting, "Stand fast until eleven o'clock!" The men seized the respite to gather around a cook fire and heat their rations. The calm was shattered by Germans firing off unspent shells. The youngest member of the gun crew, sixteen-year-old Corporal D. O. Dixon, who had lied about his age to enlist, recounted what happened to the eldest member after a shell fell among the men gathered around the fire. "We loaded Harry and the others onto the vehicles. They were buried at Caudry." The last-minute losses reduced the Vickers crew strength to the point that each survivor received a double ration of rum that day.

Two weeks before the end, Major General Charles Rhodes, fifty-three-year-old horse soldier and onetime Indian fighter, had received a note from a West Point classmate, William "Bunker" Haan, presently commanding the 32nd Division. "Hearty congratulations on making Major General," Haan had written. "Better hurry up and get a division or the SHOW will be over!" Upon receiving his second star, Rhodes had written in his diary, "Hope that promotion does not take me home, since I want to be in at the finish." Haan's felicitation on his promotion was sincere enough, though it reminded the competent but stolid Rhodes that his classmate had outraced him in reaching division command. Rhodes's hope of catching up soared when General Pershing promised him the 42nd Division, "effective at such time as operations permitted." The Rainbow was the very division for which Rhodes had set his cap. Just a bit more patience was required for the change of command since the division was actively engaged at the moment.

Before the transition took place, Rhodes was invited to dinner by the man he expected to replace, Major General Charles Menoher, who was moving up from the 42nd to take over VI Corps. Replacing Menoher augured well for Rhodes's future. Menoher had prospered by his close association with Pershing. The powerfully built, imperturbable officer had served under Cadet Captain Pershing at West Point, had been with Black Jack in the hunt for Pancho Villa, had been given the 42nd by Pershing, and now was about to get an entire corps. Rhodes longed to parallel that path.

After dinner, Menoher suggested they drive to Exermont and drop in on his brightest star, General Douglas MacArthur, commanding the division's 84th Brigade and still the youngest general in the army. MacArthur did not disappoint his reputation for the theatrical. Yes, his brigade had performed extraordinary feats, he said. The 42nd, however, had been pushed to the limits of human endurance. He told his guests that it was only a question of time before all the original Rainbow Division complement would be killed. He then went on to explain what made a great leader. "It's difficult," MacArthur said, looking straight at Rhodes, "to get soldiers into severe fighting without being led personally by officers." In the last assault, he himself had taken his brigade "through the wire." Of course, he knew that headquarters types resented him for not playing by the book, "that I wore no helmet, that I carried no gas mask, that I went unarmed, that I always carried a riding crop in my hand, that I declined to command from the rear." MacArthur's egotism was grating but rooted in truth. In eight months at the front the 42nd had been in near-constant contact with the enemy for 174 days, had fought in six major campaigns, and had taken one of every sixteen casualties suffered by the AEF. No one's exploits in the division had glowed more incandescently than those of Douglas MacArthur. He was that rarity, a courageous exhibitionist, a fearless showoff, a man who had done it all and wanted the world to know.

Two days before the armistice, Rhodes entered in his diary, "Reports reach us that the German Navy is in the hands of mutineers; that Bavaria has elected to become a republic; that the German Emperor has been asked to abdicate within twenty-four hours." Time was running out on Rhodes's dream—commanding in battle the 26,000 men of the most storied force in the AEF. At last, on the final morning of the war, with the 42nd largely out of the fight that day, Rhodes assumed command of the division. But just hours later, a courier arrived with staggering news. "By command of General Pershing, Major General Charles D. Rhodes is relieved of assignment to the 42nd Division and is assigned to command the 34th Division," the message read. It was more galling than Rhodes could bear. The 34th was a skeleton division. The worst blow was yet to come. He was to turn over his command immediately to Douglas MacArthur. Attached to the order was a personal letter from Pershing's deputy chief of staff, a Colonel Eltinge, saying, "I am sure you will understand the circumstances which made it necessary to assign MacArthur to the command of this division." For the life of him, Rhodes could not understand why, except that while his flame burned dutifully MacArthur's blazed.

BY THE DAWNING light, Elton Mackin watched stretcher bearers taking the wounded down to the Meuse. Caught in the leafless rushes along the riverbank were the bodies of men shot off the pontoons during the night. The ground was littered with caps, punctured helmets, blankets, rifles, and smashed machine guns spilling intestines of unspent ammunition belts. Amid the debris were drying pools of brown-red blood. At first the marines were puzzled by eight-foot poles topped with sprigs of vegetation that they found along the riverbank. Once across the river, they understood. Enemy gunners knew that when the Americans reached the markers, they had come within range, and the intervals between the poles marked the field of fire assigned to each gun. The system had been primitive but effective.

A voice was shouting over the continuing bursts of enemy artillery. Mackin spied a runner calling out, "Armistice at eleven o'clock!" Dropping exhausted to the ground, he explained that at that hour they were to stop and "wait for orders." Mackin had been tagged for medical evacuation three times. But each time the war within himself, his hope for survival vying with hunger for the esteem of his fellows, had led him to tear up the evacuation ticket and stay. Mackin took one last glance back at the wounded and the dead. Then the marines began moving forward through wispy patches of fog toward the heights above the village of Pouilly, close enough to the enemy to hear guttural shouting.

IT TOOK UNTIL 9:20 A.M., nearly three and a half hours, before word of the armistice seeped from Pershing's headquarters to the 2nd and 89th Divisions crossing the Meuse. By then the two divisions had nearly 60 percent of their men on the east bank. Word of the cease-fire was passed from division headquarters to subordinate units dispersed over three miles of gulleys, patches of forest, and meandering streams by messengers who moved as far as they could on motorcycles, then on horseback, and finally on foot.

In the realm well above where doughboys like Elton Mackin struggled to survive, the usually levelheaded Lieutenant General Hunter Liggett explained to his First Army staff why the men must keep fighting. "There was a big operation planned from Lunéville to come off on the fourteenth of November," Liggett noted, referring to the forthcoming Metz campaign, "and in order to better our situation when we stopped fighting on the front we were on, we should continue that so as to make it easier for that operation." To Liggett the assault he was pressing that morning was merely the continuation of the now unnecessary campaign that had been under way for the past six weeks to cut the Sedan-Mézières rail line and split the German Army in half.

The men across the Meuse, shivering in soaked uniforms, hungry, and exhausted, the water in their canteens icing over, responded to the order to form up with the unreflecting obedience of cattle. General Liggett had provided the high-level strategy for their continuing advance. Subordinate commanders found less lofty reasons to keep going. Stenay was a still-occupied town on the east bank of the river. The 89th Division's commander, Major General William M. Wright, was determined to take Stenay because "the division had been in the line a considerable period without proper bathing facilities, and since it was realized that if the enemy were permitted to stay in Stenay, our troops would be deprived of the probable bathing facilities there." Thus, placing cleanliness above survival, Wright sent his 179th Brigade to take Stenay in the war's last hour. Stenay had a further appeal to Wright: it was perhaps not Berlin, but it did possess modest value as a prize as it had recently been the headquarters of the kaiser's son Prince Rupprecht. General Wright ordered his division to go it alone. His officers were not to seek any assistance from the rival 90th Division, posted to their right, in taking Stenay. The town, normally with a population of 3,000, was now down to some 850 inhabitants cowering in their cellars in expectation of an American bombardment. The commanding officer of the 90th Division, Major General Henry Allen, had his own ambitions. Allen, who had known of the signing for more than three hours, transmitted an order to one of his brigade commanders to "push patrols as far as possible into Stenay before 11 o'clock." The brigade commander passed along the order with even greater fervor, telling the regiments under him not only to penetrate Stenay but to take Baâlon as well and "clean up the towns."

Major Hanford MacNider's battalion was among troops ordered to cross the Meuse near Mouzay over one of the few surviving bridges. On arriving with 2,000 men at the bridgehead, MacNider was appalled by the concentration of machine-gun fire that the Germans were laying down. The bodies of the first men to attempt the crossing were piled at the foot of the bridge. To press on, MacNider knew, would lead to useless slaughter. So little time remained before the fighting would end. What was the point? He withdrew his men. The battalion took no further casualties that morning. MacNider was never disciplined for what some would consider disobedience and others call common sense.

Machine guns in the hundreds spiked the hills above Stenay, raking the attackers. Still the Americans pressed forward. Finally, just before eleven o'clock, the first troops of the 90th Division entered the town from the south, while the rival 89th Division entered from the north. En route, elements of the 89th had been passing through Pouilly when a 10.5 cm howitzer shell landed in their midst. Twenty Americans had been wounded or killed outright. The doughboys found the streets of Stenay deserted except for some fifty dead Germans. Slowly, cellar doors began to open and the dazed citizens of the town began to come out. They disappeared into their houses and began unfolding the tricolor from their windows. Church bells clanged. The townsfolk returned to the streets bearing bread, wine, and cheese for their liberators, kissing them, and cheering themselves hoarse. Prince Rupprecht had commanded from a schoolhouse, now a shambles littered with charred papers. A doughboy corporal picked up a soiled proclamation and began to read from it: The German Army can "never be beaten, will win gloriously and have all their desires fulfilled if they resist." The document had been issued by Field Marshal Hindenburg at the start of the Meuse-Argonne offensive. Stenay would be the last town taken by the Americans in the war.

ELEVEN O'CLOCK WAS fast approaching when Sergeant Rudolph Forderhase heard his captain calling to him through the smoke clouding the field. Forderhase approached to find two German boys standing alongside their machine-gun pit, arms raised. Speaking the smattering of German he had learned at home, Forderhase was curious to know why they had given up without firing a shot. The young soldiers looked puzzled. Didn't the Americans know that the war would soon be over? "We see no reason to sacrifice our lives, or yours," one explained. German artillerymen on the heights above the Meuse were less disposed to turn the other cheek. As long as the Americans kept shelling, they returned fire and drew more fire in response. The Germans were finally forced to pull back, bodies tracing their retreat. As eleven o'clock approached, remnants of the 174th Infantry Regiment gathered in the woods at a point midway between Mouzon and Stenay. This German unit had gone into action with more than 3,000 men. On this last day, 327 were left standing.

IN CROSSING THE Meuse that morning, the 2nd, 89th, and 90th Divisions suffered 1,130 casualties, 792 seriously wounded and 127 dead. General Liggett had justified pressing on by citing the future assault against Metz. "This offensive would have cut the German Army in two, and . . . in my judgment would have brought about a capitulation in the field of everything north of that break," he had said. It was odd reasoning for exposing men to death: to seek a capitulation on November 14 that had already been won by November 11.

31

"Little Short of Murder"

NOVEMBER 11, 1918. Americans who led nocturnal lives—reporters on morning newspapers, cabdrivers, night-shift nurses, short-order cooks in all-night diners, and policemen on the graveyard shift—knew about the war's impending end before hundreds of thousands of doughboys that morning. At 2:50 A.M., a State Department spokesman read a short statement to drowsy, hastily summoned journalists: "The Armistice has been signed. It was signed at 5:00 A.M. Paris time and hostilities will cease at 11 o'clock this morning Paris time." Because of the time differential then in use, 5:00 A.M. in Paris was midnight on the U.S. East Coast. The Associated Press wire service flashed the news to subscriber papers all across America. *The New York Times* early edition, on the street by 4 A.M., three cents a copy, carried a headline in bold seventy-two-point type: ARMISTICE SIGNED, END OF THE WAR! People were stirred from sleep by church bells, factory whistles, firehouse sirens, and newsboys shouting "Extra! Extra!" down deserted streets. Only four days before, the world had been fooled into frenzied celebration by the false armistice. This mistaken revelry had not, however, dulled the edge of anticipation when the real moment came. Crowds began pouring from their homes into the streets. A New York merchant caught the holiday mood in the sign he hung in his shop window: "Closed for the Kaiser's Funeral."

However, the *Times*'s jubilant "End of War" headline was premature. The men sent into action after the armistice signing but before 11:00 A.M. still had hours to go.

THE NEW ENGLANDERS of the 26th Yankee Division were taking casualties from German Maxims at the very moment their neighbors back in Boston, Providence, and New Haven began spilling into the streets. For the 26th, whose order to attack had been first rescinded and then reinstated, the first wave had already left the trenches and was pushing ahead some five miles beyond the Meuse River. Earlier that morning, the division's chief of staff, Colonel Duncan Major, had sought clarification from the French II Colonial Corps, under which the American division served, asking why the 26th had to attack. He received no explanation but merely a reiteration of the order. He observed no similar activity in the French lines. For Albertine Connell, awaiting the signal for the next wave to go over the top, his consuming thought was "Not me, not now." He looked up, scanning the sky for the reassuring "freight train," as he called it, of shells roaring overhead in support of the assault. Edwin James, a correspondent of *The New York Times* covering the 26th, was stunned by the scene. "Reaching the front this morning, expecting to find quiet reigning in view of the imminence of the cessation of hostilities, I found the attack in full swing," James reported. "With every gun we had going at full speed, and roaring in a glorious chorus, singing the swan song of Prussianism."

Connell Albertine heard someone cry out, "Litter bearers! Hurry! Hurry!" Chaplain de Valles beat him out of the trench, running in the direction of the cry. When Albertine caught up, he found the priest bent over a doughboy he knew only as Gerrior. "By the time we got him on a litter and were trying to get him back to more safe cover," Albertine recalled, "he had died. Chaplain de Valles administered the last rites of the church, and without any ceremonies we began to dig a shallow grave with our bayonets."

German shells began exploding uncomfortably close, heaving dirt and fragments of hot metal onto the burial party. "The chaplain decided we had better move," Albertine remembered of the moment, "so we ran back to the brow of the hill leaving the dead soldier covered except for his toes, which were sticking up about four inches." Once safely sheltered, Albertine glanced at his watch. It was ten minutes before eleven.

Had Lieutenant Harry Rennagel stayed in the hospital one more day, he would have been spared the final fate of the 26th. Having heard the swell of armistice rumors, Rennagel returned to the trenches to find his comrades jubilant, then suddenly plunged into stunned silence when the attack order was renewed. At 10:35 A.M., bayonets fixed, they went over the top. At 10:55 A.M., a *Minenwerfer* shell exploded a dozen yards from Rennagel. "I hurried over and there lay five of my best men, one fatally injured, with a hole near his heart. 'Lieutenant, I'm going fast,' he said. 'Don't say I'll get better, you know different.' " With his last breath, the man told Rennagel, "You know we all expected things to cease today, so I wrote my girl, we were to be married when I returned."

The first two charges had been beaten back. On the third attempt, the enemy machine guns were overrun. The dead Germans, sprawled about their weapons, belied a favorite bit of battlefield lore, that the enemy were chained to their guns. Bursts of artillery merely entangled them in ammunition belts and cooling tubes. In this morning's final push, the 26th had so far taken 192 casualties, 15 killed. With minutes left, battery commanders allowed the men to attach ropes to the lanyards of the guns. More than 200 doughboys managed to get a hand on a rope. An officer, eyes glued to his watch, held a handkerchief over his head. When he dropped it, they were to yank the rope. Every man could claim that he had fired the last shot of the Great War.

CAPTAIN LEBRETON HAD thought ahead. The French 163rd Infantry Regiment must have a bugler, one who could sound "cease fire" when the moment came. His unit, operating north of the 26th Division, had just received word of the armistice, and Lebreton assumed that his men had fought their final offensive. No one could remember the last time a bugle call had been heard. With the German machine-gun fire still heavy, Lebreton dispatched a runner to locate private Octave Delalauge, rumored once to have been a bugler. A surprised Delalauge crawled his way back to the captain through shell holes and barbed wire on all fours, a bugle dangling from his neck. Lebreton asked him if he knew the cease-fire. The soldier answered that he had not played it since 1911 on the firing range. The captain whistled the first notes for him while Delalauge fumbled in his pockets for his mouthpiece. He found it and tried to sound a note, but the mouthpiece was clogged with tobacco. Lebreton became impatient. The armistice was fast approaching.

The end did not arrive in time for Lieutenant Moulin, commanding the 5th Company, 171st Infantry. Moulin was among those who, four days before, had watched the German staff cars emerge from the mist at Haudroy bearing the Erzberger peace delegation. On Armistice Day, Moulin waited out the end with four enlisted men not far from the railroad car where, hours before, the adversaries had finally signed. One of the last shells fired by an opposing battery killed all five men. They would not be the last to die. Joseph Albert Trebuchon, a twenty-five-year-old runner from the Lozère region, came to the front line bearing welcome news for the chilled, hungry troops posted near the tiny village of Vrigne-Meuse. Trebuchon reached the regimental command post, located in a shell crater, and reported that the cooks had prepared hot soup, which would be served at 11:30 A.M. As he spoke, a sniper's bullet toppled Trebuchon into the crater. It was 10:50 A.M. He would be counted the last *poilu* to die in the war.

MAJOR GENERAL RHODES'S West Point classmate Bunker Haan received a call at 6:50 A.M. from III Corps headquarters that the armistice had been signed. Haan faced a dilemma. His 32nd Division, already across the Meuse, had been ordered to go over the top at seven o'clock and advance seven miles in the direction of Longuyon. Haan had chosen the hour with care. Attacks in the dark invited disaster. Daylight this morning was due at 6:45 A.M. Seven A.M. should provide just enough light. He could hear his artillery laying down the advance barrage and was continuously shaken in his bunker by the enemy's retaliatory fire. He studied a map tacked onto the supporting timbers. His division, occupying hilly terrain overlooking a plain, was nicely positioned for jumping off. But Haan also realized, should he choose not to go, that the same deployment should provide a protective position for his men in these last hours. While he was on the phone talking to corps, a signalman informed him that his subordinate commanding the 63rd Brigade was on another line, eager to move forward and straighten out a dent in the front. Haan took the phone and informed the brigade commander that he did not intend to risk men's lives on this last morning to tidy up a map. He had made up his mind. He was calling off the attack. Haan also ceased his artillery barrage, and by 7:25 A.M., his guns had fallen silent. He mounted his horse to inspect the front near the village of La Petite Lissey. To his dismay, though his guns had stopped, the enemy continued a heavy shelling. "I counted the shots as they exploded, and there were from seventeen to twenty-two a minute," Haan recalled. "I gave instructions then and there to transmit to the artillery commander . . . to open up as heavy artillery fire as he could on the enemy batteries." His guns were to fire ten rounds for every German shell fired. The superior force produced the desired effect. The German shelling diminished and then ceased altogether. Haan's troops remained in place, and the division's guns finally stopped. Thus, the 32nd Division waited out the last hours of the war. How many men's lives were saved by Haan's decision is unknowable. The final artillery duel, however, had left fifteen American dead.

The 77th Division was ordered only to "renew hostilities in case of necessity." Its casualties on November 11: 4 killed, 79 wounded.

After being informed that the armistice had been signed, Major General Edmund Wittenmyer called off an attack set for the last hour for his 7th Division. His men would die someday, but not now with their lives barely begun. He lost no soldiers that morning.

The 5th Division occupied a stretch of the front to the left of Bunker Haan's 32d Division. Its commander, Major General Hanson Ely, no reluctant soldier and a hero of Cantigny, also asked why his men should pay with blood for a victory that had already been won on paper. Ely found a comfortable compromise: if the enemy fired an artillery shell, a machine-gun burst, or a gas missile, his division was to respond in kind, "shot for shot," but do no more. "The foe was a treacherous one, and the morale of my command would be injured if we took the enemy's fire without reply," Ely reasoned. Only the night before, the Germans had poisoned Mouzay, a town of no further strategic consequence, with clouds of phosgene gas. Some 600 civilian inhabitants, mostly women, children, the aged and infirm, had staggered out of their homes into the reeking streets. Doughboys rushed to offer spare gas masks, dampened rags, any filter available as they led the gasping townsfolk to uncontaminated ground. The people seized the hands of their saviors and kissed them. Children stared at the doughboys as if encountering exotic creatures. When the Americans expressed surprise that these children spoke German as readily as French, they were told that the occupation here had lasted for four years.

Arthur Jensen, 5th Division mule skinner and dreamer of long-deferred battlefield glory, found in the last days what he had hungered for and penned his reactions in his War Log. He was proud at how quickly he had mastered the acoustic clues for the proximity of different enemy shells, a *Minenwerfer* round, for example, from a 10.5 cm howitzer. They variously said to him, "Jensen, I'm coming to kill you" or "Jensen, where are you?" or "I'll get you yet." He tried to imagine what his mother and father were doing back in Nebraska this armistice morning. Where were they standing? What were they saying? What were they thinking? What would they think of him?

He and other wagoneers were sitting munching raw cabbage swiped from a Frenchman's garden when a motorcycle skidded alongside, the driver shouting, "War's over at eleven!" Jensen had a buddy, a fellow driver named Walt, who had taken a wagon to the rear for rations and was overdue. Jensen anxiously scanned the rutted road and finally spied his friend, only to see a shell explode above him. Miraculously, Walt survived unscathed and came in on foot. But, he told Jensen, he had already had a closer call that morning. The company cook had been ladling out corn willy and hardtack when, just as Walt stepped out of the chow line, the man was killed by a shell fragment. Jensen listened wide-eyed. That was just the kind of story to take back home.

General Ely's 5th Division had suffered 142 casualties in the previous twenty-four hours. No purpose would be served by more bloodshed, and the general held his units in place. But the artillery exchange up to the last minute took its toll. That morning the 5th lost another 14 dead and 442 seriously wounded. Ely's 11th Brigade had been too far advanced to get the word to stop fighting. As the men moved forward under cover of fog, the roar of artillery inexplicably stopped. The sun began burning off the mist, leaving the Americans naked to German gunners on the hills. To the dough-boys' astonishment, a white flag rose above an enemy dugout and an officer came forward. "My good sir," he asked in British-accented English, "what are you doing? Don't you know the armistice goes into effect at 11 o'clock?"

RADIO RECEIVERS IN the 33rd Division's headquarters had been crackling incessantly for two days. To officers on the staff of Major General George Bell, traffic intercepted from the Eiffel Tower had provided a running account of developments: the Erzberger mission's arrival, the turmoil inside Germany, the kaiser's abdication. Then on Sunday evening during supper in the staff mess came the message most eagerly awaited: Berlin had authorized the peace mission to sign the armistice. One excited junior officer asked permission to inform the division's brigades. His superior stopped him, pointing out that the message merely stated that the Germans had authority to sign, not that they had signed. Nevertheless, credible reports were soon flying among the division's units that the war was about to end. Doughboys in convoys, normally transported to the front in resigned silence, rumbled past General Bell's headquarters singing, shouting, and hurling amiable obscenities at one another and at soldiers trudging along the road.

None of this jubilation, however, affected Bell's intentions. He had 28,000 men deployed along an eight-mile front southeast of Verdun. In his view, the remaining hours would provide the opportunity to display his division's fighting élan. At 5 A.M., his 65th Brigade was to move out and take the towns of Riaville, Pintheville, Maizeray, and Harville; his 66th Brigade was to leave from Saint-Hilaire and take Butgnéville. All of them were strongholds on the Hindenburg Line. Bell believed he faced not a disintegrating foe but die-hard resistance. As he later put it, the loss of these points was, to the Germans, "synonymous with the fall of Metz and every effort was therefore bent to hold them until the bitter end." The only flaw in Bell's reasoning was the fact, known to a commander at his level, that under the armistice terms, the Germans had agreed to give up Metz along with the whole of Lorraine.

Bell's frontline troops knew only what was visible from a trench and nothing of the issues being debated in the rear. The order to the division to take the towns strung before them was still in place. In the darkness before dawn, noncoms began shouting, kicking sleepy doughboys, and herding the men into attack positions. In order to achieve surprise, the division was to advance without an artillery barrage first blasting the way. The sector was eerily silent but for a distant rumbling. The fields to be crossed before reaching the enemy's high ground had become a quagmire under the incessant rains. The men, shivering with cold, stepped out, sinking ankle deep into the mud. At 5:20 A.M., units of the 66th Brigade left the village of Saint-Hilaire, a half mile from their objective, Butgnéville. As the men stalled before the still intact enemy wire, flares illuminated them as clearly as in daylight. Slammed by mortars and machine-gun fire, the doughboys began pulling back and by 9 A.M. were again in Saint-Hilaire, where they had started, minus the men piled before the wire.

In the meantime, 33rd Division headquarters had learned at 7:50 A.M. that the armistice had indeed been signed. General Bell, finally convinced that the enemy intended to capitulate, issued an order "to stop the advance immediately and to cease all firing." The order, however, crept slowly to units far afield and already engaged. The men who had emerged from Saint-Hilaire had taken their casualties and been driven back while the message that would have saved them was still making its way to the front. They were preparing for a second push on Butgnéville when Bell's order finally reached them and "Recall" was sounded at 9:45 A.M. As a historian of the division would later put it, "Our regimental wireless had picked up sufficient intercepted messages during the early hours of the morning to make it certain that Armistice had been signed at 5 o'clock that morning; and the fact that the prearranged attack was launched after the Armistice was signed . . . caused sharp criticism of the high command on the part of the troops engaged, who considered the loss of American lives that morning as useless and little short of murder."

At 33rd Division headquarters, staff officers broke out champagne and toasted one another's health. The men still in the line needed only to hold on for less than two hours. Circumstances, however, conspired to defeat General Bell's change of heart. Though the infantry assault had eventually been broken off, the Americans' aggressiveness had poked the hornet's nest and German shells continued to rain down. Captain Robert Casey, an artillery officer with the 33rd, recorded in his diary that in the last hour, a shell hit a sawmill, the blast and splinters killing twenty men and wounding thirty-five more. His next entry read, "The war has twenty-three minutes still to go." Another shell blasted a soup kitchen, killing another fourteen doughboys and wounding four more.

AT 9:15 A.M., Major General Hay, commanding the 28th Infantry Division, finally yielded to pleas from his subordinate commanders and countermanded an earlier order for his forces to keep fighting. Still, he sought a middle ground to protect him from the appearance of quitting the fight without authorization from his superiors. His compromise was to maintain artillery fire. Major General Frederic D. Evans, under Hay as commanding officer of the 55th Brigade, protested that artillery fire begets artillery fire. Hay, however, insisted. Thus, with fifty minutes left, the artillery duel was still going on, with Evans's brigade alone losing 191 killed or wounded, mostly to retaliating German batteries.

PERSHING HAD GIVEN his 37th Division to Foch as a gesture to satisfy the marshal's desire to have American troops take part in breaking the Hindenburg Line at its northern anchor in Belgium. On October 16, the 37th was pulled from the Meuse-Argonne in midbattle and dispatched to the Schelde River to serve under the French XXXIV Corps. The doughboys forced a crossing of the Schelde on November 4. When the division was relieved that day, its war appeared over. But when Foch issued his November 9 fight-to-the-last dictum, the 37th was sent back into the line. The commanding officer, Major General C. S. Farnsworth, bowed to the French commander's order to launch an attack at 10 A.M. on November 11. As General Farnsworth recorded in his after-action report, the French "directed strong patrols be pushed forward as rapidly as possible and to advance until 11:00 A.M." Regiments of the 91st and 93rd Divisions were also engaged in Flanders on that last day. They encountered only the erratic fire of an enemy falling back in disarray. In that final hour, the casualties for these three divisions were thus fairly light: 25 dead and 208 wounded.

Back in the Meuse-Argonne, the commander of the Second Army, General Bullard, felt his sense of history quicken as his orderly wakened him that morning. As he would recount in his memoirs, "I regarded this fighting as the last day of the war, so I went early, with an aide, to near the front, to see the last of it, to hear the crack of the last guns in the greatest war of all ages. . . . Our men showed great zest in the striking of the last blows against the enemy."

Earlier, Bullard had relayed to his subordinate commanders Marshal Foch's order stating that the armistice was to take effect at 11 A.M. By passing this word along without elaboration, he believed that he had left it to these subordinates to decide whether or not to keep fighting. The implication may have been there, but not the words. Some of his generals chose to fight on, they said, in order to pressure the enemy into signing the armistice. But Bullard had held Foch's message in his hand as early as 6:30 that morning reporting that the terms had been signed. No further pressure was needed. Obviously, men would die among the units still engaged, and Bullard that morning had gone out to watch the show.

Of sixteen American divisions engaged on the western front on armistice morning, the commanders of seven judged the war essentially over upon receiving word of the signing and stopped; but the commanders of nine divisions decided that the war must go on until the last minute, with predictable results to the lives entrusted to them.

32

The Fate of Private Gunther

NOVEMBER 11, 1918. Mons had powerful symbolic significance for the British Expeditionary Force. There the army had suffered a wrenching loss in the earliest days of the war. To the high command, reclaiming the Belgian city in these final hours would turn a stain of defeat into a badge of honor. The hunger for retribution, however, eluded foot soldiers of the Canadian 42nd Battalion, the Royal Highlanders. The day before, knowing the war was all but over, Will Bird had begun to pack his souvenirs, a pearl-handled Lugar, binoculars, a pickelhaube helmet, and, most prized, the regimental kilt that had been worn only once, borrowed by Bird's pal Bob Jones for a visit to a brothel. Now Jones was dead, killed in the last twenty-four hours along with Tom Mills, just after Sergeant Studholme had informed the disbelieving Canadians that they were to retake Mons. Crossing a bridge into the city, the Canadians came upon the bodies of three men of the London Rifle Brigade killed earlier that morning. Each wore the Mons Star, which meant that they had fought in the 1914 retreat, surviving for four years only to die in the same place on the last day of the war.

By dawn of the eleventh, the Canadian 2nd and 3rd Divisions entered what appeared to be a dead city but for the flames crackling from burning houses. The men clanged their rifle barrels along the iron grillwork that barred the windows of surviving homes. Faces began to appear, cautiously at first, then openly. Soon the streets were filled. Women rushed to be the first to kiss a liberator. The people of Mons began kicking the bodies of their dead German occupiers into the gutter. By 7 A.M., the Canadians were forming up for a triumphal march to the town square, led by bagpipers whose wail sent the crowd into paroxysms of cheering. The Belgians tossed out flowers and dropped small tricolors, flags of red, yellow, and black, down the soldiers' gun barrels. The Canadians shouted back, *"Guerre finie! Boche napoo!"* The crowd broke into the national anthem, "La Brabançonne." The carillon in the bell tower of the city hall broke into a ponderous chiming of "Tipperary."

Since it was not yet eleven o'clock, time remained for a final act of retribution. The 5th Royal Irish Lancers had been among those driven from Mons in August 1914. The cavalrymen, so inconsequential thus far in trench warfare, sought one last bid for glory. Canadian infantry stood aside to let the Lancers clatter through Mons en route to Saint-Denis to the northeast, where they were to seize the high ground above that city. As the sleekly groomed horses and proud-necked riders passed through the Grande Place a Belgian priest shouted, "We saw you going; but we knew you would be back." Seventeen miles northeast of Mons, at Lessines, another cavalry unit, the 7th Dragoons, mounted a charge at 10:50 A.M. The action was necessary, their commander had explained, to capture a key bridge should the Germans renege on the armistice in the remaining ten minutes. The horsemen, brandishing swords, went galloping down a tree-lined road, pennants flying. German machine-gun fire exploded from concealed emplacements, and cavalrymen began to topple from their horses.

The 5th Irish Lancers arrived at Saint-Denis just in time to see the backs of the fleeing German defenders and to suffer the last British casualty of the war, Private G. E. Ellison, killed in its waning moments. He would eventually rest in a military cemetery a few steps away from plot L/14196, holding the remains of Private J. Parr, Middlesex Regiment. Parr, a messenger shot off his bicycle on August 21, 1914, had been the first Briton to die in the war.

Still, the victory in the Mons sector had come relatively cheap. In the last forty-eight hours, the Canadian Army had lost 280 men, light by the accounting of this war—except, as one soldier put it, "to those who were killed and their families." Just beyond Mons, the Canadian 2nd Division was still attacking an enemy holed up in a row of miners' houses. A sniper shot rang out at 10:58 A.M. and struck Private George Price, 38th Northwest Infantry Battalion. Price was officially declared the last Canadian to die in the war.

Under terms of the armistice, the Canadians could have marched unopposed into Mons on November 12. Why they did not was explained by the commander of all Canadian forces, General Sir Arthur Currie: "The reason Mons was taken was that we obeyed the orders of Marshal Foch that we should go on until we were ordered to stop." Canada's place in history further spurred Currie. As he later put it, "It was a proud thing . . . that we were able to finish the war where we began it, and that we, the young whelps of the old lion, were able to take the ground lost in 1914." Among the young whelps who died making Currie's case were Tom Mills and Bob Jones.

The retaking of Mons, site of the first retreat, might be seen as poetic closure. It could also symbolize futility. The British Army was back where it had started on the western front—some 700,000 lives later.

RESIDENTS OF EAST Baltimore woke up on November 11 to the banging of pans and kettles and the hooting of factory whistles. If anything, the mood in this heavily German part of town was even more joyous than elsewhere. Sons of these families had proved their loyalty to America and were no longer killing their own kind, even brothers and cousins, back in the old country.

Some 3,775 miles away, word of the armistice had yet to penetrate the 313th Regiment, Baltimore's Own, facing the 31st Prussians in one of the farthest reaches of the western front. At sixteen
minutes to eleven, a panting runner finally reached the men with
word that the armistice had been signed. The 313th had already
taken its assigned objective that morning, the town of Ville-
devant-Chaumont, and now stood before the ridge of the Côte
Romagne. The brigade commander, Brigadier General William
Nicholson, ordered that there would be "absolutely no let-up" until
11 A.M. Thus Private Henry Gunther and Sergeant Ernie Powell
found themselves on the slope, hugging the earth for its shallow
protection against exploding shells. Along the crest Prussian machine gunners, knowing the end was imminent, eyed the advancing
Americans with mingled disbelief and wariness.

Sergeant Powell would never understand what compelled Henry
Gunther to rise up and charge the enemy. Gunther had never been
seduced by dreams of battlefield glory. He had lost his sergeant's
stripes and been broken to private for urging a friend, in a censored letter, to stay out of the war. His pointless gesture might have
been a last desperate effort to eradicate the stain. Whatever the impulse, Gunther kept advancing, bayonet fixed. The German gunners reluctantly fired a five-round burst. Gunther was struck in the
left temple and died instantly. The time was 10:59 A.M. General
Pershing's order of the day would record Henry Gunther as the
last American killed in the war.

ALL ALONG THE front, the shriek and whine of explosives of
every caliber and destructive ingenuity howled over the heads of
infantrymen on both sides. It was as if celebrants at a county fair
wanted to shoot off all the fireworks before the festivities ended.
Gun crews worked so feverishly that they were bathed in sweat despite the November chill. "The guns are so hot that the paint is
rising from them in blisters," one artilleryman noted. The ran-
domness of the blasts, however, did not reduce their lethality. A

German officer reported that two of his men were killed by American artillery fire at 10:57 A.M. As the final minutes ticked away, men of the 26th Division watched the officer's handkerchief drop and yanked the rope attached to the lanyard of a 75 mm cannon. Technically, each could indeed go home claiming to have fired the last shot of the war.

Captain Harry Truman, following his orders, had said nothing to the crew of Battery D about an armistice until his watch read precisely 11 A.M. Just before, he had completed his test firing of the new "D" shell with its reported 30 percent increased range. Its effectiveness could be measured in the target village of Hermeville, rubble reduced to rubble for the last time. As he later wrote to Bess, "I fired 164 rounds at [the enemy] before he quit this morning. . . . I knew that Germany could not stand the gaff. For all their preparedness and swashbuckling talk they cannot stand adversity." At the appointed hour, the needles from the AEF sound recording stations, which a minute before had been gyrating wildly, instantly went flat. "It was so quiet it made me feel as if I'd suddenly been deprived of my ability to hear," Truman recalled. He felt a mingled surge of relief and pride. Of the 194 Battery D men who had arrived with him in France seven months before, all had survived.

OUTSIDE DAMVILLERS IN the French sector of the Meuse-Argonne, Lieutenant Lebreton of the 163rd Infantry jabbed his foot into the huddled form of Octave Delalauge. The bugler rose uneasily as shells continued to burst. He began sounding the cease-fire. His wavering notes, barely audible at first, pierced the cold morning air sharply as the guns fell silent. Finally standing erect, Delalauge played the stirring "Au Drapeau" ("To the Flag"). From every shell hole in earshot Frenchmen rose and began a hoarse rendering of "The Marseillaise." One man jumped out crying, *"On les a eus!"* ("We've had 'em!") Another shouted, "I won the war!"

SECONDS BEFORE ELEVEN o'clock, Australian troops near Mons crouched low to escape a withering hail of bullets from a machine gun. Exactly on the hour, a huge German rose alongside the gun, took off his helmet, bowed, turned, and walked off. An Australian signalman watched a German coming forward to surrender and recalled, "It was a chap—a big tall man—and he had his jaw shot away and he's got another bloke with broken legs or something— he's got this chap on his back. He's staggering back along the road and when they saw me they had to put up one hand [to salute], you know, and it made me ready to cry . . . the stupidity of the whole thing."

Connell Albertine of the 26th Division had buried a man in the war's waning hours. He had returned to his trench and was awaiting his platoon's turn to follow the others over the top, when suddenly all went strangely still. Had the brass changed the time for the assault? Why wasn't the artillery firing? Were they to leave the trenches naked to the enemy? He heard muffled shouts rising from the French lines and saw helmets flung into the air. He could now make out their cries. *"Finie la guerre! Finie la guerre!"* A captain from Albertine's battalion came running down the trench. "The war is over!" he yelled. "An armistice has been signed." From the moment nine months before when the grave marker bearing the name "Albertine" had been thrust into his hand in a French cemetery, he had never felt the premonition of death lifted from him until now. The import of the moment penetrated slowly. A historian of Albertine's division reported that the men greeted eleven o'clock "dumbly, as if in a dream. There was no rejoicing, no noisy jubilation; the men were stupid with fatigue and the reaction which follows a too prolonged tension of the nerves. Eleven o'clock and end of being killed!" Chaplain de Valles dropped to his knees. His clerk knelt beside him "and prayed and thanked Almighty God," Albertine remembered. "We then, being very excited, started shouting and hugging and kissing each other. We ran into no-man's-land and stood there, stunned by the quiet, a quietness we had never known." The chaplain wandered off by himself. Albertine followed de Valles's unsteady footsteps. The priest assured his assistant that he was fine and then collapsed. He was carted off the field to an aid station, emotionally drained by the unceasing stress of the past months.

The 29th Division had just been returned to the front after suffering heavy earlier losses and to ready itself for the Metz offensive, which, to one infantryman, F. C. Reynolds, "sounded like a death sentence." When the eleventh hour arrived, he recalled, "You can imagine—no, you can't imagine, it is impossible for anyone to imagine who did not experience it, the sense of relief and pure joy that came in our hearts. . . . At first we took it quietly. The feeling of gratitude was too deep for noisy expression. Instead of running out in the street, yelling, and turning a hand spring, we felt like stealing away into some lonely spot and crying for sheer joy." A soldier in the 42nd Division remembered, "We didn't know what to do first, to cheer or to pray. I guess we really did both in the same breath."

Cries could be heard from the German lines: *"Der Krieg ist über!"* shouted with a joy that sounded of victory rather than defeat. Heads began appearing above the parapets, then figures, then clusters, then whole companies. The Germans began singing, flinging their rifles, helmets, ammunition belts, and bayonets toward the American lines. A bearded soldier appeared with a concertina, playing and goose-stepping along the parapet. Dozens joined behind him. They clasped hands and danced in circles, flinging their arms and legs about in abandon.

Orders against fraternization had been issued to all units of the AEF. General Liggett reminded his First Army that the "arrangement is an armistice only and not a peace." Further, "All communication with the enemy is forbidden before and after the termination of hostilities." The order became harsher as it moved down the chain of command. Fifth Division headquarters warned, "An officer offending will be sent to division headquarters under guard." General Summerall warned all divisions under his V Corps that "intercourse with the enemy is an act of treason and is punishable by death." Curiosity, though, proved stronger than fear. Doughboys sent to drive stakes into the ground marking their farthest advance encountered Germans coming toward them, smiling shyly. A trade began to flourish as at no time since the Christmas truce of 1914: cigarettes for sausages, chewing gum for rye bread, coffee for chocolate. As they swapped souvenirs, the Germans expressed surprise at how many doughboys spoke their language. They asked the Yanks about an uncle, an aunt, a cousin in Milwaukee, New York, or Saint Louis. "Hell," one American said, clapping a hand on a German shoulder, "my mother and father were both born in Germany." Henry Gunther too, his body now resting in a burial collection point, had had family in Germany.

A BOMB BECAME stuck in the rack of a Nieuport. The American pilot rocked his aircraft furiously to shake it loose. Finally the missile went sailing over the village of Souilly. Below, thirty-eight-year-old Colonel George C. Marshall, operations officer of the 1st Division, was having breakfast in a house commandeered as headquarters. A powerful explosion shook the room and slammed Marshall against the wall and to the floor. In that split second, he thought he had been killed. Marshall survived the friendly fire to become, as army chief of staff, a key architect of victory in World War II and later the secretary of state who fathered the Marshall Plan to revive war-stricken Europe, which won him the Nobel Peace Prize in 1953. His brush with death had occurred in the war's last half hour.

The town of Marchéville was partly liberated, with the American 33rd Division holding the western edge, and partly still occupied, with the 365th Prussian Infantry on the eastern edge. The cost to the American division that morning had been 284 casualties, including 17 dead, according to a subsequent army report. But a chaplain with a burial party on the scene recalled collecting 26 bodies just on the road outside Saint-Hilaire, a mile and a half from Marchéville. As the smoke of battle lifted, a captain from the German regiment approached the American lines, asking to speak with Colonel Berry. The man spoke a cultivated English and wore the Iron Cross. He complained to Berry, politely but firmly, that the Americans had entered Marchéville after eleven o'clock in violation of the armistice terms that directed both sides to stop in place at that hour. He was exposing himself to disciplinary action if he did not rectify this matter. As they spoke, soldiers from both armies were roving the fields of the Woëvre Plain sorting out their dead. Waving his arm over the carnage, the German remarked that the American attack that morning had been a "foolish affair." He himself had known for weeks that the war was coming to an end and had taken no unnecessary risks with the lives of his men.

GEORG BÜCHER WONDERED if his getting a gas mask onto Walter, the replacement who had clung to him so desperately, might have saved the boy. When the fighting stopped, Bücher and his comrades received a chilly welcome from their captors. The Americans "didn't seem pleased that we still had hand grenades hanging from our belts and rifles in our hands," he recalled. When a doughboy refused to shake his hand, Bücher concluded, "The Americans were too embittered . . . which wasn't surprising, for they had attacked three times and had been beaten back with heavy losses."

The reaction of men to their salvation, whatever the uniform, was essentially the same: muted disbelief succeeded by euphoria. Lieutenant Pat Campbell, a Briton, recalled, "I felt excited and happy but in an uncertain subdued way. . . . I wanted to be with my friends, but none of those of my age were left in the brigade." And so Campbell wandered off alone, "without going anywhere."

Corporal Frank Richards and the other two survivors of his original unit of Royal Welch Fusiliers had beaten odds of survival that he had once placed at twenty thousand to one. Thus far in the war he had endured nothing more serious than a case of hemorrhoids. Still, he had not dared to count himself saved until the last moment. The two cooks he had seen sprawled amid the wreckage of their wagon had perished less than two hours before the end. When the shooting did stop, he and his pals holed up in the ruins of a cellar and played cards. "We had accumulated a lot of money during the last few months and had been unable to spend it." He got up hours later, "stony broke" and without a murmur of complaint.

To Captain Vivian de Sola Pinto, "The war produced as much grim farce as nobility." His observation was affirmed that last morning when a fellow officer squatting in a latrine was killed by a shell at 10 A.M. When the cease-fire at last arrived, de Sola Pinto halted his men outside Perquise. A smiling German officer appeared and came forward to warn him where the road was mined. In the town, the Fusiliers were greeted by a hunchback who jumped from the cheering crowd and began playing "The Marseillaise" on an accordion. As he dismissed his company, de Sola Pinto was irked to hear men grumbling. The day had turned windy and bitter cold. No wine was to be had, they complained. Another Fusilier shot back at one of the grumblers, "Put a sock in it. After what we've heard today, I could sleep like a bird in a tree!" A regiment of West Yorkshires approached Maubeuge, the first major French city south of Mons, to find an old man standing in his doorway in a moth-eaten uniform dating from the Franco-Prussian War, a three-cornered hat perched on his head, his arm locked in a salute, croaking out "The Marseillaise."

After the fighting ended, Sergeant Will Bird sat sipping a celebratory glass of wine in a café when one of his men, Old Bill, appeared in the doorway, beckoning to him. Outside he found Jim Mills, "wild-eyed, white as if he had been ill." Old Bill warned Bird, "He says he's going to shoot whoever arranged to have his brother killed for nothing. He's hoping Currie comes here today. If he doesn't, he's going to shoot the next higher-up. He says his brother was murdered." Bird took the problem to his superior, who proposed a soldierly solution. His mates were to take Mills out, get him drunk, and keep him out of General Currie's way. This was the shining hour for the commander in chief of the Canadians and was not to be marred by a grief-crazed soldier. Earlier that day Currie had led the victory parade through Mons—properly, it seemed to him, since his Canadians had ended the war here for the British where it had begun.

In field hospitals, the patient load on November 11 was indistinguishable from any other day. Stretchers bearing broken bodies still backed up outside the receiving stations. Makeshift operating tables remained bloody and full. The only indication that the day was different was the tears of nurses, long inured to death, watching doctors at this late date still relegating men to the moribund ward.

CORPORAL HITLER LEARNED of the end in a military hospital in the town of Pasewalk in Prussia, where he was recovering from a mustard gas attack that had temporarily blinded him. His 16th Bavarian Reserve Infantry Regiment had been gassed by the British near Ypres in mid-October. Hitler, his face a puffy, unrecognizable mass, his voice hoarse, his eyes leaking profusely, had had to be led to the aid station with a file of other blinded men, each clasping the shoulder of the man ahead. In the hospital the inflammation and swelling of the eyelids began to recede and broad outlines of shapes had started to emerge. But the pain, which Hitler described as "piercing in my sockets," continued unbearable. Hitler would later claim that his evacuation from the front had ended the happiest chapter of his life. In the trenches he had escaped from an aimless existence. He had come to know comradeship, purpose, the respect of his fellows. Before being felled by the gas, he had received his fifth battlefield decoration. His bravery, however, had never translated into further promotion. The untidy, slouching corporal was judged by his superiors as a good soldier but no leader.

With his sight returning, Hitler's spirits began to revive from the funk of depression common to gas victims. Then, on November 9, an elderly pastor visited the hospital. The patients were assembled in a hall to hear the clergyman's message, delivered in a voice broken by sobs. The kaiser had abdicated that day, the Hohenzollern dynasty was finished; Germany was now a republic. Barely able to go on, the old man told the dazed patients that the war was lost and Germany must throw itself on the mercy of its victors. "It became impossible for me to sit still one minute more," Hitler recalled. "Again everything went black before my eyes; I tottered and groped my way back to the dormitory, threw myself on my bunk, and dug my burning head into my blankets and pillow." The shock of defeat had blinded him again. A Berlin psychiatrist who treated Hitler, Dr. Edmund Forster, concluded that his blindness had returned because the patient was "a psychopath with hysterical symptoms." For Hitler, the moment became an epiphany. As he would later romanticize it, the prewar unemployed drifter saw himself at a professional crossroads. "The great vacillation of my life, whether I should enter politics or remain an architect, came to an end. That night I resolved that, if I recovered my sight, I would enter politics," and "a miracle came to pass." His sight returned.

There was little doubt in Hitler's mind as to who had authored Germany's downfall. No matter that the officer who had pinned the Iron Cross on him was First Lieutenant Hugo Guttman, a Jew and a highly decorated soldier himself. No matter that 12,000 of Guttman's coreligionists had died fighting for Germany. To Hitler, Jews and Marxists had cost Germany the war. He was not alone in his bitterness at the defeat. Hermann Göring had become an air ace and the leader of the "Flying Circus," successor to the late Baron Manfred von Richthofen. On November 11, a courier handed Göring a dispatch informing him that Germany had surrendered. He was to turn over his squadron to the French at an airfield near Strasbourg. They could go to hell, he responded. His commanding officer threatened a court-martial. Göring sent a few token aircraft to the French and led the rest of the squadron back to a field at Darmstadt. As he neared the end of the field, he slewed the plane around until the wingtip struck the ground. He kept churning until the Fokker was ground to junk. The rest of the Flying Circus pilots followed his lead.

WHILE IT WOULD have provided a neat, dramatic curtain for the blast of conflict to have been silenced in an instant, wars are disorderly affairs. After 11 A.M., German lieutenant Thoma, 19th Uhlans, at Inor, three and a half miles north of Stenay, headed toward the Americans to ask, now that it was all over, if they required quarters for their troops. Doughboys of Company L, 356th Regiment, still uninformed of the cease-fire, watched the lieutenant approach and shot him. The regiment's telephone lines to headquarters had been snapped by enemy shell fire. "I was therefore out of touch with brigade," Colonel Robert Allen, commanding the regiment, explained. "The last element of my command ceased fighting approximately 15 minutes after noon." Colonel Allen's report ended, "There were some casualties in my command between 11 and 12:15 and many more among the enemy, but I am unable to give a complete number." The 89th Division's records, including those of the 356th, subsequently showed a total of 300 casualties for that morning, with 61 dead and 239 seriously wounded. As late as 4 P.M., an American colonel named Mott received a telephone call from his French counterpart, "complaining of failure of Americans to stop firing at Stenay-Beaumont and along the Meuse." The last order to cease fire was not received by forward elements of the 2nd Division until 4:15 P.M. These Americans were returning assumed enemy fire that turned out to be blasting by AEF engineers to remove an obstruction blocking the Meuse.

The last deaths of the Great War on the western front occurred at midnight on the twelfth in Hamont, a Belgian town near the Dutch border. Retreating German troops, believing they were the last to leave the city, mined the Hamont railroad station. But one final train filled with German soldiers arrived from Antwerp. The mine went off with a roar that flung railway cars into the air like matchboxes. Hundreds of German soldiers thus died thirteen hours after the armistice went into effect.

The shadows of global conflict extended deep into Africa. Part of the kaiser's empire, German East Africa, was defended by a combative general, Paul Emil von Lettow-Vorbeck, who had earned fame as "the African Hindenburg." News of the armistice penetrated the continent slowly; thus Lettow-Vorbeck was still fighting long after all was quiet on the western front. He finally learned of his nation's defeat and surrendered on November 23, the last German commander to yield in the war.

33

"This Fateful Morning Came
an End to All Wars"

NOVEMBER 11, 1918. Describing the arrival of peace, one witness recalled, "A curious rippling sound gradually rises, the sound of men beginning to cheer from the Vosges to the sea." Lieutenant Richard Dixon, British First Army, en route to England on leave, wondered, as his boat entered Folkestone harbor, at the shriek of sirens. Shipyard workers and crews on vessels crowding the port were shouting, "The bloody war's over! And it was," Dixon remembered of that day. "We had left France with a war on and arrived in Blighty with a peace on. . . . It took some getting used to, this knowledge. There was a future ahead for me, something I had not imagined for some years. . . . No more slaughter, no more maiming, no more mud and blood, and no more killing and disembowelling of horses and mules—which was what I found most difficult to bear. No more of those hopeless dawns with the rain chilling the spirits, no more crouching in inadequate dugouts scooped out of trench walls, no more dodging of snipers' bullets, no more of that terrible shell-fire. No more shovelling up bits of men's bodies and dumping them into sandbags; no more cries of 'Stretcher-bear-ER!,' and no more of those beastly gas masks and the odious smell of pear drops which was deadly to the lungs, and no more writing of those dreadfully difficult letters to the next-of-kin of the dead."

That same day, when Montgomery Belgion had witnessed the routine horror of seeing a dead man stripped naked by peasants, his regiment was at long last pulled from the line. Badly mauled companies were now commanded by subalterns and platoons by sergeants. During the withdrawal, Belgion passed by "sleek, well fed officers" arriving from England, men whom he suspected the power wielders had been holding back for the next big push. Command of his company was turned over by a "lieutenant five feet high" to "an upstanding, bridge-playing captain of distinctly higher social status." To Belgion, the war had nicked but not cracked class barriers.

As the numbness of disbelief wore off, the joy of the men began to emerge as from a patient coming out of anesthesia who realizes that the operation has been a success. An American pilot in stylish breeches and silk scarf jumped into a muddy crater and twirled about like a dervish, singing out, "I've lived through the war!" On the first night of peace, the crash of artillery was supplanted by flares, Very lights, rockets, and star shells of every color and pattern, their detonation now a pyrotechnic spectacle rather than the preamble to slaughter. All over France and Belgium, bells tolled from every church steeple, train whistles hooted, sirens wailed, and regimental bands paraded, with the music becoming more discordant as townsfolk plied the musicians with wine and cognac. Doughboys tore down street signs the Germans had hung in occupied towns. "Kaiser Wilhelm Strasse" became "President Wilson Street" and "Pottsdamerplatz," "Broadway." A *poilu* shouted to Americans in the 80th (Blue Ridge) Division, *"Finie la guerre!"* To which one grinning southerner answered, "Well, for lawd's sake, don't start another one unless you can finish it yourself!" A doughboy in a unit that had never heard a shot fired in anger advised his pals, "When getting ready to leave for home, hit your helmet with an awful dent in the side with an axe so you can show the proud ones what peril you endured at the battle of vin ordinaire." Captain Harry Truman watched in astonishment at the speed with which the French battery next to his switched its narrow-gauge railway from hauling rounds of ammunition to hauling cases of wine. All night long the French gunners kept him awake with drunken shouts of *"Vive President Wilson! Vive le capitaine d'artillerie américaine!"* A trench lyricist fashioned the latest verse to "Mademoiselle from Armentières":

> We may forget the gas and shells,
> We'll never forget the mademoiselles,
> Inky dinky parlay voo!

The New York Times's Edwin James caught the mood in a lead that particularly pleased him: "In a twinkling of the eye four years of killing and massacre stopped as if God had swept his omnipotent finger across the scene of world carnage and cried, 'Enough!' " The celebration swelled outward, seeming to increase in intensity with distance from the trenches. In Paris, Georges Clemenceau, the seventy-seven-year-old Tiger of France, rose in the Chamber of Deputies and ignited thunderous applause simply by reading the armistice terms the Germans had bowed to. Forty-eight years before, as a young deputy, Clemenceau had opposed surrendering to Germany during the Franco-Prussian War. Now, Alsace-Lorraine, given up in that conflict, was to be returned, making France again "one and indivisible." The news sent the Chamber into near hysteria. Afterward, Clemenceau took refuge from the tumult in his residence in the rue Saint-Dominique. With him was his friend, the Impressionist Claude Monet, to whom the prime minister expressed relief that the burden of war had been lifted from him so that he could now take on the more difficult task of winning the peace. "Yes," the painter responded with his own priorities. "Now we shall have time to get on with that monument to Cézanne."

That morning the deputies passed an order of the day to be posted throughout the country, urging people to cast off the pall of the past four years and rejoice. Workmen immediately began removing the blue paint from streetlamps that had dimmed the City of Light to confound German bombers. Crowds jamming the Place de la Concorde, the Champs-Élysées, the Hôtel des Invalides, the Tuileries gardens celebrated, "not with liquor," one participant observed, but rather, "everybody seemed literally intoxicated with joy." People joined hands, dancing in circles and singing "Madelon." At the Café de Paris, patrons danced on the tables. Young girls, housewives, grandmothers, even men kissed soldiers indiscriminately. "Germs were freely exchanged," one rouge-smeared participant noted. People clambered onto cars, taxicabs, buses, delivery trucks, riding running boards, hoods, and roofs, while drivers leaned on their horns, inching their way through impenetrable crowds. An American ambulance driver abandoned his vehicle as souvenir hunters stripped everything removable until only the naked chassis remained. Civilians dragged captured German cannons, machine guns, even aircraft that had been on display up the Champs-Élysées. Boys shimmied up gun barrels that rose twenty feet high.

The novelist Mary Roberts Rinehart, in Paris as a correspondent, noted, among the revelers, "too many women shrouded in black for whom the victory has come too late." Crippled veterans, trying to dance on one leg, "broke my heart." Heber Blankenhorn, in Chaumont, Pershing's AEF headquarters, also detected a dark edge to the revelry. At a ceremony in the town hall, amid silk-hatted dignitaries and bearded bankers, he spied a French lieutenant, emaciated, wry-necked, his expression dour. "I saw he had the *Croix de Guerre,* with many palms and stars, and the *Médaille Militaire.* . . . Also, he had an artificial arm and one artificial leg." In Belfort, Madame Naegelen had tried to put on a good face during the celebration to please her hero son, René. But on returning home, she gazed at the photograph of the dead Joseph and clapped her hands over her ears to seal off the merrymaking outside. René closed the shutters, "to shut out the world, its cruel joys and light."

MINUTES BEFORE ELEVEN, a shaggy-maned figure stepped from the doorway of Number 10 Downing Street to face a flag-waving, exultant throng. Prime Minister Lloyd George's expression was serene as he waited for the cheers to abate. At eleven o'clock, he told the crowd, the war would be over. "You are entitled to rejoice. The people of this country and of their Allies and the people of our overseas dominions and of India have won a glorious victory." At the stroke of eleven, Londoners thrilled to the long-absent sound of Big Ben atop Parliament tolling the hour for the first time since August 1914. Later that afternoon the prime minister echoed in the House of Commons the sentiment that had fired the nation's zeal when Britain had first gone to war: "I hope we may say that thus, this fateful morning, came to an end all wars."

From Saint Paul's to Oxford Circus and down Whitehall to Victoria Street, the surging masses snake-danced, hoisted men in uniforms onto their shoulders, and belted out endless choruses of the raffish "Knees Up, Mother Brown": "Knees up, knees up, don't let the breeze up." Motorbikes built for two labored under four, five, a half-dozen riders. At the Queen Victoria Memorial, little boys plopped themselves down in the ample stone lap of the old queen's statue and no bobby chased them off. That afternoon, pelted by a cold drizzle, King George V in naval uniform and Queen Mary emerged onto the balcony at Buckingham Palace. The king was not particularly eloquent, and his words were barely audible except to those within a stone's throw. "With you, I rejoice," he began. "Thank God for the victories which the Allied armies have won and have brought hostilities to an end." Whether they heard him or not, his subjects roared deliriously. Sir Edward Grey had said on the day Great Britain had gone to war, "The lamps are going out all over Europe." This day they began to burn once again.

Some faces on the fringes remained subdued. General Sir Henry Wilson found himself walking home to Eaton Place after dining with Lloyd George and Winston Churchill. He was circumventing the crowd still packed thickly before Buckingham Palace when he saw an elderly, well-dressed woman sobbing quietly. The general approached. "You are in trouble," he said. "Is there anything I can do for you?" "Thank you, no," she replied. "I am crying, but I am happy, for now I know that all my three sons who have been killed in the war have not died in vain."

Wilfred Owen had left the Craiglockhart Hospital in August passed fit for service and returned to the 2nd Manchesters. One week before the armistice, his battalion ran into fierce resistance near Cateau. Owen led his men across the Sambre Canal under heavy fire. The poet who had branded as "the old lie" the idea that it was sweet and fitting to die for one's country died that day. He was twenty-five. His parents received Form B.104-82a notifying them of his fate as the bells were tolling on Armistice Day.

That morning a VAD nurse burst into the Queen Alexandra Hospital annex where Vera Brittain was cleaning out dressing bowls. "Brittain, Brittain," she cried out, "It's all over. Do let's come out and see what's happening." Vera followed her mechanically into the street. "With a half-masochistic notion of 'seeing the sights' . . . I made a circular tour to Kensington by way of the intoxicated West End. With aching persistence my thoughts went back to the dead and the strange irony of their fates—to Roland, gifted, ardent, ambitious, who had died without glory in the conscientious performance of a routine job; to Victor and Geoffrey, gentle and diffident, who, conquering nature by resolution, had each gone down bravely in a big 'show.' "

After her brother, Edward, had been badly wounded and won the Military Cross fighting with the Sherwood Foresters on the Somme, Vera had felt relief at his transfer in November 1917 to what she believed to be a safer front, Italy. The magnificent Alpine scenes, picturesque villages, and his cheery messages in postcards he sent her reassured Vera that Edward was secure. Four months later she had left her hospital post in France at her father's insistence. He needed her at home because Mrs. Brittain had "crocked up," as he put it, when she could not get decent domestic help. Vera subsequently rejoined the VAD and was assigned to the Queen Alexandra. She was at home on June 22 when "there came the sudden loud clattering at the front-door knocker that always meant a telegram." Edward had been killed in action in the Battle of Asiago on June 15, 1918. "For a moment, I thought that my legs would not carry me," she recalled of that day. She handed the telegram to her father and then "I remembered that we should have to go down to Purley and tell the news to my mother." Edward, her "musical, serene, lover of peace," had died, one of his men later wrote her, taking a trench from the Austrians. He was "keeping a sharp lookout on the enemy when he was shot through the head by a sniper, he lived only a few minutes," the soldier informed her.

Early in the war she had written to Roland Leighton, wondering where she might find herself at the end, among those rejoicing in the triumph or watching the celebration with a broken heart. Wandering about Whitehall on Armistice Day, she thought "how completely everything that had hitherto made up my life had vanished with Edward and Roland, with Victor and Geoffrey. The War was over; a new age was beginning; but the dead were dead and would never return. . . . In that brightly lit, alien world I should have no part. All those with whom I had really been intimate were gone."

IN THE BRONX, more than 800 draftees were waiting for a train that would take them to Grand Central Station and thence to Fort Wright for training before being shipped to France. Mothers, fathers, wives, sweethearts, and awed younger siblings had gathered at the station to bid tearful good-byes. When the draftees arrived at Grand Central, a beaming Martin Conboy, director of their draft board, was waiting with thrilling news. An armistice had been signed, Conboy announced. The army did not need them. They could go home.

The celebration this Monday differed in tone, if not magnitude, from that of the previous Thursday's false armistice. The earlier word had struck like a thunderclap, emotional manna from Heaven. Today's news was rather like an anticipated holiday. Still, a cacophony of automobile horns, fire alarms, tugboat whistles, church bells, and air-raid sirens rent the air. Workers arriving at factories and offices found they had the day off. Children were sent home from school.

New York mayor John F. Hylan ordered a bond-drive parade,

fortuitously already scheduled, to go forward. Marchers wound their way up Fifth Avenue, across Forty-second Street, then up Broadway. Bands from the police, fire, and sanitation departments paraded, too, belting out "Over There," "Tipperary," "Pack Up Your Troubles." Elephants conscripted from the Hippodrome led the way. Enrico Caruso, in town to perform Saint-Saëns's *Samson and Delilah,* leaned out of his window from the Hotel Knickerbocker and sang a Neapolitan-accented version of "The Star-Spangled Banner" to wild applause.

The celebrants found a unifying theme in demonizing "Kaiser Bill." Wilhelm II was burned in effigy in Central Park and hung from countless lampposts. Even in predominantly German Yorkville, a dummy kaiser was paraded in a coffin. Storefronts blossomed with placards proclaiming, "Poor Bill. Rest in Pieces" and "Me und Gott Haf Dissolved Our Partnership." A truck carried a sign reading, "We've Got the Kaiser Canned This Time." On the back was a papier-mâché head of the deposed emperor set on a metal drum. Judge William Wadhams announced that one William Hohenzollern was a fugitive from justice and instructed the clerk of the court to issue a bench warrant for his arrest. Another judge of the General Sessions released thirty young defendants convicted of minor crimes, explaining, "It is a time when all men should begin their lives anew."

A rare solemn note intruded. At Liberty Hall on the corner of Broadway and Seventh Avenue, an ivory-skinned, rosy-cheeked English beauty mounted the platform and began singing the Doxology in a pure, sonorous voice to a briefly hushed audience. An elderly black man sat on the steps of City Hall weeping, telling passersby that he had been born a slave on a Virginia plantation and had now given two sons, killed in France, to the country that had set him free. But for most, the mood was uninhibited abandonment, noise as an emotional release, expressed in joyous vindictiveness toward the leader of the fallen foe.

Among the New York crowd was a German who not long before had fought in the enemy uniform. In the last days of the war the few survivors of his Pioneer Battalion 30 had been sent back to Germany to quell a socialist revolution that Lothar Lanz would have eagerly embraced. Lanz, the ex-miner and deserter, had hated the army, hated the war, hated most of all the imperial regime in whose cause he had risked his life. Lanz had seen his pacifist tendencies perverted by the kill-or-be-killed imperative of survival. He had shown unwonted skill in hand-to-hand fighting, stabbing, gouging, cleaving with animal ferocity. And when, during Verdun, he could no longer take the conflict raging within him, he had left. Holland had at first seemed a safe enough haven. But he would feel safer still with an ocean between him and Germany. And so he had managed to stow away on the *Zyldyk,* a small steamer of the Holland-America Line headed for New York. He took along seven pounds of bread and a ten-quart can of water and spent the next eighteen days hidden in the ship's coal bunker. In New York, he had gone to work for the American Socialist Party to break the "capitalist caste," which he believed had provoked a war "in which the working class of Europe is now bleeding to death." Armistice Day found him marching with the Socialists toward Carnegie Hall, where they planned a rally to celebrate the fall of the Hohenzollern dynasty and the apparent triumph of the German revolution over capitalism. They had reached Thirty-fourth Street when soldiers and sailors tore into their ranks, trampling on the red flags and beating up men and women alike. For Lanz, the class struggle went on.

PRESIDENT WILSON HAD not gone to bed until one in the morning on the eleventh, working on decoded messages reporting the tag ends of the armistice negotiations. He had managed to slip in two hours' sleep when he was awakened with word that the cease-fire had been signed. The president declared a government holiday and took to his desk to polish the remarks he planned to deliver before a joint session of Congress later in the day. Wilson's objective was to establish once again that America's entrance into this war had been not the extension of mindless barbarism to yet another country but a crusade, or, as he would tell the lawmakers, a historic opportunity to achieve "disinterested justice, embodied in settlements which are based on something better and more lasting than the selfish competitive interests of powerful states." He was already planning to travel to Europe to make sure that the politics of vindictiveness did not derail the politics of world betterment. As he later put it, "I think there should be one man at this peace table who hasn't lost his temper."

All day long people continued their revelries in big-city avenues and small-town streets. And everywhere the kaiser's fall provoked contemptuous amusement. In one Illinois town, people stuffed an effigy of the kaiser inside the hearse of an undertaker reputed to harbor German sympathies. They then burned the effigy and the hearse. In Chicago, where one million people jammed the Loop, sixty automobiles were stolen by joy riders. In Cedar Rapids, Iowa, William L. Shirer, a fifteen-year-old high school student, lamented the hijinks in a town where gold stars hung in windows and amputees hobbled through the streets. Around the corner from his home, his cousin's husband was slowly dying from lungs burned out in a gas attack while outside townsfolk behaved like drunken sailors. Within twenty years, Shirer would become an influential correspondent in Europe and then write his masterful account of the next war, *The Rise and Fall of the Third Reich*.

The celebration-cum-carnival, the air of abandonment, the brief suspension of conventional restraints and sexual taboos, the drinking, singing, shouting, horn blowing, and effigy burning spilled over into the small hours of the next morning before finally waning. The next day, millions of Americans awoke groggily from a national hangover.

BACK IN FRANCE, men who would soon return to humdrum lives and men who would go on to famous careers sat on the parapets of trenches, jammed the estaminets, played cards, or merely walked in silence contemplating the future. Darryl Zanuck, a sixteen-year-old private who had lied his way into the army, would go on to produce film classics, including a biography of his commander in chief entitled *Wilson*, and, later, *The Longest Day*, *All About Eve*, and *The Snows of Kilimanjaro*. Another Hollywood figure, the actor Adolphe Menjou, serving at war's end as a captain in the 5th Division, would later convincingly portray a cynical Great War French general in *Paths of Glory*. Alexander Woollcott, finishing his latest story for *The Stars and Stripes*, awoke on November 11 in the cellar of a ruin on Montfaucon Hill. He was walking toward the rear when he came upon a replacement company headed for the front. He called out, "Don't you know the war's over at 11 o'clock?" A skeptical sergeant shouted back, "Yeh? What time is it now?" Sergeant Alvin York, who had entered the army in obscurity and was ending it in celebrity, found himself in a rest area in Nancy on November 11. York, who had done his share of hell-raising before discovering Jesus, was upset to see every doughboy, it seemed, with a bottle under one arm and a girl on the other. York had a sandwich and a lemonade that night and was in bed by nine.

The armistice aroused the poet in Arthur Jensen, who at the end found the action he had craved. Encountering the greenish carcasses of four German dead, he was prompted to imagine what these men might say to their American conquerors and wrote:

> We are the dividends of war;
> We're what you came to Europe for.
> Our cause is lost; we died in vain,
> And now we're rotting in the rain.

The poem "Peace—November 11, 1918" by George Patton, now a lieutenant colonel and pioneer of tank warfare, shrank from the thought of a world without war:

> We can but hope that e're we drown
> 'Neath treacle floods of grace,
> The tuneless horns of mighty Mars
> Once more shall rouse the Race

When such times come, Oh! God of War
Grant that we pass midst strife,
Knowing once more the whitehot joy
Of taking human life.

Joe Rizzi, 35th Infantry, was no poet but a love-starved romantic immigrant son from the Midwest who saw the world in black and white. After passing through newly liberated towns, Rizzi wrote in his diary, "We learned that the French women had married some of the Germans. This was one of the things very hard for us to understand—married to an enemy and happy!"

Sergeant Bill Triplet had fought the war with the same 35th, but with none of Rizzi's earnest innocence. An incorrigible wiseacre, Triplet had survived with the quip as his armor. On a grueling march the night before the armistice he had swilled too much cognac, he said, to keep it from another friend who "would get drunk and lose his newly won chevrons." Of a friend gassed and sent to the rear, Triplet commented, "They'd finally gotten tired of him, given him a bottle of cough syrup, and sent him back to duty." Beneath the facetiousness, the war's end had delivered Triplet a troubling blow. He had come to love the army. For weeks he had been sweating out orders to Officer Training School, a move that would open a military career to him. When he learned of the armistice, he wrote, "I felt terrible. Peace!" The army would need no more ninety-day wonders. The armistice "shot the damned war right out from under me."

The commander in chief of the American Expeditionary Forces felt cheated too. Contemplating the end, an unsmiling Black Jack Pershing mused aloud, "What I dread is that Germany doesn't know that she was licked. Had they given us another week, we'd have *taught* them." Later he would add with ominous prescience, "They never knew they were beaten in Berlin. It will have to be done all over again." Pershing's battlefield acumen would be hotly debated in the years to come. But his iron will—some called it pigheadedness—had scored one victory. Had he yielded to the pressures of Haig and Foch, American forces would have been parceled out as bodies to fill out the British and French ranks. Instead, at Pershing's insistence, the AEF emerged as a unified force that, in the war's last chapter, tipped the scales to Allied victory.

Pershing's French colleague, the Tenth Army commander, General Charles Mangin, known as the "eater of men" for his profligate squandering of troops, reacted to the timing of the peace with equal unhappiness. "The armistice," Mangin said through tears, "should have been signed in Berlin. The Germans will not admit they are beaten." Admittedly the enemy had yielded to harsh demands, but who, Mangin wanted to know, would enforce the terms? "A coalition," he argued, "has never survived the danger for which it was created. It is a fatal error and France will pay for it."

That Field Marshal Haig, on the last day, gathered his top commanders at Cambrai to discuss postwar athletic programs to keep the troops out of mischief reflected the man's habitual serenity—or, some might say, his obliviousness to the tides of history. Lloyd George could be scathing toward Haig and his generals, complaining that they had never known the stench, filth, death, and maiming that their chess moves produced, "not even through a telescope." Yet Lloyd George had never employed his own authority to reverse Haig's military decisions that he privately deplored. A far more insightful portrait of Haig emerged from the pen of Winston Churchill, who described him as "a great surgeon before the days of anaesthetics, versed in every detail of such science as was known to him, sure of himself, steady of poise, knife in hand, intent upon the operation, entirely removed in his professional capacity from the agony of the patient, the anguish of relations, or the doctrines of rival schools, the devices of quacks, or the first-fruits of new learning. He would operate without excitement, or he would depart without being affronted; and if the patient died, he would not reproach himself." Patients had died in the hundreds of thousands, but Haig left the field of battle serene in the knowledge that his duty as a soldier had been fulfilled. The enemy had been defeated. What happened after that was not in his realm but in that of the politicians.

34

Greater Losses Than on D-Day

Away from the fraternizers and souvenir swappers, with the music of a military band heard dimly in the distance, a burial party of the 366th Regiment, 92nd Division, went about its work in a hastily laid out cemetery on the edge of Pont-à-Mousson. The grave diggers, like the soldiers they were burying, were all black. The dead had fallen in the three charges launched armistice morning from the Bois de Voivrotte, the last in the final half hour. Major Warner Ross wandered the battleground with "my face so swollen I could only see a little with one eye. My ears had been bleeding and I had to be yelled at to hear . . . and my voice refused to work." In ironic contrast to the wasteland around him, a limousine arrived to drive him back to regimental headquarters. On the way, Ross recalled, he passed by the burial detail, working over "a row of dead and pieces of dead." Assignment to a black outfit had not been considered a career plus for white officers in the AEF, and earlier accusations of poor performance, even cowardice, by these units had not enhanced the assignment. But what Ross had experienced in the past twenty-four hours led him to describe "my heroic battalion— the battalion that had earned undying fame for itself, its regiment, its brigade, its division and for the American colored race."

The official army casualty report issued after the war would list the 92nd's total losses for November 11 at 319, with 17 dead. The official report was challenged by the division's artillery chief, General Sherburne, who reported 52 dead and 393 wounded, gassed, or missing between November 10 and 11, most lost on the eleventh. Evidence contradicts the official last-day casualty figures for other divisions as well. Clarence Richmond, who had quit the University of Tennessee in 1917 to join the 5th Marines, had been assigned to a team of stretcher bearers for the last ten days. Late on the morning of November 11, he found himself searching the banks of the Meuse River near Mouzon for men wounded while crossing the flimsy footbridges as Elton Mackin had done. "Near the small bridge," he wrote in his war diary, "the river was strewn with our dead. I counted about twenty-five within a distance of a hundred yards." On the opposite side of the river, where the crossing had begun, Richmond wrote, "the dead were more numerous. Here we had suffered our greatest casualties. As many as four and five dead could be seen around many single shell holes." The 5th Marines were just one of the four regiments comprising the 2nd Division engaged in the river crossing, but the official postwar army report shows only 22 killed in action for the entire division on that last day.

Similar discrepancies abound. The official figure provided by the army shows no battle deaths on the last day for the 28th Division, which had not advanced but continued to fire its artillery across the Woëvre Plain, provoking German retaliatory fire. Yet one brigade commander alone reported 191 killed or wounded that morning. Likewise, the 33rd Division reported only 17 killed in action. But artillery captain Robert Casey claimed that within his sector alone 34 men were killed in the last twenty-three minutes of the war. One statistic emerges clearly, whatever the source: the numbers of men killed in the nine divisions in the Meuse-Argonne sector that continued fighting to 11 A.M. ran as high as four and a half times more than those in the seven divisions that halted after the signing.

War is envisioned on an heroic scale, but for those who do the fighting it is random mayhem, as lofty as a worm burrowing into the earth, and not that dissimilar. That last day, a head cocked an inch to the left or right, being summoned by the sergeant, occupying a particular spot in a trench, being sent to the rear with a fever, or going to the latrine: any of these trifles determined whether a man would live another half century or not live out the day. Clarence Richmond tried to make sense of the carnage: "I asked myself the question why had all this loss of life been permitted when those high in command knew that an armistice was pending? From one standpoint it seemed a needless waste of life." Yet in the end, Richmond sought solace in the ordinary soldier's assumption that surely his superiors knew what they were doing. And so he closed his diary with "On the other hand, Germany was not yet decisively beaten, and every blow was needed to make her realize that a victory was not for her. Looking at it from that viewpoint, one had to grant the wisdom of the attack."

All day long the contrasting reactions to the armistice continued, celebration alongside contemplation and sorrow. One soldier described the burial of comrades killed that morning at a place called Moulleville Farm: "A huge grave, much in the shape of a horseshoe, was dug; the dead bodies wrapped in blankets were laid around this grave. A chaplain held the regular service, after which the bodies were placed side by side in the grave. A farewell volley was then fired over the graves, and as the graves were being filled in, taps were blown. . . . It was a most touching and impressive scene."

Father Francis Duffy, recovering from exhaustion at the aid station, was puzzled by his emotions at the end. "I had always believed that the news of victory and peace would fill me with surging feelings of delight," the chaplain of the Fighting 69th recalled. "But it was just the contrary. . . . I could think of nothing except the fine lads who had come out with us to this war and who are not alive to enjoy the triumph. All day I had a lonely and an aching heart. It would be a lesser thing to have killed myself than to go back to the mothers of the dead who would never more return." On sailing for France the regimental roster had shown 3,500 men.

Duffy calculated that at the end only some 600 of the original contingent had survived.

The most remembered verse of the war, John McRae's lines on the poppies of Flanders field, had ended with a call for still more sacrifice to avenge the fallen:

> Take up our quarrel with the foe,
> To you from failing hand we throw
> The torch . . .

The Canadian Army physician, driving himself mercilessly, had died from pneumonia abetted by exhaustion ten months before the end. By then his call for heroic retribution rang hollow. More prevalent was the soldiers' yearning just to get it over with and go home in one piece.

The two last casualties of Will Bird's platoon, Tom Mills and Bob Jones, were laid out in state in the Mons city hall in a room covered with black drapery. Alongside them were two other Canadians who had died in the last twenty-four hours, Privates Daigle and Brigden. As the battalion history recorded the ceremony: "A great throng of people paid their tributes and heaped the room with wreaths and flowers. . . . Practically the entire city followed to the graves." The pageantry helped Jim Mills's rage to subside to grief. The gratitude of the Belgian mourners lifted his brother's death from pointlessness to at least a place, however infinitesimal, in the victory.

According to the most conservative estimates, during the last day of the war, principally in the six hours after the armistice was signed, all sides on the western front suffered 10,944 casualties, of which 2,738 were deaths, more than the average daily casualties throughout the war. Putting these losses into perspective, in the June 6, 1944, D-Day invasion of Normandy, nearly twenty-six years later, the total losses were reported at 10,000 for all sides. Thus the total Armistice Day casualties were nearly 10 percent higher than those on D-Day. There was, however, a vast difference. The men storming the Normandy beaches were fighting for victory. Men dying on Armistice Day were fighting in a war already decided.

Numbers are lifeless. The minimal 320 Americans lost in those hours and how they died included Jasper Boon from Missouri, taking Stenay; Americo Di Pasquale from Pennsylvania, who won the Distinguished Service Cross posthumously on the Côte de Romagne, where Henry Gunther also died; Martin Bollhorst from Illinois, attacking near Ville-de-Chaumont, body never recovered; Russell Lyon from New Jersey, crossing a pontoon bridge over the Meuse; James Irby from Alabama, of the all-black 92nd Division, emerging from the Voivrotte woods into machine-gun fire. All were under age twenty-five.

Throughout four years of war, casualties on both sides on the western front averaged 2,250 dead and almost 5,000 wounded every day. Had Marshal Foch accepted Matthias Erzberger's plea to stop the fighting on November 8 while negotiations were under way, likely, 6,750 lives would have been spared and nearly 15,000 maimed, crippled, burned, blinded, and otherwise injured men would instead have gone home whole. All this sacrifice was made over scraps of land that the Germans, under the armistice, were compelled to surrender within two weeks.

The Great War on the western front took place on an astonishingly small canvas. The ground over which the bulk of the battles raged was only about eighty-five miles wide, a relatively modest battleground but a rather large cemetery, considering the 3,258,610 killed there and the 7,745,920 wounded, for total losses of 11,004,530 men. By comparison the fighting in the western campaigns in World War II ran more than 625 miles, from Normandy into the heart of Germany. Gavrilo Princip's assassination of Archduke Franz Ferdinand had eventually led to deaths from military action on all fronts between 1914 and 1918 totaling conservatively 8,364,700. The wounded totaled 21,436,000, of which an estimated 7 million were permanently maimed, for a grand total of 29,800,700 battle casualties. Another 6,276,000 civilian deaths were attributable to the war. For the army of the dead who could not be identified, Rudyard Kipling devised the words to be chiseled on countless British headstones: "A Soldier of the Great War Known unto God." The body of the author's son, Second Lieutenant John Kipling of the Irish Guards, missing since Loos in 1915, was not identified until years later, and then only tentatively. The numbers of sons, fathers, husbands, and brothers killed in the millions defy comprehension. The measure of loss must be made personal, as in the grave marker that read simply, "To the world he was a soldier, To me he was all the world."

In France, the war created 600,000 widows and left nearly one million children fatherless. In England three men were killed in World War I for every man killed in World War II. Before the war, the population of the British Isles had been growing by 10.4 percent annually. In the immediate years afterward, it rose by only 4.7 percent annually. The proportion of unmarried to married women in that country increased to the highest percentage ever. In 1921, in the age group twenty to thirty-nine, there were fifty-five women for every forty-five men, condemning tens of thousands of women to spinsterhood.

In the American Expeditionary Forces, the 26,000 men killed in the Meuse-Argonne represented the greatest loss in a single battle to that point in the nation's history. One of every five West Pointers in action in France was killed. The Germans had more men killed and wounded at Verdun, 325,000, than all the 230,000 men deployed in the field at Stalingrad twenty-six years later. More than 66,900 Germans lost limbs. The dimensions of loss can perhaps be appreciated visually. If one were to stand on a street corner at 9 A.M. and watch the spirits of the British dead march by four abreast, the column would be 97 miles long and would take twenty hours, or until five the next morning, to pass. The French dead would take an additional fifty-one hours and the Germans another fifty-nine hours. Considering all the dead on the western front, this parade would last from 9 A.M. Monday to 4 P.M. Saturday and stretch 386 miles, roughly the distance from Paris halfway through Switzerland or from New York to Cleveland.

So staggering were the losses that Lloyd George had once confided to the editor of *The Manchester Guardian,* "If the people knew, the war would be stopped tomorrow." Nine years after the war, Winston Churchill looked back and observed: "It was not until the dawn of the twentieth century of the Christian Era that war began to enter into its kingdom as the potential destroyer of the human race. The organisation of mankind into great states and empires, and the rise of nations to full collective consciousness, enabled enterprises of slaughter to be planned and executed upon a scale and with a perseverance never before imagined. . . . Without having improved appreciably in virtue or enjoying wiser guidance, it has got into its hands for the first time the tools by which it can unfailingly accomplish its own extermination. . . . Science unfolded her treasures and her secrets to the desperate demands of men, and placed in their hands agencies and apparatus almost decisive in their character." Years afterward, while prime minister, Churchill, contemplating the potential losses of an invasion of Nazi-occupied Europe and reflecting on the abattoirs of the Somme and Passchendaele, looked about the House of Commons "at the faces that are not there," the generation that had perished between 1914 and 1918.

Yet an anomaly persists, a sentimental reverie expressed by so many who survived. Some have described an emotion approaching ecstasy. Subaltern Gillespie, of the Argyll and Sutherlanders, wrote home, "My dear Daddy . . . it will be a great fight and, even when I think of you, I would not wish to be out of it. I am very happy and, whatever happens, you will remember that." So glorious a spectacle did Gillespie find war that he suggested that a road be built afterward all along no-man's-land with shady trees and seats for pilgrims. Eleven days after suggesting this idea, in September 1915, Gillespie was killed leading his company in a charge. Another British subaltern, Charles Edmonds, wrote, "Horror and discomfort, indescribable as they are, were not continuous. . . . As for the danger, it must be remembered that most men like adventure. . . . It is one of the strange attributes of the mind that we enjoy what makes our flesh creep." And as for dying? "To die young," Edmonds reflected, "is by no means an unmitigated misfortune; to die gaily in the unselfish pursuit of what you believe to be a righteous cause is an enviable and not a premature end." From the opposing trenches a parallel sentiment arose. Ernst Jünger recorded, during the heat of the March 1918 German offensive, that he and his comrades had gone "mad and beyond reckoning; we had gone over the edge of the world into superhuman perspectives. Death had lost its meaning." Yet the same young officer, after leading his company over a British position, could not bring himself to shoot a prostrate Tommy who waved a family photo in his face. What many proud veterans came to resent after the war was the pitying drone of handwringers and pacifists who reduced their experience to meaninglessness. "It appeared that dirt about the war was in demand," one wrote. "Every battle a defeat, every officer a nincompoop, every soldier a coward."

Religionists also succumbed to the narcotic of the battlefield. The priest–stretcher bearer Pierre Teilhard de Chardin had gone through the war without a scratch or a day's illness and lived to become a major twentieth-century philosopher. Of his feelings on Armistice Day Teilhard wrote his cousin, "The atmosphere I feel around me is going to become more oppressive and more uninteresting. What I have to do is to master this external sense of flatness by a more intense than ever interior life and vision." Father Francis Duffy had said that he would have preferred to kill himself rather than face the families of the dead of his Fighting 69th Infantry. At the same time, he could say that his ministry in the trenches "had been full of life and activity, and take them all in all, years of happiness. There never was a moment when I wanted to be any place other than where I was."

So indelible were their experiences that even natural adversaries Adolf Hitler and Anthony Eden, the latter having lost two of his brothers in the war, found common ground during a dinner just before World War II. The British foreign minister and the German dictator discovered that they had faced each other across the lines at Villers-Bretonneux in France. Issues of state were set aside while the two old soldiers sketched maps on the backs of menus and swapped accounts of long-ago days in the trenches.

Admittedly, these are the reactions of men capable of giving articulate expression to their experiences. Likely more common among ordinary men was the observation made by the writer Ian Hay, who summed up the character of the Tommy as "trust coupled with absolute lack of imagination which makes the British soldier the most invincible in the war. . . . He settles down to war as down to any other trade and is chiefly concerned, as in peacetime, with his holidays and creature comforts."

Long after the war, a former American second lieutenant, James Aldous, caught in a few lines the sentiment of ordinary men in extraordinary circumstances:

> It wasn't much.
> A scramble up a bank, a foot or two;
> A hundred yards as if you said
> "Look, post a letter for me, will you?"
> Just fifty years ago. A summer's day
> Not screaming as the poets like to say,
> Because shock numbs, and anyway it's rare;
> But frightened, naturally, and tense,
> And, until the end, rather enjoying it.

Whether among the expressive or the inarticulate, the war bound men in an unspoken fraternity. "And then there was comradeship," Charles Edmonds recalled, "richer, stronger in war than we have ever known since." Echoed repeatedly was the sentiment that never again would a man know the selfless sharing, the reliance on comrades when the stake was life itself, the elevating feeling of being part of something larger than oneself, or the adrenaline rush that makes a man most alive when he is closest to death. The Frenchman Henri Desagneaux wrote in his diary the day after the guns went silent, "It's back to the pettiness of peacetime: parades, exercises, spit and polish etc." The intense kinship explains why soldiers safely out of the fight went back voluntarily, as did Siegfried Sassoon, who hated the stupidities of the war but could not resist its siren call. He left Craiglockhart Hospital only to be mistakenly wounded by one of his own men near the end.

Well after the war this sense of an exclusive brotherhood persisted for Richard Dixon, who had learned of the peace on a boat entering Folkestone harbor. He would later write, "It has always been difficult for me to be wholly at ease with those men who were unfortunate enough to escape the experience of war, it is quite impossible to convey this in its essence, for they persist in believing men like me to be as they are." Upon meeting fellow veterans, Dixon felt at instant communion. "I can at once proceed upon certain indefinable assumptions and I know that, upon certain matters and certain subjects, no explanations will be necessary, may be taken for granted from the start." Dixon's sense that those not involved could never understand was confirmed in Vera Brittain's experience upon returning to Oxford. She found herself among a generation who had not tasted the war firsthand and recorded in verse the indifference, even derision, she encountered from younger classmates:

> You threw four years into the melting pot.
> "Did you indeed," these others cry.
> "Oh well, the more fool you."
> And we're beginning to agree with them.

The passage of enough years would eventually erode even the most jagged memories. In old age, after a life rich in civic achievement, Captain Griffith of the Welch Fusiliers wrote, "Events in retrospect have died into words on the printed page, incapable of producing anything but a 'Yes, that was how it was' by way of reaction. No more dreams of being involved. And as it all recedes, almost beyond recall, it has become something impersonal, as remote as the Trojan War. The sorrow of losing comrades who did not survive the war has turned into the sorrow of losing those who did survive it and whom I have outlived."

35

"Only the Dead Have
Seen the End of War"

What had it all been about? One of the most esteemed chroniclers of the war, A. J. P. Taylor, offers a judgment unsentimental but, on the whole, positive: "The First World War failed to produce Utopia, resembling in this every human endeavour since the beginning of time. . . . On a more prosaic level, it did rather better than most wars, though no doubt the price was excessive. The subjects of the Hapsburg Empire obtained their national freedom; some of the subjects of the Ottoman Empire started on the same path. The war postponed the domination of Europe by Germany, or perhaps prevented it. The most practical war aim was the one most completely achieved. Belgium was liberated." Viewed in a global context, Taylor did not see even the physical and human loss as so devastating: "On a map of Europe, the areas of destruction appear as tiny black spots: northeastern France, parts of Poland, and Serbia, a remote corner of Italy." As for the loss of life, "Young males could be more easily spared than at any other time in the world's history, brutal as this sounds."

As Taylor points out, dynasties did tumble in Germany, Austro-Hungary, Russia, and Turkey. But durable democracies were not necessarily their successors; look at Nazi Germany and the Soviet Union. The dismantling of the Austro-Hungarian Empire left hate-ridden ethnic clans that were still warring more than eighty years later and gave the word "balkanization" its pejorative meaning. In the end, how much did it benefit the ordinary Berliner, Viennese, or Muscovite to be ruled no longer by a Hohenzollern or a Hapsburg or a Romanov but instead by nonroyal absolutists, a Hitler or a Stalin?

Countering Taylor's essentially positive view is Sir John Keegan's grim verdict that the First World War was "tragic and unnecessary" and that along with the hideous waste of life it "destroyed the benevolent and optimistic culture of the European continent and left, when the guns at last fell silent four years later, a legacy of political rancour and racial hatred so intense that no explanation of the causes of the Second World War can stand without reference to those roots."

The balance sheet of the war is not easily tallied. Germany was driven from France and Belgium, and twenty-one years of peace on the European continent did follow. But the magnitude of the war that began in 1939—taking more than five times as many lives—made a mockery of the rallying cry, "The war to end all wars." No war had begun with grander pomp or pride or loftier promise than the Great War. It quickly sank and essentially remained in a slough of meaningless carnage. Again and again the word "horror" is employed to distill its nature. A Canadian, William Peden, one of five brothers who served, would later write, "Looking back over the years and wondering, I ask myself the question, what was I fighting for in the First Great War which took the lives of two of my brothers, myself and another wounded, which ultimately cost him his life also?" Rudyard Kipling had an answer for Peden: "If any question why we died / Tell them because our fathers lied." As one observer put it, British soldiers "went to war with Rupert Brooke but came home with Siegfried Sassoon."

While the pain of individuals would fade and the generation that fought the war eventually disappear, the conflict's historical repercussions continue to reverberate. It has been argued, and persuasively, that the major accomplishment of World War I was to produce World War II. The logic runs thus: the victors imposed a harsh peace on Germany in 1919 through the Treaty of Versailles; the treaty's vengeful spirit ignited in Germans a sense of persecution; persecution provided the soil of discontent in which Adolf Hitler was able to sow his rise to power; and Hitler's megalomaniacal ambitions brought on World War II. The Versailles terms were indeed a bitter pill for Germans to swallow. Article 231 of the treaty required the loser to assume guilt for a war brought about by "the aggression of Germany and her allies." Compounding the bitterness, Article 232 demanded reparations from Germany to "make compensation for all damage done to the civilian population of the Allies and Associated Powers and to their property during the period of the belligerency." The verdict of war guilt handed down against Germany seems hard to fault. France did not invade Germany, Germany invaded France. Britain did not violate Belgian neutrality, Germany did. Russia did not declare war on Germany, Germany declared war on Russia. Nor was it incomprehensible to anyone familiar with the devastation France suffered as the primary battlefield of the war in the west that the victors would want recompense. However, more farseeing Allied representatives at Versailles might have recognized that whatever Germany's guilt, whatever the case for reparations, punishment is a poor foundation for future amity.

But even had Versailles not assigned guilt or exacted reparations, would this have banked the fires of German discontent? Hitler and his malignant charisma are inseparable from Germany's launching a second world war. It is doubtful that even a peace without punishment would have satisfied the Nazi leader's appetite for power and talent for acquiring it. It is hard to imagine Hitler, even under a more lenient Versailles agreement, forsaking the exploitation of issues that allowed him to come to power. The German military, he argued, had not been beaten in the field but "stabbed in the back." This was patent nonsense. Otto Brautigan, a Great War veteran, certainly no enemy of Hitler, who later became a senior figure in the Nazi Ministry for the Occupied Eastern

Territories, dismissed the thesis of betrayal by the home front. "The soldier at the front rejected the legend of the stab in the back from the beginning," Brautigan stated. "In an honest fight which had lasted four years, we succumbed to the superior strength of our enemies and to the lack of indispensable equipment caused by the blockade."

The imaginary betrayal, however, served Hitler well. From his earliest gifted rabble-rousing he proclaimed, "It cannot be that two million Germans should have fallen in vain. . . . No, we do not pardon, we demand—vengeance!" A German soldier had put it more plainly on Armistice Day. Sam Van Tries was an American balloon observer who visited the German lines to swap souvenirs. He was exchanging American cigarettes for a German razor with an erstwhile enemy who told him, "You didn't lick us. We knew when to quit. We'll be back in twenty years."

More accurately, it was the Allied generals whose guns were spiked by their civilian leaders. Foch and Pershing regretted that Germany had been allowed to give up on her feet rather than on her knees. Foch had not wanted to stop on November 11. Pershing had feared that the Germans would not believe that they had been beaten and that someday the job would have to be done over. Were they right? Could World War II have been avoided if unconditional surrender rather than a conditional armistice had ended World War I? Would an Allied victory parade down Unter den Linden have torn out, root and branch, the last vestiges of German militarism? It can be argued that this is what unconditional surrender and occupation achieved after the Second World War: the extirpation of Nazism followed by the implantation of a durable German democracy. Similarly, the morality of dropping two atomic bombs on Japan may provoke eternal debate. But it cannot be denied that their detonations brought the war in the Pacific to a swift conclusion, followed by Japanese democracy.

But before this neat equation—total victory is good, conditional victory is suspect—is accepted, it is well to remember that the conditional surrender of Germany in 1918 did initially produce democracy. The Weimar Republic had a fairly decent fourteen-year run before succumbing to hyperinflation, a worldwide depression, and a demagogue's genius for scapegoating, inflaming old wounds, and planting dreams of ethnic superiority. Even a thorough defeat of Germany on her soil in 1918 could not likely have staved off Hitler's rise. Why would crushing, total defeat have produced less bitterness, less demand for vengeance than the terms of the Treaty of Versailles? Hitler's program was lebensraum and anti-Semitism. Versailles merely provided the prod of resentment that Hitler used to herd the German people toward a policy not unlike the kaiser's, the pursuit of power and influence commensurate with Germany's stature as a great nation.

The last day of the war provided chilling closure. The ending, in its ferocity, bloodiness, and uselessness, contained the entire war in microcosm. The fighting went on for the hollowest of reasons: no one knew how to stop it. Graveyards were the chief legacy of World War I. Nowhere is this depressing conclusion more evident than among the dead who fell during the last day, the last hour, even the last minutes. Why had the great powers not exhibited the prudence and goodwill that, as Keegan said, could have spared the world so ghastly a calamity? How did the noble rallying cry "The war to end all wars" become a bitter jest? Were any lessons of peace learned on the bloodied fields of the western front or other battlegrounds of World War I? Considering what followed, the even more catastrophic conflict of 1939–1945, and what has happened since, it seems not. Since 1945, approximately 50 million lives have been lost to wars between nations, wars of independence, civil wars, coups, and insurrections, as many as died in World War II. The most depressing lesson of World War I is that people once believed in a war to end all wars and now no one does. For America alone, World War II has been followed by wars in Korea, Vietnam, Panama, Grenada, Bosnia, Kosovo, Somalia, and Afghanistan, and two wars against Iraq. A hard-eyed reading of history demonstrates that periods of conflict somewhere on the globe are more prevalent than periods of peace. Indeed, one student of warfare has calculated that the world has been entirely at peace for only 8 percent of recorded history. The Greek philosopher Plato said, "Only the dead have seen the end of war."

Something, it seems, persists in the human makeup, genetic or so culturally ingrained as to be virtually genetic, that drives mankind to fight. Just five months after the guns went silent in 1918, the war's most caustic poet, Siegfried Sassoon, asked in "Aftermath":

> Do you remember the rats; and the stench
> Of corpses rotting in front of the front-line trench—
> And dawn coming, dirty-white, and chill with a hopeless rain?
> Do you ever stop and ask, "Is it all going to happen again?"

It would happen again and again. Consider the analogy of a length of rope. It can be used to save a man or hang him. The rope itself is neutral. Given its apparent inevitability, perhaps we must judge war similarly. It is the purpose to which force is applied that determines its justification. Is it to stop aggression, free the subjugated, topple a despot, or end economic exploitation? Or is it to commit aggression, subjugate a people, impose tyranny, and carry out economic exploitation? We shrink from accepting war as a rational path to resolving earthly differences. But we are forced to accept—if five thousand years of recorded history tell us anything—that more often than not conflict is the solution mankind chooses. As we look over the graves of those who died a useless death in the last moments of a senseless war, we can only hope, with more optimism than history supports, that just causes will outnumber the unjust.

EPILOGUE: MARCHING HOME

On April 28, 1919, crowds jammed the sidewalks of New York's Fifth Avenue to cheer the returning 165th Infantry Regiment, still popularly the "Fighting 69th." Leading the victory parade was Wild Bill Donovan, now a full colonel and commanding the regiment. Rather than dress uniform, Donovan had the men wear battle garb, steel helmets and leggings with bayonets fixed as if going into action. Alongside Donovan marched the regiment's chaplain, Father Francis Duffy, who wrote of that day, "There were 615 gold stars on the white banner which led the regiment up the avenue, each star for a valiant comrade who 'went west.' " After the war, Donovan would go on to earn a fortune as a New York lawyer, and in World War II he became America's first spymaster when President Franklin D. Roosevelt appointed him director of the Office of Strategic Services, the forerunner of today's Central Intelligence Agency.

The black 369th Regiment had already staged its victory parade the previous February up the same Fifth Avenue. "These Negroes have helped to win the war," *The Jewish Daily News* editorialized. "Let us hope that their unflinching courage in the face of death will be remembered. Color, after all, is of no consequence." *The New York Herald* marveled that "less than two years ago many of these bemedalled veterans were parlor car porters, apartment house helpers, restaurant waiters, shipping clerks, bell boys, truck drivers and what not." Standing in a touring car holding a bouquet of *fleurs-de-lis* and waving to the crowd was Henry Johnson, onetime redcap who had driven off two dozen Germans attempting to breach the lines in the Meuse-Argonne, killing four of the enemy and suffering twenty wounds himself. When the shouting faded, Johnson returned to civilian life physically depleted, a troubled man drifting from job to job. He turned to drink and died virtually penniless in 1929. Though Johnson had earned one of France's highest decorations, the Croix de Guerre with gold palm, a campaign to win the Medal of Honor for him has thus far not succeeded.

Soldiers of Johnson's stripe and other blacks who fought courageously in France had little influence on postwar racial policies in the military. The War Department decided that in the future blacks would serve mainly as laborers. They were barred from such elite branches as aviation. By 1940, black soldiers numbered 5,000 men and 5 officers, only 2 percent of the army. Thirty years would have to pass after World War I before black and white soldiers would parade side by side when another Great War veteran, President Harry S Truman, desegregated the U.S. military. Eventually, the army would become the most integrated institution in the country, well ahead of corporations, the professions, universities, and churches. By 1989, the chairman of the Joint Chiefs of Staff, the highest position in the U.S. military, would be an African American, four-star general Colin Powell.

William Triplet at age eighteen had essentially gone from Sedalia High School in Missouri into the trenches with the 35th Division, where he faced doughboy trials with breezy insouciance. Under his flippancy lay a deep attraction to the soldiering life. Triplet was briefly a civilian while preparing himself for a long-cherished dream, to enter West Point, which he did in 1920. His career took him through World War II to his retirement in 1954 with the rank of colonel. Joe Rizzi, also of the 35th, served with the Construction Battalions, the Seabees, during World War II and subsequently became a successful contractor in Tarrytown, New York.

The Kentuckian Alex McClintock had headed north in 1915 to join the Canadian Army before the United States entered the war. McClintock was seriously wounded at Desire Trench and mustered out just as his fellow Americans were arriving in France. He wrote a jaunty yet harrowing account of his war entitled *Best o'Luck,* which won him instant celebrity. Barely healed, he again enlisted, this time in the U.S. Army, was commissioned a first lieutenant, and eagerly awaited orders to France. But his wounds were not all bodily, and, much to his frustration, he was found unsuited for combat and not allowed to ship out with his division. The thwarted soldier went AWOL. A month later, McClintock's body was found in a shabby Manhattan hotel room where he had shot himself.

Douglas MacArthur's career continued its rocket-propelled ascent. He became superintendent of West Point, army chief of staff, commander of Allied forces in the Southwest Pacific in World War II, and virtual proconsul during the occupation of Japan, his forty-eight-year career ending when he was dismissed by President Truman in an epic clash of civilian versus military authority during the Korean War. His Great War reputation as an officer close to and revered by his men faded in 1932 when, as chief of staff, he personally led troops in crushing the "Bonus Marchers," World War I veterans who had come to Washington in the midst of the Depression asking for early payment of a promised reward for war service. MacArthur used tear gas against men, some of whom he had once commanded, and led a force putting torches to the lean-tos, tents, and packing crates where the veterans had taken shelter.

George S. Patton, also involved in the suppression of the Bonus Marchers, continued a career marked by brilliance and flamboyance and easily became the most controversial and indiscreet general that the U.S. Army produced during World War II. His genius for war, demonstrated by his swift conquest of Sicily and headlong rush through France, was, however, clouded by his slapping two soldiers suffering from what had been called shell shock in the first war and battle fatigue in the second. Patton died at age sixty in a mundane traffic accident in Germany in 1945 just after World War II ended—hardly the death this mystic warrior would have orchestrated.

General Pershing returned to the United States full of honors, the first American to hold the rank of general of the armies, becoming chief of the army in 1921. When Congress created an agency to build and maintain overseas cemeteries, Pershing became the first chairman of the American Battle Monuments Commission, serving from 1923 until his death in 1948. His burdens in France had been eased by the love of his twenty-three-year-old mistress, the artist Micheline Resco. After the war they exchanged transatlantic visits. "Michette" moved to America in 1940, when World War II broke out, and six years later Pershing, then eighty-four, ill, and confined to Walter Reed Hospital, married Micheline, then age fifty-two. The general died two years later.

President Woodrow Wilson's crusade after Versailles to have the United States ratify the League of Nations ran aground on the reef of his own inflexible idealism and the opposition of the chairman of the Senate Foreign Relations Committee, Henry Cabot Lodge. Wilson rejected even reasonable compromises, and Lodge refused to budge. Hence, the United States failed to enter the League. Wilson suffered an incapacitating stroke in 1919, his presidency largely managed thereafter by his wife, Edith, and White House aides. Wilson died in 1924.

Henry Gunther, of Baltimore's Own 313th Infantry, officially the last man to die in the war, had his sergeant's rank restored and was posthumously awarded the Distinguished Service Cross. Henry D. Gunther Post 1858 of the Veterans of Foreign Wars in Baltimore honors his memory.

René Naegelen, decorated veteran of Verdun, was at home in Belfort at the war's end with his mother, grieving over the loss in battle of another son, Joseph. Naegelen had gone into the war a pacifist and come out more so. He became managing editor of the

Socialist Party newspaper, *Populaire de Paris,* wrote a best-selling memoir of his war years, was elected to the French parliament, fought in the Resistance in World War II, and was commended by General Dwight Eisenhower "for brave conduct while acting under my orders in the liberation of his country, 1944–1945."

Pierre Teilhard de Chardin, priest and stretcher bearer, had wrestled with the anomaly of a beneficent, all-powerful God permitting war's horrors. After the conflict, he went on to become a leading paleontologist involved in the research that found the Peking man. He wrote the acclaimed *The Phenomenon of Man,* in which he sought to reconcile evolution with Christian theology.

Marshal Ferdinand Foch, commander of Allied forces at the war's end, was made a Marshal of France and participated in negotiating the 1919 Treaty of Versailles. There his chief objective was to block the possibility of a resurgence of German militarism. Henri Pétain, wildly popular for stopping the Germans at Verdun, lived too long to sustain his heroic stature. After Germany invaded France in 1940, Pétain, at the age of eighty-four, became premier, surrendering half of his country to the Nazis and becoming chief of state of the fascistic rump Vichy government. After the war, Pétain was tried and sentenced to death for treason. Charles de Gaulle, the provisional head of government and a fellow veteran of Verdun, commuted Pétain's sentence, and the leader who had put spine into France with the rallying cry "They shall not pass" died in disgrace at age ninety-five.

A grateful nation awarded Field Marshal Douglas Haig a gift of £100,000 and made him an earl. Haig devoted the rest of his life to organizing the British Legion of Great War Veterans and raising funds for disabled servicemen. His resistance to new ideas and fidelity to the old are demonstrated in something he wrote eight years after the war: "I believe that the value of the horse and the opportunity of the horse in the future are likely to be as great as ever. Aeroplanes and tanks are only accessories to the men and the horse." Haig died in 1928 at age sixty-seven.

The British prime minister, David Lloyd George, sought at Versailles a bridge between Wilsonian idealism and the French thirst for vengeance. He fell from power in 1922 and never held public office again. After his wife, Margaret, died in 1941, Lloyd George married his wartime confidante, secretary, and mistress, Frances Stevenson. He died in 1945 at age eighty-two. Thirty years later, his letters to Frances were published under the title *My Darling Puss.*

R. C. Sherriff, who had initially been denied a commission for not having attended the right schools and who so insightfully inventoried the insanity of assaults over open ground against barbed wire, machine guns, and artillery, wrote *Journey's End,* a play that palpably caught the smell and feel of trench life and became a hit in London and New York. Sherriff also became a successful screenwriter, his credits including *Goodbye, Mr. Chips* and *The Invisible Man.*

The Royal Welch Fusiliers produced a constellation of brilliant postwar writers. The brightest was Siegfried Sassoon. The poet who had authored the most cutting poetry to come out of the war went on to write the semifictional *The Complete Memoirs of George Sherston.* Sassoon, so reckless of life in battle, died in bed in his eightieth year. His onetime second in command, Vivian de Sola Pinto, became a distinguished professor of literature and served again in World War II.

Robert Graves, at one point left for dead in a moribund ward, wrote an enduring trench classic, *Goodbye to All That,* and is perhaps best remembered for his fictional account of ancient Rome, *I, Claudius,* subsequently an acclaimed television series. After the war, Frank Richards, the perennial private, showed Graves a handwritten memoir describing his experience in the trenches. Graves found the manuscript a rough gem and helped Richards find a publisher for *Old Soldiers Never Die,* an instant success. Graves wrote the introduction. Richards never went back to the Welsh coal pits from which he had sprung. Graves's eldest son, David, was killed in World War II.

After completing her education at Oxford, Vera Brittain joined the faculty of the university, where she taught until 1922, then began a full-time writing career. In 1925, ten years after the death of her fiancé, Roland Leighton, she married another Great War veteran, George C. G. Catlin, a political scientist who taught at Cornell University in the United States and by whom she had two children. In 1933, she published her classic wartime memoir, *Testament of Youth*. Brittain described herself as a member of "the breakthrough generation of women who have transformed a track to the future into a highway for our successors to tread." She died in 1970 at age seventy-seven.

The physician Geoffrey Keynes, who had used his experiences on the battlefield to advance medicine, particularly in the area of blood transfusions, was again in uniform in World War II, becoming senior consulting surgeon to the Royal Air Force and ultimately attaining the rank of air vice marshal.

Fritz Nagel, from the wealthy Bremen tobacco family, had never believed Americans would go to war against Germany. Afterward, contemptuous of proletarian romantics and their dreams of a workers' utopia in Germany, Nagel emigrated to the United States, where his older brother, an AEF veteran, lived. He spent the rest of his life as a businessman in Paducah, Kentucky.

Herbert Sulzbach, whose pride in the German Army persisted to the war's last day, also left his native land but for rather different reasons. Sulzbach had written a scathing letter to the Berlin paper *Der Tag,* criticizing the Nazis as he watched the cloud descending over his fellow German Jews. By 1938, he had fled to England with his wife, the niece of the noted conductor Otto Klemperer. In World War II the much-decorated German officer volunteered and served as a private in the British Army. He wrote a vivid and successful memoir of his service in the trenches entitled *Two Living Wars.*

Fritz Haber had gone into the war an international hero for his work on the mass production of ammonia for the manufacture of agricultural fertilizers. But his role in inventing poison gases during the war tarred him in many eyes as a war criminal. He was ultimately rehabilitated and awarded the Nobel Prize in chemistry for his earlier peacetime contributions to science. Haber's service to his homeland counted for nothing in Nazi Germany, and the Jewish scientist fled in 1933, dying in exile.

Ernst Jünger had enlisted fresh out of high school and despite enduring the worst the war could offer (including twenty wounds) long remained a trench romantic, as evidenced by his semifictional novel *Copse,* glorifying war as the ultimate in human experience. His most famous book became the autobiographical war memoir *Storm of Steel.* Politically Jünger was all over the lot, at times a hero of the German right, the French left, and early environmentalists. The Nazis courted him in the 1920s and 1930s, then banned his books in the 1940s. He nevertheless served with the German forces in World War II. He later rejected militarism completely and became a world peace activist. Jünger died in 1998 at age 103.

Count Wolf-Heinrich von Helldorf, who had taken the Allies' armistice demands from Compiègne Forest through the lines to German headquarters at Spa, eventually became the police chief of Berlin. Helldorf was hanged for his involvement in the July 20, 1944, assassination attempt on Hitler.

Kaiser Wilhelm II, under the Treaty of Versailles, faced charges as a war criminal, but the Netherlands, where he had fled after his abdication, refused to give him up. He died in comfortable exile in Doorn, at age eighty-two, after Nazi Germany had conquered the nation that had given him refuge.

The lives of two giants of the war and an obscure corporal eventually intersected with disastrous results for the world. The German Army chief of staff, Erich Ludendorff, had been Germany's virtual dictator in the latter part of the war only to flee disguised by a false beard to Denmark at the end. On his return to Germany, Ludendorff immersed himself in ultranationalist politics and marched with Adolf Hitler in the unsuccessful 1923 "Beer Hall putsch" intended to seize control of Bavaria. The next year, Ludendorff became a Nazi member of the Reichstag. He subsequently had a falling-out with Hitler and died powerless in 1937 at age seventy-two. Ludendorff's superior, Field Marshal von Hindenburg, was elected Germany's president in 1925 and reelected in 1932. The following year, the nearly senile head of state was persuaded by conservatives to name Adolf Hitler chancellor, in effect Germany's prime minister, with the argument that they could control the upstart. When Hindenburg died in 1934, Hitler seized total power.

The German emissaries who were handed the hapless task of ending the war in 1918 at Compiègne Forest were subsequently branded by Hitler the "November Criminals," chief among them Matthias Erzberger, the Socialist who had signed the armistice. Erzberger was assassinated by right-wing zealots in 1921. Prince Max of Baden, who had been appointed chancellor in October 1918 and had essentially ousted the kaiser, also won the unforgiving wrath of rightists and militarists. His noble birth, however, spared him from a violent end and he died in 1929 at age sixty-two.

Gavrilo Princip, whose pistol had ultimately led to nearly 9 million military and more than 6 million civilian deaths, was tried for the murders of the Archduke Franz Ferdinand and his wife, Sophie, but escaped execution because of his youth at the time of the crime. He died of tuberculosis in an Austrian prison in April 1918 at age twenty-four.

In 1955, a powerful explosion rocked the earth near Ploegsteert Wood in Belgium. One of the twenty-one mines planted in 1917 under the German lines along the Messines Ridge had failed to explode at the time but went off thirty-eight years later during a rainstorm, presumably when a bolt of lightning struck a tree. One last unexploded mine remains, its exact location unknown and its hidden potency serving as something of a symbol of the Great War's underlying power to influence events down to the present day.

ACKNOWLEDGMENTS

I could not have written this book without the expertise and generous investment of time by numerous people. At the National Archives, Mitchell Yockelson unearthed a wealth of invaluable material and also reviewed the manuscript, much to my profit. Others at the Archives who guided me were longtime friends William Cunliffe, John Taylor, and Larry MacDonald, as well as Tim Nenninger and Rod Ross. Another invaluable resource was the U.S. Army Military History Institute at Carlisle, Pennsylvania, under the able direction of Richard Sommers. Among his staff, Katherine Olson was enormously helpful to me, and David Keough, Jay Graybeal, and Randy Hackenburg provided valued assistance, the latter two helping to find appropriate photos.

My research took me to the Imperial War Museum in London, where fellow author Malcolm Brown generously assisted me and Michael Paterson promptly filled my every request. The American Battle Monuments Commission, on which I am privileged to serve, is a storehouse of information on World War I. The Commission's chairman, General P. X. Kelly; its secretary, General John Herrling; and Executive Director Kenneth Pond aided me importantly, as did Brigadier General William Leszczynski, Jr., director of the Commission's European Region. Marty Sells of the Commission

staff provided useful photographs. Joseph P. Rivers, superintendent of the American Meuse-Argonne Cemetery, shared his ency-
clopedic knowledge of that battlefront with me. David Atkinson,
superintendent of the American Somme Cemetery, and his associate, Muriel Defrenne, were mines of information and provided a
tour of the Somme sector. Philip De La Mater, superintendent of
the American Aisne-Marne Cemetery, provided a most helpful
tour of his sector.

Superintendent Rivers also introduced me to Colonel Alain
Bernède, a deeply informed French Army historian. Further infor-
mation on the French role in the war was arranged for me by my
longtime friend Ambassador James Malone Rentschler, by Colonel
Frederic Guelton, and by Colonel J. C. Aumoine of the French
Army history office. Those who aided me with the German phase
of my research included Dr. Peter Kaspar, Olaf Hamann of the
Berlin Staatsbibliothek, and Katharina Kloock of the German
American Historical Institute. Sandrine Volpato of the Volksbund
Deutsche Kriegsgräberfürsorge helped me with photo research.

The various western front associations are a remarkable source
of information on the war. Among members who aided me were
Len Shurtleff, president of the U.S. branch of the WFA; Chris
Baker, former chairman of the WFA–United Kingdom; and Christina
Holstein, who provided valuable leads. For providing information
on Canadian forces in World War I, I thank Douglas Fisher and
Derek Blackburn.

The Library of Congress staff assisted me on this as well as previous works. I am particularly indebted to Margaret Krewson, for-
merly of the Library and presently Washington representative of
the Society for German-American Studies; Prosser Gifford, director of scholarly programs; his assistant, Lester Vogel; and David
Wigdor, assistant chief of the Manuscript Division. The historian
of the U.S. Senate, Richard Baker, promptly met my every request
and helped me find long-neglected material that proved invaluable.

At my alma mater, the State University of New York at Albany,

I am deeply indebted to the library director, Meredith Butler, and to William Young for his indispensable research assistance. Among those who assisted me at the State Library of New York were Jean Hargrave, Elaine Clark, Melinda Yates, Vicki Weiss, and Kathi Stanley, along with V. Chapman Smith, former director of the New York State Archives.

My local Guilderland Public Library includes several assiduous researchers in the reference section. Among those who helped me on numerous occasions were Thomas Barnes, Rosemary Englehardt, Margaret Garrett, Gillian Leonard, Maria Buhl, Eileen Williams, and Mary Alingh.

Two indispensable partners in this project have been my wife, Sylvia, and my daughter Vanya Perez, who were involved in the researching, editing, and preparation of the manuscript.

Other colleagues who gave generously of their time and knowledge in reviewing the manuscript included Bernard F. Conners, Robert Cowley, Robert Ferrell, Tanya Melich, Dennis Showalter, David R. Woodward, and my literary agent, Esther Newberg, who represents me so well.

I received assistance with photographs from Donna Williams of the Maryland Historical Society and Clarence Deaver of the Henry Gunther Post, Veterans of Foreign Wars in Baltimore. Colonel William Smullen gave me inestimable help in my map research. Donna Salsich provided useful information on wartime medical care.

The book contains an extensive bibliography of works consulted. However, I want to especially acknowledge four that were my constant companions throughout the project: Stanley Weintraub's *A Stillness Heard Round the World*, A. J. P. Taylor's *The First World War*, John Keegan's *The First World War*, and Malcolm Brown's *The Western Front*. Needless to say, the accuracy of the final work remains my sole responsibility.

Finally, I have benefited from the outset of this project from the guidance, enthusiasm, and seasoned judgment of my Random House editor, Robert Loomis.

APPENDIX: CASUALTY STATISTICS

Consistent casualty statistics from World War I (as for most wars) are not easily obtained. Countries compiled their casualty figures on different bases and covering different periods. German casualty records for the last days of the war pose a particular challenge because the armies were in retreat, facing defeat, and returning to a homeland in chaos. I have used conservative casualty figures for all the belligerents, preferring to err on the low rather than the high side and thus avoid presenting an inflated picture.

The principal sources consulted for casualty figures used here are Ellis and Cox's definitive *The World War I Databook; The British Official History—Military Operations—France and Flanders 1918, Volume 5; Official History of the Canadian Army—Canadian Expeditionary Force, 1914–1918; AEF Monthly Report on Casualties, November 1918; Hearings Sub-committee No. 3, House of Representatives, 1920; Service Historique de L'Armée de Terre, Ministère de la Defense* (France); *Verlustliste, Staatsbibliothek Zu Berlin* (German); *The Oxford Companion to American Military History;* German Historical Institute, Washington, D.C.; The Western Front Association, *Trenches on the Web* (www.worldwar1.com); and the U.S. Army Military History Institute, Carlisle, Pennsylvania.

NOTES

Source notes are keyed to the book's page number and a quotation or phrase on that page. Citations from books, periodicals, and other attributed sources begin with the author's name followed by the title and page numbers. Sources are fully identified in the bibliography. Frequently used sources are abbreviated as follows:

ABMC: American Battle Monuments Commission, *American Armies and Battlefields in Europe*

IWM: Imperial War Museum, London

MHI: U.S. Army Military History Institute, Carlisle, Pennsylvania

MHQ: MHQ:The Quarterly Journal of Military History

RG 120: Record Group 120, National Archives

RG 407: Records of the Adjutant General's Office, National Archives

Sub-committee 3: Select Committee on Expenditures in the War Department, U.S. House of Representatives, *Hearings Before Sub-committee No. 3.*

USAWW: *United States Army in the World War, 1917–1919: Meuse-Argonne Operations*

INTRODUCTION

xv "little crosses": RG 407, Letter, Livermore to Fuller, November 12, 1919.

xvii "The First World War": John Keegan, *The First World War*, p. 3.

xvii "They fought because": Trevor Wilson, *The Myriad Faces of War*, p. 850.

xviii "a mistress": Niall Ferguson, *The Pity of War*, p. 361.

1: THE DESPERATE HOURS

4 "An indescribable feeling": Connell Albertine, *The Yankee Doughboy*, pp. 10–11.

5 John B. de Valles: Ibid., pp. 105, 230–231.

6 "Kill them!": Ibid., p. 125.

6 "Why?" Dowell asked: Sub-Committee 3, pp. 1769–1773.

7 "I expected my casualties": Ibid., p. 1774.
7 "When the orders came": Frank Freidel, *Over There*, p. 216.
9 "On Monday morning": Will R. Bird, *Ghosts Have Warm Hands*, pp. 13–14.
9 "the War is over": Ibid., pp. 210–214.
10 "regretted that no other": J. R. Harvey, *The History of the 5th (Royal Irish) Regiment of Dragoons*, p. 435.
11 "I'm hit. I'm hit": Bird, *Ghosts Have Warm Hands*, pp. 215–217.
12 "in such a cowardly way": Herbert Sulzbach, *With the German Guns*, pp. 31–33.
13 The youths had been cut down: Robert Cowley, "Massacre of the Innocents," *MHQ*, spring 1998, pp. 38–41.
13 "I find this sign": Sulzbach, *With the German Guns*, pp. 243, 250.

2: THE BOY WHO BLEW UP THE WORLD
16 The archduke's gesture: Robert K. Massie, *Dreadnought*, pp. 859–860.
17 The young Bosnian: Stephen O'Shea, *Back to the Front*, p. 21.
18 "the dangerous little viper": Massie, *Dreadnought*, pp. 857, 860–861.
19 "the most formidable document": Ibid., p. 866.
19 "There is nothing": Ibid., p. 868; A. J. P. Taylor, *The First World War*, p. 16.
21 "It cannot but end": Massie, *Dreadnought*, pp. 883, 887.
22 "repel by all means": Ibid., p. 907.
23 "We shall send them": Ibid.

3: "A LOVELY WAR"
25 "I am not ashamed": Niall Ferguson, *The Pity of War*, p. 174.
26 "looked at it": John Toland, *Adolf Hitler*, p. 58.
26 "Now everything depended": Fritz Nagel, *Fritz: The World War I Memoirs of a German Lieutenant*, pp. 16–17.
27 "Part of our men": J. Koettgen, trans., *A German Deserter's War Experience*, p. 18.
28 "there was a gallantry": George A. Panichas and Sir Herbert Read, *Promise of Greatness*, p. 334.
28 "Almost any other sort": John Keegan, *Face of Battle*, p. 216.
29 "a lovely war": Panichas and Read, *Promise of Greatness*, p. 68.
30 "I'm sorry, but": Ibid., p. 136.
30 "Officers had to be made quickly": Ibid., p. 139.
31 "This, the greatest of all wars": Phillip Knightley, *The First Casualty*, p. 83.
32 "Women were crying": Henri Desagneaux, *A French Soldier's War Diary*, pp. 3–4.
33 "long, weary struggle": J. M. Bourne, *Who's Who in World War I*, p. 209.

4: "GOYA AT HIS MOST MACABRE"
34 "Goya at his most macabre": Panichas and Read, *Promise of Greatness*, pp. 72, 84.
35 "Revolution is brewing": Desagneaux, *A French Soldier's War Diary*, p. 104.

36 That the war would descend: Keegan, *The First World War,* pp. 30–31, 80; Taylor, *The First World War,* p. 20.

37 "When looking at": Koettgen, trans., *A German Deserter's War Experience,* pp. 4, 8, 15.

38 "Murder, lust, and pillage": Knightley, *The First Casualty,* p. 83.

38 "About 220 inhabitants": *Current History, The New York Times,* February 1918, pp. 346–347.

39 Still, at this stage: Richard Holmes, *The Western Front,* p. 22; John Toland, *No Man's Land,* p. 17; Taylor, *The First World War,* p. 25.

40 "In our hurry": John W. Kress, *The Great Adventure,* pp. 15–16.

40 "The attack directed": Harry L. Smith and James R. Eckman, *Memoirs of an Ambulance Company Officer,* pp. 3–5.

41 "The Race to the Sea": Taylor, *The First World War,* pp. 34–35.

41 Moltke promptly had: Bourne, *Who's Who in World War I,* p. 209.

42 "amiable enough": Alan Clark, *The Donkeys,* p. 13.

5: UPON A MIDNIGHT CLEAR

43 "our regiment handled itself": Toland, *Adolf Hitler,* p. xvi.

43 "the greatest and most unforgettable": Niall Ferguson, *The Pity of War,* p. 174.

44 "When somebody in the crowd": Fritz Kreisler, *Four Weeks in the Trenches,* pp. 3–4.

45 "the extraordinary lack of hatred": Ibid., p. 17.

46 "Two men would take a dead soldier": Koettgen, trans., *A German Deserter's War Experience,* p. 2.

48 "Were these things improper": Ibid., p. 3.

48 "This hour is one": Knightley, *The First Casualty,* p. 81.

49 "Don't shoot! Don't shoot!": Will R. Bird, *The Communications Trench,* p. 133.

50 "Merry Christmas": Frank Richards, *Old Soldiers Never Die,* p. 47.

50 "After they had recovered": Bird, *The Communications Trench,* p. 134.

51 "There was no sort": Stanley Weintraub, "The Christmas Truce," *MHQ,* winter 1993, p. 81.

51 more than 1,000,000 casualties: Ian Westwall, *World War I Day by Day,* p. 47.

52 "I had two men shot": Rudolf Binding, *A Fatalist at War,* pp. 16, 35.

6: "THE GOD WHO GAVE THE CANNON GAVE THE CROSS"

54 The generals began using: Paul Fussell, *The Great War and Modern Memory,* pp. 2, 9.

55 "The effects of the successful": Binding, *A Fatalist at War,* p. 64.

55 By 1915, with the western front: *Fritz Haber: Chemist and Patriot;* see www.windows/desktop/fritzshaber.htm.

56 "Blindness, deafness, loss of voice": Malcolm Brown, *The Imperial War Museum Book of the First World War,* p. 79.

57 "He gazed at my uniform": Panichas and Read, *Promise of Greatness,* p. 184.

58 "The Soldier": Tim Cross, *The Last Voices of World War I*, pp. 52–58.
58 "We had been instructed": Panichas and Read, *Promise of Greatness*, p. 85.
58 "If then a man happened": Koettgen, trans., *A German Deserter's War Experience*, p. 19.
59 "looked on as a 'soft number' ": Teilhard de Chardin, *The Making of a Mind*, p. 26.
60 "If there were a good God": Ibid., p. 63.

7: THE THREE MUSKETEERS
61 "if I shall be one": Vera Brittain, *Testament of Youth*, p. 460.
62 "represented all that was": Ibid., p. 23.
62 "I was kicked, hounded, caned": Alan Bishop and Mark Bostridge, eds., *Letters from a Lost Generation*, p. 3.
63 "a lofty assumption": Brittain, *Testament of Youth*, p. 81.
63 "Women get all the dreariness": Ibid., p. 104.
64 "Yes, I should": Ibid., p. 116.
64 "a really terrible": Ibid., pp. 215–16.
65 "Shall be home": Ibid., p. 232.

8: A SCAR FROM BELGIUM TO SWITZERLAND
67 "Imagine a broad belt": O'Shea, *Back to the Front*, p. 16.
67 "Dig a trench shoulder-high": Barrie Pitt, *1918: The Last Act*, p. 8.
68 "formed a sandbag club": Guy Chapman, *A Passionate Prodigality*, pp. 39–40.
68 No-man's-land was: *MHQ*, summer 1996, p. 32.
68 "that short and dry word 'raid' ": *In Flanders Field: Museum Guide*, p. 5.
69 "Let me try to picture": John W. Kress, *The Great Adventure*, pp. 107–109.
70 "Soldiers of the Republic": Panichas and Read, *Promise of Greatness*, p. 169.
71 "Their faces and hands": Malcolm Brown, *The Western Front*, p. 86.
71 "You can't destroy": Panichas and Read, *Promise of Greatness*, pp. 141–142.
72 By the time these offensives: Taylor, *The First World War*, p. 99; Westwall, *World War I Day by Day*, p. 67.
72 "Gerrard, a charming": Chapman, *A Passionate Prodigality*, p. 65.
74 "the tunic torn": Brittain, *Testament of Youth*, p. 251.

9: EVERY INCH A SOLDIER
76 "very often the best": Robert Blake, ed., *The Private Papers of Douglas Haig*, p. 340.
77 "as good a general": Alan Clark, *The Donkeys*, p. 192.
78 "Why not?": Blake, ed., *The Private Papers of Douglas Haig*, pp. 16–20.
78 "If anyone acted": Taylor, *The First World War*, p. 107.

10: "THEY SHALL NOT PASS"
80 "Joseph had been entrusted": Panichas and Read, *Promise of Greatness*, pp. 175, 180.

81 In choosing the ancient city: O'Shea, *Back to the Front,* p. 165.
82 "You may not think": Taylor, *The First World War,* pp. 121–122.
83 "My two friends": Panichas and Read, *Promise of Greatness,* pp. 170, 181.
84 "A machine gunner has been blinded": Desagneaux, *A French Soldier's War Diary,* pp. 21, 30.
84 Verdun did not mark: Panichas and Read, *Promise of Greatness,* pp. 62–63.
85 "Her thin gray hair": Herbert Ward, *Mr Poilu,* p. 68.
86 While the word caught: John Brophy, *The Long Trail,* p. 165.
87 "and on the following morning": Koettgen, trans., *A German Deserter's War Experience,* pp. 17–18.

11: "WHAT DID YOU DO IN THE GREAT WAR, DAD?"
90 "You won't catch me complaining": Panichas and Read, *Promise of Greatness,* p. xviii.
92 Of 1,959 passengers and crew: ABMC, p. 9.
92 "Germany surely must": Gary Mead, *The Doughboys,* p. 31.
92 "There is such a thing": Ibid., pp. 32–33.
93 "What a lesson it is": Keegan, *The Face of Battle,* p. 221.
94 "I shall never think": Denis Winter, *Death's Men,* p. 62.
94 "would eventually fuel": Keegan, *The Face of Battle,* p. 221.
95 "The only things legitimate": Alexander McClintock, *Best O'Luck,* p. 50.
96 "At a little before daybreak": Ibid., p. 20.
96 "the great leveller": Keegan, *The First World War,* p. 398.
98 "The Western Front was known": Pitt, *1918: The Last Act,* p. 12.
98 "The temptation to get out": Brown, *The Western Front,* p. 160.
99 "Lovely evening": Panichas and Read, *Promise of Greatness,* pp. 313–314, 320.
100 "Oh, death, sir, I suppose": Chapman, *A Passionate Prodigality,* p. 73.

12: "TOMORROW I SHALL TAKE MY MEN OVER THE TOP"
101 "One can hardly find words": Sulzbach, *With the German Guns,* p. 232.
101 "We understood each other": Ibid., pp. 32, 75, 172.
103 "I feel that every step": Fussell, *The Great War and Modern Memory,* p. 29.
104 "How long could this last?": Malcolm Brown, *The Imperial War Museum Book of the First World War,* p. 65.
104 "speech was of course impossible": Laurence Housman, *War Letters of Fallen Englishmen,* p. 62.
104 "The wire has never been": Fussell, *The Great War and Modern Memory,* p. 29.
105 "It is utterly impossible": Brown, *The First World War,* p. 63.
105 "I'm writing this letter": Housman, *War Letters of Fallen Englishmen,* pp. 106–107.
105 "The Hun is going to get": Brown, *The First World War,* p. 232.
106 "too much hard work": Brown, *The Western Front,* pp. 188–189.
106 "I should say that": McClintock, *Best O'Luck,* p. 5.

107 "I gave the men": Winter, *Death's Men,* p. 176.

107 Suddenly the earth shook: Westwall, *World War I Day by Day,* p. 101.

108 "They're coming": James Hannah, *The Great War Reader,* p. 124.

108 "even the heaviest shells": Fussell, *The Great War and Modern Memory,* pp. 44–45.

109 "the kind commonly called heavenly": Ibid., p. 29.

109 Before Montauban: IWM, Robert Cude, *Diary,* pp. 36–38.

109 "They looked as though": O'Shea, *Back to the Front,* p. 93.

110 "Leave me, would you?": Hannah, *The Great War Reader,* p. 182.

110 "I laid my head": Ibid., p. 47.

110 "Then I heard": Keegan, *The First World War,* p. 295.

110 "men going to the glory": Winter, *Death's Men,* p. 185.

111 "A man dies": Hannah, *The Great War Reader,* p. 87.

111 "We knew it was pointless": Ibid., p. 56.

112 "This cannot be considered": Blake, ed., *The Private Papers of Douglas Haig,* p. 54.

112 "The men are much too keen": Brown, *The Western Front,* p. 196.

113 "I remember thinking": Alden Brooks, *As I Saw It,* p. 195.

113 "He neglected to tell": Panichas and Read, *Promise of Greatness,* p. 301.

114 "spared from the ward": Brittain, *Testament of Youth,* p. 282.

115 "For conspicuous gallantry": Ibid., p. 286.

116 "The French and British attacks": Sulzbach, *With the German Guns,* p. 10.

116 "power-driven, bullet proof, armed engine": Bourne, *Who's Who in World War I,* p. 280.

117 "This is the first time": McClintock, *Best O'Luck,* pp. 26–27.

118 "it seemed the rest of us": Ibid., pp. 34–36.

118 "on our first bombing raid": Ibid., pp. 4–5.

119 "put that bloody cigarette out": O'Shea, *Back to the Front,* p. 68.

119 "I am glad to be going in": Freidel, *Over There,* p. 102.

120 "lions led by donkeys": Richard Holmes, *The Western Front,* p. 13.

13: "HINDENBURG! THE NAME ITSELF IS MASSIVE"

122 "Let Joffre, the deputies": Desagneaux, *A French Soldier's War Diary,* pp. 34–35.

122 "palatial setting": William Hermanns, *The Holocaust,* pp. 138–139.

123 "Hindenburg!": Winston Churchill, *Great Contemporaries,* p. 67.

124 "a happy marriage": Paul von Hindenburg, *Out of My Life,* p. 62.

127 "The machine gun was": Taylor, *The First World War,* p. 86.

127 "I ought not": Frances Stevenson, *Lloyd George: A Diary,* p. 93.

130 "When you are a soldier": Brittain, *Testament of Youth,* p. 306.

130 "with bulging packs": Fussell, *The Great War and Modern Memory,* p. 83.

131 "They ought not to publish": Henri Barbusse, *Under Fire,* pp. 310–311.

132 "The hardest part": McClintock, *Best O'Luck,* p. 96.

14: "KEEPING THE WORLD SAFE FOR DEMOCRACY"
133 "Hostilities will cease": RG 120, Boxes 30–31.
133 "Germany's morale": USAWW, v. 10, pp. 28–30.
134 "Supply sergeants were": Ernest Powell, Baltimore Sun, March 9, 1969.
134 "On our first day": Ibid.
136 "shall make war together": Mead, The Doughboys, p. 425.
137 "chin shaking, face flushed": Meirion and Susie Harries, The Last Days of Innocence, p. 71.
137 "We have no selfish ends": Ibid., p. 72.
138 "I feel that you are putting": Ibid.
138 "because our submarines": Keegan, The First World War, p. 372.
139 Canada, as a dominion: Veterans' Affairs, Canada, Canada in the First World War, p. 19.
140 "No-man's-land, so often": Winter, Death's Men, p. 185.
141 "and he had such beautiful eyes": Brittain, Testament of Youth, p. 342.
141 "it was somewhat disconcerting": Ibid., p. 374.
142 The man President Wilson chose: Laurance Stallings, The Story of the Doughboys, p. 4.
142 "plainly of the estate": Mead, The Doughboys, p. 118.
143 At age forty-five, Pershing made: Thomas Fleming, "Iron General," MHQ, winter 1994, p. 59.
144 "Wire me today": Ibid., p. 60.

15: ACTS PREJUDICIAL TO MILITARY DISCIPLINE
146 "One and a half million Frenchmen": William Manchester, American Caesar, p. 95.
147 "While French soldiers endured": Holmes, The Western Front, p. 77.
147 "the industrialization of murder": O'Shea, Back to the Front, p. 128.
147 "Goodbye to life": Ibid., p. 127.
148 "On the tenth": Panichas and Read, Promise of Greatness, p. 174.
148 "I had five court-martialled": Desagneaux, A French Soldier's War Diary, p. 39.
148 "Pétain enters, cold, stern": Ibid., pp. 48–49.
149 "Two hundred men": Barbusse, I Saw It Myself, pp. 77–80.
150 Of the thousands convicted: Anthony Babbington, For the Sake of Example, p. 190; Nicolas Offenstadt, "French Executions," www.shotatdawn.org.uk.
150 "An example is needed": Babbington, For the Sake of Example, p. 182.
150 "The following men": IWM, A Manx Soldier's War Diary, p. 27.
151 "The thing that had been": Ibid., pp. 28–29.
152 "Dearest Mother Mine": Babbington, For the Sake of Example, pp. 102–105.
153 "bantam division": Julian Putkowski, www.durham.gov.
153 "The General then began": Max Hastings, ed., The Oxford Book of Military Anecdotes, p. 338.
153 "Shot at Dawn": Fussell, The Great War and Modern Memory, p. 176.
153 "I don't like the sea": Harry Kendall, A New York Actor on the Western Front, p. 96.

154 German troops faced: Christoph Jahr, "German Executions," www.shotat dawn.org.uk.

154 Shell shock, new: Hannah, *The Great War Reader*, pp. 84, 85; Brown, *The Western Front*, pp. 162–163; Eric J. Leed, *No Man's Land*, p. 175.

156 "This soldier absented himself": Will Judy, *A Soldier's Diary*, pp. 350–351.

16: DOUGHBOYS

157 "I just got notice": Harry S Truman, "World War I Letters from Harry to Bess," www.whistlestop.org.

158 "After reading all the books": Robert H. Ferrell, ed., *The Autobiography of Harry S Truman*, p. 27.

159 "made arrangements": David McCullough, *Truman*, p. 103.

160 "I did not believe": Joseph Rizzi, *Memoirs of a Doughboy*, pp. 1–2.

160 "Many times": Harry L. Smith, www.ukan/edukansite/ww_one/memoir.html.

160 "were both rarin' ": Arthur E. Jensen, *The War Log of an Underdog*, p. 1.

161 "just couldn't wait": Kenneth Gearhart Baker, "Oatmeal and Coffee," pp. 31–32.

162 "Don't join the 69th unless": Francis P. Duffy, *Father Duffy's Story*, p. 13.

162 "Donovan is a man": Ibid., p. 25.

164 "No bedding, Mr. Secretary?": Kelly Miller, *Kelly Miller's History of the World War for Human Rights*, pp. 530, 533.

164 "It should be well known": Ibid., pp. 537–538.

166 Country boys turned out: Mead, *The Doughboys*, p. 71.

166 "You can sew brass buttons": William Seaver Woods, *Colossal Blunders of the War*, p. 5.

166 "Uneducated except in army affairs": Arthur H. Joel, *Under the Lorraine Cross*, p. 9.

167 The American soldier was almost immediately: John Toland, *No Man's Land*, p. 20; Mead, *Doughboys*, p. 67.

17: "SWEET AND NOBLE TO DIE FOR ONE'S COUNTRY"

168 By the summer of 1917: Westwall, *World War I Day by Day*, pp. 133, 137; Taylor, *The First World War*, pp. 188–189.

170 "Gentlemen, we may not make history": www.expage.com/page/history/1; www.spartacus.schoolnet.co.uk/fwwmessines.html.

170 "We saw what might have been doors": www.spartacus.schoolnet.co.uk/fwwmessines.html.

171 "You cower in a heap": Hannah, *The Great War Reader*, p. 296.

171 "We often talked": Ernst Jünger, *The Storm of Steel*, p. x.

172 "It was only once": Fussell, *The Great War and Modern Memory*, p. 91; Bourne, *Who's Who in World War I*, p. 248.

172 "Good-morning; good-morning!": Rupert Hart-Davis, ed., *The War Poems of Siegfried Sassoon*, p. 78.

173 "I'd like to see a tank": Panichas and Read, *Promise of Greatness*, p. 342.

173 "That splendid erect form": Ibid., p. 79.

173 "I am not protesting": Bourne, *Who's Who in World War I*, pp. 213, 258.

174 "Dulce et Decorum Est": O'Shea, *Back to the Front,* pp. 171–172; *In Flanders Field: Museum Guide,* p. 27.

175 "We regret to announce": Hannah, *The Great War Reader,* p. 195.

176 "Probably none": Panichas and Read, *Promise of Greatness,* p. 82.

176 "The common dress": Mead, *The Doughboys,* p. 100.

176 "Lafayette, we are here!": Freidel, *Over There,* p. 137; Stallings, *The Story of the Doughboy,* p. 20.

177 "I was much struck": Blake, ed., *The Private Papers of Douglas Haig,* pp. 12–13.

177 "that son of a bitch": Mead, *The Doughboys,* p. 99.

178 "Even this war can't keep it out": Ibid., p. 111.

178 The chemistry between artist and subject: Ibid., pp. 111–112; Thomas Fleming, "Iron General."

18: "OVER THERE"

180 It was as if: Leed, *No Man's Land,* p. 99.

180 "no intention of entering": Panichas and Read, *Promise of Greatness,* p. 8.

180 "If you stood on the platform": R. G. Dixon, *The Wheels of Darkness,* p. 26.

180 "A steam saw was cutting": Hannah, ed., *The Great War Reader,* p. 86.

181 "If a careful search": O'Shea, *Back to the Front,* p. 43.

182 "faint, long, sobbing moans": Keegan, *The First World War,* p. 364.

182 "An amusing part": IWM, Cude, *Diary,* p. 77.

182 "Fritz commenced shelling": Brown, *The Western Front,* pp. 202–203.

182 "I miss the theatre": IWM, Cude, *Diary,* p. 97.

183 "I move off": Ibid., p. 77.

184 *"Nichts essen, nichts trinken"*: Keegan, *The First World War,* pp. 363–364.

184 "Did I really": Winter, *Death's Men,* p. 228.

185 "ever since I have been": Brown, *The First World War,* pp. 70–71.

186 "He is twenty-three": Bird, *Ghosts Have Warm Hands,* p. 123.

186 "He told me that": Ibid., p. 30.

187 "Major General Lipsett": Ibid., pp. 20–21.

187 "One for every week": Panichas and Read, *Promise of Greatness,* p. 150.

189 "If people really knew": Knightley, *The First Casualty,* p. 109.

189 "The soldiers were beating": Panichas and Read, *Promise of Greatness,* p. 564.

190 "Say lootenant": Ibid., pp. 78–79.

190 "It was better in France": Chapman, *A Passionate Prodigality,* p. 139.

191 "We'd always been told": Brown, *The First World War,* p. 223.

191 Tommies were dying: John Ellis and Michael Cox, *The World War I Databook,* p. 270.

192 "Thirteen days": Wilbur C. Peterson, *Memories of Rainbow,* p. 2.

192 "I think they marched": Baker, "Oatmeal and Coffee," pp. 50–51.

193 "The Germans were": Jensen, *The War Log of an Underdog,* p. 83.

193 "into the war too late": Bullard, *Personalities and Reminiscences of the War,* pp. 86–87.

194 "They looked larger": Brittain, *Testament of Youth,* pp. 420–421.

194 The Americans were pouring: Mead, *The Doughboys,* pp. 125–126.

195 "He would calmly advise": William S. Triplet, *A Youth in the Meuse-Argonne*, p. 56.

196 The 16th Infantry Regiment: Stallings, *The Story of the Doughboys*, p. 24.

198 "Here lie the first soldiers": Harries, *The Last Days of Innocence*, pp. 4–5.

199 "As he spoke to me": Binding, *A Fatalist at War*, p. 196.

199 "to have a good look": Ibid., p. 145.

19: "IF THIS IS OUR COUNTRY, THEN THIS IS OUR WAR"

202 To launch that attack: Sub-committee 3, pp. 1837–1838.

202 the attack order remained: Ibid., 1834–1835.

203 "If this is our country": Miller, *Kelly Miller's History of the World War for Human Rights*, p. 541.

204 "General Pershing is in some doubt": USAWW, vol. 2, p. 413.

204 "Our government seemed": Bullard, *Personalities and Reminiscences of the War*, pp. 292–298.

205 "The 92nd Division (colored)": Charles D. Rhodes, *Diary of the World War*, p. 56.

205 "I'se gwin to buy me": Mead, *The Doughboys*, pp. 76–77.

206 "Don't worry about me": Theodore Roosevelt, Jr., *Rank and File*, pp. 111–113.

206 "Reports in hand": Miller, *Kelly Miller's History of the World War for Human Rights*, p. 532.

207 "had twice run away": Bullard, *Personalities and Reminiscences of the War*, pp. 292–293.

208 "How to Stop the War": Chester D. Heywood, *Negro Combat Troops in the World War*, pp. 212–213.

208 "During seven months": Ibid., p. 228.

208 "one of absolute horror": Sub-committee 3, p. 1837.

209 "I at once put every agency": Ibid., p. 1805.

209 The 366th's advance from: Ibid., pp. 1809–1810.

20: LUDENDORFF'S GRAND GAMBLE

210 "We are just": Ernst Kielmeyer, *Diary of Ernst Kielmeyer* (unnumbered).

214 He intended first to hit: Woods, *Colossal Blunders of the War*, p. 101.

214 "The enemy is rather threatening": Blake, ed., *The Private Papers of Douglas Haig*, p. 294.

214 "I have never seen him": Toland, *No Man's Land*, p. 47.

215 "can only mean": Kielmeyer, *Diary of Ernst Kielmeyer* (unnumbered).

215 "you can't put a lot": Keegan, *The First World War*, p. 398.

216 "The overpowering desire": Toland, *No Man's Land*, pp. 15, 21.

217 "Gentlemen, a great victory": Ibid., p. 254.

217 Ludendorff pressed on: Westwall, *World War I Day by Day*, p. 160.

218 "naturally, he is Ludendorff's son": Toland, *No Man's Land*, p. 57.

218 "He shows it off": Binding, *A Fatalist at War*, p. 160.

218 "My old enthusiasm": Sulzbach, *With the German Guns*, p. 165.

219 Mass surrender: Ferguson, *The Pity of War*, p. 372.

219 "Such an action": Fussell, *The Great War and Modern Memory*, pp. 177–178.

220 "volunteering for the most difficult": Toland, *No Man's Land*, p. 272.

220 "run around": Binding, *A Fatalist at War*, pp. 56–59.

222 The feisty seventy-six-year-old French premier: Taylor, *The First World War*, pp. 203–204.

222 "Perhaps, but I never fought": Bullard, *Personalities and Reminiscences of the War*, p. 155.

222 "I will fight": Churchill, *Great Contemporaries*, p. 199.

223 "To All Ranks": Brittain, *Testament of Youth*, pp. 419–420.

223 "I began to see": Binding, *A Fatalist at War*, pp. 209–210.

224 By April 29, Ludendorff's advance: O'Shea, *Back to the Front*, p. 180.

21: "A GERMAN BULLET IS CLEANER THAN A WHORE"

225 "large numbers": *USAWW*, vol. 12, p. 223.

226 "American nurses, pretty, trim": Joseph N. Rizzi, *Joe's War*, p. 140.

227 "began stripping off": Bird, *Ghosts Have Warm Hands*, pp. 23, 57.

228 "most of the Americans mistake": Jensen, *War Log of an Underdog*, pp. 111, 145, 164–165.

229 "Officers are not permitted": Mead, *The Doughboys*, p. 201.

229 "who could not have continued": Bullard, *Personalities and Reminiscences*, p. 183.

230 "The man who enlists": James E. Agate, *L. of C.*, pp. 16–17.

22: BAPTISM IN CANTIGNY

231 Should he fight on?: ABMC, p. 515.

232 "The division commander definitely": Sub-committee 3, p. 1824.

232 "I felt, since the Armistice": Ibid., p. 1801.

233 "I stopped our machine gun": Ibid., p. 1825.

233 "We never knew": Mead, *The Doughboys*, pp. 160–161.

234 "It's the orders you disobey": Manchester, *American Caesar*, p. 101.

235 "hard for me to conceive": Ibid., p. 94.

235 "a bully fellow": Hugh Ogden, Papers, MHI (unnumbered).

235 "Father, why didn't you": Duffy, *Father Duffy's Story*, p. 81.

236 "Every man in the town": Ibid., pp. 68–69.

237 "but my chiefest joy": Ibid., p. 96.

237 "Our bodies were burnt": Freidel, *Over There*, pp. 102–103.

237 "They lay as they fell": Toland, *No Man's Land*, p. 122.

238 "be handed down": Brown, *The First World War*, p. 76.

238 "One after another": Duffy, *Father Duffy's Story*, p. 75.

238 "He performed a dance": Ernst H. Hinrichs, *Listening Post*, p. 51.

239 "The Jerries were laughing": Triplet, *A Youth in the Meuse-Argonne*, p. 98.

239 "Illiteracy, while not essential": Ibid., p. 263.

240 "a long column of men": Dixon, *The Wheels of Darkness*, pp. 64–66.

240 "We had the Americans": Teilhard de Chardin, *The Making of a Mind*, p. 218.

241 "great self-contained American Army": Blake, ed., *The Private Papers of Douglas Haig*, p. 307.

241 "I remembered the tradition": Bullard, *Personalities and Reminiscences of the War*, p. 141.

242 "The notion that": Jünger, *The Storm of Steel*, p. 98.
242 "When the wind is right": Mead, *The Doughboys*, p. 237.
242 "Back in America": James T. Duane, *Dear Old "K,"* pp. 67–68.
244 "the Million Dollar Raid": Ibid., pp. 69–71.
244 "My Dear Mother": Balbino R. Flores, *The New York State "Boys" in the World War*, p. 31.
245 "We would have to hold out": Panichas and Read, *Promise of Greatness*, pp. 94–95.

23: "DO YOU WANT TO LIVE FOREVER?"
246 "The news from the front": Binding, *A Fatalist at War*, pp. 244–245.
247 "Should the Americans": ABMC, p. 49.
248 "the best brigade": Toland, *No Man's Land*, p. 278.
248 "great strapping fellows": Holmes, *The Western Front*, p. 203.
248 "plodding their way back": Toland, *No Man's Land*, p. 278.
249 "Come on you sons of bitches!": Mead, *The Doughboys*, pp. 246–247.
249 "Hey, Pop": Elton S. Mackin, *Suddenly We Didn't Want to Die*, pp. 17–18.
250 "Fix bayonets!": Ibid., p. 28.
250 "Have you ever watched": Ibid., pp. 20, 55.
251 "Want the job, son?": Ibid., pp. 68–69.
251 "We had to go out": Mead, *The Doughboys*, pp. 249–250.
252 "The 2nd American Division": ABMC, p. 31.
252 "If those in front of us": Mead, *The Doughboys*, p. 252.

24. "I DON'T EXPECT TO SEE ANY OF YOU AGAIN"
254 "Rumors of enemy capitulation": Stanley Weintraub, *A Stillness Heard Round the World*, p. 95.
256 "Armistice signed and takes effect": RG 120, Boxes 30, 31.
256 "We spent our nights": Albertine, *The Yankee Doughboy*, p. 143.
257 "the finest soldiers": Ibid., pp. 154–155.
258 "We erected our own": Duffy, *Father Duffy's Story*, p. 223.
259 "I have no vision of gods": www.blockhead.com.
261 "I started counting": Baker, "Oatmeal and Coffee," pp. 50–51.
261 "My God!": Triplet, *A Youth in the Meuse-Argonne*, pp. 125–126.
262 "It made my blood tingle": Jensen, *The War Log of an Underdog*, p. 164.
262 "Hurry, here comes the king!": Judy, *A Soldier's Diary*, pp. 118–119.
263 "noisy, hot, airless and bumpy": Brown, *The First World War*, p. 86.
264 "As the sun set": Taylor, *The First World War*, pp. 232–234.
264 "It is sadly tragic": Toland, *No Man's Land*, p. 346.
265 "continues to be a mystery": Harries, *The Last Days of Innocence*, p. 276.
265 "Their attacks were undoubtedly brave": Mead, *The Doughboys*, p. 189.
265 "Many German people": Fritz Nagel, *Fritz: The World War I Memoirs of a German Lieutenant*, pp. 96–97.
266 "the capacity for leadership": Toland, *No Man's Land*, p. 381.

25: "DO YOU WISH TO TAKE PART IN THIS BATTLE?"

268 "infantry, artillery, aviation": ABMC, p. 26.

268 "Do you wish to take part": Fleming, "Iron General," p. 70.

269 "a shave and a haircut": RG 407, p. 264.

269 "those army meals": A. Draper Dewees, *Fifth Corps Headquarters*, p. 29.

270 "with a single cupful": Peterson, *Memories of Rainbow*, p. 7.

272 "get out and dash": Joel, *Under the Lorraine Cross*, p. 72.

272 "Germany and her allies": *Current History, The New York Times*, October 1918, p. 131.

273 "We few fellows cannot hold up": MHI, 42nd Division Intelligence Summary, September 1918.

273 "five hundred shots": Mead, *The Doughboys*, p. 296.

274 "Last night was satisfactory": Rhodes, *Diary of the World War*, p. 43.

274 "Wave after wave of Europeans": Don Smythe, *Pershing: General of the Armies*, pp. 186–187.

275 "I had lots of fun": Jensen, *The War Log of an Underdog*, pp. 182–187.

276 "I have found out": Dewees, *Fifth Corps Headquarters*, p. 166.

277 "We stood and talked": Manchester, *American Caesar*, p. 115.

26: A CIVILIZED END TO POINTLESS SLAUGHTER

278 "the utter desolation": Clarence Johnson, *The History of the 321st Infantry*, pp. 42–43.

279 "You will advance": RG 120, Boxes 30, 31.

279 "Runners finally managed": Sub-committee 3, p. 1820.

280 "At 5:22 A.M.": MHI, Letter, Sterling Chesson to Fred Chesson, December 13, 1918.

280 The attackers ran up: ABMC, pp. 374–379.

281 "The prevailing impression": *Current History, The New York Times*, December 1918, pp. 481–483.

281 The Foch strategy: ABMC, pp. 167–170.

282 "our officers . . . arrogant": Mead, *The Doughboys*, pp. 191–192.

283 "which is reasonable": Dewees, *Fifth Corps Headquarters*, pp. 93–94.

283 "Let me assure you": Flores, *The New York State "Boys" in the World War*, p. 29.

283 "We are very proud": MHI, Letter, Mrs. Carleton Simon to Carleton Simon, Jr., September 18, 1918.

283 "I have not heard": Judy, *A Soldier's Diary*, p. 125.

284 "We give away": Jensen, *The War Log of an Underdog*, p. 243.

285 "ass over head": Rizzi, *Joe's War*, pp. 81–82.

285 "It just came out": Albertine, *The Yankee Doughboy*, p. 221.

285 "It's odd": Triplet, *A Youth in the Meuse-Argonne*, p. 195.

286 "wild Irish and German Catholics": Ferrell, ed., *The Autobiography of Harry S Truman*, p. 46.

286 "He was a banty officer": Stallings, *The Story of the Doughboys*, pp. 133–134.

287 "They fly around": "World War I Letters from Harry to Bess," October 8, 1918, www.whistlestop.org.

287 "A single bullet took him": Triplet, *A Youth in the Meuse-Argonne*, pp. 204, 225–226.

289 After a week of fighting: Fleming, "Iron General," p. 71.

289 "The papers are in the street": "World War I Letters from Harry to Bess," October 6, 1918, www.whistlestop.org.

289 "at a time of success": Keegan, *The First World War*, p. 412.

290 "It was plain the situation": Hindenburg, *Out of My Life*, p. 322.

290 "Ludendorff stood up": Oberst von Thaer, Diary Notes, October 1, 1918, www.lib.byu.edu.

27: A PLAGUE IN THE TRENCHES

293 "Our boys just went down": Doughboy Center, Great War Society, wfa-usa.org, pp. 1–6.

293 "Every time a head": Stallings, *The Story of the Doughboys*, p. 158.

294 "Go to Hell": ABMC, pp. 337, 362–365.

294 "rushed on machine-gun nests": Thomas A. Britten, *American Indians in World War I*, p. 181.

295 "with the same emotions": Ibid., p. 100.

295 "little gun shoot fast": Ibid., pp. 106–107.

296 "he had been caught": Mackin, *Suddenly We Didn't Want to Die*, pp. 198, 208.

297 "Way up to the North": Ibid., pp. 226–227.

297 "Give me Châtillon": Manchester, *American Caesar*, p. 119.

298 "On a field where courage": Ibid., p. 120.

298 "There's nothing to it": Duffy, *Father Duffy's Story*, p. 235.

299 "Come on, we'll have them": Ibid., p. 271.

301 "I'm glad you fellows": Mackin, *Suddenly We Didn't Want to Die*, pp. 112–113.

301 "Yet that damned Boche": George S. Patton Papers, Box 60, Library of Congress.

302 "It was unpleasant amputating": Freidel, *Over There*, p. x.

302 "Rejection was almost regarded": Panichas and Read, *Promise of Greatness*, p. 198.

303 "God in his mercy": RG 407, p. 169.

303 Plague struck in 1918: Joseph E. Persico, "The Great Swine Flu Epidemic," pp. 28, 81–82; Richard Collier, *The Plague of the Spanish Lady*, p. 305.

304 "I can never forget": Panichas and Read, *Promise of Greatness, p.* 201.

305 "Every such soldier": Persico, "The Great Swine Flu Epidemic," p. 83.

28: "VICTIMS WHO WILL DIE IN VAIN"

306 "Standing on the running boards": Hugh Cecil and Peter Liddle, *At the Eleventh Hour*, p. 85.

307 "Ask these gentlemen": Weintraub, *A Stillness Heard Round the World*, p. 53.

308 "numerous victims": Ibid., p. 56.

308 "For God's sake": Toland, *No Man's Land*, p. 252.

309 "Their request is an acknowledgment": RG 120, Boxes 30–31.

309 "would jeopardize the moral position": USAWW, pp. 29–30.

310 "Admiral, may I use that?": *Washington Evening Star,* November 11, 1925; Toland, *No Man's Land,* pp. 457–458.

311 "I am ashamed to say": "World War I Letters from Harry to Bess," November 1, 1918, www.whistlestop.org.

312 "I'd learned in the Argonne": Triplet, *A Youth in the Meuse-Argonne,* pp. 245, 282.

312 "My job is keeping me": Dewees, *Fifth Corps Headquarters,* pp. 82–83.

313 "I Wore a Tulip": John Brophy with Eric Partride, *The Long Trail,* p. 47.

314 a "military atrocity": ABMC, p. 298.

316 "Some of the simple minded": Nagel, *Fritz: The World War I Memoirs of a German Lieutenant,* pp. 106–107.

316 "no intention of quitting": Weintraub, *A Stillness Heard Round the World,* p. 62.

316 "Your abdication has become": Toland, *No Man's Land,* p. 554.

317 "I shall remain at Spa": Ibid., pp. 558–561.

318 "Treason, gentlemen!": Weintraub, *A Stillness Heard Round the World,* p. 125.

318 "The enemy, disorganized": *The New York Times,* January 11, 1920.

319 "the plenipotentiaries are authorized": Weintraub, *A Stillness Heard Round the World,* p. 153.

29: "WE KNEW THE END COULD NOT BE FAR OFF"

320 Private Louis Harris: "Quiet Graves" Conference, www.shotatdawn.org.

321 "Rumors that an armistice": Weintraub, *A Stillness Heard Round the World,* p. 78.

321 "No parson was present": IWM, Cude, *Diary,* pp. 86, 198.

322 "It was all the harder": Freidel, *Over There,* p. 201.

323 "an oddly assorted crew": Flores, *The New York State "Boys" in the World War,* p. 38.

323 "would contemplate the provisioning": Weintraub, *A Stillness Heard Round the World,* pp. 156–157.

324 "The discipline of the troops": USAWW, p. 61.

325 "What an enormous difference": Weintraub, *A Stillness Heard Round the World,* p. 176.

325 "to take every advantage": Sub-committee 3, p. 716.

325 "Victory is at hand": Norman Archibald, *Heaven High Hell Deep,* p. 323.

326 "a typical American 'grandstand' finish": Weintraub, *A Stillness Heard Round the World,* p. 102.

30: "PASS THE WORD. CEASE FIRE AT ELEVEN!"

327 Brigadier General John Sherburne: Sub-committee 3, pp. 1834–1837.

328 "I won't die": Toland, *No Man's Land,* p. 576.

329 "half-sitting, half-crouching": Panichas and Read, *Promise of Greatness,* p. 297.

329 "11th November, we are staggered": IWM, Cude, *Diary,* p. 201.

330 "under angelic protection": Weintraub, *A Stillness Heard Round the World,* p. 214.

330 "Hearty congratulations": Rhodes, *Diary of the World War*, pp. 68, 56.
331 "that I wore no helmet": Manchester, *American Caesar*, p. 124.
332 "I am sure you will understand": Rhodes, *Diary of the World War*, p. 76.
333 "There was a big operation": Sub-committee 3, p. 2181.
334 "the division had been": RG 120, Boxes 30, 31.
335 "never be beaten": *The New York Times*, November 13, 1918.
335 "We see no reason": Mead, *The Doughboys*, p. 339.
336 "This offensive would have cut": Sub-committee 3, p. 218.

31: "LITTLE SHORT OF MURDER"
338 "Reaching the front": *The New York Times*, November 14, 1918.
338 "Litter bearers! Hurry!": Albertine, *The Yankee Doughboy*, pp. 228–229.
339 "I hurried over": Freidel, *Over There*, p. 217.
340 The end did not arrive: Christina Holstein, *Western Front Association Bulletin*, no. 53, February 1999.
341 "I gave instructions": Sub-committee 3, pp. 1753–1761; RG 120, Boxes 30, 31.
342 "The foe was": Sub-committee 3, p. 2352.
342 "Jensen, I'm coming": Jensen, *The War Log of an Underdog*, p. 263.
343 "My good sir": Weintraub, *A Silence Heard Round the World*, p. 171.
344 "synonymous with the fall of Metz": Sub-committee 3, pp. 1972–1973.
345 "to stop the advance": RG 120, Boxes 30, 31.
345 "Our regimental wireless": MHI, *History of the 55th Field Artillery Brigade*, p. 172.
345 "The war has twenty-three minutes": Weintraub, *A Stillness Heard Round the World*, p. 204.
346 "directed strong patrols": USAWW, pp. 459–460; ABMC, pp. 395–397.
347 "I regarded this fighting": Alden Brooks, *As I Saw It*, pp. 294–295.

32: THE FATE OF PRIVATE GUNTHER
349 "We saw you going": Rose Coombs, *Before Endeavors Fade*, p. 436.
350 "to those who were killed": Pitt, *1918: The Last Act*, p. 269.
350 "The reasons Mons was taken": Weintraub, *A Stillness Heard Round the World*, pp. 209–210.
351 Sergeant Powell would never: *Baltimore Sun*, March 9, 1969.
351 "The guns are so hot": Weintraub, *A Stillness Heard Round the World*, p. 204.
352 "I fired 164 rounds": "World War I Letters from Harry to Bess," www.whistlestop.org, November 11, 1918.
352 "We've had 'em!": Cecil and Liddle, *At the Eleventh Hour*, p. 102.
353 "It was a chap": Weintraub, *A Stillness Heard Round the World*, p. 177.
353 "dumbly, as if in a dream": Emerson Taylor, *New England in France, 1917–1919*, pp. 276–277.
353 "and prayed and thanked": Albertine, *The Yankee Doughboy*, pp. 233–235.
354 "sounded like a death sentence": F. C. Reynolds, *The 115th Infantry U.S.A in the World War*, p. 164.

354 "We didn't know": Peterson, *Memories of Rainbow,* p. 8.
354 "arrangement is an armistice only": *USAWW,* p. 400.
354 "intercourse with the enemy": Dewees, *Fifth Corps Headquarters,* pp. 88 89.
356 "foolish affair": MHI, *History of the 55th Field Artillery Brigade,* p. 173.
356 "didn't seem pleased": Toland, *No Man's Land,* p. 580.
356 "I felt excited": Ibid., p. 557.
357 "We had accumulated": Richards, *Old Soldiers Never Die,* pp. 200–201.
357 "The war produced": Panichas and Read, *Promise of Greatness,* p. 84.
357 "wild-eyed, white": Bird, *Ghosts Have Warm Hands,* pp. 220–221.
358 "piercing in my sockets": Toland, *Adolf Hitler,* p. 70.
359 "It became impossible": Ibid., p. xix.
360 "I was therefore": Sub-committee 3, p. 1813.
360 "complaining of failure": RG 120, Boxes 30, 31.
360 The last deaths of the Great War: Weintraub, *A Stillness Heard Round the World,* p. 173.
361 He finally learned: *General Aviation News,* December 5, 2003, p. 50; Bourne, *Who's Who in World War I,* p. 170.

33: "THIS FATEFUL MORNING CAME AN END TO ALL WARS"
362 "The bloody war's over!": Malcolm Brown, *1918: Year of Victory,* p. 285.
363 "sleek, well fed officers": Panichas and Read, *Promise of Greatness,* p. 296.
363 "Well, for lawd's sake": RG 407, History, 318th Infantry Regiment, Box 34.
363 "When getting ready": Hugh Ogden, Papers, MHI, p. 68.
364 "In a twinkling of an eye": *The New York Times,* November 14, 1918.
364 "Now we shall have time": Holmes, *The Western Front,* p. 287.
365 "I saw he had": Heber Blankenhorn, *Adventures in Propaganda,* pp. 139–140.
365 "to shut out the world": Panichas and Read, *Promise of Greatness,* p. 180.
366 "You are entitled": *The New York Times,* November 13, 1918.
366 "With you, I rejoice": *The New York Times,* November 12, 1918.
366 "You are in trouble": Toland, *No Man's Land,* p. 593.
367 "Brittain, Brittain": Brittain, *Testament of Youth,* p. 461.
367 "there came the sudden": Ibid., pp. 438–440, 462–463.
369 "Poor Bill. Rest in Pieces": *The New York Times,* November 12, 1918.
370 "in which the working class": Koettgen, trans., *A German Deserter's War Experience,* p. xxiv.
371 "I think there should be": Clifton Daniel, *Chronicle of the 20th Century,* p. 245.
372 "We are the dividends of war": Jensen, *War Log of an Underdog,* p. 264.
372 "We can but hope": Carlo d'Este, *A Genius for War,* pp. 270–271.
373 "We learned that the French": Rizzi, *Joe's War,* p. 123.
373 "would get drunk": Triplet, *A Youth in the Meuse-Argonne,* pp. 282–284.
373 "If only they had given us": Harries, *The Last Days of Innocence,* p. 421; Fleming, "The Iron General."
374 "The armistice should have": Weintraub, *A Stillness Heard Round the World,* p. 175.

34: GREATER LOSSES THAN ON D-DAY

375 "my face so swollen": Warner A. Ross, *My Colored Battalion*, pp. 78–79.

376 "Near the small bridge": Clarence Richmond, www.en.com/users/robin/wardiary/diary21.html.

376 Similar discrepancies: Sub-committee 3, pp. 1824–1825, 1850; RG 120, Boxes 30, 31.

377 "A huge grave": L. M. Zimmerman, *Echoes from the Distant Battle-field*, p. 58.

377 "I had always believed"; Duffy, *Father Duffy's Story*, p. 304.

378 "A great throng of people": Beresford Topp, *The 42nd Battalion, CEF,* p. 296.

378 According to the most conservative: See Appendix for sources of casualty figures.

378 Putting these losses into perspective: Chambers, *The Oxford Companion to American Military History*, p. 203.

379 Throughout four years of war: Ellis and Cox, *The World War I Databook*, pp. 269–270.

379 "A Soldier of the Great War": O'Shea, *Back to the Front*, p. 52.

380 In France, the war created: Knightley, *The First Casualty*, p. 109; Keegan, *The First World War*, pp. 6–7.

381 "If the people knew": Knightley, *The First Casualty*, p. 109.

381 "It was not until the dawn": Winston Churchill, *The Gathering Storm*, pp. 38–39.

381 "at the faces": Joseph E. Persico, *Roosevelt's Secret War*, p. 279.

381 "My dear Daddy": Winter, *Death's Men*, pp. 224, 263.

381 "Horror and discomfort": Charles Edmonds, *A Subaltern's War*, pp. 194–200.

382 "mad and beyond reckoning": Holmes, *The Western Front*, pp. 16–17.

382 "The atmosphere I feel": Teilhard de Chardin, *The Making of a Mind*, pp. 250–251.

382 So indelible were: Winter, *Death's Men*, pp. 20–21.

383 "trust coupled with": Ibid., p. 223.

383 "It wasn't much": Lyn Macdonald, *To the Last Man*, pp. xv-xvi.

383 "And then there was": Edmonds, *A Subaltern's War*, p. 195.

383 "It's back to the pettiness": Desagneaux, *A French Soldier's War Diary*, p. 104.

384 "It has always been difficult": Dixon, *The Wheels of Darkness* (unnumbered).

384 "You threw four years": Winter, *Death's Men*, p. 247.

384 "Events in retrospect": Panichas and Read, *Promise of Greatness*, p. 293.

35: "ONLY THE DEAD HAVE SEEN THE END OF WAR"

385 "On a map of Europe"; Taylor, *The First World War*, p. 279.

386 "tragic and unnecessary": Keegan, *The First World War*, p. 3.

386 "Looking back": www.worldwar1.com/peden/history.htm.

388 "The soldier at the front": Weintraub, *A Stillness Heard Round the World*, pp. 195–196, 325.

388 "It cannot be": Keegan, *The First World War,* p. 3.

390 "Do you remember the rats": Hart-Davis, ed., *War Poems of Siegfried Sassoon,* p. 143.

EPILOGUE: MARCHING HOME

391 "There were 615 gold stars": Martin J. Hogan, *The Shamrock Battalion of the Rainbow,* p. 279.

391 "These Negroes have helped": Reid Badger, *A Life in Ragtime,* pp. 4–5.

392 When the shouting faded: *Times Union* (Albany, N.Y.), February 10, 2002.

395 "I believe that the value": James McWilliams and R. James Steel, *Amiens: Dawn of Victory,* pp. 273–274.

399 In 1955, a powerful explosion: O'Shea, *Back to the Front,* p. 52; Fussell, *The Great War and Modern Memory,* p. 14.

BIBLIOGRAPHY

BOOKS

Agate, James E. *L. of C.* London: Constable and Company Ltd., 1917.

Albertine, Connell. *The Yankee Doughboy.* Boston: Branden Press, 1968.

Archibald, Norman. *Heaven High Hell Deep.* New York: Albert and Charles Boni, 1935.

Ayres, Leonard P. *The War with Germany: A Statistical Summary.* Washington, D.C.: U.S. Government Printing Office, 1919.

Babbington, Anthony. *For the Sake of Example: Capital Courts-Martial, 1914–1920.* London: Secker and Warburg, 1983.

Badger, Reid. *A Life in Ragtime.* New York: Oxford University Press, 1995.

Barber, J. Frank. *History of the Seventy-ninth Division, A.E.F., During the World War.* Lancaster, Pa.: Steinman and Steinman, 1922.

Barbusse, Henri, translated by Brian Rhys. *I Saw It Myself.* New York: E. P. Dutton and Company, 1929.

———, translated by Fitzwater Wray. *Under Fire.* New York: E. P. Dutton and Company, 1917.

Barzun, Jacques. *From Dawn to Decadence: 500 Years of Western Cultural Life.* New York: HarperCollins, 2000.

Benwell, Harry A. *History of the Yankee Division.* Boston: Cornhill Company, 1921.

Binding, Rudolf, translated by Ian F. D. Morrow. *A Fatalist at War.* Boston: Houghton Mifflin, 1929.

Bird, Will R. *The Communications Trench.* Toronto: CEF Books, 2000.

———. *Ghosts Have Warm Hands.* Toronto: Clark, Irwin & Company, 1968.

Bishop, Alan, and Mark Bostridge, eds. *Letters from a Lost Generation: The First World War Letters of Vera Brittain and Four Friends.* Boston: Northeastern University Press, 1998.

Blackburne, Harry W. *This Also Happened on the Western Front*. London: Houghter and Stoddard, 1932.

Blake, Robert, ed. *The Private Papers of Douglas Haig, 1914–1919*. London: Eyre and Spottiswoode, 1952.

Blankenhorn, Heber. *Adventures in Propaganda*. Boston and New York: Houghton Mifflin Company, 1919.

Bourne, J. M. *Who's Who in World War One*. London and New York: Routledge, 2001.

Brittain, Vera. *Testament of Youth: An Autobiographical Study of the Years 1900–1925*. New York: Macmillan, 1935.

Britten, Thomas A. *American Indians in World War I*. Albuquerque: University of New Mexico Press, 1997.

Brooke, Geoffrey. *The Brotherhood of Arms*. London: William Clowes and Sons, 1941.

Brooks, Alden. *As I Saw It*. New York: Alfred A. Knopf, 1930.

Brophy, John, with Eric Partridge. *The Long Trail*. New York: André Deutsch, 1965.

Brown, Malcolm. *The Imperial War Museum Book of the First World War*. Norman: University of Oklahoma Press, 1991.

———. *1918: Year of Victory*. London: Sidgwick and Jackson, 1998.

———. *The Western Front*. London: Pan Books, 1993.

Bullard, Robert Lee. *Personalities and Reminiscences of the War*. Garden City, N.Y.: Doubleday, Page and Company, 1925.

Cecil, Hugh, and Peter Liddle. *At the Eleventh Hour: Reflections, Hopes and Anxieties at the Closing of the Great War, 1918*. South Yorkshire, U.K.: Leo Cooper, 1998.

Chambers, John Whiteclay, ed. *The Oxford Companion to American Military History*. New York: Oxford University Press, 1999.

Chapman, Guy. *A Passionate Prodigality*. New York: Holt, Rinehart and Winston, 1966.

Churchill, Winston. *Great Contemporaries*. New York: W.W. Norton and Company, 1990.

———. *The Second World War*. Vol. 1, *The Gathering Storm*. Boston: Houghton Mifflin, 1948.

Clark, Alan. *The Donkeys*. New York: William Morrow & Company, 1962.

Clouting, Benjamin. *Tickled to Death to Go: Memoirs of a Cavalryman in the First World War*. Staplehurst, U.K.: Spellmount, 1996.

Coffman, Edward M. *The War to End All Wars: The American Experience in World War I*. New York: Oxford University Press, 1968.

Coombs, Rose E. B. *Before Endeavours Fade*. London: Battle of Britain Prints, 1986.

Collier, Richard. *The Plague of the Spanish Lady*. New York: Atheneum, 1974.

Corrigall, D. J. *The History of the Twentieth Canadian Battalion*. Toronto: Stone and Cox, 1935.

Daniel, Clifton. *Chronicle of the 20th Century*. Mount Kisco, N.Y.: Chronicle, 1987.

Davis, Henry Blaine, Jr. *Generals in Khaki*. Raleigh, N.C.: Pentland Press, 1998.

Desagneaux, Henri, edited by Jean Desagneaux, translated by Godfrey J. Adams. *A French Soldier's War Diary*. Morley, Yorkshire: Elmfield Press, 1975.

d'Este, Carlo. *A Genius for War*. New York: HarperCollins, 1995.

Dienst, Charles F. *History of the 353rd Infantry Regiment*. Chicago: 353rd Infantry Society, 1921.

Dolden, A. Stuart. *Cannon Fodder: An Infantryman's Life on the Western Front, 1914–1918*. Dorset, England: Blanford Press, 1980.

Duane, James T. *Dear Old "K."* Boston: Thomas Todel Company, 1922.

Duffy, Francis P. *Father Duffy's Story*. New York: George H. Doran Company, 1919.

Edelman, Bernard. *Centenarians: The Story of the 20th Century by the Americans Who Lived It*. New York: Farrar, Straus & Giroux, 1999.

Edmonds, Charles. *A Subaltern's War*. New York: Minton, Balch & Co., 1930.

Ellis, John, and Michael Cox. *The World War I Databook*. London: Aurum Press, 1993.

English, George H., Jr. *History of the 89th Division*. War Society of the 89th Division. Denver: Smith-Brooks Printing, 1920.

Farwell, Byron. *Over There: The United States in the Great War*. New York: W. W. Norton and Company, 1999.

Feilding, Rowland. *War Letters to a Wife*. London: Medici Society, 1929.

Ferguson, Niall. *The Pity of War*. New York: Basic Books, 1999.

Ferrell, Robert H., ed. *The Autobiography of Harry S Truman*. Boulder, Colo.: Colorado Associated Press, 1980.

Flores, Balbino R. *The New York State "Boys" in the World War*. Albany: New York State Department of Education, 1935.

Freidel, Frank. *Over There: The Story of America's First Great Overseas Crusade*. Philadelphia: Temple University Press, 1990.

Fussell, Paul. *The Great War and Modern Memory*. New York and London: Oxford University Press, 1975.

Hallas, James H. *Doughboy War: The American Expeditionary Force in World War I*. London: Lynne Rienner Publishers, 2000.

Hannah, James, ed. *The Great War Reader*. College Station: Texas A & M University Press, 2000.

Harlowe, Jerry. *Your Brother Will*. Ellicott City, Md.: Patapsco Falls Press, 1992.

Harries, Meirion and Susie. *The Last Days of Innocence: America at War, 1917–1918*. New York: Random House, 1997.

Hart-Davis, Rupert, ed. *War Poems of Siegfried Sassoon*. London: Faber and Faber, 1983.

Hastings, Max, ed. *The Oxford Book of Military Anecdotes*. New York: Oxford University Press, 1986.

Harvey, J. R. *The History of the 5th (Royal Irish) Regiment of Dragoons*. Aldershot, England: Gale and Polden, 1923.

Hermanns, William. *The Holocaust: From a Survivor of Verdun*. New York: Harper and Row, 1972.

Heywood, Chester D. *Negro Combat Troops in the World War: The Story of the 371st Infantry*. New York: AMS Press, 1969.

Hogan, Martin J. *The Shamrock Battalion of the Rainbow: A Story of the "Fighting Sixty-Ninth."* New York: D. Appleton and Company, 1919.

Holmes, Richard. *The Western Front*. New York: TV Books, 1999.

Housman, Laurence, ed. *War Letters of Fallen Englishmen*. London: Victor Gollancz, 1930.

Jennings, Peter, and Todd Brewster. *The Century*. New York: Doubleday, 1998.

Joel, Arthur H. *Under the Lorraine Cross*. Lansing, Mich.: privately published, 1921.

Johnson, Clarence Walton. *The History of the 321st Infantry*. Columbia, S.C.: R. P. Bryan Company, 1919.

Judy, Will. *A Soldier's Diary*. Chicago: Judy Publishing Company, 1930.

Jünger, Ernst. *The Storm of Steel*. London: Chatto and Windus, 1929.

Keegan, John. *The Face of Battle*. New York: Viking Press, 1976.

———. *The First World War*. New York: Alfred A. Knopf, 1999.

Kendall, Harry. *A New York Actor on the Western Front*. Boston: Christopher Publishing House, 1932.

Knightley, Phillip. *The First Casualty*. New York and London: Harcourt Brace Jovanovich, 1975.

Koettgen, J., trans. (author anonymous). *A German Deserter's War Experience*. New York: B. W. Heubsch, 1917.

Kreisler, Fritz. *Four Weeks in the Trenches: The War Story of a Violinist*. Boston and New York: Houghton Mifflin, 1915.

Kress, John W. *The Great Adventure*. Privately published, 1962.

Leed, Eric J. *No Man's Land: Combat and Identity in World War I*. London: Cambridge University Press, 1979.

Lunt, James. *The Scarlet Lancers*. London: Leo Cooper, 1993.

Macdonald, Lyn. *To the Last Man: Spring 1918*. New York: Carroll and Graf, 1998.

Mackin, Elton S. *Suddenly We Didn't Want to Die*. Novato, Calif.: Presidio, 1993.

Manchester, William. *American Caesar*. New York: Dell, 1978.

Massie, Robert K. *Dreadnought*. New York: Random House, 1991.

McClintock, Alexander. *Best O'Luck*. Ottawa: CEF Books, 2000.

McCullough, David. *Truman*. New York: Simon and Schuster, 1992.

McWilliams, James, and R. James Steel. *Amiens: Dawn of Victory*. Toronto: Dundurn Press, 2001.

Mead, Gary. *The Doughboys: America and the First World War*. Woodstock and New York: Overlook Press, 2000.

Miller, Kelly. *Kelly Miller's History of the World War for Human Rights*. Unpublished manuscript, 1919.

Muller, E. Lester. *The 313th of the 79th in the World War*. Baltimore, Md.: Meyer and Thalheimer, 1919.

Nagel, Fritz, edited by Richard A. Baumgartner. *Fritz: The World War I Memoirs of a German Lieutenant*. Huntington, W. Va.: Der Angriff Publications, 1981.

Nicholson, G. W. L. *Canadian Expeditionary Force, 1914–1918*. Ottawa: Queen's Printer, 1964.

O'Shea, Stephen. *Back to the Front: An Accidental Historian Walks the Trenches of World War I*. New York: Walker and Company, 1996.

Palmer, Alan. *Victory 1918.* New York: Atlantic Monthly Press, 1998.

Panichas, George A., edited with Sir Herbert Read. *Promise of Greatness: The War of 1914–1918.* New York: John Day Company, 1968.

Parsons, W. David, *The Spanish Lady and the Newfoundland Regiment.* St. John's, Newfoundland: St. John's Medical History Society, 1992.

Pattullo, George. *Horrors of Moonlight.* New York: Allston and Depew, 1939.

Persico, Joseph E. *Roosevelt's Secret War.* New York: Random House, 2001.

Pitt, Barrie. *1918: The Last Act.* New York: W. W. Norton & Company, 1962.

Powell, Colin L., with Joseph E. Persico. *My American Journey.* New York: Random House, 1995.

Putkowski, Julian, and Julian Sykes. *Shot at Dawn.* London: Leo Cooper, 1989.

Reynolds, F. C. *The 115th Infantry U.S.A. in the World War.* Privately published, 1920.

Richards, Frank. *Old Soldiers Never Die.* London: Berkley Publishing Corporation, 1966.

Rizzi, Joseph N. *Joe's War: Memoirs of a Doughboy.* Huntington, W.Va.: Der Angriff Publications, 1983.

Rohl, John C. G., translated by Jeremy Gaines and Rebecca Wallach. *Young Wilhelm: The Kaiser's Early Life, 1859–1888.* Cambridge, U.K.: Cambridge University Press, 1998.

Roosevelt, Theodore, Jr. *Rank and File: True Stories of the Great War.* New York: Charles Scribner's Sons, 1928.

Ross, Warner A. *My Colored Battalion.* Chicago: Warner A. Ross, 1920.

Sanborn, Joseph B. *The 131st U.S. Infantry in the World War.* Chicago: privately published, 1919.

Sassoon, George, ed. *Siegfried Sassoon: The War Poems.* London: Faber and Faber, 1983.

Schneider, A. *Company E.* Privately published, 1919.

Smith, Harry L., with James R. Eckman. *Memoirs of an Ambulance Company Officer.* Rochester, Minn.: Doomsday Press, 1940.

Stallings, Laurance, condensed and adapted by M. S. Wyeth, Jr., from *The Doughboys. The Story of the Doughboys: The AEF in World War I.* New York: Harper and Row, 1963.

Stevenson, Burton, ed. *The Home Book of Quotations.* New York: Dodd, Mead and Company, 1964.

Stevenson, Frances, edited by A. J. P. Taylor. *Lloyd George: A Diary.* New York: Harper and Row, 1971.

Sulzbach, Herbert, translated by Richard Thonger. *With the German Guns: Four Years on the Western Front, 1914–1918.* Hamden, Conn.: Archon Books, 1981.

Sutliffe, Robert Stewart. *The Seventy-first New York in the World War.* Privately published, 1922.

Taber, John. *The Story of the 168th Infantry.* Iowa City: State Historical Society of Iowa, 1925.

Taylor, A. J. P. *The First World War.* New York: Berkley Publishing Group, 1970.

Taylor, Emerson Gifford. *New England in France, 1917–1919: A History of the 26th Division, USA.* New York and Boston: Houghton Mifflin, 1920.

Teilhard de Chardin, Pierre, translated by René Hague. *The Making of a Mind: Letters from a Soldier Priest.* New York: Harper and Row, 1965.

Thorne, Henry G., Jr. *History of the 313th U.S. Infantry.* New York: Wynkoop Hallenbeck Crawford Company, 1920.

Toland, John. *Adolf Hitler.* Garden City, N.Y.: Doubleday & Co., 1976.

―――. *No Man's Land: 1918, the Last Year of the Great War.* Garden City, N.Y.: Doubleday & Co., 1980.

Topp, Beresford. *The 42nd Battalion, CEF: Royal Highlanders of Canada.* Montreal: Gazette Printing Co., 1931.

Triplet, William S., edited by Robert H. Ferrell *A Youth in the Meuse-Argonne.* Columbia: University of Missouri Press, 2000.

Tucker, Spencer C., with Laura Maiysek Wood and Justin D. Murphy, eds. *The European Powers in the First World War: An Encyclopedia.* New York and London: Garland Publishing, 1996.

Van der Kiste, John. *Kaiser Wilhelm: Germany's Last Emperor.* Stroud, U.K.: Bodman Sutton Publishing Co., 1999.

von Hindenburg, Marshal, translated by F. A. Holt. *Out of My Life.* London: Cassell and Company, 1920.

Ward, Herbert. *Mr Poilu.* London: Hodder and Stoughton, 1916.

Weintraub, Stanley. *A Stillness Heard Round the World.* New York and Oxford: Oxford University Press, 1985.

Westwall, Ian. *World War I Day by Day.* Osceola, Wis.: MBI Publishing Company, 2000.

Williams, Charles H. *Sidelights on Negro Soldiers.* Boston: B. J. Rimmer Company, 1923.

Wilson, Trevor. *The Myriad Faces of War.* Cambridge, England: Polity Press, 1986.

Winter, Denis. *Death's Men: Soldiers of the Great War.* London: Penguin Books, 1979.

Woods, William Seaver. *Colossal Blunders of the War.* New York: Macmillan Company, 1930.

Zimmerman, L. M. *Echoes from the Distant Battlefield.* Boston: Gorham Press, 1920.

ARTICLES

Baker, Kenneth Gearhart. "Oatmeal and Coffee." *Indiana Magazine of History* 97, no. 1 (2001).

Cowley, Robert. "Massacre of the Innocents." *MHQ: The Quarterly Journal of Military History,* spring 1998.

Fleming, Thomas. "Iron General." *MHQ: The Quarterly Journal of Military History* 7, no. 2 (winter 1994).

Frazer, Elizabeth. "The Last Fight." *Saturday Evening Post,* February 8, 1919.

James, Edwin L. "End of War." *Current History, The New York Times,* December 1918.

Paschall, Rod. "The Belfort Ruse." *MHQ: The Quarterly Journal of Military History,* autumn 2002.

Persico, Joseph E. "The Great Swine Flu Epidemic." *American Heritage*, June 1976.

Stevenson, Mathew. "Roads to Sarajevo." *Harper's*, February 2002.

Weintraub, Stanley. "The Christmas Truce." *MHQ. The Quarterly Journal of Military History*, winter 1993.

DOCUMENTS

American Armies and Battlefields in Europe. American Battle Monuments Commission, Washington, D.C.: United States Government Printing Office, 1938.

Les Armées Françaises dans la Grande Guerre. Tome VII, deuxième volume. Paris: Imprimerie Nationale, 1938.

Canada in the First World War. Ottawa, Ont.: Veterans Affairs Canada, 2000.

Cude, Robert. *Diary of Sergeant T. H. Cude*. London: Imperial War Museum.

Dewees, A. Draper. *Fifth Corps Headquarters*. Carlisle, Pa.: U.S. Army Military History Institute (unpublished and undated).

Dixon, R. G. *The Wheels of Darkness*. (unpublished and undated), Imperial War Museum.

Harrison, Lee, Jr. *The Amateur Soldier*. Carlisle, Pa.: U.S. Army Military History Institute (unpublished and undated).

Hearings Before Sub-committee No. 3. Select Committee on Expenditures in the War Department. Vols. 2 and 3. Washington, D.C.: U.S. Government Printing Office, 1920.

Hinrichs, Ernst H. *Listening Post*. Carlisle, Pa.: U.S. Army Military History Institute (unpublished and undated).

History of the Fifty-fifth Field Artillery Brigade. (No author, no publisher), 1920.

In Flanders Field: Museum Guide. Ieper, Belgium, 1998.

Jensen, Arthur E. *The War Log of an Underdog*. Carlisle, Pa.: U.S. Army Military History Institute (unpublished and undated).

Kielmeyer, Ernst. *Diary of Ernst Kielmeyer, 8th Battery, 26th Reserve Field Artillery Regiment*. Carlisle, Pa.: U.S. Army Military History Institute (unpublished and undated).

Ogden, Hugh. Papers. Carlisle, Pa.: U.S. Army Military History Institute (unpublished and undated).

Peterson, Wilbur C. *Memories of Rainbow*. Carlisle, Pa.: U.S. Army Military History Institute (unpublished and undated).

Rhodes, Charles D. *Diary of the World War*. Carlisle, Pa.: U.S. Army Military History Institute (unpublished and undated).

The Second Division: 1917–1919. Newied am Rhein, Germany: Privately published, 1919.

Siepmann, Harry. *Riding with the Guns*. London: Imperial War Museum (unpublished manuscript), 1919.

United States Army in the World War, 1917–1919, Meuse-Argonne Operations. Washington, D.C.: Department of the Army, Historical Division, 1948.

The World War: The 358th Infantry. (No author, publisher, or date.)

INDEX

Afghanistan, 389
African Americans, 163–65, 327–28,
    391–92
    American prejudice against,
        203–8
    casualties of, 375–76
    patriotism of, 164, 203
"Aftermath" (Sassoon), 390
Agate, James, 230
airships, 93
Aisne River offensive, 139
Aitkin, Private, 251
Albertine, Connell, 3–6, 15, 54, 89,
    256–57, 285, 292, 338–39,
    356–57
    first combat experience of, 4–5
Aldous, James, 383
Alexandra, Queen Consort of
    England, 78, 214
Algonquin, 137
All About Eve, 372
Allen, Henry, 334
Allen, Robert, 360
Allenby, Edward, 305
Allies, *see specific countries*
All Quiet on the Western Front
    (Remarque), xix

Alsace-Lorraine, 36, 39, 41, 125, 290,
    364
Alvord, Benjamin, 177
American Battle Monuments
    Commission, 394
American Expeditionary Forces
    (AEF), xv, 133, 156, 313, 314,
    327, 332, 374
    African American troops of, *see*
        African Americans
    arrival in Europe of, 176–77,
        194–95, 225–29
    at Belleau Wood, *see* Belleau Wood,
        Battle of
    in Cantigny offensive, 241–42
    casualties of, 260–61, 296–97, 300,
        331, 380
    Chaumont headquarters of, 177–78
    equipment of, 195
    execution of deserters in, 321
    first artillery fire by, 233
    first combat of, 196–98
    first raid of, 233–34
    German assessment of, 252, 265–66
    hit and run raids by, 242–44
    influenza epidemic in, 303
    Ludendorff's assessment of, 265

American Expeditionary Forces
  (*cont.*)
  in Meuse-Argonne offensive, *see*
    Meuse-Argonne offensive
  Pershing named commander of, 144
  rawness of, 239–40
  songs of, 270
  training of, 195–96
  vice and, 226–29
  in voyage to Europe, 167, 191–94
  see also specific units
Ames, Oliver, 259
Andrée (French civilian), 228
Arab Bureau, British, 120
Archibald, Norman, 325
"Archives of Reason, The," 67
armistice:
  allied opposition to, 308–9
  authorization to sign, 318–19,
    343–44
  celebration of, 350, 363–71
  continued war planning and,
    311–12
  Erzberger mission and, 306–9,
    315–16, 323, 340, 343
  mass desertions and surrenders and,
    323, 329
  Metz offensive and, 311–12, 313,
    324–25
  military careerists' reaction to, 326
  news of, 337–38
  Pershing's opposition to, 308–9,
    324–25, 373–74, 385
  premature celebration of, 310
  prospects for survival and, 321–22
  signing of, 323–24
  terms and conditions of, 307–8,
    323
  Wilhelm II's abdication and,
    315–18
Army Form B.104-82a, British, 114,
  367
Army Form B.164-82a, British, 185
Arras offensive, 139–41, 146
Artists' Rifles, British, 174
Asiago, Battle of, 367

Asquith, Herbert Henry, 23, 78, 119,
  127
Asquith, Raymond, 119
Associated Press, 337
Astor, Lady, 263
atomic bomb, 388
Austin, Francis Reed, 232–33
Australia, 119, 226
Austria-Hungary, 15, 16, 32, 79, 213,
  290, 307, 385–86
  armistice sought by, 305
  casualties of, 42, 51–52
  Italy's declaration of war against,
    79
  onset of war and, 18–19, 23
  Romania's declaration of war
    against, 145

Baden, Max von, 291, 304, 306, 399
  Wilhelm's abdication and, 316–18
Bailey, Charles, 279
Bairnsfather, Bruce, 8
Baker, Kenneth, 161, 163, 192, 261
Baker, Newton D., 144, 164, 165–66,
  249
Baldwin, Hiram, 250, 300
"balkanization," 385–86
Ballou, Charles C., 164–65, 202, 205,
  207–9
Baltic, 167, 176, 192
Balzac, Honoré de, 85
Bangalore torpedo, 97
barbed wire, 66, 67–68, 71, 97, 110,
  113, 273
Barbusse, Henri, 131, 149
Barnett, Correlli, 189
battle fatigue, 394
Bavaria, 332
bayonet, 239
Beer Hall putsch, 398
Belgian Congo, 125–26
Belgion, Montgomery, 112, 181, 329,
  362
Belgium, 22–23, 24, 27, 66, 89–90,
  122, 125, 179, 363, 385–86, 399

atrocities against civilians in, 38–39
casualties of, 42, 51
Bell, George, 343–45
Belleau Wood, Battle of, 247–52, 260, 296
casualties in, 251
German counterattack in, 250
Marine advance in, 248–50
Berend (German soldier), 122
Bernstorff, Johann Heinrich von, 136
Berry, Colonel, 355–56
Bessborough, Harry, 330
Best O'Luck (McClintock), 393
Bettemps, Maurice, 38
Bill (British officer), 99
Binding, Rudolf, 52, 223–24
end of war and, 246–47
fatalism of, 198–99
gas attack witnessed by, 55, 57
Richthofen visited by, 218
Bird, Steven, 9
Bird, Will, 9, 11, 15, 35, 185–87, 226–27, 348, 357, 378
as sniper, 186–87
Bishop, Billy, 140
Black Hand, 16
blacks, *see* African Americans
Blankenhorn, Heber, 365
Blenk, Karl, 109–10
Bliss, Tasker, 262
Blücher, Princess, 264
Bluebird (U.S. soldier), 295
Blunden, Edmund, 68–69
Boer War, 58, 78
Bollhorst, Martin, 379
Bonus Marchers, 393
Boon, Jasper, 379
Bordeaux, Paul, 198
Bosch, Carl, 55
Bosnia, 15, 389
Boston Globe, 4, 256
Boswell, Percy, 105, 112
box barrage, 243
box respirator, 56
"Brabançonne, La," 349
Bradow, Gil, 296

Brautigan, Otto, 387–88
Breckinridge, Robert M., 206–7
Brest-Litovsk, treaty of, 213–14
Briand, Aristide, 82, 123, 133
Brigden, Private, 378
British Expeditionary Force (BEF), 54, 76, 103, 140, 213, 348
at Le Cateau, 40
punishments for desertion and cowardice in, 150–54
in retreat from Mons, 8–9, 35, 39, 54
see also specific units
British Legion of Great War Veterans, 395
British Medical Journal, 154
Brittain, Edward, 62–64, 75, 114–16, 141, 367–68
Brittain, Vera, 61–65, 74–75, 114–16, 140–42, 194, 223, 367–68, 384
postwar career of, 396–97
Brodie, John L., 72
Brooke, Rupert, xi, 28, 57–58, 92, 386
Brown, J., 110
Brown, Ray, 218
Bruchmüller, Georg, 215
Bryce, James, 38
Bryce Report, 38–39, 90
Bücher, Georg, 322, 328, 356
Bulgaria, 32, 290
Bullard, Robert Lee, 142, 193–94, 204–5, 207, 208, 222, 229, 232, 241–42, 251–52, 296, 346–47
Bulletin 35, 164–65
Burns, Private, 6
Byng, Julian, 199, 214

Cambridge, duke of, 78
Campbell, Pat, 316
Canada, 92, 226
casualties of, 139, 140, 184, 350
Cantigny offensive, 241–42, 247, 260
Capelle, Eduard von, 138
Caporetto, Battle of, 200

Carranza, Venustiano, 136
Carter, Sergeant, 196
Caruso, Enrico, 369
Carver, Christian, 104
Casey, Robert, 345, 376
Cassel, F. L., 104
Castelnau, Noël de, 39
casualties:
 abandonment of, 46–47, 58
 in Arras offensive, 139–40
 at Belleau Wood, 251
 "blessed wound" and, 84–85, 115
 in Cantigny offensive, 242
 at Caporetto, 200
 in Champagne and Loos offensives, 72
 at Chemin des Dames, 146–47
 citations and, 115–16
 compilation of, 312–13
 daily rate of, 379
 in first month of war, 41–42
 in first year of war, 51–52
 on last day of war, 378–79
 in Ludendorff's offensives, 217–18, 224, 256, 264
 at Messines Ridge, 170, 171–72
 in Meuse-Argonne offensive, 296–97, 300, 336, 380
 modern weapons and, 41
 Native American, 295
 odds of survival and, 98
 at Passchendaele, 181, 183, 184–85
 at Saint-Mihiel, 274
 at Saint-Quentin tunnel, 281
 at Second Ypres, 77
 septic poisoning in, 58
 at the Somme, 112, 114, 119
 treatment of, 58, 115, 302–3
 at Verdun, 86, 122–23, 380
 in war, 327, 379
 see also specific countries
Cates, Clifton, 248
Catholic Center Party, German, 306
Catlin, George C. G., 397
Central Intelligence Agency, 391

Central Powers, 32
 see also specific countries
Chamber of Deputies, French, 364
Chaplains' Corps, U.S., 5
Chapman, Edward, 105
Chapman, Guy, xviii, 68, 72, 100, 112, 190
Charreton (French soldier), 121
Château-Thierry, Battle of, 5, 260
Chemin des Dames, 146–47
Chesson, Sterling, 280
chlorine gas, 56
Choctaw Indians, 295
Christmas truce of 1914, 48–52, 53, 172, 198–99
Churchill, Winston, xvii, 23, 67, 94, 188, 366
 Clemenceau and, 222–23
 Gallipoli campaign and, 79
 Haig described by, 374
 on Hindenburg, 123–24
 tank development and, 117
 on war, 381
civilians:
 atrocities against, 38–39
 flu deaths among, 304
 gassing of, 342
Civil War, U.S., 163–64, 167, 251, 265
Clarke, George G., 5, 89
class, social, 93–96, 130, 363
 conscription and, 93–94
Clegg, Harold, 56
Clemenceau, Georges, 222–23, 252, 288, 308, 364
Cloete, S., 112–13
Cloud, Joseph, 295
communication trenches, 66
Conboy, Martin, 368
Complete Memoirs of George Sherston, The (Sassoon), 396
Congress, U.S., xv, 394
 see also House of Representatives, U.S.; Senate, U.S.
conscription, 93
 class barriers and, 93–94

in Great Britain, 93–94, 241
in U.S., 165–66
Cooper, Duff, 77
Cooper, H. E., 69 70
Cooper, Howard, 237
Copse (Jünger), 398
Côte-de-Châtillon assault, 297–98
Council of State, Belgian, 22
coup de mad, 243
Craiglockhart Hospital, 155, 367,
    384
creeping barrage, 107–8
Croix de Guerre, 35, 206, 365, 392
Cromwell, Oliver, 94
Cude, Robert, 105–6, 112, 182,
    321–22, 329
Currie, Arthur, 350, 357–58
Custer, George, 167

Daigle, Private, 378
Daily Express, 170
Daily Mail, 63
Daily Telegraph, 188
Dalmatia, 79
Daly, Daniel Joseph, 249
Darrow, Clarence, 90
da Vinci, Leonardo, 117
D-Day invasion, 378–79
de Gaulle, Charles, 395
Delalauge, Octave, 340, 352
Denmark, 291, 398
Derby, Lord, 93
Desagneaux, Henri, 31–32, 248, 383
in final hours of war, 35
mutinies and, 148–49
at Verdun, 83–84, 121–22
Desire Trench, 393
de Sola Pinto, Vivian, 28–30, 292,
    396
Christmas truce and, 50
disillusionment of, 175–76
enlistment episode and, 29–30
in final hours of war, 34–35, 357
Gallipoli experiences of, 34
on Sassoon, 173

wounded, 190
Deutsche Bank, 12
Deuxième Bureau, 310
de Valles, John B., 5–6, 7, 54, 89,
    256–57, 338–39, 356–57
Dewees, Draper, 269–70, 276,
    282–83, 312–13
Di Pasquale, Americo, 135, 379
dirigibles, 191
Distinguished Service Cross, 298, 374,
    379
Dixon, A. G., 180
Dixon, D. O., 330
Dixon, R. G., 240
Dixon, Richard, 362, 384
Donovan, William J. "Wild Bill," 162,
    235, 237, 259–60
Duffy's description of, 162–63
in Kriemhild-Stellung assault,
    298–99
leadership of, 235–36
nickname of, 163
postwar career of, 391
doughboy, 195
possible origins of term, 167
Dowell, Cassius M., 6–7
Doyle, Arthur Conan, 281
dreadnoughts, 21, 88
Drews, Herr, 316
Drum, Hugh, 176
Dual Alliance, 21
Duane, Jim, 242–44
Dubail, Auguste, 39
Du Bois, W. E. B., 164, 203
duckboards, 66–67, 183, 284, 307
Duffy, Francis, 162–63, 235, 236,
    238, 258–59, 299, 377–78, 382,
    391
"Dulce et Decorum Est" (Owen),
    174–75
Dupin, Lieutenant, 121

East Kent Regiment, British, 105, 322
East Prussia, 41, 42, 124
Ebert, Friedrich, 318

Eden, Anthony, 382
Edgington, William, 40
Edmonds, Charles, 381–82, 383
Edwards, Adrian, 244–45
egg bombs, 97
Eighth Army, German, 123
8th East Surreys, British, 109
8th Moroccan Light Infantry and
    Zouaves, French, 59
8th Warwickshire Regiment, British,
    181–82
18th Division, French, 196
80th Division, U.S., 363
80th Infantry Regiment, French, 120
81st Division, U.S., 278–79
82nd Division, U.S., 292
82nd Reserve Division, German, 241
83rd Brigade, U.S., 297
84th Brigade, U.S., 276, 297, 331
85th Battalion, Canadian, 117
87th Infantry Battalion (Grenadier
    Guards), Canadian, 92
89th Division, U.S., 256, 333–35,
    336, 360
Einem, Karl von, 102
Einstein, Albert, 122
Eisenhower, Dwight D., 395
11th Brigade, U.S., 343
11th Jaeger Battalion, German, 38
11th Sherwood Foresters, British, 64,
    115, 141, 367
Eliot, T. S., 92
Ellison, G. E., 349–50
Eltinge, Colonel, 332
Ely, Hancock, 342–43
Enfield rifle, 195, 293
Engall, John Sherwin, 105
Enright, Tom, 197–98, 233
Erzberger, Matthias, 306, 308, 315,
    318–19, 323, 324, 379, 399
Eva (Jensen's girlfriend), 227
Evans, Frederic D., 232–33, 346

Falkenhayn, Erich von, 81, 86, 122,
    124–25

Farnsworth, C. S., 346
Fatalist at War, A (Binding), 198
Field Order 5, 202
Field Order 105, 3
"field postcard," 129
Fifth Army, British, 152, 180, 214,
    217, 221
V Corps, U.S., 254, 269, 276, 282,
    297, 312, 314, 354
5th Division, U.S., 342, 343, 354,
    372
Fifth Guards, Prussian, 288
5th Marine Regiment, U.S., 248–49,
    300, 376
5th Royal Irish Lancers, British, 9, 10,
    35, 76, 349–50
15th Regiment, U.S., 204
55th Brigade, U.S., 232, 346
57th Infantry Regiment, French,
    85–86
Fighting 69th, see 165th Regiment,
    U.S.
First Army, British, 362
First Army, French, 180
First Army, U.S., 198, 314, 326, 333,
    354
1st Army Corps, British, 77
I Corps, U.S., 292
1st Division, U.S., 176, 193, 196,
    222, 229, 241, 260, 314, 355
1st Newfoundland Regiment,
    Canadian, 139
1st Royal Dragoons, British, 48
1st West Yorkshire Regiment, British,
    96–97
fire trench, 66, 95
Fixon, Jess, 295
Fleming, Ian, 67
Fleming, Valentine, 67
flamethrowers, 84, 321
Flying Circus, 218, 359
Foch, Ferdinand, 4, 178, 194, 201,
    225–26, 263, 266, 314, 347,
    350, 373, 388, 395
    appointment as commander-in-chief
    of, 221–22

armistice negotiations and, 306–10,
315, 318–19, 323–24, 379
battle cry of, 40
fight-to-the-end order of, 318, 325,
328–29, 346
Pershing's confrontation with, 268
Siegfried Line strategy of, 279–80,
281
Fokker aircraft, 218
food, 269, 282
Forderhase, Rudolph, 335
Forster, Edmund, 359
Fort Des Moines, 164
Fort Douaumont, 82, 123
Fort Riley, 303
Fort Vaux, 83, 123
Foster, Reginald Francis, 99
Fourth Army, French, 205, 314
4th Royal Sussex Regiment, British,
64
Fourteen Points, xvi, 290, 291, 308
42nd Battalion Royal Highlanders
(Black Watch), Canadian, 9, 348
42nd Division (Rainbow Division),
U.S., 161–62, 233, 260, 273,
276, 297, 314, 330–31, 332, 354
44th Reserve Division, German, 171
415th Infantry Regiment, French, 121
Fox, Frederick "Itchy," 251
France, 36, 66, 159, 213, 290, 311,
385–86, 387
armistice celebration in, 363–65
in attempt to recover Alsace, 39
casualties of, 51, 77, 86, 119, 122,
128, 139, 146–47, 184, 380
German occupation of, 102–3
mutiny among troops of, 147–50
onset of war and, 18, 21–24
patriotism and enlistments in,
31–32
submarine warfare and, 126, 136
U.S. entry into war and, 138–39
Wilson's peace initiative rejected by,
125–26
Franco-Prussian War (1870), 39,
119–20, 123, 307, 311, 364

Franz Ferdinand, Archduke of
Austria, 15–17, 24, 36, 379, 399
assassination of, 16–17
Franz Josef, Emperor of Austria
Hungary, 15–18
Frederick II (the Great), King of
Prussia, 153, 316
French, John, 42, 76–77, 78, 79
Haig's replacement of, 76–77
French Foreign Legion, 92
Frost, Robert, 89
Fuller, Alvan T., xv

Gallagher, Jim, 298
Gallieni, Joseph, 41
Gallipoli campaign, 34, 79, 172
gangrene, 58
gas warfare, 90, 98, 237–38, 288,
328, 342, 397
effects of, 56
first British use of, 71
first successful use of, 55
Hitler as victim of, 358–59
limitations of, 57
masks in, 56, 57
Gaudy, George, 85–86, 245
Gaupp, Corporal, 211
General Order No. 35, 156
Genon, Gilda, 38
George V, King of England, 20, 78,
214, 262–63, 366
George Washington, 191
German East Africa, 361
Germany, Imperial, 32, 36, 79, 145,
305, 385–86, 387
alleged atrocities by, 38–39, 90,
160, 193
armistice sought by, 289–91, 292,
see also armistice
Britain's naval arms race with, 21
casualties of, 41–42, 51, 77, 86,
119, 122, 140, 184, 224, 264,
380
in first combat against Britain, 39
France occupied by, 102–3

Germany, Imperial (*cont.*)
  home front unrest in, 246–47, 264, 289, 317, 343
  Italy's declaration of war against, 79
  onset of war and, 18, 19, 21–24
  patriotism in, 25–28
  Russia's peace agreement with, 213–14
  U.S. declaration of war against, 138
  U.S. relations with, 89–92
  Wilhelm II's abdication and, 316–18
  Wilson's peace initiative rejected by, 125–26
  Zimmermann telegram controversy and, 136–37
Germany, Nazi, xvii, 385, 398
Germany, Weimar, 389
Gerrard (British soldier), 72
Gerrior (British soldier), 338
Gibbs, Philip, 188–89
Giles, Sergeant, 196
Gillespie, Subaltern, 381
Goethals, George, 265
Goggins, Peter, 152
"Goodbye Broadway, Hello France," 270
Goodbye, Mr. Chips, 396
Goodbye to All That (Graves), 396
Göring, Hermann, 359
Gotha bombers, 93, 191
Gough, Hubert, 152, 180, 214, 221
Grant, A., 107
Graves, David, 396
Graves, Robert, 98, 174, 190, 191, 396
Great Britain, 57, 126, 159, 179, 213, 387
  armistice celebration in, 365–66
  casualties of, 42, 51, 77, 119, 140, 183, 184, 217, 380–81
  class barriers in, 93–94, 130, 363
  conscription in, 93–94, 241
  execution of deserters by, 320–21
  in first combat against Germans, 39
  first gas attack by, 71
  Gallipoli campaign and, 79
  German bombing of, 93, 191
  German naval arms race with, 21
  influenza epidemic in, 304
  onset of war and, 21–23, 24
  patriotism and enlistment in, 29–31, 93
  postwar demographics in, 380
  submarine warfare and, 126, 136
  U.S. citizens volunteer in, 92–93
  U.S. entry into war and, 138–39
  Wilson's peace initiative rejected by, 125–26
Great Depression, 393
Greater Serbia Kingdom, 15
Greer, Allen, 203
Grenada, 389
Grenfell, Julian Henry Francis, 48
Gresham, James B., 197–98, 233
Grey, Edward, 19, 21, 23, 366
Griffith, Captain, 384
Groener, Wilhelm, 291, 317, 324
Gruebl, Olga, 134
Gunther, Henry N., 134–36, 267, 351, 355, 379, 394
Guttmann, Hugo, 220, 359

Haan, William "Bunker," 330, 340–41, 342
Haber, Frau, 56
Haber, Fritz, 55–56, 397–98
Habsburg dynasty, 305, 385
Hague Convention, 219
Haig, Dorothy Vivian, 78
Haig, Douglas, 76, 127, 150, 152, 172, 182, 188, 194, 199, 213, 223, 224, 241, 266, 329, 373
  Arras offensive and, 139
  background of, 77–78
  Churchill's description of, 374
  Foch championed by, 221–22
  French replaced by, 76–77, 79
  Passchendaele offensive and, 179–80, 181, 183, 184, 189

Pershing appraised by, 177
postwar career of, 395
promotion to field marshal of, 120
Somme offensive and, 103, 112,
    113, 120
Wilson on, 214
win-the-war strategy of, 168
Haig, Henrietta, 78
Halstead, Frank, 279
Hampshire, HMS, 127, 153
Handel, George, 61
hand grenades, 97, 208
Harbord, James, 166, 177,
    247–48
Harris, Louis, 320–21
Hassell, Gordon, 263
Hay, Ian, 383
Hay, L., 182
Hay, William H., 231–33, 346
Hays, Merle, 197–98, 233
Helldorf, Wolf-Heinrich von, 315,
    322–23, 398
helmets, 72, 282
Hermanns, Wilhelm, 122
Hernia, the, 267
Hertling, Georg von, 289–90, 291
Herzegovina, 15
High Seas Fleet, German, 88
Hill, A. V., 57
Hill, Margaret Keynes, 57
Hindenburg, Paul von, 123–25, 266,
    291, 319, 335
  armistice and, 289–90
  Churchill on, 123–24
  Ludendorff's relationship with,
      124–25
  rise of Hitler and, 399
  Wilhelm II's abdication and,
      317–18
Hindenburg Line (Siegfried Line),
    125, 146, 278–82, 297
  British breakthrough on, 199–200
Hinds, John, 127
Hinrichs, Ernst, 238–39
hit and run raids, 242–44
Hitler, Adolf, 27

Christmas truce disapproved of by,
    52
decorations awarded to, 220, 266,
    358, 359
defeatists resented by, 266
Eden and, 382
end of war and, 358–59
enlists in army, 25–26
gassed, 358–59
Ludendorff and, 398–99
in Ludendorff offensive, 219–20
stab-in-the-back theory of, 387–88
wartime heroism of, 43
wounded, 118–19, 266
Hodgdon, Raymond F., 303
Hohenzollern dynasty, 13, 122, 359
Holler, Sergeant, 121
Holmes, Richard, 147
Holsten (German soldier), 122–23
Honourable Artillery Company,
    British, 112
Horace, 174
Hotchkiss machine guns, 195
Hötzendorf, Count von, 18
Housatonic, 126
House of Commons, British, 21, 366,
    381
House of Representatives, U.S., 137,
    138
Howard, Roy, 310
Howet, Stephen, 93–94
Hunter, Dan "Pop," 249
Hutchinson, Graham Seton, 219
Hylan, John F., 368–69

I, Claudius (Graves), 396
"I Have a Rendezvous with Death"
    (Seeger), 92–93
Illinois, 137
India, 69, 78, 119
Indians, *see* Native Americans
"In Flanders Fields" (McRae), 73,
    378
influenza epidemic, 303–5
"In the Pink" (Sassoon), 188

Invisible Man, The, 396
Iraq, 389
Irby, James, 379
Ireland, 90
Iron Cross, 220
Italy, 79, 305, 367, 385
   casualties of, 200
   declaration of war by, 79

Jackson, Andrew, 164, 222
Jackson, Ernest, 320–21
Jacobs, T., 215
James, Edwin, 338, 364
Japan, xvii, 136, 388, 393
Jenkins, Paul, 135
Jensen, Arthur, 160–61, 163, 193,
   227, 262, 268, 275–76, 284,
   292, 299–300, 342–43, 372
Jensen, Walt, 160
Jewish Daily News, 391
Jews, 220, 316, 359, 397
Joel, Arthur, 166–67
Joffre, Joseph, 81–82, 86, 103, 122,
   123, 188, 224
Johnson, Clarence, 278
Johnson, Henry, 205–6, 392
Joint Chiefs of Staff, 392
Jones, Bob, 10, 11, 35, 185, 348, 350,
   378
Journey's End (Sherriff), 30, 396
Judy, Will, 262–63, 283
Jünger, Ernst, 171, 216, 242, 382,
   398
Justice, Moses, 205
Jutland, Battle of, 88

Kaiser's Battle, *see* Ludendorff's
   offensives
Kayes, John, 259
Keddie, James, 55–56
Keegan, John, xvii, 28, 94, 386, 389
"Keep the Home Fires Burning," 270
Kelly, "Little Eddy," 235–36
Kerr (British officer), 112

Keynes, Geoffrey, 57–58, 302–3, 304,
   397
Keynes, John Maynard, 57
Kielmeyer, Ernst, 210–12, 214–15,
   217
Kiggell, Launcelot, 188
Kilmer, Aline, 259
Kilmer, Joyce, 236–37, 259–60
King's Liverpool Regiment, British,
   106
King's Own Regiment, Bavarian, 25
King's Own Yorkshire Infantry,
   British, 105
King's Royal Rifle Corps, British,
   140
Kipling, John, 380
Kipling, Rudyard, 379–80, 386
Kitchener, Lord, 29, 30–31, 79, 127,
   153
Klemperer, Otto, 397
"Knees Up, Mother Brown," 366
Koch, Lance Sergeant, 220
König, 13
Korean War, 389, 393
Kosovo, 389
Kreisler, Fritz, 44–46
Kriemhild-Stellung assault, 297–98
Krupp Works, 221, 271
Kuhn, Joseph E., 133
Ku Klux Klan, 164

Lacotte Hill, 202, 209
Lafayette, Marquis de, 176
Lafayette Escadrille, 161
Lambert, General, 170
Lancaster Fusiliers, British, 105
Lancet, The, 155
Lansing, Robert, 136–37, 310
Lanz, Lothar, 27, 36–37, 58, 70
   cavalry charge witnessed by, 47
   Christmas truce and, 49, 51
   as deserter, 88
   in firing squad, 47–48
   first combat experience of, 37
   in U.S., 370

at Verdun, 86–88
wartime experiences of, 46–48
Larson (American officer), 186
Laurent, Second Lieutenant, 121
Lawrence, Thomas Edward, 120, 305
League of Nations, 394
Lebreton, Captain, 339–40, 352
Le Cateau, 40
Lee-Enfield rifle, 39
Leighton, Clare, 74
Leighton, Roland, 61–65, 74, 140,
    367, 368, 397
Lettow-Vorbeck, Paul Emil von, 361
Leviathan, 191, 304
Liberal Party, British, 38, 126
lice, 268–69, 282
Liggett, Hunter, 292, 314, 326,
    333–34, 336, 354
Limmer, Walter, 48
Lippmann, Walter, 92
Lipsett, Major General, 187
"Little Grey Home in the West,"
    270
Livermore, George K., xv
Lloyd George, David, 23, 168, 170,
    177, 179–80, 183, 188–89, 214,
    238, 365–66, 374, 380–81
    becomes prime minister, 126–27
    postwar career of, 395–96
    War Cabinet of, 127
Lloyd George, Margaret, 396
Lodge, Henry Cabot, 309, 394
London Rifle Brigade, British, 49, 348
Longest Day, The, 372
Loos offensive, 72, 77, 78
Lost Battalion, 294
Ludendorff, Erich, 212–13, 214, 217,
    221, 240–41, 247, 253, 257,
    264, 271, 272–73, 289, 290,
    303–4
    AEF assessed by, 265
    Hindenburg's relationship with,
        124–25
    postwar career of, 398–99
    resignation of, 391
Ludendorff, Erich (stepson), 218

Ludendorff's offensives, 212–19
    AEF's arrival and, 225
    Allied counterstrike in, 263–64
    casualties in, 217–18, 224, 256,
        264
    concept of, 212–13
    fifth (Second Battle of the Marne),
        253, 256–57, 263
    first, 215–18, 219, 268
    Foch's re-emergence and, 221–22
    fourth, 252–53
    French counterattack in, 256–59
    German advance in, 216–17
    Hitler in, 219–20
    looting and loss of discipline in,
        223–24, 246
    "Paris gun" in, 221
    prisoners of war in, 219
    second, 218, 223
    shelling strategy of, 215–16
    stalled, 221, 223–24
    third, 240–41, 245
    Wilhelm II's observation of, 216,
        217
Ludwig III, King of Bavaria, 25
Lusitania, 90–91
Lyon, Russell, 379

MacArthur, Douglas, 162, 276–77,
    314, 332
    in AEF's first raid, 233–34
    Bonus Marchers and, 393
    in Côte-de-Châtillon assault,
        297–98
    leadership of, 331
    in Ourcq engagement, 260
    Patton's exchange with, 276–77
    postwar career of, 393
McCabe, Sergeant, 250–51
McCauley, John, 151, 153–54
McClintock, Alexander, 92, 93,
    95–96, 98, 106, 117–18, 119,
    132, 161, 393
McCoy, Frank, 235, 257–58
MacDonald, John, 152

Machine Gun Corps, British, 330
machine guns, 11–12, 77, 109–10,
    112, 195, 255, 259
McIver, George, 278–79
Mackin, Elton, 249, 254–56, 296,
    332–33, 376
  POW incident and, 300–301
MacNider, Hanford, 334–35
McRae, John, 73, 378
"Madelon," 270, 365
"Mademoiselle from Armentières,"
    270, 364
Major, Duncan K., 6–7, 338
Manchester Guardian, 189, 381
Mangin, Charles, 311, 374
Manning (British soldier), 111
Manual of Military Law, 100
March, Peyton, 304–5
Marine Corps, U.S., 249, 251
Marne, First Battle of the, 41
Marne, Second Battle of the, 253,
    256–57, 263
Marshall, George C., 198, 273, 326,
    355
Marshall Plan, 355
Mary, Queen of England, 366
Maslin, Henry, 263
Mason, Captain, 185–86
Massachusetts National Guard, 4
Massacre of the Innocents at Ypres
    (Der Kindermord bei Ypern),
    12–13
Masurian Lakes, Battle of, 124
Matbern, Private, 38
Maud'huy, General de, 153
Max, Prince, see Baden, Max von
Maxim, Hiram, 11–12
Maxim machine guns, 11–12, 109,
    255, 259
May, Charles, 182
Maze, Paul, 180
Médaille Militaire, 80, 365
Medals of Honor, 281, 294, 298, 299,
    392
Megiddo, Battle of, 305
Memorial to the Missing, 185

Menjou, Adolphe, 372
Menoher, Charles T., 234, 331
Merrill, J. N., 207
Messines Ridge assault, 168–72,
    179
  casualties in, 170, 171–72
  tunnel fighting in, 169–70
Metz offensive, 311–12, 313,
    324–25, 333, 336
Meuse-Argonne offensive, 54,
    281–89, 292–97, 324, 333,
    346–47, 376, 392
  casualties in, 296–97, 300, 336,
    380
  Côte de Châtillon attack in,
    297–98
  gas warfare in, 288, 297
  Kriemhild-Stellung attack in,
    297–99
  Lost Battalion legend of, 294
  Meuse River crossed in, 254–56
  Native Americans in, 294–96
  objective of, 297
  scale of, 294
  Sedan as objective in, 281–82,
    313–14
  Stenay attack in, 334–35
Mexico, 144
  Zimmermann telegram and,
    136
Meyer, Jacques, 84
Meyers, Charles S., 154–55
Michael, Operation, see Ludendorff's
    offensives
"Million-Dollar Raid," 244
Mills, Jim, 9–11, 357, 378
Mills, Ogden, 178
Mills, Tom, 9–10, 11, 35, 185, 348,
    350, 378
Mills bombs, 97, 106, 116
Minenwerfer (minniewerfer), 97, 185,
    235, 238, 339, 342
"Missing of the Somme, The"
    (monument), 119
Missouri National Guard, 158
Mitchell, William "Billy," 272

Mojave Indians, 295
Moldavia, 193
Moltke, Helmuth von, 22, 33, 36, 38–41, 81, 124
  Schlieffen Plan modified by, 40–41
Molwitz, Battle of, 153
Monet, Claude, 364
Mons offensive, 348–50
Montenegro, 15
Montgomery, Thomas, 164
Moran, Lord, 94, 154
Morgan, Glyn, 48
moribund ward, 115, 303, 358, 396
Mormal Forest, 322
Morrell, Ottoline, 173
Morrell, Philip, 173
Morrison, Sybil, 191
mortars, 97
Mott, Bentley, 324
Mott, Colonel, 360
Moulin, Lieutenant, 340
Mudd, Jack, 185
Mudd, Lizzie, 185
Munro, Hector Hugo, 119
Murry, John Middleton, 173
"Musical Evening in Coon-Town, A," 205
mustard gas, 54, 56, 96, 184, 209, 238, 297
mutiny, 147–50, 332
  punishments for, 149–50
My Darling Puss (Lloyd George), 396

Naegelen, Joseph, 80–81, 147, 365, 394
Naegelen, Madame, 365
Naegelen, René, 70–71, 72, 80–81, 83, 121, 147–48, 365
  postwar career of, 394–95
Nagel, Fritz, 26–27, 40, 41, 316, 397
Nagel, Karl Friedrich Rudolf, 265–66
Napoleon I, Emperor of France, 153

Napoleon III, Emperor of France, 307
National Association for the Advancement of Colored People, 161
National Guard, U.S., 138
  Missouri, 158–59
  mobilization of, 161–62
Native Americans, 165
  casualties of, 295
  code talking of, 295–96
  in Meuse-Argonne offensive, 294–95
  warrior image of, 295
Navy Cross, 300
Netherlands, 88
  Wilhelm II's exile in, 319, 398
Nevill, W. P., 109, 112
Newfoundland, 119, 139
New Orleans, Battle of, 164
New York Herald, 90, 391–92
New York Times, 132, 309, 337–38, 364
New York Times Magazine, 237
New Zealand, 119, 226
Nicholas II, Czar of Russia, 19, 20, 21, 213
  abdication of, 213
Nicholson, William, 133, 351
Ninth Army, French, 40
IX Corps, French, 314
19th Uhlans, German, 360
90th Division, U.S., 334–35, 336
91st Division, U.S., 346
92nd Infantry Division, U.S., 164, 201–5, 208, 327–28, 375–76, 379
93rd Division, U.S., 204, 205, 208, 346
Nivelle, Robert, 123, 128, 139, 146, 148, 224
Nobel Peace Prize, 355
Nolan, Dennis, 274
no-man's land, 68
  generals' view of, 100
Norris, George, 138
November Criminals, 399

Oberndorff, Alfred von, 307
"Observations of the Conditions of an Armistice with Germany," 318
Occasional Oratorio (Handel), 61
Office of Strategic Services, 391
Ogden, Hugh, 235
Oklahombi, Joe, 294
Old Bill (Canadian soldier), 357
"Old Contemptibles," 39
Old Soldiers Never Die (Richards), 396
Olympic Games, 195
103rd Regiment, U.S., 6
104th Infantry Regiment, U.S., 3–6, 89, 256, 257
106th Regiment, French, 83–84
107th Infantry Regiment, U.S., 281
108th Regiment, French, 147
110th Engineers, U.S., 163, 226
129th Field Artillery, U.S., 157–58, 159
140th Regiment, U.S., 196, 239, 261, 282
141st Infantry Regiment, U.S., 294
157th Brigade, U.S., 135
157th Division, French, 208
157th Field Artillery, U.S., 205
163rd Infantry Regiment, French, 339–40
165th Regiment, U.S. (Fighting 69th), 162, 235, 237, 238, 382
  casualties of, 377–78
  in Kriemhild-Stellung attack, 298–99
  at Second Marne, 258–60
  in victory parade, 391
167th Infantry Regiment, U.S., 295
168th Regiment, U.S., 298
171st Infantry Regiment, French, 306, 340
174th Infantry Regiment, German, 336
179th Brigade, U.S., 334
Order 12257, 102
Ottoman Empire, *see* Turkey
Ourcq engagement, 260–61

"Over There," 160, 195, 270, 369
Owen, Wilfred, xi, 174, 367

pacifism, 191
"Pack Up Your Troubles in Your Old Kit Bag," 270, 369
Palmer, J. W., 71
Pals, 31
Panama, 389
Pankhurst, Sylvia, 153
"Paris gun," 221
Parker, Frank, 314–15
Parr, J., 350
Passchendaele, Battle of, 172, 179–82, 186, 189, 217, 381
  casualties in, 181, 183, 184–85
  Memorial to the Missing of, 185
  Sherriff wounded in, 187–88
  terrain of, 181
Paterson, Major, 157
Paths of Glory, 372
patriotism:
  of African Americans, 164, 203
  in Austria, 44
  British enlistments and, 29–31
  and distance from battlefield, 283
  fraternal solidarity and, 31
  French mobilization and, 31–32
  German, 25–28
  Hitler's enlistment and, 25–26
  Kreisler's experience and, 44–46
  as personal salvation, 25–26
  romanticism and, 44–46
  U.S. enlistments and, 159–63
  youthful idealism and, 28–29, 48
Patton, Anne "Nita," 178
Patton, George S., 177, 178, 276–77, 326
  MacArthur's exchange with, 276–77
  poems by, 301, 372–73
  postwar career of, 393–94
Pawnee Indians, 295
"Peace—November 11, 1918" (Patton), 372–73

Pearce, Sergeant, 186–87
Pearce, Thomas, 279
Peden, William, 386
Pegler, Douglas, 117
Pershing, Helen Frances Warren, 143
Pershing, John J., xv, 133–34, 142–43, 162, 163, 164, 167, 179, 192, 194, 198, 201, 204, 206, 208, 225, 241, 252, 262, 266, 294, 304, 311, 312, 313–14, 330–31, 332, 346
  armistice opposed by, 308–9, 324–25, 373–74, 385
  background and personality of, 142–43
  Belleau Wood and, 247–48
  Chaumont headquarters of, 177–78
  Foch's confrontation with, 268
  Haig's appraisal of, 177
  and "Lafayette, we are here" remark, 176–77
  Meuse-Argonne offensive and, 288–89
  named AEF commander, 144
  postwar career of, 394
  Resco and, 178, 394
  Saint-Mihiel offensive and, 267–68, 274–75
Pershing, Warren, 144
Pétain, Henri-Phillipe, 82, 86, 148–49, 214, 221–22, 266, 395
Peterson, Wilbur, 192, 193, 270
Pfander, Eugen, 210
Phenomenon of Man, The (Teilhard de Chardin), 395
Philadelphia Public Ledger, 90
phosgene gas, 54, 56, 96, 215, 342
Pilditch, P. H., 301–2
Pioneer Battalion 30, German, 27, 36–37, 86, 370
Plato, 390
Plumer, Herbert, 152, 168–69, 170, 180
Poetry, 237

poilus, 85–86, 87, 131–32, 167, 195, 225
  mutiny by, 147–50
  Verdun and reputation of, 85–86
Poincaré, Raymond, 32, 176
"Point of View, The" (Swinton), 68
poison gas, see gas warfare
Poland, 125–26, 214, 385
Pompie (German soldier), 238
Populaire de Paris, 395
Post Office Rifles, British, 98
Pourtales, Count, 22
Powell, Colin, 392
Powell, Ernest, 134–36, 267, 351
President Lincoln, 191–92, 193
Price, George, 350
Prince, Norman, 161
Princip, Gavrilo, 16–17, 24, 379, 399
prisoners of war, 257
  captured by York, 293–94
  descriptions of, 281, 323
  executions of, 219–20, 264
  in Ludendorff offensive, 219
propaganda leaflets, 272
prostitution, 226–27
Punch, 72–73
Putnam, Israel, 267

Rabelais, François, 85
"Race to the Sea, The," 41
raids, 68–70, 98
  first recorded, 69
  hit and run, 242–44
  in Somme offensive, 117–18
Railway Transportation Service, French, 32
Ranghart, Major, 202
rats, 238–39
Rawlinson, Henry, 103
Reader, Alec, 98–99
Recklinghausen, Earl, 252
Red Cross, 283, 288
Reed, John, 92
Reichstag, German, 154, 321, 398
Reinhardt, Kurt, 101–2, 219

religion, 59–60
Remarque, Erich Maria, xix
Rennagel, Harry G., 7, 339
Resco, Micheline, 178, 394
reserve trench, 66, 97
Reynolds, F. C., 354
Rhodes, Charles D., 205, 274,
    330–32, 340
Richards, Frank, 50, 53–54, 172,
    356–57, 396
Richardson, Victor, 62, 64, 75,
    140–41
Richmond, Clarence, 376–77
Richmond (Virginia) Times-Dispatch,
    91
Richthofen, Manfred von, 218, 359
Rinehart, Mary Roberts, 365
Rise and Fall of the Third Reich, The
    (Shirer), 371
Rivers, W. H. R., 155
Rizzi, Joe, 160, 163, 193, 226, 373
    in Meuse-Argonne offensive,
        284–86
    postwar career of, 392–93
Roberts, Needham, 206
rolling barrage, 244, 285
Rollins, Chaplain, 243
Romania, 307
    casualties of, 220–21
    surrender of, 220
    war declared by, 145
Romanov dynasty, 213
Roosevelt, Archie, 258
Roosevelt, Franklin D., 391
Roosevelt, Kermit, 258
Roosevelt, Quentin, 257–58
Roosevelt, Theodore, 143, 164, 257,
    258, 309
Roosevelt, Theodore, Jr., 258
Ross, Major, 298
Ross, Warner, 328, 375
"Rouge Bouquet" (Kilmer), 236
Rough Riders, 143, 164
Royal Air Force, 218
Royal Army Medical Corps, British,
    57

Royal Field Artillery, British, 71, 104
Royal Scots Regiment, British, 264
Royal Warwickshire Regiment,
    British, 69
Royal Welsh Fusiliers, British, 29, 34,
    53, 172, 356, 396
Rupprecht, Prince of Germany, 334,
    335
Russell, Bertrand, 173
Russia, Imperial, 36, 40–41, 272,
    385, 387
    casualties of, 42, 51
    Germany's peace agreement with,
        213–14
    onset of war and, 18, 19, 21, 22–24

Saint-Mihiel offensive, 5, 267,
    271–74, 282
    casualties in, 274
    plan of, 271–72
    U.S. bombardment in, 273–74
Saint-Quentin Canal, 280–81
Salvation Army, 282–83
Samsonov, Alexander, 42
sandbags, 67–68, 96, 284
Sargent, John Singer, 238
Sassoon, Hamo, 172
Sassoon, Siegfried, xviii, 109, 172–74,
    175, 188, 383–84, 386, 390, 396
Saturday Evening Post, 249
"Sausage Machine," 98
Sawkins, A. E., 209
Sazonov, Sergei, 22
Schaffer, Paul, 285–86
Schlieffen, Alfred von, 33, 36
Schlieffen Plan, 22, 33, 39–41, 124
    concept of, 36
    Moltke's modification of, 40–41
Schröder, Hans, 237
Schwaben Redoubt, 111
Schweiger, Walter, 90
Scott, C. P., 189
Second Army, British, 152, 169, 180
Second Army, U.S., 202–3, 204, 232,
    241, 346

Second Champagne, Battle of, 70, 72
II Colonial Corps, French, 6–7, 338
2nd Division, Canadian, 348–50
2nd Infantry Division, U.S., 166,
    247–48, 251–52, 333, 336, 360,
    376
2nd Manchester Regiment, British,
    174, 367
2nd Middlesex Regiment, British, 114
Seeger, Alan, 92–93, 119, 161
Seeley (British officer), 111
Senate, U.S., 138
    Foreign Relations Committee of,
        394
    Military Affairs Committee of, 143,
        144
Serbia, 15, 24, 52, 385
    Austrian ultimatum to, 18–19
    casualties of, 42
7th Battalion, British, 322
7th Bavarian Landwehr Regiment,
    German, 197
7th Division, U.S., 342
7th Dragoons, British, 349
7th Worcestershires, British, 63, 74
17th London Regiment, British, 322
71st Regiment, U.S., 303
73rd Hanoverian Fusiliers, German,
    216
77th Division, U.S., 263, 294, 314,
    341–42
79th Division, U.S., 133, 284
Sharpe, William, 216
Shaw, George Bernard, 205
shell shock, 154–56, 303, 393–94
Sherburne, John H., 201–3, 208,
    327–28, 376
Sherman, William Tecumseh, 251
Sherriff, R. C., 29, 71–72, 113
    postwar career of, 396
    wounding of, 187–88
Shirer, William L., 371
Shroeder (German soldier), 123
Siegfried Line, see Hindenburg Line
Signal Corps, U.S., 161, 163
Silk Stocking Boys, 162

Silver Star, 260, 300
Simon, Carleton, 283
Sixth Army, French, 245
6th Cheshires, British, 51
VI Corps, U.S., 202, 331
16th Infantry Regiment, U.S., 196
16th London Regiment, British, 105
16th Reserve Infantry, Bavarian, 25,
    43, 358
63rd Brigade, U.S., 341
63rd Frankfurt Field Artillery
    Regiment, German, 12, 101
65th Brigade, U.S., 344
66th Brigade, U.S., 344
Smith, Harry L., 160, 163
Smith-Dorrien, Horace, 42
sniping, 186–87
Snows of Kilimanjaro, The, 372
Social Democrat Party, German, 318
Socialist Party, French, 70, 394–95
Socialist Party, U.S., 370
"Soldier, The" (Brooke), 57–58
Soldiers' Councils, 316
"Soldier's Declaration, A" (Sassoon),
    173–74
soldiers and soldiering:
    African American, see African
        Americans
    "blessed wound" sought by, 84–85
    close-combat weapons of, 97
    duality in experiences of, 189–90
    equipment burden of, 106
    executions for cowardice and
        desertion of, 150–54, 320–21
    food and, 269
    gallantry on battlefield and, 183–84
    imminent death and, 106–7
    language of, 128–29, 238
    McClintock on, 132
    mutiny by, 147–50
    Native American, see Native
        Americans
    officers and politicians scorned by,
        129–30, 187–88, 190, 282
    pastimes of, 182–83
    poilu figure and, 85–86

soldiers and soldiering (*cont.*):
  qualities of good, 230
  sense of kinship of, 383–84
  shell shock and, 154–56
  songs of, 270
  souvenir hunting by, 276, 288, 311
  tobacco and, 269–70
  trench community of, 94–96
  vermin and, 238–39, 268–69, 270,
    282
  vice and, 226–30
  see also trench warfare; trenches
Somalia, 389
Somme offensive, 103–19, 139, 169,
    381
  British failings in, 113–14
  casualties in, 112, 114, 119
  end of, 119
  initial British assault in, 106–12
  initial French assault in, 112
  monument to missing of, 119
  opening bombardment in, 103–4,
    108–9, 113
  pace of advance in, 108–9, 130–31
  raids in, 117–18
  tanks in, 117
  zero hour in, 106–7
Sophie, Archduchess of Austria, 16,
    399
South Africa, 119
souvenir hunting, 276, 288, 311
Soviet Union, xvii, 385
Spad aircraft, 257, 328
Spanish-American War, 138, 143, 164
Sparks, Lee, 165
Spears, Edward, 153
Springfield 1903 rifle, 195
Staff College, British, 78
Stahl, Fräulein, 20
Stalingrad, Battle of, 380
Stanton, C. E., 176
Stars and Stripes, 205, 262, 372
State Department, U.S., 337
Stegmaier, Albert, 215
Stevenson, Frances, 126, 127, 396
Stewart, Edgar, 134

stick bombs, 97
Stokes mortar, 322
Stones, William, 152
Storm of Steel (Jünger), 398
Struvay, Clara, 38
Stuart, Edgar, 267
Studholme, Sergeant, 9–10, 348
submarine warfare, 88, 126, 136–38,
    291
  against neutral shipping, 90–91,
    137
  against troop ships, 192–93
  Zimmermann telegram and, 136–37
Suez Canal, 79
Suicide Club, 97
Suicide Squad, 251
Sulzbach, Emil, 12
Sulzbach, Herbert, 12–14, 15, 101,
    218–19, 228–29, 292, 397
  disillusionment of, 101–2
  at Somme, 102–3, 116
Sulzbach, Rudolf, 12
Summerall, Charles P., 254–56, 297,
    314–15, 354
  take-no-prisoners order of, 297–98
support trench, 66, 95, 97
Supreme War Council, Allied, 133,
    241, 262, 309
Swinton, Ernest, 68, 116–17
Switzerland, 66
Szogyeny-Marich, Count L. de, 18

Tag, Der, 397
tank warfare, 77, 277
  concept of, 116–17
  interior of, in battle, 263–64
  in Siegfried Line breakthrough,
    199–200
  at Somme, 117
Tannenberg, Battle of, 124
Taylor, A. J. P., xvii, 86, 385–86
tear gas, 55, 215, 297, 393
Teddy (British soldier), 321
Teilhard-Chambon, Marguerite,
    59–60

Teilhard de Chardin, Pierre, xviii, 35, 121, 240, 292, 382
  bravery of, 59
  drafting of, 32
  on lack of religious conviction, 59–60
  postwar career of, 395
  promotion of, 59
  as stretcher-bearer, 58–59
Tenth Army, French, 311, 374
10th Battalion, British, 320
10th Calvary, U.S., 143
10th Division, German, 273
Testament of Youth (Brittain), 397
"There'll Be a Hot Time in the Old Town Tonight," 310
Third Army, British, 199, 214, 217, 329
Third Army, German, 102
III Corps, U.S., 156, 340
3rd Division, Canadian, 185, 187, 348–49
3rd Tyneside Irish, British, 110
13th Royal Fusiliers Regiment, British, 68
30th Division, U.S., 280–81
31st Regiment, Prussian, 351
XXXII Corps, French, 202
32nd Division, U.S., 330, 340–41, 342
XXXIII Corps, French, 204
33rd Division, U.S., 262, 263, 343, 345, 355–56, 376
XXXIV Corps, French, 346
35th Division, U.S., 157–58, 163, 196, 226, 284–87, 373, 392
37th Division, U.S., 284, 346
38th Northwest Infantry Battalion, Canadian, 350
39th Garwahl Rifles, British, 69
306th Machine Gun Battalion, U.S., 294
307th Infantry Regiment, U.S., 294
308th Infantry Regiment, U.S., 294
311th Machine Gun Battalion, U.S., 135

313th Regiment, U.S., 133–35, 267, 351, 394
314th Regiment, U.S., 133
315th Regiment, U.S., 135
321st Infantry Regiment, U.S., 278–79
323rd Infantry Regiment, U.S., 279
328th Infantry Regiment, U.S., 292
356th Regiment, U.S., 360
365th Regiment, Prussian, 355–56
365th Regiment, U.S., 202, 203
366th Regiment, U.S., 202, 203, 208–9, 327–28, 375
367th Regiment, U.S., 207–8
368th Regiment, U.S., 206, 207
369th Regiment, U.S., 205, 391
Thoma, Lieutenant, 360
Thomas, David "Tommy," 172
Thurlow, Geoffrey, 64, 75, 114–15, 141
Ticonderoga, 193
Times (London), 29, 114, 115, 281
Tirpitz, Alfred von, 21
tobacco, 269–70
toilet paper, 270
Tommy, 167, 195, 226
  character of, 383
  origin of term, 131
Transylvania, 145
Trebuchon, Joseph Albert, 340
"Trees" (Kilmer), 237
Trench of the Bayonets, 122
trench foot, 183
trench warfare, trenches, 66–72, 313
  artillery bombardment in, 96–97
  barbed wire in, 67–68
  brotherhood of, 185, 190–91
  camaraderie of, 283–84
  daily life in, 94–97, 183
  duckboards in, 66–67
  emotional pull of, 98–100
  fatalism of, 130–31
  finding one's way in, 95
  German design of, 108–9, 275
  ideal design of, 66–67
  no-man's-land in, 68–69

trench warfare, trenches (*cont.*)
  passivity of, 71–72
  raids in, 68–70
  rats in, 238–39
  sandbags in, 67–68
  stench of, 96
  see also soldiers and soldiering
Trenche de Bosphore, 8, 11, 13, 89
Trieste, 79
Triplet, William, 195–96, 239,
    261–62, 282, 312, 373
  in Meuse-Argonne offensive, 285,
    287–88
  postwar career of, 392
Truman, Bess Wallace, 157–58, 159,
    285, 287, 289, 291, 311, 352,
    364
Truman, Harry S., 157–59, 163, 289,
    291, 311, 352, 363–64, 392, 393
  description of, 286–87
  in Meuse-Argonne offensive,
    286–87
Tumulty, Joseph, 137
Turkey, 32, 79, 120, 145, 290, 307,
    383
  armistice signed by, 305
  declaration of war by, 42
Tuscania, 192–93, 261
22nd Manchesters, British, 152
24th Battalion, British, 320
25th Reserve Division, German, 241
26th Division, U.S., 3, 6–7, 14, 54,
    89, 121, 162, 242, 257, 283,
    285, 352, 353
26th Regiment, U.S., 260
26th Reserve Artillery, German, 211
27th Division, U.S., 280–81
28th Division, U.S., 231–32, 346, 376
28th Infantry Regiment, U.S., 242
29th Division, U.S., 354
Two Living Wars (Sulzbach), 397
Tyrol, 79

U-boat 20, 90–91
Ukraine, 214

Ulmer (German soldier), 211–12
Ulster Division, British, 111
United Press, 310
United States, 88, 392
  anti-German prejudice in, 134
  armistice celebration in, 350,
    368–70
  casualties of, 89, 197–98, 232, 251,
    260–61, 274, 281, 300, 336,
    339, 341–42, 343, 346, 355,
    375–76, 378–79
  declaration of war by, 137–38
  draft lottery in, 165–66
  first casualties of, 197–98
  German relations of, 89–92
  patriotism and enlistments in,
    159–63
  postwar conflicts of, 389
  Zimmermann telegram controversy
    and, 136–37
  see also American Expeditionary
    Forces

Van Tries, Sam, 388
Vaughan, Edwin, 181–82
venereal disease, 226
Verdun, Battle of, 81–87, 92, 103,
    112, 124–25
  attrition strategy of, 81–82, 86,
    121–22, 123
  casualties in, 86, 122–23, 380
  flamethrower use in, 84
  poilu figure and, 85–86
  tacit cease-fire in, 86–87
  Trench of the Bayonets in, 122
Versailles Treaty, 387–89, 395
Veterans of Foreign Wars, 394
Vichy France, 395
Victoria Cross, 140
Vietnam War, 389
Vigilancia, 137
Villa, Pancho, 144, 162, 163, 167,
    331
Vimy Ridge offensive, 139–40,
    146

Vittorio Veneto, Battle of, 305
Volpatte, Private, 131
Voluntary Aid Detachment (VAD), 61, 64, 367
von Thaer, Colonel, 290
von Tubeuf, Colonel, 220

Wadhams, William, 369
Walt (U.S. soldier), 343
Walter (German soldier), 328, 356
War Cabinet, British, 127, 180
War Department, U.S., 226, 392
War Ministry, French, 310
War of 1812, 164
Warren, Francis E., 143, 144
Washington, George, 163
Waugh, Alec, 28
Weimar Republic, 389
Wells, H. G., 31
Wemyss, Rosslyn, 323–24
West Yorkshire Regiment, British, 320
Weygand, Maxime, 307, 308
Wharton (U.S. soldier), 261
Whittlesey, Charles W., 294
Wiedemann, Fritz, 266
Wilde, Oscar, 62
Wilhelm, Crown Prince, 82, 86
Wilhelm II, Kaiser of Germany, 12, 39, 41, 81, 122, 123, 125, 295, 369
    abdication of, 13, 316–18, 332, 343, 359
    armament workers addressed by, 270–71
    armistice negotiations and, 315–16
    birth defect of, 20
    in exile, 319, 398
    Ludendorff's offensive observed by, 216, 217
    onset of war and, 18, 19–23, 24
    personality of, 20–21
Williams, Ernie, 51
Williams, Private, 106

Wilson, Albert, 154
Wilson, Edith, 394
Wilson, Henry, 214, 310, 366
Wilson, Woodrow, xvi, 4, 8, 133–34, 142, 144, 145, 159, 165, 194, 207, 258, 272, 370–71, 394
    Fourteen Points of, xvi, 290, 291, 308
    German peace initiative and, 290–91, 292, 307, 308
    influenza decision of, 304–5
    peace without victory initiative of, 125–26, 127
    "too proud to fight" speech of, 91–92
    U.S.'s entry into war and, 136–38
Wilson, 372
Wilson administration, 91
Winterfeldt, Detlev von, 308
Wipers Times, 175
Wittenmyer, Edmund, 342
Wolf Telegraph Agency, 317–18
Woollcott, Alexander, 259, 372
World War I:
    assessment of, 385–86
    cavalry in, 47, 349–50
    conditional vs. unconditional victory in, 388–89
    effect of modern weapons in, 41–42
    extent of battleground in, 379
    as global crusade, 31
    historical repercussions of, 386–89
    last American to die in, 351
    last British casualty in, 349–50
    last Canadian to die in, 350
    last deaths in, 360
    last French soldier to die in, 340
    last German to die in, 361
    see also specific battles and offensives
World War II, xvii, 355, 379, 382, 393, 395, 396, 397, 398
    deaths in, 389
    World War I as prelude to, 386–87
Wright, William M., 334

Yealland, Lewis, 155
Yeats, W. B., 28
YMCA, 283
York, Alvin, 292–94, 372
Young, Charles G., 206–7
Young Hawk, Joe, 294–95
Ypres, First Battle of, 12–13
Ypres, Second Battle of, 73, 77, 139

Ypres, Third Battle of, see
    Passchendaele,
    Battle of
Yser, Battle of the, 59

Zanuck, Darryl, 371–72
zeppelin airships, 93
Zimmermann, Arthur, 136
Zyldyk, 370